Red International and Bl

Black Critique
Series editor: Anthony Bogues

This series concerns radical black thought and politics, both historical and contemporary. The volumes explore and interrogate the ways in which radical black thinkers, activists and artists have formulated political, social and artistic ideas and practices. The series includes critical texts on the present conjuncture facing Africa and the African Diaspora in the Caribbean, North America, Europe and other parts of the world.

The main objective of the series is to produce a body of work which challenges conventional critical theory and foregrounds a radical tradition oftentimes marginalized.

Also available:

Edited by Amber Murrey
A Certain Amount of Madness:
The Life, Politics and Legacies of Thomas Sankara

Red International and Black Caribbean

Communists in New York City, Mexico and the West Indies, 1919–1939

Margaret Stevens

PLUTO PRESS

First published 2017 by Pluto Press
345 Archway Road, London N6 5AA

www.plutobooks.com

British Library Cataloguing in Publication Data
A catalogue record for this book is available from the British Library

ISBN 978 0 7453 3727 2 Hardback
ISBN 978 0 7453 3726 5 Paperback
ISBN 978 1 7868 0163 0 PDF eBook
ISBN 978 1 7868 0165 4 Kindle eBook
ISBN 978 1 7868 0164 7 EPUB eBook

This book is printed on paper suitable for recycling and made from fully
managed and sustained forest sources. Logging, pulping and manufacturing
processes are expected to conform to the environmental standards of the
country of origin.

Typeset by Swales & Willis
Simultaneously printed in the United Kingdom and United States of America

This book is dedicated to the people without shoes

Contents

Figures

Abbreviations

ABB	African Blood Brotherhood
AAAIL	All-American Anti-Imperialist League
ACLU	American Civil Liberties Union
AFL	American Federation of Labor
ALWF	American League Against War and Fascism
AME	African Methodist Episcopal
ANLC	American Negro Labor Congress
AIL	Anti-Imperialist League
APP	All People's Party
BGLU	British Guiana Labor Union
BWI	British West Indies
CIO	Committee for Industrial Organization
Comintern	Communist International
CPA	Communist Party of America
CPC	Communist Party of Cuba (also PCC *Partido Comunista de Cuba*)
CPH	Communist Party of Haiti (also PCH *Parti Communiste Haïtien*)
CPM	Communist Party of Mexico (also PCM *Partido Comunista de México*)
CPPR	Communist Party of Puerto Rico (also PCPR *Partido Comunista de Puerto Rico*)
CPUSA	Communist Party of the United States
ECCI	Executive Committee of the Communist International
HPU	Haiti Patriotic Union (also UPH *Union Patriotique d'Haïti*)
ILD	International Labor Defense (also DOI *Defensa Obrera Internacional*)
ILW	International Longshoreman Workers
Inprecorr	*International Press Correspondences*
IRA	International Red Aid (also MOPR *Mezhdunarodnoye Obshtchestvo Pomoshtchi Revolutzioneram*)
ITUCNW	International Trade Union Committee of Negro Workers
IWW	International Workers of the World
KKK	Ku Klux Klan
KMT	Kuo Min Tang
LSNR	League of Struggle of Negro Rights

NAACP	National Association for the Advancement of Colored People
NCCL	National Cuban Confederation of Laborers (also
	CNOC *Confederación Nacional de Obreros Cubanos*)
NMU	National Maritime Union
NNC	National Negro Congress
NYPD	New York Police Department
Kresintern	Peasant International of the Soviet Union
RILU	Red International of Labor Unions
TLO	Toussaint L'Overture
TUUL	Trade Union Unity League
UMW	Union of Marine Workers
UNIA	Universal Negro Improvement Association
WIDC	West Indian Defense Committee
WP	Workers (Communist) Party
YCL	Young Communist League

Acknowledgements

Tony Bogues is the visionary behind the concept of a series on black radicalism, and the placement of my book in this series is only because of his enduring support for my work which began while he was the advisor of my thesis. I thank him for the mentorship which was an admixture of research, teaching, conference presentations and conversations about my topic. He cemented the partnership with Pluto Press and introduced me to David Shulman, the commissioning editor, who shepherded this work through its most critical stages of publication. The Pluto team then finished the job. Thank you.

I have been able to grow with and learn from an exceptional global community of students, faculty and staff who made my graduate and subsequent academic career exciting, intellectually stimulating and relevant. The training that I received from my other thesis advisors—Paget Henry and Paul Buhle—from the Departments of Africana Studies and American Civilization at Brown University remains the formative core of my work. I have taken tremendous leadership from Ani Mukherji and Matthew Quest who were my department colleagues and have gone on to produce critical work about anticolonial internationalism and working-class emancipatory politics. The friendship and camaraderie that I enjoyed with Jeannette Lee, Jermain McCalpin and Andreas Woods made my time in Providence enjoyable and helped to advance my thinking on black radicalism. Professors Robert Lee and Elliott Gorn always showed interest in my transnational approaches to "American" history. Finally, the office support from Jean Wood in the Department of American Civilization was present from my initial days of entry into the department until the final hour of my completion of graduate school. The Center for Caribbean Thought at the University of the West Indies Mona Campus in Jamaica allowed me to meet Professor Rupert Lewis and my colleague Maziki Thame both of whom continue to help expand my understandings of and approaches toward Caribbean radicalism. English Professors Grover Furr and Gregory Meyerson deeply contributed to my understanding of Marxist epistemology and Communist history. Above all, Gerald Horne has stood unequivocally in support of my research, writing and publications and helped me think scientifically about the centrality of black labor in the class struggle that has ensued over the past 500 years.

The librarians, staff and archivists who facilitated the research component of my work cannot go unacknowledged. Many thanks to the librarians at the

Schomburg Center for Research in Black Culture who patiently saved my photocopies in spite of sometimes months-long absences on my part. The staff at the National Library of Jamaica also ensured that my materials were safely kept and delivered to me in a timely manner. Above all, the archivists and staff at the U.S. National Archives in Maryland, particularly the now deceased Walter Hill, were vital in ensuring that I found accurate and relevant information that laid the basis for much of the research that is presented in this project. Lastly, the librarians and staff of Rockefeller Library at Brown University were also patient and understanding as I checked out cartloads of materials that sometimes did not return to the library on the timeliest basis.

Insofar as the personal is political, a solid community of friends and colleagues based out of Newark, New Jersey, helped push this work through its most critical stage from dissertation into book. My closest friends—Tasha Meggett, Latisha Coe, Maiga Hunter, Jenn Kohl and Hajar Shirley—checked in to make sure I was handling the stress of working and writing. Currently at Essex County College where I teach history, my colleagues Jen Wager, Eileen Defreece, Rebecca Williams, Jina Lee and Christopher Rivera are the reason I stay committed to teaching and writing in the city where I came of age. My scholar-activist community with Shelagh Patterson, Emanuel Martinez and Kamika Bennett has inspired me to stay in the game and see the power of my approach.

Of course, my family was just as much an intellectual and political support base for this project as the aforementioned individuals and institutions. My brother, Adam Stevens, is the finest "organic intellectual" that I know, and his commitment to education for liberation has been pivotal for my dedication to same. My father, Houston Stevens, is living proof of the heroic tradition this book discusses. My mother, Barbara Foley, has been my friend, colleague, mentor, advisor and, well, my mother. Without her, this book would not have been possible.

Introduction

A truth little known and even less understood is that black workers in the West Indies were critical to the historical development of Communism between World War I and World War II. This revolutionary praxis was not a provincial phenomenon; rather, Communists and black workers in the Anglophone, Francophone and Hispanophone Caribbean as well as in New York City and Mexico were collectively implicated in an eruption of progressive forces whose magnitude was manifested at local, hemispheric and indeed global levels. Several points must be made plain. First, the anti-racist legacy of Communism cannot be fully assessed without examining the struggles of black workers in the colonial outposts of empire. Second, it is incumbent upon scholars of twentieth-century black radicalism not to offer revisionist paradigms—i.e. paradigms that retroactively obscure or even worse, erase, the Communist organizations which often anchored the fight for freedom from racist oppression in which so many black working people were historically engaged.

Red International and Black Caribbean brings coherence to an under-acknowledged network of organizations, individuals and Communist parties between 1919 and 1939, referred to herein as the "interwar period," that were headquartered in New York City and Mexico as well as in certain parts of the British West Indies, Haiti and the Afro-Latin Caribbean islands of Cuba and Puerto Rico. I refer to this geopolitical space as the "Black Caribbean." Mexico's thematic function in the book is unique yet indispensable, precisely because of its position as the first people-of-color Communist hub in the hemisphere; as such, this renders it a critical force—at times an anchor and at times as a counterweight—to the Communist Party of the United States (CPUSA) for experimenting with Communist praxis in largely peasant-based and non-white spaces. In so doing, this book describes the inner workings of one aspect of a revolutionary global political network that emerged in the wake of the Bolshevik Revolution under a Moscow-based umbrella called the Third International, or the Communist International (Comintern), designated at times herein as the "Red International."

What follows is an organization-based history. A collection of roughly one dozen groupings—five of them Communist parties and six of them radical Communist-led organizations—form the thematic core of this investigation. The CPUSA, based in New York City, operated in tandem with the Communist parties then operating in Mexico, Cuba, Puerto Rico and Haiti as well as with Comintern affiliate organizations in the British West Indies. While we are careful not to occlude the role of European-based Communist parties in the trajectory of radicalism for black workers in the Caribbean, we make a case for the fact that the CPUSA played a critical role in the activities of Communist parties in Mexico, Cuba, Puerto Rico and Haiti as well as non-Communist organizations in the British West Indies. Not only did Communist parties lead black workers in the Caribbean but in turn, black workers' uprisings and struggle in the Caribbean pushed Communists and their vision of world revolution to the left.

In addition to examining actual Communist parties in the region, we look at Communist-led "front" organizations that were designed to extend Communist political influence beyond the relatively small spheres of individual parties and into the larger mass of workers in the regions under question. As such, the Anti-Imperialist League (AIL), International Labor Defense (ILD), American Negro Labor Congress (ANLC), League of Struggle of Negro Rights (LSNR), International Trade Union Committee of Negro Workers (ITUCNW) and the National Negro Congress (NNC) were all organizations that were deliberately created to carry out the political strategy of the Communist International at different points in the years from 1925 to 1939. Each of these organizations had some kind of outpost or headquarters in New York City—either in lower Manhattan or uptown in Harlem. Taken together, these organizations offer historians and political theorists a new vantage point from which to assess not only Communist praxis but also the radicalism of black workers across the region.

Newspaper history is inseparable from this focus on organizations in the Comintern network, rather than an issue to be treated in a different study. The reason is simple: a century ago, and really up until the past decade, many organizations promoted their ideas, described their actions, and debated important political strategies by way of newspapers which were the optimal mechanism for communication of the written word to large numbers of people. The various newspapers are not only an important object or medium of expression for the organizations, but they are also an archive for Communist history in the same way that surveillance reports from the US State Department are archives. In this way, this book offers an extremely close reading of leading presses published by Communists and also newspapers and writings from black radicals in the network of Communist organization though not directly within the International itself. The emphasis on newspapers outside of western metropoles alongside an analysis of largely New York-based newspapers allows for a fuller analysis of this newspaper history and its role in black anti-colonialism and anti-racism in the interwar period. This focus on newspapers complements our emphasis on organizations and parties, and illuminates the Communist history as praxis, and the role of black working-class struggle also as a constant interplay between emancipatory ideas and militant action.

The primary contradiction with which this work is preoccupied is the following: the medium through which Communists collectively organized between World War I and World War II, the Comintern, reinscribed rather than overturned several of the weaknesses embedded in the capitalist oppression that it was dedicated to challenging. First, it created individual, distinct national parties that would, in turn, act as a coalition, under the direction of the Soviet Union, as a means of forging international classless society. And while such a mobilization opened the door to hitherto nonexistent opportunities for coordinated, systematic efforts toward fighting racism, colonialism and fascism, each of these parties and even the Soviet Union was to some degree bound within the limitations of a nation-state social construct that negated elements of this emancipatory project. Second, the Comintern created individual organizations, committees and bureaus for addressing what it termed the "colonial" and "Negro" questions, rather than threading the anti-racist and anti-colonial struggles into the fabric of every aspect of the world socialist project. In other words, the fight to liberate people of color around the world from racism and colonialism became a subsidiary—though always significant—struggle within the Communist movement rather than the fundamental basis for uniting all oppressed peoples. Examination of the years from 1919 to 1939 in the region in question points toward the tremendous pioneering efforts in social, political and economic empowerment for black workers in this Communist matrix; at the same time, this book reveals that the Comintern in significant ways succumbed to elements of the very racism and national chauvinism that it in so many ways had weakened.

Red International and Black Caribbean places black workers in the Caribbean at the center of a narrative about Communism—and this alone is significant. But this work also makes four major interventions in historical methodology in general and Communist and black radical history in particular that must be highlighted. First, it refutes the revisionist tendency to theorize twentieth-century black radicalism as a "tradition" of "great men" which ultimately dismisses the role of black workers as a class and also the collective organizations through which they mobilized forces and grew in consciousness—often alongside non-black comrades. Second, while it is true that western metropoles such as Paris, London, Hamburg and New York City were operational hubs for Communist engagement with anti-racism and anti-colonial internationalism, this story places emphasis instead on the fluid interplay of radicalism between these metropoles and colonized and semi-colonized epicenters in Cuba, Haiti, Puerto Rico, Jamaica, British Guiana and Mexico that contributed to the total force of the Communist International. Third, this narrative complicates the tendency to posit a false dichotomy between Communism and Garveyism with respect to black radical workers. In short, the Garvey movement, under the Jamaican pioneering black internationalist Marcus Garvey's leadership, was politically opposed to many of the critical tenets of workers' power that the Communists put forward from the post-World War I days of the African Blood Brotherhood (ABB) through the labor struggles of the 1930s. At the same time, however, when examining the lived experiences of many black radical workers, it becomes evident that from the Caribbean vantage point, they often straddled between and within these organizational poles rather than being anchored solely at one end or the other. Finally, this project is cautious not to join the seemingly hegemonic tendency toward anti-Stalinist rhetoric in academic works and attempts a more even-handed, objective approach to the Soviet Union and to Moscow-based Comintern leadership.

Ultimately, the spatio-temporal shift to the "Black Caribbean" in this book casts the entire political trajectory of global Communist periodization from 1919 to 1939 in a new light, illuminating it with developments in the Caribbean, Mexico and Harlem. That is: some of the first "bolshevization" campaigns took place among Mexican peasants in Vera Cruz; the sharpest class-against-class tensions of the "Third Period" were manifest in Scottsboro campaigns in Haiti; the most grassroots and radical "Popular Front" sit-down strikes of the late 1930s were arguably in sugar plantations in Barbados, and some of the fiercest displays of fascist genocide in the world first took place at the border of Haiti and the Dominican Republic. Using the lens of this hemispheric space allows us to see Communist interwar history through a richer and more complex set of practices and contradictions. Moreover, shifting our emphasis away from the West and onto this space allows us to reconceive the general "red line" of history in a healthier, more objective—because it is more anti-racist—manner.

Indeed, tracing this "red line" takes us past, or prior to, October 1917. How might we begin to draw parallels between the nineteenth-century African Djuka maroons of Dutch Guiana, or the Kromanti maroons of Jamaica, and the Bolsheviks in Russia after World War I? Just as the former peoples had to forge treaties and make compromises with their colonial slave masters as a means of winning peace and developing their own societies absent of racist chattel slavery, so too did the new Union have to strike deals with western imperialists as it developed its internal capacity for socialism. The hemispheric lens of this project, therefore, opens up an abundance of ways to understand the contradictions of revolution and freedom that have been born of class struggle in the immediate and distant past that we often refer to blankly as "modernity."

The roughly one dozen political organizations that form the core of this study are plotted thematically on a spatio-temporal axis. That is, specific Communist organizations and parties are featured in relevant chapters, and these organizations are the anchoring mechanism for the narrative in each chapter. In turn, the chapters are defined chronologically by major historical conjunctures during the 1919–39 interwar period of global Communist activity. The term "periodization" is applied to the ways in which Communist history is commonly marked by strategic shifts in the Comintern's orientation toward global working-class struggle, ensuing fascism and socialist transition. Since Communist mass organizations rose and fell according to these strategic shifts in political organization, their presence in the book is necessarily determined by the periods in which they were formed and liquidated by the Comintern. While this book does not seek to reconfigure or shift the common-held periodization of Communist praxis in the period from 1919 to 1939, it does suggest that shifts in political strategy were often in response to rather than in anticipation of working-class resistance to imperialism and racist exploitation in regions like the Caribbean. In other words, radical workers at the periphery of empire often pushed the Communist movement into a more radical direction—and not just the reverse.

Coupled with the chronological demarcations are a series of geographic shifts in emphasis within the Caribbean-US-Mexican space. Emphasis is placed upon which organizations and parties appear to have been most sharply engaged in questions such as peasant-based uprising, anti-racist campaigns, anti-American imperialist movements, and labor organizing in specific places. In this way, the tracing of anti-colonial and anti-racist struggles, and the "red line" of history, are themselves unevenly mapped through time and space. Take Haiti as an example. Chapter 3 reveals how class struggle in Haiti in 1929 makes it a vanguard locale for shaping Communist anti-racist activity across the United States. But in 1937, as the final chapter reveals, Haiti re-emerges when the fascist attacks on Haitian workers in the Dominican Republic make this same island the forefront of Communist political retreat.

The book is divided into three sections that help bring coherence to the political networks operating across the US, Mexico and the Caribbean. Part I "Bolshevism in Caribbean Context" consists of three chapters; it extends from 1919 to 1929 and focuses primarily on the ways that radical black workers in the West Indies played an important role in the formation of Communism in the United States. Chapter 1 uncovers the impact of labor struggles emanating from the Caribbean which informed the growth of the African Blood Brotherhood as well as "New Negro" newspapers such as *Emancipator* and *Crusader*. This post-war process presents one critical aspect of the geopolitical genesis of Communism's intersection with black workers' resistance in the hemisphere.

Insofar as the Communist Party of Mexico is formed at roughly the same time as its US counterpart, Chapter 2 is organized around the work of the

Communist Party of Mexico, WP, All-American Anti-Imperialist League, and these groups' relationships with Mexican peasants and Latino workers in Cuba and Puerto Rico. This aspect of the hemispheric Bolshevism has a dialectical interplay with US-based Communism and partially informs the spread of Communist parties several years later in Haiti. Chapter 3 places Haiti and New York City as the central geographical locales, and the focus shifts to the anti-racist praxis embodied by the workers' uprising in Haiti in 1929. The Communist mass organizations which emerged in this context, beginning in 1925, were again the Anti-Imperialist League, but also the International Labor Defense, and the American Negro Labor Congress as well as the Haiti Patriotic Union. This first segment of the book therefore introduces a cast of radical characters, some of whom become foundational members of the anti-racist and anti-colonial struggles of the Communist movement during the interwar period, including: Richard Moore, Otto Huiswoud, Navares Sager, Grace Campbell, Henri Rosemund, Rose Pastor Stokes, Manuel Gomez and Wilfred Domingo.

Part II, "Two Steps Forward," not only presupposes "One Step Backward"— which will soon come—but also implies that this particular phase of interwar Communist movement, from 1930 to 1934, is indeed a representation of some of the finest work of the Comintern in advancing anti-racist and anti-capitalist struggle. Chapter 4, "Scottsboro in Every Country," depicts how Cuba displaced Mexico as the hub of Communist and anti-racist praxis in the hemisphere. The US, Mexican and Cuban Communist parties as well as Anti-Imperialist League and International Labor Defense are the anchoring organizations. Chapter 5 describes the headway that Communists made among black workers in the British West Indies and Haiti during the period of Scottsboro campaign organization, but also as black radical organizations emerging out of Trinidad and British Guiana began to overtly collude with Comintern forces at the global level. The Communist Party of Haiti and the CPUSA, in addition to the International Labor Defense, League of Struggle for Negro Rights, British Guiana Labour Union and Trinidad Workingman's Associations are all critical for this understanding.

Part III, "Race, Nation and the Uneven Development of the Popular Front," traces the years from 1935 to 1939 and captures both the apparent militancy and latent potential of the intense labor uprisings across the British West Indies in the wake of the invasion of Abyssinia in 1935, and also the tragic implications of popular front collusion with non-Communist progressives in Cuba, Mexico and Puerto Rico in the same period. Chapter 6 focuses on the British West Indies and the transition from the ITUCNW to the NNC and a series of "defense leagues" based out of Harlem such as the Jamaica Defense League, as well as radical newspapers such as the *Barbados Observer*, which all become part of the popular front network of anti-racist organizations. In Chapter 7, the Communist Party of Puerto Rico becomes critical to understanding anti-racist praxis in Spanish Harlem led by the CPUSA at the attendant internal networks of Communist collaboration between Puerto Rico, Cuba and Mexico. At the same time, this chapter introduces how the "50 per cent law" in Cuba in 1935 is at first denounced but ultimately supported by Communists and contributes to the mass deportation of Jamaican and Haitian workers back to their countries. Finally, Chapter 8 unveils the tragic flaw in the Comintern's efforts toward fighting racism by returning to the question of Haiti during the period of Jacques Roumain's persecution and subsequent release from jail but, with Communist parties in retreat, the massacre of over 30,000 Haitian workers with little response from Communists in the Black Caribbean matrix.

Ultimately, no one was immune to the force of Russia's revolution, and yet, not every instance of class struggle and racial consciousness equally resulted in the creation of Communist cells of organization, much less actual Communist parties aligned with and part of the Third International. Nor can Communist growth be seen as the sole or primary litmus test in every instance for possibilities at achieving emancipation. Certainly when the Russians won in 1917, as did the Haitians in 1804, common folk suffering under the bitter lash of socio-economic exploitation identified with the new victors. Just as non-wage enslaved Africans from New Orleans to Sao Paolo looked to Haiti in the nineteenth century, wage enslaved Africans looked to Russia in the twentieth. But, as we will see in what follows, in the aftermath of World War I they also continued to look to Africa, the "fatherland," or sometimes called the "motherland," as they had for centuries prior. An affinity for the former did not altogether erase an ideological and felt generation-based commitment to the redemption of the latter. Hence, the political and geographical landscape for imagining emancipation was varied and vast in 1919. So the Bolshevik experiment in social transformation was relevant to anyone interested in fighting back. And this was true on the docks in Jamaica just as it was true on the soap boxes of 135th and Lennox.

By denying today's youth around the world, and in the Western Hemisphere in particular, access to this complex, heroic, and at times tragic history, they have been prevented from engaging as proactively as possible in overturning the crumbling infrastructure that is today the late capitalist order. The youth of today have inherited membership into a working class which experiences not just the successes but just as significantly the failures of what the last century's social movements did not achieve: unions are gone or deeply weakened; police brutality is the modern form of lynching; the drug economy has become the single most viable form of economic sustenance for poverty-stricken masses whether it be in Mexico or New Jersey; public schools in urban centers have been stripped of any meaningful enterprises; natural disasters kill countless more humans than modern technology makes admissible, while forced migration the world over has displaced more people than ever before in human history.

The progeny of the working class around the world has little understanding of or pride in their class history, origin and historical function; indeed, it has been shattered before they have learned to "like" Black Lives Matter protests on Facebook. Any youth aged 21 or younger growing up in almost any nation on the planet has had nearly their whole life subsumed by some degree of military conflict. While today's strongest capitalist power in the world refuses to allow its judicial system to indict the vast majority of police officers engaged in the sustained and systemic murder of youth of color, Communists prevented nine young black men from Scottsboro, Alabama, from being executed in racially segregated Jim Crow courts over eighty years ago. Though time moves forward, political possibility does not always do the same.

Ultimately, the preponderance of mass bourgeois consciousness has stripped today's youth of any sense of pride in the successes that organized class struggle achieved in the past hundred years. In the face of interminable political repression from colonial and fascist authorities, in the face of internal political weaknesses wrought in large part by national chauvinism and sustained racist thinking, in the face of being relative novices in the art of organizing along multiracial lines and seizing state power and the means of production in the name of workers' control, Communists and radical workers before World War II fought valiantly to pioneer almost every significant social and political right that the workers of today enjoy. Yet the average young American today—or young person from any part of the world—when asked to name famous black people in history would more than likely mention Martin Luther King, Malcolm X, and perhaps Barack Obama. If Haitian, the youth might prefer to name Toussaint L'Ouverture; if Jamaican, Marcus Garvey or Michael Manley; if Trinidadian, Eric Williams; if Cuban, Jose Marti or Fidel Castro. But what knowledge do any of these youth have of George Padmore, Otto Huiswoud, Richard Moore, Claudia Jones, Henri Rosemund, Rose Pastor Stokes, Wilfred Domingo, or Sandalio Junco, all of whom, as we will see, were critical in the global struggle to raise the consciousness of workers in the fight against racism and colonialism from a socialist vantage point? What is more, each of these unsung revolutionaries committed to transcending boundaries of nation—even as they fought for the right to national independence—were all in some sense part of the "red line" of history. In short, the Communist International was an experiment in social transformation that was unparalleled in humankind—positively visionary in scope and decisively heroic in action. This book is an attempt to describe one set of factors in a much larger equation which scholars and activists alike have yet to fully compute.

PART I

BOLSHEVISM IN CARIBBEAN CONTEXT

CHAPTER 1

The Dark World of 1919

*What, then, is this dark world thinking? It is thinking that as wild
and awful as this shameful war was, it is nothing to compare with
that fight for freedom which black and brown and yellow men must
and will make unless their oppression and humiliation and insult
at the hands of the White World cease. The Dark World is going
to submit to its present treatment just as long as it must
and not one moment longer.*
W.E.B. Du Bois, *Darkwater*, 1920

In April of 1919, Jamaican dock workers shut down the ports of United Fruit, an American company, and Atlantic Fruit, a British company. Their demand was basic but radical for the time: a wage increase exceeding 100 percent of their present earnings. As the strike extended into May, the representative of the American Consul who was stationed in Jamaica and anxiously witnessing this strike reported confidently to his superiors in Washington, DC that the owners of these companies had "diverted several of their vessels to other ports for loading or discharge." And yet the strikers continued their protest into June, inspiring even "the women laborers employed in loading bananas aboard ship, whose wages had been increased" to strike again "at the last moment for a further increase to forty-nine cents per hundred stems." The strike wave then spread into the island's interior by means of the railway workers with such force that the colonial Governor "sternly cautioned" the workers "not to strike and thus seriously affect the Island's trade as well as foreign trade." Instead, he averred, the "proper course for laborers to adopt" was to allow "representatives to present their grievances to a Board" of representatives of the British colonial government who would be appointed by none other than the Governor of Jamaica himself. But the soul rebels persisted.[1]

Labor unrest on the island of Jamaica continued through the final days of 1919. Fast losing grip of its working population—from the ports, to the railroads, to the fruit industry inland, and now to the policemen with guns—

the British colonial apparatus on the island was far from secure at the close of World War I, as revolutionary upheaval at the local and global levels was on the rise. A series of strikes under the leadership of the island's longshoremen climaxed on Christmas Eve which "was chosen as an opportune date for a tie-up of transportation and shipping facilities," presumably because of the holiday commerce. What had the appearance of a spontaneous strike, however, was the outcome of earlier "strikes in the middle of December when the city police of Kingston practically went off duty for a few hours." As we can see in hindsight, it was clearly part of a year-long campaign of labor rebellion on the island, and workers were gaining courage with each win. It had become what is referred to as a general strike. In other words, Jamaican workers were collectively shutting down critical sectors of the colonial economy on the island, namely the ports, farming produce, and communications, thus strengthening their class power.[2]

But the workers' struggle in 1919 was not an isolated phenomenon in Jamaica alone; rather, it was representative of its time. Social and economic historical development does not always move forward in even increments of progressive change, and indeed, the year 1919 marked a qualitative leap forward in the development of militant protest arising from the ranks of the laboring classes the world over. The sense of group consciousness and collective interest evident among Jamaica's women banana pickers was not accidental, and while it might have been spontaneous in manifestation, it was part of an international trend in which everyday black people across the hemisphere had begun to rise up and demand their freedom—from social and racial dehumanization and persecution manifested on job sites, in housing, in public spaces and in government service work. Moreover, rebellions of black workers across the Caribbean and elsewhere were actually part of a wave of well-documented uprisings around the world in the wake of the proletarian-led Bolshevik Revolution in Russia of 1917. From India to China, South Africa, Mexico, Britain, the United States and beyond, the international working class was becoming more aggressive about demanding that their exploitation at the point of production amount to better wages and quality of life. So the surge of sometimes sporadic and sometimes coordinated class struggle demonstrated by black laborers in places like Jamaica which emerged at the close of World War I cannot be isolated politically or historically from the global Communist movement led by the socialist state of Russia under the direction of the Bolshevik Party and its leader, Vladimir Lenin.

What manifested in 1919 as spontaneous and disconnected protests across the colonized islands inhabited for the most part by black laborers in the Caribbean, was the beginning stages of a fundamentally new dimension in the anti-racist and anti-colonialist struggle in both the Caribbean itself and across the Western Hemisphere, impacting radical movements in cities as far away as New York City and Tampico, Mexico, and becoming interwoven into the fabric of the Comintern. The ubiquitous nature of this unrest in 1919, however, did not result in the even development of Communist Party organization across the hemisphere. The particular conditions in each region under investigation were critical to shaping the manner in which race and nation played into the effectiveness of Communist strategies for working-class emancipation. So the constant dialectical interplay between internal and external factors in shaping the Communist movement across this region is the primary dynamic through which this history unfolds.

By 1930, Comintern leadership based in Moscow would come to see how the working class, as it was positioned in places like Cuba, could serve as the vanguard force in the global struggle to dismantle systems of capitalist economic domination. The Communist Party based in New York City in the 1920s and 1930s would enter into new frontiers in the hemisphere because of Moscow's strategic mandate which would indicate that the strength of worker-led struggle emanating from within the Caribbean made it ample ground for Communist organization to take root; New York City would be the regional coordinating center. Throughout the 1930s, Harlem-based black Communists like James Ford traveled to places like Cuba to help direct the tide of civic unrest, climaxing in the 1933 coup, toward fighting racism and advocating for pro-Soviet state power. So the strike of Jamaican workers merits our close examination in part because it is reflective of working-class black militancy in the Caribbean that would one day inform the Communist outlook toward political expansion across the hemisphere—even though Jamaica never actually formed a Communist Party during the interwar period. The colonial periphery was indeed to become central to this global experiment for workers' organization and socialist transformation.

Absent a consolidated Communist organizational base within the black working class of Harlem or the Caribbean in 1919, black radical newspapers were critical, namely *Crusader*. Uprisings and protest were the most concrete form of expression for the wave of radicalism evinced by black people in the Caribbean and the US. The African Blood Brotherhood, the organizational arm of *Crusader*, became the political foil of the Universal Negro Improvement Association, an organization led by Marcus Garvey, and the political trajectories of both organizations were largely determined by developments concerning militant black workers in the Caribbean. Reciprocally, these organizations and their attendant papers deeply impacted the ways that black radical and Communist ideas would be disseminated across the hemisphere. As early as 1919, reportage of protests and uprisings which occurred in the Caribbean made its way to Harlem's radical papers, indubitably shaping the language, sentiment and overall scope of imaginative possibility for liberation of black people that was emergent in the postwar era from the Harlem headquarters. And it was the constant interplay between class-based rebellion and political propaganda that would give rise to the uneven development of a Communist movement across the region between 1919 and 1939.

Mexico offered a budding Communist party with deep roots by 1924 in the indigenous peasantry and an urban-based industrial population whose growth was driven by significant foreign investment capital, and had historically been a major political influence across Latin America. In Cuba, a Communist party would form a few years later in 1925, but here too the postwar period initiated a budding Communist movement which, perhaps even more than Mexico, would soon draw upon the intense angst and radical labor uprising of black working-class people in its efforts to defend Soviet Russia and spread the ideology of workers' power to the outposts of American empire.

CLASS STRUGGLE IN THE WEST INDIES AND MEXICO AFTER WORLD WAR I

My father and mother, they are British, and they
have to say, "God Save the King," but I am a Cuban,
and I can say, "God curse the King!"
Daily Worker, August 1924

Proletarios de todos los Paises, Unios!
El Machete, 1924

Radicalism in the West Indies

As depressed postwar local economies slashed jobs and wages, and as battle-hardened and politically informed veterans returned home from fighting in World War I, nearly every outpost in the Caribbean joined in the wave of workers' uprisings across the globe in 1919. Jamaica was just one case. Cuba, Puerto Rico, Haiti, Trinidad and British Guiana were among the places hit by this wave of resistance. British Guiana, the only South American colony included in this study, is a useful point of entry into the overview of workers' militancy in the Caribbean after World War I because of its specific internal conditions: there was already a labor movement dating back to the beginning of the 1900s; there was a multiracial working class of largely Indians and Africans that, when united, formed a powerful threat to the colonial apparatus, and there was a union leadership of radicals that were open and willing to engage with Communist-affiliated organizations based in the US, Mexico, Europe and Moscow over the coming decades.

British Guiana had experienced its own series of strikes as early as 1905, and from this foundation grew a commitment to organized labor that would last through much of the twentieth century. As a colony that was comprised of a large peasant base, considerable industry concentrated in the port towns, and relatively high illiteracy, it shared certain conditions with Russia. However, Russia had an organized workers' political party intent on seizing power, and British Guiana did not. But the legacy of Labour Party syndicalism in England impacted its colonial subjects to varying degrees, so it was not entirely uncanny when in 1920, according to one report, there occurred in "town and country" a series of "frequent strikes among the different trades in Georgetown, and lately these strikes have extended to the rural districts mainly to different classes of labor employed on the sugar estates." What was peculiar, however, was that in the history of this British colony whose population was dominated by a division between black city dwellers and a mix of black and East Indian rural peasants, such unity among "different classes of labor" on the sugar plantations was unparalleled for its time.[3]

By chance, certain individuals are born into this world like Henry Critchlow of British Guiana. By chance, such individuals like Critchlow, now known as the father of the labor movement in today's independent Guyana, have the drive to band together with a few courageous pioneers and create fighting organizations like the British Guiana Labor Union. The British Guiana Labor Union (BGLU) founded in 1917 was to become the chief mechanism through which the Comintern established influence in this colony by way of its active leadership embodied in the figure Henry Critchlow. Certain historical circumstances had to be underway in order for the Critchlows of the world to realize their potential. He was athletic, handsome, well-liked—even by the British: as a college athlete he played cricket with them in his off-time as a dock worker. He was not a Bolshevik or member of such Communist-affiliated groups like the Harlem-based African Blood Brotherhood and perhaps had never heard of Lenin in 1917 when he helped form the BGLU.

However, the BGLU, the first official labor union founded in the Caribbean, was initiated by a man who for all intents and purposes was to become part of the growth and development of the Communist movement and would shape the colony's subsequent development into a radical epicenter for multiracial unity, independence and workers' rights in the years to come. Certainly by the 1920s he had heard of Stalin, reigning leader of the Soviet Union once Lenin passed away, and during the Depression in the early 1930s he would travel to Germany to visit with George Padmore, fellow West Indian and then leader of the International Trade Union Committee of Negro Workers (ITUCNW) based in Hamburg to coordinate labor activities. The effort to align the causes of labor and union rights in British Guiana with the larger struggle against capitalist super-exploitation and racism the world over was to be led actively by the Profintern, or Communist International umbrella network of labor unions, by way of Padmore's ITUCNW. But without Critchlow's founding of the

BGLU during World War I, coordinating the work of the ITUCNW in the 1930s with local strikes in British Guiana among largely black urban workers would not have been possible. In other words, the degree to which workers would be receptive to Communism was always contingent upon the particular pre-existing, or internal, political history and experience of the region in question. The Communist leader of Guyana's formal independence, Cheddi Jagan, would emerge in part from this tradition; so, too, would the black populist leader Forbes Burnham. But in 1919, this historic process—at once global and local—was formative and not yet set.

As in British Guiana, labor movements rocking Trinidad and Jamaica in December of 1919 augured greater insurrection in the coming period and opened doors for interest in Harlem's varied "New Negro" radicalism. These small-scale postwar uprisings forced the hand of the British and American rulers in the region, causing increased unity and conflict between these competing ruling authorities over military and economic domination in the Caribbean. From literally day one in 1920, the US State Department was considering naval intervention in Trinidad unless British colonial military forces were able to protect the American and British white inhabitants from the wrath of the protesters then being led by the Trinidad Workingmen's Association. United States Consulate officials in the coming weeks were reassured only by reports that Americans living in Trinidad had been recruited to work with "colonial vigilantes" to put down the strikes. In Jamaica as well, the white troops stationed on the island were considered to be the main reason the "mobs" had not yet attacked the American Consulate. The conservation of capitalist property relations and state power in the hands of white colonial ruling elite British and, to a lesser degree, Americans required that all-out brute force be wrought against the rebels.[4]

In this way, British and American rulers required an alliance of coercive measures in spying, anti-sedition legislation and flexing military muscle to reinforce their mutual need for subjecting Caribbean laborers to racist conditions in which maximum profit could be generated from underpaid labor, mass unemployment and brutal dispossession of land, all well before the ostensible start of the "Great Depression" with the Wall Street stock market crash of 1929. Existing alongside British colonial enterprise, then, was the United States finance capital's forward expansion through Wall Street banks into Haiti and Puerto Rico after World War I, and attendant with this was increased American military aggression to consolidate this financial base overseas. So Haiti and Puerto Rico also experienced unrest among the masses in 1919 as a result of brutality faced in the fields, on the production lines, and at the hands of soldiers, all representing American empire's financial and political collusion with the islands' ruling elites.

The *Daily Worker* then published by the Workers (Communist) Party in Chicago described conditions in Puerto Rico by 1920 wherein "the wage workers were shifting from the tobacco factories to the sugar and coffee fields with the periodical unemployment" and hence bringing about "the awakening of their class consciousness with the sequel: spasmodic strikes." As such, the paper reported that Puerto Rico's general strike in 1919 was "ruthlessly crushed" such that by 1920 "over 90 per cent of the total production of the Puerto Rican tobacco, coffee and sugar" was imported by the United States.[5]

Also reported in the *Daily Worker* was a contemporaneous strike in Haiti against American Marines on the island, which resulted in the deaths of 2,300 islanders as reported in the paper, though by 1924 the total had risen to 3,000. While this coverage of the Caribbean was marginal relative to other strike coverage in the pages of the *Daily Worker*, it reflects the fact that since its inception, as an ideological mechanism for communicating Communist propaganda, this paper and its attendant party made small-scale efforts to identify with the causes of labor in the West Indies. In particular, since the *Daily Worker*'s chief object of contention was the financiers running the banks and Wall Street corporations which, in turn, directed US foreign policy, this paper made special efforts to elucidate instances of workers' discontent in those regions in the Caribbean suffering disproportionately from US military and economic rule. Cuba, Mexico, Puerto Rico and Haiti, all deeply intertwined in American hemispheric expansion of military bases and investments in the nineteenth and especially twentieth centuries, were therefore key.

What this brief overview of laborers' unrest in the region indicates is that at a minimum, political frustration with the US military and traditional British colonial domination was mounting in the postwar West Indies. Communists in the United States, as evidenced by *Daily Worker*, were not aloof to these developments. Rejection of American military and economic domination that was fast mounting in Haiti and Puerto Rico would also lay the foundation for evidence of sympathies to the Red International, ultimately manifesting in the form of Communist parties in both of these West Indian islands in 1930 and 1935, respectively. In turn, these Communist movements would be directly linked to Communist organizations that were at first based in Chicago and later in New York City. It was Mexico, however, where the groundwork for a non-European-Anglo-based Communist politics in the hemisphere first emerged explicitly, helping to spur Communist efforts in the Anglophone, Francophone and Hispanophone Caribbean.

Origins of the Communist Party of Mexico and All-American Anti-Imperialist League

Four major issues in the Mexican Communist movement emerged in the postwar period that would have ramifications for the Comintern in relationship to black laborers in the Caribbean. First, the Mexican experiment demonstrates how "foreign" and "domestic" leaders always worked together to establish Communist headquarters outside of Moscow. Second, Mexico demonstrates that peasant-based, non-industrial centers were always a critical though not unproblematic demographic that helped spark Bolshevik consciousness beyond Moscow. Third, the Mexican bourgeoisie's ambivalent relationship with workers' control of the state demonstrates how Communists from inception wavered between collaboration and hostile opposition to bourgeois leaders of governments as they themselves contested for seizing control of state power. Finally, American elite economic enterprise was ever fearful of workers' uprisings under Communist influence because of adverse impacts on their profit margin, and Mexico demonstrates how vigilant American imperialists would be about suppressing Communism in the hemisphere—for our purposes in relation to black laborers in the Caribbean.

The Mexican "Red Menace" to American economic and political hegemony was in part personified by the transnational activism of Manabendra Nath Roy, leading representative of the Communist International who attended a Comintern convention in 1920 as a delegate of the "Mexican Soviet" with a passport reporting him as Mexican. This East Indian Communist reportedly fled to China and later to California, finally landing in Mexico by 1918 with his "American wife" and helping to found the Communist Party of Mexico (CPM). Just as factors within a geographical region such as British Guiana or Cuba are critical to the origins of "indigenous" radicalism, so too did the CPM include within it the trademark of Bolshevism emanating from the East and settling in the West—i.e., from India and China to Mexico via the United States.[6]

But as is the case with any formation of Communist cells outside of Bolshevik Russia, non-Mexican foreign agitators like Roy were not the primary basis for the construction of a Communist party in Mexico. Local surveillance reports from September of 1920 offered anonymous and possibly alarmist accounts of Mexican labor leaders who "entered the National Palace and unfurled a red and black flag and professed anarchist speeches from the balcony advocating destruction of public and private property and a Bolshevik revolution." Moreover, though some claims were clearly sounder than others, unsubstantiated State Department reports noted that certain "insiders" warned of Communist infiltration penetrating into the presidential office itself. In 1921, an anonymous "messenger," claiming himself privy to the "plans of the six local leaders for the coming social revolution" in Mexico, charged that Lincoln Steffens of the CPUSA was offering personal advice to President Obregon on conceding power to a Bolshevik "Council of Six." This "provisional communist government" was ostensibly prepared in 1921 to "overthrow Obregon in twenty four hours."[7]

Notwithstanding such apocryphal US intelligence briefings on Bolshevik control over the Mexican state apparatus, there is evidence that demonstrates the considerable impact that radical syndicalism had over portions of the country. The American Consulate at Guadalajara reported in June of 1921 that anarchists with a Bolshevik plan for implementing Communism in the region were also responsible for recent May Day clashes with the Catholic Church. Even into 1923 American "residents" in Ciudad de Carmen lamented that their city had been "controlled by the Reds" for the past "several years" and causing "continuous annoyances" in the form of "murder, robbery and imprisonment of Americans." The president of the Lagun Corporation, an American enterprise with 650,000 acres of timber lands in the State of Campeche and headquartered in Ciudad de Carmen, was personally "inclined to recommend" the establishment of an American Consulate; however, the Division of Mexican Affairs was "of the opinion that the establishment of an office would be dangerous" precisely because it might "become a target for Red activities thus involving us in some sort of international difficulty," possibly even inciting the intervention of Soviet Russia.[8]

In the early formation of the Comintern, part of the Leninist theory was that progressive governments in semi-colonial or colonial regions could be allies in the fight against capitalism. This was a political tenet that factored sharply into the Mexican Communist movement from the beginning. The Mexican government, then under the leadership of President Calles, was engaged in a series of national agrarian reforms that dated back to the Constitution of 1917. In particular, on the question of national land confiscation, a pinnacle of the Mexican Revolution of 1910, it was commonly known that the "Land Law devised the whole of the land to be national property, and admitted of a distribution of the property, of the large estate owners among the farmers." Therefore, the Mexican government, at the provincial and national levels, had been considered by the CPM as a primarily revolutionary government such that whatever shortcomings were found on the part of the current president were attributed by Mexican Communists to foreign rather than domestic factors— namely the "resistance of the United States and England" to this national reform in land distribution.[9]

But the Communists' faith that national rulers of semi-colonized capitalist economies like Mexico would enforce the redistribution of private lands to the hands of the tilling mass was misplaced. US finance capitalists helped President Calles undo these land laws. Communists in Mexico had been "soft" on Calles rather than seeing him as an enemy of the workers of Mexico. They incorrectly surmised that his interests would lie more with defending the economic needs of Mexican workers than with the needs of American and other ruling-class forces. But they were wrong. So the Congress of the League of Agricultural Communities of the State of Vera Cruz, a peasant-based organization that affiliated itself with the Moscow-based Communists, held a meeting in December 1924 in which it resolved to join the Peasant International of the

Soviet Union (called the Kresintern), making a feeble yet not insignificant blow to US business enterprise in the state and across Mexico, while helping to consolidate a Communist headquarters in Mexico.

One month after the CPM proclaimed "Viva la Revolucion Mundial!! Proletarios del todos los Paises, Unios!" in their leading periodical, *El Machete*, to celebrate the anniversary of the 1917 revolution in Russia, the *Daily Worker* in the US reported that the Mexican peasant league of Vera Cruz had joined the Kresintern:

> Resolved: To acknowledge the absolute necessity of organizing nationally and internationally for the protection of common interests; To line itself up with the Peasant International in Moscow, which stands for the overthrow of capital; The Peasant International in Moscow is the only organization which responds to all hopes and demands of the toilers. Hail to the land and to freedom![10]

We will see how this decision to join the Kresintern made by primarily Indian peasants in Mexico challenged the hitherto biased assumptions of Communists in Mexico and the United States, who were not entirely convinced of the strategy of taking political leadership from this largely Aztec-descended demographic of peasants that were now self-proclaimed Bolsheviks though they had not officially joined the ranks of the CPM. Independent peasant direct control over the production and distribution of land—absent an industrial Communist party counterpart within the Third International to complement, strengthen and direct this process—brought with it a series of political and cultural tensions that the Communists based in the US and Mexico would inescapably confront. Alas, there was no "little red book" to consult in these matters. Such early experiments conducted by peasants as these Mexican Indians who were expressing an affinity with Soviet Russia's social experiment would inevitably push to the surface embedded chauvinisms based on race and notions of "backward" peoples that US-based Communists would at times demonstrate even though they were justified in their insistence upon party formation. But a recurring theme is that these are the lessons of history and that actors at the moment do not have the objective hindsight to see.

With all of its contradictions, Mexico's early Communist movement demonstrated that the Red International could become integrated into the lives and activism of myriad demographics of oppressed people—city industrial workers and rural peasant dwellers—who lived in close proximity to the United States "colossus to the North." Historians and cultural theorists alike have often acknowledged the impact of Mexico as a site of resistance and radicalism for black radicals and intellectuals, and this impact is reflected, as we will see, in the pages of New Negro newspapers of time like *Crusader*. But nowhere in this western hemispheric space would the confluence of Red and Black forces linking New York to the Caribbean be as strongly manifested as in Cuba's eastern province of Oriente, where Afro-Cubans and black immigrants from across the basin formed the backbone of the sugar industry.

Cuban Bolshevism and Black Working-class Unrest

It was in Cuba's sugar industry and outlying districts, concentrated on the island's mountainous "Black Belt" Oriente side—the eastern side that faces out toward Haiti to the east and Jamaica to the south—where evidence of postwar unrest among black laborers would come to engage Communism, though not until the 1930s. In the eastern province of Oriente, Cuba, immigrant laborers were relatively underpaid on the island compared to the average pay accorded a native Cuban, and those super-exploited black immigrants from across the West Indies who came in search of a relatively more thriving economy than their own were subjected to the historic position of last hired and first fired. Rebellions like the 1912 uprising led by Afro-Cuban peasants demonstrated that Cuba was far from immune to class unrest among black people, whether of a "domestic" or "foreign" variety. But just as the Cuban elites made every effort to violently put down the insurrection of Afro-Cuban peasants in the years before Communism was a political force in Cuba, so too did the reactionary Cuban rulers—with support from the American military and sugar barons— go to great lengths to prevent black workers from organizing in and alongside Communists in Cuba and beyond.

As World War I came to a close, the War Department reported on December 28, 1918 that in Camaguey, Cuba the "situation here again [is] very alarming" and warned that a "general strike may be declared about January second" for a repeal of the "obligatory military service law." But the "unmistakable feeling of uneasiness present among all classes" was considered "purely political." Months later, the "strike situation" remained "unchanged" in the heavily black-populated region "West of Santa Clara" where sugar cultivation had ground to a halt. Bringing the lifeblood of Cuba's economy, sugar, to its knees—if only briefly—these workers were considered loose cannons since War Department officials conjectured a possible "alliance with [the] Cuban Army."[11]

Subsequent to Cuba's string of protests in 1919, US intelligence circles immediately began assessing the degree to which Cuban laborers, and black workers especially, might fall under the leadership of not only anti-government "*Cuba libre*" parties and adjoining divisions of the Cuban military but also under Bolshevik leadership. Intelligence officials had good cause for consternation. As early as April of 1919, correspondences among American military officials indicated that there was some degree of Bolshevik leadership in the current strikes. The magazine *El Hombre Nuevo*, or *The New Man*, was being disseminated among the sugar workers by local members of the International Workers of the World, pre-eminent radical organization of workers' economic and political rights. Although not affiliated directly with the Third International, the IWW, or "Wobblies," was a grassroots labor organization based in the United States, with an ideology of multiracial and international class unity whose membership was composed of some Communists. Therefore, the IWW's conscious attempt to penetrate and radicalize Cuban laborers beginning as early as 1919 is part of the process that helped spark Bolshevik activity of this period, particularly among the black sugar workers on the island.[12]

In addition to the work of the IWW, US State Department correspondence on Communist influence in the labor movement in April of 1920 revealed a series of newspaper clippings, which indicated for one official that "Bolsheviks may find fertile soil here and there." This official concluded that the "extreme statements as are contained in these clippings are more the result of oratorical inspiration" rather than "convictions held by the masses of the workers." And yet one of these newspaper reports revealed that when the "question of sending delegates to the Pan-American Conference of Labor to be held in Mexico came up for discussion" among Cuban labor leaders, a "motion was presented to instruct the delegates ... that the Cuban proletariat considers Soviet Russia a tower of light illuminating the Universe and enlisting Cuba's solidarity." This early Mexico-Cuba alliance which had emerged in the labor movement, in affinity with Soviet Russia, was an initial gesture for bridging the Caribbean-Mexican radical collaborations in the years to come.[13]

The financial depression in Cuba by 1920 hit the sugar industry hardest and targeted the largely black immigrant labor population and left "thousands of immigrant laborers [that] came to Cuba to work in harvesting the sugar crop" in dire conditions and "so seriously affected labor of all classes that thousands of these immigrants [began] making the greatest effort to return to their native lands" like Barbados and Haiti. Many immigrants suffering from unemployment were unable to leave the island where they were subjected to linguistic and racial discrimination for "lack of sufficient funds to pay their passage." Some would stay and join the ensuing movement.[14]

But the black working-class unrest in postwar general strikes that rocked Haiti, Jamaica, Trinidad and British Guiana did not result in pro-Russian nuclei such as emerged in Cuba and Mexico; for this we turn to the organization of the African Blood Brotherhood among Harlem's "New Negroes" and its relationship to the rising Garvey movement to better understand the political evolution of Marxism across this demographic. Thus far we have seen a wide-angle snapshot of just some of the ripple effects that reached the shores of the Caribbean in the wave of resistance culminating at the close of World War I. It would be a mischaracterization to clothe this political wave in the blanket term "Bolshevik" or Communist.

Certainly, notions of Bolshevism varied place to place, community to community, person to person. Jamaican longshoremen informed the radicalism of Harlem's New Negroes in 1919. At the same time, what do we make of the fact that "Bolshevik" is exactly what one would-be Communist, Jamaican radical pioneer Wilfred Domingo, would label West Indian militants in the postwar period, as he reported coverage of strikes in places like Dutch Guiana in his short-lived Harlem-based paper, *Emancipator?* How did black people in Santo Domingo, in Cuba, in Panama, in Haiti, in Trinidad, in British Guiana, in Panama see this Russia as they read *Crusader?* Did all this talk of proletarian internationalism and the "Bolsheviki" coming out of Harlem inform their politics in the yard? The simple answer is: absolutely. But the more difficult task is to demonstrate how so, and with what significance.

NEGROES OF THE WEST INDIES AND AMERICA, UNITE!

Negroes of the West Indies and America, Unite!
You have nothing to lose but your chains!
You have life, liberty and the pursuit of happiness to gain!
Challenge, 1919

The short-lived black radical newspaper called *Challenge* (not to be mistaken for two subsequent newspapers with the same name) reflects an ideological admixture in the masthead above that is itself astounding. It celebrates the bourgeois values of "life, liberty and the pursuit of happiness," which are the cornerstone of individualism and private property in the Euro-American tradition of John Locke and Thomas Jefferson juxtaposed with the *Communist Manifesto*'s declaration that the "chains" of wage slavery would be destroyed by the "gains" of united workers' worldwide revolution. But the subjects of this cause were none other than "Negroes of the West Indies and America"—occluding the notion of the "worker" and replacing it with a hemispheric, race-based rather than class-based, unity. As such, this hodgepodge framework within which liberation was proclaimed represents a microcosm of the contradictions and forces at work in the political movement that was the New Negro Harlem scene of 1919. How do we interpret this epigraph in *Challenge*, much less its historical context at the time of its circulation—or lack of? Do the terms "Diaspora," or "Black Internationalism," "New Negro," or "Garveyism," or "Bolshevism" for that matter, sufficiently *name* the political stand, much less accurately *describe* the significance of this phenomenon embodied most clearly by the newspaper movement based in Harlem?

What we do know is that while white South African miners declared "white workers of the world, unite!" radicals in Harlem declared "Negroes of the West Indies and America, unite!" It is precisely here where the significance of the post-World War I movement in Harlem and the attendant rise of newspapers is critical: it laid the basis, in part, for a period of anti-racist political orientation and development of organizations from 1925 through 1939, and these organizations would fall explicitly within the Communist political network or else advocate for some degree of black workers' united local interests with the cause of Soviet Russia. Cyril Briggs's *Crusader* and Wilfred Domingo's *Emancipator* are the main papers in which "Caribbean militants in Harlem" comprised an editorial staff that encouraged social experimentation with ideas of human emancipation that took Bolshevism seriously as a praxis through which to achieve this emancipation.

In articulating and promoting the growing causes of workers' empowerment the world over, through the explicit lens of "Negro first!", these two papers conveyed a level of sophistication, substance, passion, intelligence and candor that would be out of place today. This political expression took myriad forms: short fiction, letter-writing, editorials, poetry and even advertisements. Ultimately, these papers functioned in several capacities: as media for cultural representation, as forums for political education and debate, as advertisers for black-owned business and cooperatives, as tribunes for heralding Africa's redemption from colonial occupation alongside Russia's Bolshevik alternative, and as pragmatic recruitment tools for organizations like the African Blood Brotherhood and, by 1921, for the Communist Party.

Well known is the existence of these papers and their Harlem headquarters. However, what is significant here is the manner in which the Caribbean loomed large in these papers as a site of struggle, a site of social engagement, a site of political organization, and a site where one could dream of social alternatives to the deeply racist, economically exploitative world that capitalism had engendered, from Harlem to across the hemisphere—and globe. That is, the Caribbean was not simply where many of these Harlem New Negro radicals were from, but, more importantly, it was a critical regional epicenter that prompted the growth and spread of black radical ideas as expressed in the papers of the time. We see this in the "foreign correspondence," the ads, and the editorials.

Crusader's circulation across the region, which encompassed the South American mainland of Panama and heavy on islands in the British West Indies as well as in Harlem, evoked various interpretations, understandings and reactions to Soviet Russia's rise. Harlem was an organizing and political center of thought for radical editors like Cyril Briggs, but it cannot be seen as a locale that was representative of a totalizing perspective of radicalism for black people across the region. You stood on a soap box, you started a co-op, or you started a newspaper. If inspired, and having the time on your hands—more than likely meaning you were a single or married man who was not responsible for running daily domestic duties—you boarded a subway car train and headed downtown to the Rand School and enjoyed mental wrestling with white people of ethnic Polish, Irish, German, Slavic, or other European extraction—Christian or more likely Jewish—and engaged a world of emerging Communist sentiments. This all after you spent some time helping to build Universal Negro Improvement Association forums and plans out of Liberty Hall in Harlem. Then you wrote for your own paper.

In the Panama Canal, however, you wrote in to any one of Harlem's papers after you had already read someone else's copy of *Negro World*, *Crusader*, or *Messenger*, and had just fought incessantly with racist white American canal workers who saw you as the enemy of their economic security. Nearly any alternative coming from Harlem sounded like a winning plan. Any of these figures could be characterized as a New Negro.

Wilfred Domingo's *Emancipator* seems to have remained primarily local in Harlem, and yet, one element that set *Emancipator* apart among New Negro journals of its time is the fact that upon its inception this paper took especial interest in the labor struggles at the point of production for black people in the Caribbean and linked them with struggles emanating from Soviet Russia. This same Wilfred Domingo would never actually join the Communist Party, but he was a seminal figure in the movement bridging Communism in the US, Soviet Russia, and black working-class militancy in the Caribbean during the interwar period and well beyond. Domingo's trajectory merits a full-length biography in itself, but for our purposes, the main point is that Domingo's experience as Garvey's first editor of *Negro World*, then rejection of this movement in favor of Bolshevism, was critical to pushing Cyril Briggs and other West Indian Harlem radicals toward the Workers (Communist) Party.

Crusader at first established itself as a literary link for African Americans and West Indians in 1918. Unlike the immediately pro-Bolshevik consciousness put forward in *Emancipator*, *Crusader* morphed into a more pro-Bolshevik stance over time rather than taking this position from the outset. As early as September of 1918, it was politically committed to "awaken the American Negro to the splendid strategic position of the Race in the South American and West Indian Republics" in the form of "nation-building," "the unhindered pursuit of happiness," and "free development and the highest advancement." An article entitled "The Black Man's Burden" in October 1918 raised commentary on intra-island chauvinism and "foolish native pride" within the Anglophone, primarily British, West Indies. While hardly a call for Bolshevik internationalism, this observation about British West Indians was apparently meant to posit black West Indian unity within the Caribbean and beyond as an antidote to the racist demoralization fostered by colonialism. Notably, however, there was no expressed call for analogous solidarity efforts among Francophone and Spanish-speaking black people in the Caribbean.[15]

Though the paper was only printed in English so far as evidence shows, *Crusader* by way of short fiction attempted to bridge the linguistic and cultural differences between Spanish-speaking and Anglophone black people even before it started to take its distinctly left turn toward Bolshevik-style advocacy for workers' control of production. Since its beginnings, the paper ran a series of "Punta, Revolutionist" stories, accounts of a Puerto Rican mulatto and patriot named "Punta," and its significance lies in its insistence upon a pro-black consciousness while asserting regional/national pride, in this case from both the American and Puerto Rican perspectives.[16]

This fictitious account was written by an obscure Danish West Indian figure named Romeo L. Dougherty, arriving on Ellis Island in 1915 by way of the passenger ship *Comao* from a port in Puerto Rico, 33 years of age by 1918. In a very concrete way, he had witnessed in his own life experience traversing the region from the Caribbean to Harlem the need for regional race unity. Cyril Briggs and other eminent Communists in the African Blood Brotherhood organizational base would later in the 1930s lead a Communist-led cross-border, multilingual political collaboration linking such demands as freedom for Puerto Rican political prisoners with anti-eviction campaigns in Spanish Harlem. The Anti-Imperialist League and International Labor Defense and actual Communist parties in Puerto Rico and Harlem had their seeds sown, in part, through visionary articles like "Punta" printed in *Crusader*.[17]

Sympathy toward the Bolshevik project became much more visible in *Crusader* at the very moment when the paper's distribution in the Caribbean was emerging. One could conclude from this observation that entry into a demographic of militant Caribbean workers indeed encouraged the Harlem-based editors to offer a more class-based analysis. The May 1919 issue which ran a "Punta, Revolutionist" saga also featured two markedly more class-oriented political positions taken by the editors: criticism of W.E.B. Du Bois as an "Old Crowd" Negro and praise for Bolshevism as an alternative to the ills of rampant slumlord culture suffered by so many tenants in Harlem. One article forewarned that the "landlords and real estate agents of Harlem are doing their merry best to increase the converts of Bolshevism in that district." Another article guaranteed a "series of articles treating of the history, geography, people, government, politics laws and industries of the West Indies," in order to facilitate the "better understanding of the West Indian Negro by his American brother." Therefore, the "better understanding" on the part of "his American brother" that *Crusader* editors were promulgating, if seeking an honest exposé of current events, would necessitate an accounting for the labor revolts being manifested by Jamaican dockworkers of the time, as well as disgruntled Harlem tenants.[18]

But the "better understanding of the West Indian Negro by his American brother" would reveal in an October 1919 issue of *Crusader* that the view from the outposts of colonialism in places like the Canal Zone in Panama did not always mirror the way liberation and struggle were being articulated by Marxist-inclined black radicals in Harlem. While the Harlem editors of *Crusader* proclaimed "assuredly we are Bolshevists" but "Negro first," they were speaking mainly on behalf of "those who insist on thinking for themselves and agitating for their rights," and, moreover, "'those bad agitators, who [were] not content that the people shall forever be enslaved in the clutches of the cut-throat, child-exploiting, capitalist-imperialist crew." So what did rank-and-file "bad agitators" in Panama, who were inspired by the concept of an ABB and wanted to join the movement, have to say?

One correspondent from the Panama Canal Zone who got word of the "announcement of the organization of the African Blood Brotherhood for African liberation and redemption" did not explicitly mention Bolshevism, capitalism, or imperialism. Rather, he requested to have his name placed "at the head of the list, or as near to the head as you may deem fit," and "in bold Roman type," no less, as he considered himself to be "one of those Negroes who is prepared to go to the limit—and then some—for the liberation of my Race and redemption of the Fatherland—Africa." Months later, another Canal Zone resident joined the ABB in order to "hasten the redemption of the Fatherland." What moved these Anglophone black migrant workers in the Canal Zone to join the ABB was racial "redemption," but they were seeing Africa rather than Russia as the symbolic site and land upon which their blood would be shed for the betterment of their people.[19]

In this way, *Crusader*'s Canal Zone sympathizers were sickened and tired of seeing fellow black people degraded in every shape and form as testimonies in the 1920 Universal Negro Improvement Association (UNIA) convention in Harlem will reveal shortly. At the same time, however, what is critical to understand is that the intense labor uprising underway in the Canal Zone was a key factor which motivated these black workers to join the pro-labor mission of the ABB. Their loyalties to African liberation could not be separated from their economic hardship as super-exploited laborers in a depressed postwar economy, and their desire to seek better working conditions at the point of production meant that they too were engaged in a class struggle against a bitterly racist outpost of American empire, though their letters indicate that they understood this struggle in terms of racial redemption distinctly linked to the African continent, rather than class-based empowerment in alignment with the growing Moscow-based Bolshevik movement.

Understanding that black laborers in the Canal Zone were not in a position to see worker-based unity with prejudiced white counterparts as a viable option, *Crusader* began to run more articles in the paper aimed at educating black readers about the ways in which American capitalists and their military were the enemy rather than white workers as a whole. More explicit editorial challenges to US military expansion in the Caribbean became pronounced, and in a "sage" but inaccurate prediction at the end of 1920 about possible "military intervention in Mexico," then under the control of American "oil companies," *Crusader* advocated for "solidarity among the American working class generally." Just as the Communist movement was consolidating in places like Tampico, Mexico, *Crusader* editors in Harlem placed squarely before their readers the following: the "only question for the Negro, then, is how shall he act to prevent war with Mexico? That has already been answered—Economic power and direct action …. Join the IWW …" Whether the IWW was weak or not, *Crusader* was advocating for working-class unity across borders, uniting Mexicans suffering from American "oil companies" into common cause with "American working class generally."[20]

In an effort to win more black readers to solidarity along class rather than race lines, *Crusader* editors illuminated instances of anti-racist white people who sought common cause in this liberation—and demonstrating against racist American imperial control in the Caribbean was critical to illustrating this class-oriented perspective. In 1920, the paper featured an "ex-Marine" who described his experiences in "San Domingo," where he had "seen" and "participated in" injustice that was "committed on the natives" which he attributed, in turn, to "foolish" youth and "capitalist propaganda." This veteran's testimony was meant to expose not only the detrimental effects of capitalism on "foolish" American soldiers but, more profoundly, the effects of imperialism on the Dominican impoverished masses. He sought to redeem his own humanity by shaming his acts committed against an "occupied" population while the other soldiers, or his "confederates in crime," ran free.

Indeed, *Crusader* had significantly shifted its political framework by the end of 1920 such that socialism and the IWW were being heralded as strategic alternatives for American soldiers to align themselves—black and white—in their opposition to military expansion in the Caribbean. The political redemption of US-influenced republics such as Mexico, Haiti and Santo Domingo, as seen through *Crusader*, was expanding the scope of radical possibility for solidarity and a sense of shared struggle that could be embraced by everyday readers of the paper, effectively challenging racism wrought by American empire both within the US borders and in the Caribbean as well. Inevitably, however, this too would mean that alternatives to Garveyist African redemption as well would be espoused by these Caribbean militants, laying the basis for theoretical and organizational alternatives to be cast before a growing mass of black laborers who were convening at annual UNIA conventions in Harlem and also circulating through the Caribbean on the Black Star Line.

In Harlem, opposing forces were magnifying within the common cause of advocating for black empowerment among the laboring mass.[21]

The perspectives reflected by the Caribbean readers of *Crusader* demonstrate that frustrated laborers and businessmen who were indeed influenced as well by the "race movement in the United States" did not necessarily demonstrate the same approach to imagining liberation from racist colonialism as these budding Bolsheviks in Harlem. Hitting Castries, St. Lucia, as early as August of 1919, *Crusader* apparently "stirred to energy" one reader who was "about to open a cooperative association" in the spirit of the "race movement in the United States" which he hoped would "cause those of us who [were] interested in the cause to give their aid and co-operation." The point here is simply that the predilection for cooperatives as a means of skirting colonial super-exploitation and land deprivation was not as radical as the 1930s call for burning plantations, which happened as we will see in St. Kitts, but it did demonstrate that black workers and peasants like Mr. Thompson saw themselves as fundamentally intertwined with the anti-racist struggle in the United States, and *Crusader* was an important mechanism for bridging that geographical divide.

While Mr. Thompson was by no means directing his consciousness toward support for Russian-style organization of a Communist party, there was no reason that his personal conditions would have warranted such a political response. Instead, he was advocating for economic cooperatives on behalf of the working man who sought to avoid the ratchet nature of colonial work as it was manifested in his life experience on a small island. Lest we forget, islands such as St. Lucia had no substantial white working class; there was no Rand school of Eastern Europeans and Russian Jews working in local garment mills that in the evening hours were holding lectures on socialism in the yard next door. Many of these black laborers were peasants, not industrial workers, and through their ancestry they had already forged centuries of identification as native Africans in a displaced land, or as the "Calibans" of the colonial Caribbean.

The co-operative movement, whether rural land-based or urban merchant-based, was individualistic at core, and yet it did strike a blow at the racially dominated colonial business enterprise, and this desire for black consumers and entrepreneurs to seek an independent economic base which could skirt the colonial business apparatus was one form that radicalism took. Though cooperatives did not pose the same degree of challenge to finance capital's investments in the Caribbean as the general strikes that were then underway in Trinidad, Guiana, Jamaica and Haiti, they did promote a sense of group pride, courage and subversive activity—and all of these were critical preconditions for the expansion of any successful Communist alternative in the region in the coming period.[22]

In this patchwork, uneven way, *Crusader* helped form the shared sense of community and political interest that would consolidate the very same network of individuals that over the next decades would establish ties—if at times short-lived and tenuous—between Communists in New York City and their allies in the Caribbean. Self-proclaimed Socialist, Rothschild Francis, who wrote into *Crusader* as a Virgin Island representative of the New Negro movement in the May 1921 issue of the paper, would be a Communist "fellow traveler" until he was rejected as a class traitor a decade later during the Third Period shift in Comintern strategy. He disclosed the present state of violence against "a peaceful colored people, because they protested against Marines mal-treatment [sic] of their wives and children." His letter to *Crusader* was also forwarded to the Navy Secretary, select senators, and the American Civil Liberties Union, "asking them to help ... in the fight for the removal of these half civilized men of the navy from our midst." Francis had far from established himself as a capitalist-bashing Bolshevik. Still, his expressed allegiances to the political plight of jailed American Socialist Eugene Debs and his openly anti-US military stance represented a breakthrough in the international movement to overturn racial oppression suffered at the hands of lynch mobs in the United States and the US Marines in the Virgin Islands in the summer of 1921.[23]

TOWARDS AN IRRECONCILABLE CONTRADICTION: THE FALSE DICHOTOMY OF GARVEYISM AND BOLSHEVISM

If A is true, then B must be false; if B is rejected, then A must be accepted: this logical expression is the essential of the term "dichotomy." Garvey meant pro-black, or pro-race empowerment; Communism meant pro-worker, or pro-class struggle: this formulation is the essence of the false dichotomy, which is often posited between Garveyism and Bolshevism. In its most fundamental form, this false division between "black" and "worker" into mutually exclusive parts is how many—in the academy and among non-academics alike—have understood the historical relationship between Garveyism and Bolshevism that arose in the post-World War I period. Certainly, the tensions borne out through history between the Workers Party (WP)-led Communist vs. UNIA-led Garveyist movements demonstrate the irreconcilable contradictions over the question of multiracial anti-capitalist unity in the fight against racial oppression on one hand, and a commitment to promoting black-owned business and advocating for repatriation to Africa on the other hand. Ultimately, the antagonism revolved around the question of what it meant to fight against racial oppression, how to go about this struggle, and what the ultimate goal ought to be. But when Cyril Briggs, W.A. Domingo, Grace Campbell and Richard Moore liquidated the ABB and *Crusader*'s commitment to "Negro, first!" as a framework for approaching anti-racism, they did not relinquish their commitment to organizing black workers; indeed, they deepened this commitment by engaging in the development of the Comintern at the local, hemispheric and global levels.

Close examination of the newspapers and minutes from the UNIA's annual convention minutes as demonstrated in what follows reveals that the affinity for Bolshevism among ABB leaders in Harlem came from a cadre that developed at first in tandem with the rising Garvey movement embodied by the UNIA and after several years transitioned into open conflict over the viability of the Black Star Line and other organizational ventures led by the UNIA. Hence, there was a short period before the differences became more significant than the similarities when the ABB, as reflected in *Crusader*, was developing its own political and organizational framework in the US and Caribbean by working alongside the larger UNIA. Indeed, a much more accurate and useful historical lens would be one that sees the mutual penetration of individual leaders, of shared newspaper circulation, and of mass followings that, by 1924, did develop into openly antagonistic political movements vying for leverage over black working-class consciousness in the postwar period.

By 1924, Garvey's decision codified at the Harlem convention of the UNIA, to make a tactical unity with the Ku Klux Klan (KKK) in their shared goal of black peoples' repatriation back to Africa, ran directly counter to the ABB members' strategic realignment of forces officially with the Communist Party in the aftermath of the Negro Sanhendrin conference in Chicago, where direct action against racist lynching and brutality was seen as the most immediate order of business. Curiously, however, the way that this process was experienced by New Negroes in the Caribbean did not mirror how it played out in the United States. Black people in the Caribbean who had participated in UNIA enterprises— whether UNIA cooperatives, Black Star Line patronage, or the proliferation of *Negro World*—laid the basis in part for how Harlem leadership of the ABB and the paper would cast their decisive votes first for and later against the "Back to Africa" movement. For some West Indians, *Crusader* was circulated alongside the UNIA's *Negro World* and Socialist Party's *Messenger* and seen as all part of one "race" movement. For others, *Crusader* editors would give voice to the angst, distrust and political frustration of former UNIA members and disgruntled Black Star Line patrons who were turned off by the services rendered by this pioneering black pro-capitalist enterprise. Such was the messy intermingling of forces from whence the origins of Bolshevism arose for black radicals in New York and the Caribbean.

UNIA vs. ABB Leadership among Caribbean Workers

The ABB, as reflected in the pages of *Crusader*, was hardly a mass organization that single-handedly paved the way for pro-Bolshevik sympathies in Trinidad, much less across the basin. The little evidence of its Caribbean posts seems to indicate that this organization was numerically small and politically not drawn to pro-Moscow sentiments, at least not from the Caribbean vantage point. Coming from the West Indies, reports in *Crusader* dating back to 1920 from the San Pedro de Macoris post in the Dominican Republic, an important indication of ABB's praxis in the region, reflect that the membership concerns were largely of a logistical and cultural nature rather than explicitly political, much less militantly pro-Soviet. This would be true to form since the constitution of the ABB itself proclaimed the organization to be "highly centralized" with the main function as one of propaganda. In spite of Cyril Briggs's efforts to convey *Crusader*'s professed mission to strategically put the Caribbean at the center of the map of the black world and promote an organization wherein "Across All Frontiers the Negro Race is One!", it appears that in fact the leadership of the ABB was not prepared to relinquish strategic leadership to the posts in the Caribbean.

Therefore, on the question of offering what appeared to be viable alternatives to the daily grind of capitalism across the Caribbean, the UNIA's efforts toward promoting independent business enterprise and racial unity actually paved the way for wider ideological support for the ABB and its attendant newspaper in the Caribbean. In Trinidad, members of the UNIA and Trinidad's co-operative movements sought the direction and assistance of *Crusader* and other radical periodicals from Harlem which were entering the region, and did not see this commingling of papers as problematic. A local UNIA member disclosed in *Crusader* his chapter's efforts "in cooperation for [a] rice mill for the benefit of the rice cultivators of the island" under the overarching leadership of "the correspondent of Marcus Garvey, President-General." Subsequently, *Crusader* was also requested by Hermon Thompson, Trinidadian member of the UNIA, to "hand a copy of the same [letter] to The Messenger [and] The Negro World" in order to, in Thompson's words, "connect ourselves with the American Negroes in sounding our voice for the rights of our Fatherland—Africa ...." In this manner, *Crusader*, *Negro World* and the Socialist Party's *Messenger* were all seen as facilitating the process of reciprocating the flow of information across both spaces in the hemisphere. The more obvious point, however, is that the UNIA had established outposts across the basin and *Crusader* was considered an ally for the redemption of Africa, which was a fundamental basis for their political unity by these Trinidadian Garveyites.[24]

Just as mothers and children would play a key role in the membership base of the UNIA and patronizing the services of the Black Star Line, offering a distinct vantage point for understanding how Garvey was perceived in the Caribbean, returning WWI veterans of both the British colonial and US militaries also factored into the equation of those militant black workers who fall under the characterization of the New Negro. Months after returning from combat in July of 1919, one veteran from St. Lucia wrote into *Crusader*, speaking on behalf of other veterans who "were called to go to fight through the pulpit and press, but since we have returned no editor or parson [had] asked for us fair play." As a "victim of the vicious system who enlisted at the age of seventeen, and served two years in active service, returning July, 1919, and up to date have not been paid," this British colonial forces veteran-turned UNIA member sought employment as a courier for both *Crusader* and *Messenger* in order to "enlighten the people" while paying his own bills. Notable, again, is the interchangeability of these various magazines and their attendant organizations when taken from the perspective of black people such as this St. Lucian veteran.[25]

Garveyism was not an abstraction in 1919. The Black Star Line, the steamship enterprise of the UNIA, provided a pragmatic yet visionary—if dysfunctional— service to many West Indian laborers who might otherwise not have had access to intra-Caribbean transport. But every patron who utilized these services could not now and would not then have been considered a Garveyite. Those same black immigrant workers in Cuba who sought to escape from its local depressed economy in 1920 might have been overjoyed when the Black Star Line reached the island's shores, as their best hope for removal to more auspicious lands. Those same Canal Zone workers that were left disenfranchised and attacked in the racially exclusionary strikes in the Panama Canal might have just as easily found Garvey's Black Star Line as the ticket to their next escape to employment. A record of passengers who were on board SS *Yarmouth* embarking from Havana in January of 1920, included many patrons whose "last place of residence" included Panama, Barbados, Jamaica and Martinique, with mainly women and children on board. Moreover, many of these women, such as "Agatha Headly," bore Anglophone names and worked as domestic laborers. This would suggest that in terms of composition, black women workers were fundamentally the crux of the UNIA's consumer base and also sphere of influence.

At the operational level, the Black Star Line apparently not only offered options for mobility to people who might otherwise have been forced into less amenable situations; it offered them a chance to navigate the circuit of jobs, homes, families, and organizations between New York City and the Caribbean. In very concrete terms, the capacity for the UNIA, especially through the Black Star Line, to facilitate the means of transportation for black mothers and their children across the Caribbean and into New York City also laid an important foundation for the development of circuits of radicalism that the Communist movement would itself traverse in the coming period.[26]

And yet, it was this very same service, that of catering to the underemployed and sometimes altogether unemployed black masses across the region, that left Garvey's enterprise in black-owned business the object of criticism and angst at both the ideological and practical levels by patrons of its services. As *Crusader* increasingly became the outlet for political beliefs that altogether denied the legitimacy of capitalist wage-based production, as its editors swayed increasingly toward alignment with the Workers Party based in New York and the ideologies of pro-Russian socialism, the paper also became an outlet for black people who had begun to reject the Universal Negro Improvement Association's organizational culture and Black Star Line services. According to the Caribbean perspectives that were reflected in the "correspondence" pages of *Crusader*, disgruntled patrons of the Black Star Line became much more vocal in letters published by *Crusader* from both Haiti and Trinidad—two regions where Communism would make its mark in the Black Caribbean during the interwar period.

Whatever tensions existed between ABB and UNIA leadership became exacerbated by *Crusader*'s exposé, largely derived from information generated by subscribers in the Caribbean, about the problems associated with the Black Star Line. In particular, the steamship company had sparked some discontent in Haiti when, in one October 1920 account, 77 Haitians who were boarding a steamer had "complained of dirty conditions" and subsequently "were all turned off the ship." The correspondent asked that the reader "[i]magine the state of affairs … Some of the passengers were foreigners and had arranged to leave." As a result, "… the storm clouds burst. The passengers all rushed to the agency to relate the incident. Some demanded their money for paid tickets," but the "purser of the ship" was "not entirely in a position to reimburse" on account of "other heavy debts to be paid by the agency." This open complaint aired in *Crusader* suggests that the initial enthusiasm coming from some Haitian patrons for the enterprise quickly turned to scorn.[27]

The implicit ideological critique surrounding the Haitian debacle was an assertion of the failure of the UNIA's organizational model and business enterprises. This critique was grounded in larger rhetorical points made by *Crusader* editor Cyril Briggs himself in support of class antagonism—and therefore anti-capitalism—as the basis for black radical praxis. Despite the initial enthusiasm on the island of Haiti for the UNIA, what some considered to be gross operational weaknesses of this venture—and black business as a viable socio-economic alternative to racial capitalism—was strategically laid bare in *Crusader*. The supposed inability of the Black Star Line to guarantee safety and quality of life for these proud Haitian workers en route to other Caribbean regions or New York City had been revealed before the larger UNIA membership and *Crusader* readership. It is possible that such early business infractions with Haitian patrons with respect to Garvey's enterprises, coupled with obvious failures of their own Haitian rulers to provide for everyday workers, helped pave the way for more openness in Haiti in the coming period to the Comintern's alternative vision of proletarian internationalism.

In Trinidad, a historical process that provided the basis for linkages between Bolshevism and the island's black and East Indian laborers was derived from two sources: growing disillusionment with the UNIA among select Trinidadian radicals, and incessant political repression at the hands of the British colonial authorities—with American complicity—visited upon black rebels of any New Negro stripe. Indeed, *Crusader, Messenger,* and *Negro World* had been banned on Trinidad as of 1920. Months prior to the ban, P.V. Langton, one-time member of a local Trinidadian UNIA chapter, had professed that his "hope lies in the Black Star Line of steamships." But in late 1920 after the ban was in effect, he observed that the "Trinidad divisions of the UNIA [were] rotten with 'false Negroes,' in the know" and that as a result, agents within the UNIA had tipped off local authorities to a resident, Mr. R.R. Cuffee, who disseminated these same three banned papers.[28]

Letters in *Crusader* indicate that Trinidad's laborers were becoming ever more visibly demoralized from daily political suppression and economic impoverishment. This same ex-UNIA member, Langton, further remarked in *Crusader* that alongside fierce political repression faced by black propaganda disseminators, the general lot was apparently

> … wearing haggard faces, the cause being that the capitalist owners of the lands they work do not advance them in any way near to a just ration to work the land from which they must get cane for the same owners.

He rejoiced that "the laboring colored population are [*sic*] at last attempting corporation enterprises" to replace prior models plagued with "graft" and "dishonesty."[29] For professing his views, Langton was to become the victim of a house raid for handling such "seditious" literature as *Crusader*, to which he had been submitting these exposés. Much more remains to be researched about the fate of such early disseminators of Harlem-based propaganda in the Caribbean as P.V. Langton.

Two important conclusions can be drawn from the ban of all New Negro propaganda by the British colonial government in Trinidad and subsequent tensions in a local UNIA chapter over how to respond to this political repression. First, the fact that all these papers were banned demonstrates how colonial authorities felt threatened by any political formation that challenged the status quo of racist colonial oppression, which necessitated the constant and perpetual economic and social disempowerment of everyday Trinidadians. In this sense, even the UNIA's incipient rice mill venture on the island was unwelcome by the British ruling class and its colonial henchmen. But second, and related, is the manner in which the very interest in the ABB's more militant advocacy of anti-capitalism as a means of empowering the masses definitely laid the basis for the incipient Communist influence in the island in the coming period. By the 1930s, similar sedition Acts that were even more directly pinpointed against Communist periodicals, organizations and headquarters became the focus of British government intrigue in Trinidad. And as early as 1920, all measures were being made to prevent Anglophone radicals in Trinidad from finding solidarity with the Third International. US authorities were implicated in this repression for the duration of the interwar period precisely because they understood the ramifications of black working-class commitment to Communism across the hemisphere.

Seeds of Dissent in the UNIA Convention Movement: 1919–20

Even though the ABB leaders in New York City utilized *Crusader* to apply an increasingly pro-Bolshevik analysis to the struggle for ending racist oppression, the UNIA in the Caribbean and US made significantly more headway than the ABB in galvanizing thousands and thousands of black workers across the hemisphere, and nowhere is this more evident than in the annual UNIA conventions in Harlem. While Bolshevism and Garveyism were essentially born in the same epoch, ABB members were increasingly advocating for a strategy of proletarian internationalism that was based on multiracial solidarity, which was much more difficult and indeed much more experimental than even black business. A series of accounts from delegates at UNIA conventions from 1920 to 1924, including Garvey and ABB leaders, demonstrates the range of political perspectives emanating from across the hemisphere. In this way, what emerges over the four years at these conventions is ultimately the schism around direct action against racist terror, and from this break is borne a new black cadre in the WP that is comprised of former ABB members.

While Panama and the Panama Canal Zone do not factor centrally into the geopolitical terrain under investigation, the Canal Zone is instrumental for demonstrating how deeply racism acted to prevent black and white workers from uniting to attain better economic conditions. A delegate from the Colon, Panama branch of the UNIA attended the group's annual August convention in 1920 and reported on the intense labor repression of black workers in the Canal Zone as a result of their organized efforts in the labor movement under the labor union leadership of the "United Brotherhood." On the question of the UNIA's current organizing there, he testified that of

> … the people in Panama, especially in Colon—10,000 Negroes there and between 7,000 and 8,000 in Panama—a body of fully 22,000 there, for the most part coming from the various islands in the West Indies—have been accorded the worst treatment at the hands of the white man.

The delegate further revealed that when 17,000 "Negroes stepped out" during a strike

> Drawn bayonets were fixed and the workers were practically ousted from the Panama Canal by military forces. They took possession of the houses and the workers had to rent houses from the Panama Canal authorities so that they were

compelled to work for them. Women and children were ejected from their homes at the point of the bayonet, and many a man has been forced to commit suicide from the time that work ceased on the Panama Canal for them.[30]

Such an image of bloodthirsty Marines with armed bayonets fixed against unarmed black laborers, some of whom were UNIA members, is perhaps one of the most graphic and revealing historical accounts of the ferocity with which New Negroes confronted Jim Crow in the post-WWI Caribbean. In this particular instance, the UNIA was the political conduit through which such direct engagement with racist imperialism was waged, and absent a class analysis of this experience, the "white man" meant any white man—from the ones holding the guns, to the ones getting paid more at the canal, to the ones profiting from the entire process. And this experience was shared before a broader audience convened at Liberty Hall in Harlem.

While such UNIA hubs were overwhelmingly concentrated in Anglophone sectors of the black demographic in the Caribbean, singular attention to the largely Anglophone population in the Canal Zone would obscure important developments in the Spanish-speaking sectors of the basin as well. After apologizing for his hesitant English, a UNIA delegate from Puerto Rico who was one of the "few Spanish speaking delegates" to attend the universal event at Liberty Hall, gave an eloquent speech at the August convention of 1920:

> … the fact of Spanish speaking Negroes joining hands with English speaking Negroes means that language makes no difference with us as long as we are Negroes. My country is a small island 36 by 130 miles, with a population of 1,500,000 inhabitants. It is one of the most thickly populated islands in the West Indies. Ninety per cent of the inhabitants of this island are Negroes. Conditions confronting Negroes in Porto [*sic*] Rico are the same conditions of Negroes no matter where they reside. We Negroes are the same all over the world. We are beasts of burden and servants of the white man.[31]

Here was the personification of *Crusader*'s "Punta, Revolutionist" in living color, courtesy of the UNIA convention. This delegate presented an Afro-Latin Pan-Africanist perspective that was unparalleled for his time. It was an act of political education for anyone who was present and bearing witness. His declaration that Puerto Rico was 90 percent African was far from commonly accepted knowledge of that time—or even today for that matter. Additionally, it was delivered in stilted speech from a native Spanish speaker who was attempting to use language as a basis for actively challenging colonial boundaries which themselves functioned to obscure the "same conditions" that black laborers faced across the basin. This Afrocentric race vision from the Puerto Rican delegate put forward a criticism of economic exploitation since the delegate was condemning the "same conditions of the Negroes" which were characterized by their class function as the "beasts of burden and servants of the white man." This delegate did not recognize the function as "beasts of burden" was the super-exploitation of black labor and, as such, "white man," as with the Panama delegate, was a referent for finance capitalists and their henchmen. Puerto Rico, too, would provide in the coming years one of the most striking accounts of the convergence of anti-racism and the fight for Communism with respect to the Caribbean.

The UNIA, like *Crusader*, was an important point of inception for this process even though in Harlem tensions between Garveyism and Bolshevism had already begun to mount. Therefore, rather than mechanically and a-historically pitting the UNIA and ABB against one another, it is important to investigate precisely how the UNIA's transnational circuits and internationalist appeals were foundational for the entire process that linked workers from such island epicenters like Puerto Rico and the Dominican Republic with laborers and radicals in New York. The UNIA was undoubtedly foundational in the sense that it was an organization of tens of thousands if not much more, and it was run by and for black people, many of whom were black workers from across the Caribbean, and provided a concrete forum for the interpenetration of and struggle over ideas about liberation and power. And yet, the logical conclusion of the UNIA's approach was manifest by the 1924 convention, and the progressive aspects of this movement were fundamentally outweighed by the concession to the Klan.

The UNIA also lost favor in the eyes of ABB members because in the early years of conventions, Garvey would not base the annual conventions in the Caribbean, much to the chagrin of Cyril Briggs. In December of 1919, *Crusader* rebuffed any attacks on Garvey, the UNIA, or the BSL as "racial pessimism." Disregarding such criticisms as a "trial" period, the paper asserted that "Mr. Garvey [had] suffered enough persecution … to earn himself the status of a martyr … in Ethiopia's hall of fame."[32] Months later, however, in the events leading up to the annual August 1919 convention of the UNIA in Harlem that was supposed to elect "a paramount leader for the race," tension visibly mounted in the pages of *Crusader*. While acknowledging that "this announcement of an election of a paramount chief is the most important that has emanated from any Negro source," writers in the paper averred that the leader "should be accepted as such by the entire race," requiring that "all purely Negro bodies outside the UNIAACL should be invited to send delegates to the convention."

Even though Briggs was not utilizing *Crusader* yet to explicitly disagree with Garvey's leadership at the coming convention, he was absolutely attempting to widen the scope of organizations—namely to include the ABB—from which the "subjects" of this ostensible black empire were to extrapolate the "paramount leader for the race." Furthermore, Briggs also began to push for the UNIA's annual convention to choose "a point more convenient to the center of the Negro population of the world than is New York City," as this was apparently the only means of guaranteeing "a set of delegates having mandates from all the Negro communities of Africa and the New World." The ABB utilized its attendant magazine to struggle with the UNIA, and therefore Garvey and his central leadership, around two things: first, to democratize the election by inviting all groups and, second, to have it in a more geographically central location for black people in the hemisphere than New York. The explicit criticism was that Harlem was not the geographical center for black people in the hemisphere. Implicitly, the criticism was that the Caribbean was strategically central in terms of relevance, culture and political orientation. In other words, *Crusader* was "centering the periphery" in praxis as early as 1919.[33]

The immediate impetus of Briggs's approach to centralizing the convention was derived in part from the recent surge of ABB membership in the Caribbean, especially in Colon, Panama. As reported in the magazine from a Colon post meeting held in February of 1920, "a large number of enlistments [were] accepted." The *Crusader* reports would suggest that this Colon post of the ABB was the first one in the Caribbean; now numbering over a hundred members, it was most certainly a demographic that Briggs wanted to include in the coming UNIA convention where a "paramount ruler" would be selected. Additionally, a San Pedro de Macoris post of the ABB had been established in the Dominican Republic by February of 1920 which included a "Cruzian" and an "ex-general secretary of the Macoris Division of the UNIA," the latter of whom felt that "there [was] room here for many more Negro-uplifting societies." An important observation, however, is that this leader was an ex-UNIA member. Perhaps the fact that he was a former rather than current member of the UNIA suggests that already in such islands as the Dominican Republic there had begun to develop a certain degree of tension between said organizations.[34]

Towards a More Proletarian Internationalism: ABB/Communist Party of America Consolidation, 1921–22

July 1921 ushered in important advances for the greater collusion of the ABB and Communist Party of America (CPA), which would soon dissolve itself and join forces with the Workers Party, then considered a "sympathetic party" of the Comintern. In 1921, the ABB and therefore *Crusader* were inaccurately charged with leading the self-defense movement of black people in Tulsa, Oklahoma, popularly known as the "Tulsa Riot." Resulting from the Tulsa affair, the CPA agitated in New York on behalf of the black rebellion and by implication the ABB, which was based nearby in Harlem. *Crusader* in turn informed its readership about the anti-racist efforts of the CPA by publishing an account called "The Tulsa Massacre" which detailed how "Morris Sorner, forty-two, white, of 123 Ludlow Street, [was] arrested last night while distributing … circulars of an incendiary nature," signed by the "Executive Committee, Communist Party of America." In this manner, the ABB was politically tag-teaming with Communists in New York City just as it was making important alliances in the Caribbean and preparing to attend the coming UNIA convention in August of 1921. At that convention, the ABB was indeed expelled.[35]

The disbanding of *Crusader* at the beginning of 1922 led to the consolidation of the ABB leadership with the newly formed Workers Communist Party, thus widening even further the gap between UNIA and ABB strategies for black liberation. Paralleling this United States development in the Bolshevik movement was Soviet Russia's proclaimed anti-colonial policy of national autonomy for the tsar's former colonies. *Crusader* considered that this "fair-minded attitude towards the darker races and her concrete acts of friendship to them" on the part of Soviet Russia meant that this global Bolshevik epicenter was the "only power that has no skeleton of murderous subjugation and wrongdoing in her national closet—no spectre of a brutally oppressed Ireland or Haiti." In this way, the December 1921 issue of *Crusader* was also a harbinger of future alliances between the Communist movement in the US and Haiti. Communist sympathizers like Briggs were at once defending Russian Bolshevism and the Workers Communist Party on one hand and declaring "The American Negro's Duty Toward Haiti and Santo Domingo" on the other hand:

> Should the brave patriots of Haiti and Santo Domingo decide to lay down their lives for their countries ... in a death struggle with the mightiest of the imperialist thieves they will have a chance to reconquer their liberties and drive the crackers into the sea if—IF—the American Negro will forthwith recognize his duty toward the Negro republics of Haiti and Santo Domingo and the extent to which his destinies are bound up with those of the Negro peoples of these two republics ....

In its last pages, *Crusader* invoked the "duty" of African Americans as a race in their common struggle against "imperialist thieves" in Haiti and "crackers" in the Jim Crow United States. And this was to be accomplished with the active collusion of Moscow and incipient US-based hubs of Communist activity—particularly with the active support of white Reds and conscious distance of themselves from their hitherto consistent collaboration with Garvey's UNIA.[36]

Scholars often allude to the ABB/UNIA schism or "expulsion" of the ABB that resulted from the August 1921 convention as a significant breaking point between Communist and Garvey-led ideological currents in the Harlem-based movement of the New Negro. Significant in this qualitative break in the unity of black radical praxis based out of Harlem is the specific manner in which this early development helped lay the basis for a new unification of forces between Communists committed to offering an internationalist approach to the "Negro question" and the ABB radicals—largely West Indian in ethnicity—and the central role of the Caribbean in this consolidation of forces. Rose Pastor Stokes, an important Communist in the United States and of Euro-American heritage, was an important figure who arose in this context of Communist-led organization building who would come to address the fight against racism in both the United States and Caribbean, particularly Haiti, in the coming years.

At the 1921 convention, introduced by Garvey as "a lady visitor who [had] been widely made known to the public by the press the world over as belonging to that class of agitators who are endeavoring to free struggling white humanity," Rose Pastor Stokes was the delegate for the Communist Party who advocated a form of multiracial "co-operation" as "workers" since, "co-operation, in the interest of your own freedom is as necessary in relationship to the great revolutionary working class struggle of the world as it is necessary for you to build your own powerful organization (Applause)." But Garvey not only dismissed her sardonically as "a Soviet professor" among the other "white" professors at the UNIA's disposal, but also expelled the ABB outright for "fantastic misrepresentations" of the UNIA and for acting as the "paid servant of certain destructive white elements which aimed at exploiting Negroes for their own subservient ends."[37]

Little did Rose Pastor Stokes know that as a "Soviet professor" in the years to come, she would pay for this class-based "co-operation" with her own life after suffering a fatal blow from police at a protest, in part, to support Haitian strikers and students in 1929. The very nucleus of the ABB that was expelled at the UNIA convention also, in turn, by 1925 would come to lead the Communist-led American Negro Labor Congress (ANLC) that Rose Pastor Stokes supported in defense of Haiti. From its Liberty Hall headquarters in Harlem, the UNIA was therefore objectively part of the process that consolidated the relationship between Communism and the Caribbean precisely because it provided the pretext for these black radicals and Communists to unify in common action before the UNIA's mass grassroots base. Therefore, the expulsion of the ABB from the UNIA convention is historically important for several reasons. First, it forced the question of collaboration with the "white man" in relationship to the fight against racism to come to a head. Second, it steeled some of the key Reds—black and white—who would carry out the "Negro question" in relationship to the Caribbean for the duration of the interwar period. Third, it helped force the imminent demise of *Crusader* which ceased publication in December of 1921, as Cyril Briggs and other newspaper staff moved into the Workers (Communist) Party orbit.

Caribbean Responses to the ABB Expulsion from UNIA

An important letter to *Crusader* from a UNIA member in the Caribbean in Dominica also helps illuminate the manner in which the Caribbean played a role in helping to concentrate the convergence of Bolshevism and black anti-colonialism in the form of a joint ABB-Workers Party organization. In the aftermath of the August 1921 expulsion of the ABB, J.R. Casimir wrote to *Crusader* declaring that both

> The Negro World—Garvey's paper—and The Crusader—Briggs's paper—have caused the "British" fellows to tremble in their pants in the West Indies. These papers teach us a great deal about the glories of our Race, and if we follow them closely we will act as men.

Casimir also wanted to remind readers that while "admiring Garvey and Briggs and their respective publications we must also remember others who are doing much for the race in some way or other." For this particular member who was weighing in on the question of "race first" from the shores of Dominica, the unity of the race was paramount for defeating the "white bellied reptiles" of US and British imperial domination.

On Casimir's account, neither Briggs nor Garvey, headquartered in Harlem, ought to have been considered the sole representatives of this movement precisely because the struggle was not mutually exclusive of one organization versus the other. But Casimir was also arguing implicitly that "white bellied reptiles," even of the Red variety, did not belong in this struggle. Hence, the schism between ABB and UNIA members in the United States also reflected shifts in the pro-ABB sentiments of some Caribbean-based UNIA members like Casimir who had forsaken ties with whites of any political variety. We do not know whether Casimir's nationalist inclinations represented residual or still dominant thinking on the part of UNIA members across the basin. But Communists could only push the limits as far as their limited cadre could take them.[38]

1924: NEW ALLIANCES, NEW OPTIONS

The 1924 UNIA Convention, the Ku Klux Klan and the Disgrace of Garvey

The year 1924 brought to a head the open and latent tensions between the UNIA and the ABB over the fate of black workers in the hemisphere, tensions that had been only embryonic in 1919. Among the important political positions that were before New Negroes in both organizations were questions surrounding militant direct action against lynching in the United States and international solidarity with people suffering from US imperialism abroad—namely in the Caribbean. In the face of continued KKK attacks and lynching suffered by black people across the United States and concentrated in the South, some of UNIA's membership began to elicit signs of open dislike for any soft-pedaling on the lynching question. Up through 1924, the WP—which by now had infused the leadership of the ABB into its ranks—remained steadfast in its commitment toward critical co-operation with the independent organization of black people embodied in the UNIA because this had been the strategy of the Comintern for the past few years, as had been the case with Mexican Communists who supported President Calles. However, the UNIA convention of 1924 brought the final break to fruition.

The *Daily Worker* announced that the agenda at the Fourth Convention of the UNIA would include the "Back to Africa" movement and also substantive discussion of "the anti-Negro organization of America—the Ku Klux Klan," though Garvey promised a conversation "without prejudice." But the WP, decisively opposed to an objective attitude toward Klansmen, still attended the convention in the hope of bringing a militant, Communist-led alternative to the fore. The *Daily Worker* announced that the UNIA convention would bring "almost half a million Negroes together in the largest mass movement the American Negroes have ever had." Neither the WP nor its ABB recruits had anything approaching such a mass base among black workers in the US or beyond. On the ground level at the convention itself, it was actually the rank-and-file members of the UNIA rather than WP attendees who took the lead in challenging the UNIA leadership on the question of militant self-defense against lynching, which was proof enough for Communists that black workers were open to considering other options for organizational activity.[39]

On August 6, 1924, UNIA members began "initiating [a] discussion" that was "very delicate," beginning with one member from Alabama who "said the activities of the Ku Klux Klan had redounded to the benefit of the Universal Negro Improvement Association" by acting as evidence for the "Black to Africa slogan." This same claim of friendly alliance with the Klan was backed, moreover, by the "Honorable Cipriani," the "trade union leader" and delegate from Trinidad who "spoke advocating the necessity for the Negro peoples of these United States to do nothing that would antagonize the Klan." But a representative from New York, the Hon. M.E. Boyd, fired back and

> … assailed the point of view of [the] previous speaker, who, she said, had spoken as if the Klan were a friend of the Negro. However true it might be that activities of the Klan increased the membership of the UNIA, it was cowardly to acquiesce in the intolerance the Klan exhibited. Negro men must learn that their duty was to place their women in a state of independence. The race could not rise when women had to scrub the floors of white men for a living. No race rose higher than its women.[40]

This woman delegate had challenged the UNIA on the question of militant direct action against lynching. The UNIA responded in kind; it officially regarded the "alleged attitude of the Ku Klux Klan to the Negro as fairly representative of the feelings of the majority of the white people" and therefore declared that the only solution was "that of the UNIA, namely, the securing for ourselves as speedily as possible a government of our own on African soil." The WP, however non-confrontational it could be at the convention, did not adhere to the UNIA leadership's strategy of averting rather than directly challenging lynch terror in the US, much less supporting this strategy as a means toward advancing the anti-imperialist struggle in Africa itself.[41]

Tensions between the UNIA and the WP over how to challenge racism in the United States were also reflected at international level by 1924, and the Caribbean was an important site of contestation. The WP posed questions in the *Daily Worker* for its readers and also presumably for UNIA sympathizers over which international association black workers ought to side with in order to fight racism most effectively. While reporting on developments at the 1924 convention, the *Daily Worker* "fraternally" suggested "that there is another international league which is far more potent to give aid to the classes and races struggling for freedom," since the "League of Nations is the international organization for the purpose of holding down all suppressed classes and peoples" and, in contradistinction, the "Communist International is the international league for the liberation of all suppressed classes and peoples." Garvey, however, had deliberately chosen to align the UNIA with the League of Nations rather than with the Comintern, even though the nations represented therein were responsible for dictating the very terms of racial colonialism that so many UNIA members desired to challenge.[42]

A series of letters written by Garvey on August 3, 1924, in the early days of the UNIA convention indicates the opportunistic manner in which he articulated his movement to the current ruling nations in order to gain their favor and demonstrate his distance from class antagonism, much less Bolshevism. His letter addressed to US President Coolidge communicated his "best wishes of the 400,000,000 Negroes of the world" and thanked him and the white race for "the friendship you have shown that portion of our people that forms a part of the nation" in order to arrive at a "speedy solution" to racial inequality. He also greeted the British colonial officer, Ramsay MacDonald and Italian fascist dictator, Benito Mussolini. While kindly calling upon Mussolini and MacDonald to withdraw their colonialist forces from Africa and other regions where black workers were under their rule, he also conveyed to President Louis Borno of Haiti his

> ... deep sympathy with the indignation of the people of Haiti in the matter of the rape of the country through the forcible occupation by an alien race. We shall work along with the patriots of Haiti to free her from the yoke of exploitation. Long live free and independent Haiti—the pride of the Black race of the Western world.

One point of contestation surrounding Garvey's assertions about Haitian independence was clear for the WP at that time: its vision of what it meant to "work along with the patriots of Haiti to free her from the yoke of exploitation" was looking increasingly different from that of the UNIA.[43]

Communists sought to differentiate themselves from the UNIA by demonstrating their more aggressively anti-imperialist and anti-capitalist methods, and, in order to do so, they had to mingle with black people at the convention itself. While attending the convention, Robert Minor, leading member of the WP at the time, was able to capture and record in the *Daily Worker* a striking story that documented struggles against racism in Jamaica and Cuba as revealed by a "Negro delegate from Jamaica" named R.H. Bachelor, who attended the 1924 UNIA convention. What the WP was doing, in part, by participating in the convention was to use the experiences of black workers across the hemisphere in order to educate readers of the paper about what the fabric of racism felt like.

In his intimate account of the colonial conditions in which Jamaicans suffered, Bachelor recounted "an American lady who seemed to get morbid pleasure in forcing a colored boy of exceptional brightness to read to his fellow pupils in a church these stories of the Negroe's inferiority," but the boy "refused" and "walked out of the church, calling upon the other children to follow." Twenty-one did. Bachelor's disclosure of the complex interrelation of race, nation and culture continued in the Caribbean as he also "told of eight thousand Jamaican Negro laborers who were shipped to Cuba to work. 'They slaved for inhuman hours by day, and then at night they had no houses to live in .... worked themselves beyond human endurance for one dollar a day,'" all while continuing to sing, "God Save the King." That is, except for

> ... a little boy born of these Jamaican parents on Cuban soil, and he grew up old enough to talk and to think ... [and] said, "My father and mother, they are British, and they have to say, 'God Save the King,' but I am a Cuban, and I can say, 'God curse the King!'"

Such was an example of the modest attempts made by the *Daily Worker* to voice the daily concerns and struggles against racial oppression faced by black laborers who were living both as migrant workers within the colonial Caribbean as well as in their own native "independent" lands like Cuba.[44]

The commentaries at the 1924 convention of the UNIA from Trinidad's pre-eminent labor leader, Captain Cipriani, and Jamaican UNIA member, R.H. Bachelor, elucidate the political undercurrents circulating through the Caribbean with which the Comintern would have to contend in the coming period. Self-identifying "socialist" leaders like Cipriani who celebrated May Day and spoke of internationalism were not in agreement with Communists who, aligned with the Third International, advocated for direct action against lynching as the primary solution to racially motivated hate crimes that were so rampant in the United States. But Communists who sought to make political inroads in Trinidad would inevitably have to grapple with the strong undercurrent of "social-democratic" ideology that leaders like Cipriani represented. In the case of Cuba, Bachelor's testimony about the plight of everyday Jamaican domestic and migrant laborers placed before Communists like Robert Minor the problem of translating Bolshevism into a political language that would be amenable to this transnational, multilingual demographic of black migrant workers on the island and across the region.

Seeds of Haitian Revolution Sown at the Negro Sanhendrin, 1924

The Bolshevik movement emerging out of Russia had not yet consolidated its own power on the ground, wrapped up in a bitter "War Communism" period of mass famine and "white shirt" counter-revolution, in 1919. So the ideology of workers' power could never spread successfully to counter the hegemonic norms of racial, cultural, national, ethnic, linguistic and gender divisions imposed by competing capitalist elites and reinforced within the global workforce without a unified political agenda where party organization under a Bolshevik banner of "proletarian internationalism" could be waged. Therefore, part of what is so fascinating about the first historical interval in Communist development described in this chapter from 1919 to 1924 relative to the Caribbean is the simultaneously anarchistic yet formulaic nature of this initial process. That is, a climax in protest in 1919 led to a gestation period through 1924 during which time seeds were sown that by 1925 would give birth to a new stage of radicalism with the emergence of a new set of united front mass organizations and Communist parties operating under the banner of the Third International, as the next chapters uncover.

From the global perspective, by 1924 there was a marked progression in the Third International's strategic mission of linking the national liberation struggles of the colonies and semi-colonies with the proletarian struggles in imperial centers. Peasants, industrial laborers and radical intellectuals from Mexico, the West Indies and New York were all brought into this process of increasing collaboration between movements at the "periphery" and "centers" of American empire. The Communist movements then under way in China and South Africa played an important role in the influence of the Third International on brown and black proletarians in the western hemisphere—namely in Mexico and the West Indies. By 1924, we would see the same South Africa whose white mineworkers were in the global vanguard of racial oppression become one of the world's leading hubs for a new multiracial center of proletarian might, with the Communist Party of South Africa at the center. While Soviet Russia was proclaiming that it had become the "centre of gravitation and attracted the Oriental nations to itself," an even more significant development for the Third International was taking place on a global scale with direct ramifications for the spread of Bolshevism among people of color: China and South Africa were indeed emerging as Red hubs with their own gravitational pulls. Therefore, the "shades" of Bolshevism in 1924 looked quite different from the international perspective than in 1917, with important implications of their own for the development of Communism in Mexico and the Caribbean.[45]

But Communists were not the only ones that were crystallizing the issues of civil rights and black exploitation in the US. Dr. Kelly Miller of Howard University organized an "All-Race Conference" in 1924, and Communists in attendance became more convinced than ever of the need to form their own organization for directly engaging the fight against racism. The ABB and WP leadership had emerged from the "Negro Sanhedrin," the conference's more popular name, held in February in Chicago, with apparently much more political clout than before; they were poised to try and mount a more concerted opposition to the UNIA, whose political base in the black community had thrived consistently up to that time. By July, the *Daily Worker* pointed out that

> Practically the same radical proposals which were made to the Negro Sanhedrin conference last February in Chicago by the Workers Party delegation and sympathizing elements which were down to defeat before the onslaught of the combine of federal office holders, real estate speculators who had profit by segregation of their own race, and proprietors of employment agencies, have been brought before this conference by Robert Minor, of the Workers Party, who is seated as a delegate.[46]

This anti-racist platform of the WP purported to place racism in the United States at the forefront of its political agenda along with "sympathizing elements" in the black liberation struggle, particularly ABB representatives. But the material basis had not yet been laid for political organization around the "Negro question" under WP leadership. The American Negro Labor Congress was not yet in operation as a Communist-led organization that could practically carry out the theory of united action against racism within and beyond the borders of the United States. Once the ANLC was formed in 1925, it would focus particularly on Haiti, where the convergence of racism and American imperialism was the most pronounced.

* * *

Generally speaking, with the exception of periodic newspaper coverage of US Marines atrocities in Haiti, during the formative years of the Workers (Communist) Party in the United States ranging from 1919 to 1924, efforts to lead the political mobilization of US workers against the hegemony of American empire were relatively negligible. A 1924 assessment of the "colonial work" of the WP noted that "the American League has done practically nothing in this important phase of our activity despite great possibilities and despite definite directives sent you." It was therefore proposed by the Political Secretariat from Moscow, the leading political body of the Communist International, that the Central Committee of the WP "must immediately make connections with the Leagues and Communist groups in the American Colonies and Latin America;" and further still, "work in closest contact with the Negro committee," because "the young Negro masses are the most important base for [the] general anti imperialist activity within the USA." At the same time as the WP was being commissioned to carry out this internationalist collaboration between the "young Negro masses" in the United States and Communist nuclei in the colonies, it was also pushing its trade-union organization, the Trade Union Educational League, to "seek to destroy the [American] workers' faith in the capitalist system and to turn their eyes towards the establishment of a communist society through the dictatorship of the proletariat."[47]

Richard Moore, Otto Huiswoud and Cyril Briggs, the others who formed the core of the ABB-WP nucleus of black radicals in New York City, would soon become directly involved in the growth of the ANLC which, in turn, would move its headquarters to New York City just as attention to developments in the Caribbean was intensifying. These new comrades working within the ANLC in the years leading up to the Wall Street crash in 1929 would attempt to place the class interests of the black worker increasingly at the center of their political strategy for working-class liberation. However, it was not WP-aligned black Communists alone who paved this path between New York and the Caribbean in the post-WWI period. As we will see, Haiti loomed large in this process.

CHAPTER 2

Hands Off Haiti!

*There never was a race that, weakened and degraded by
such chattel slavery, tore off its own fetters, forged them
into swords, and won its liberty in the battle field, but one,
and that was the black race of St. Domingo.*
Wendell Phillips, 1861

*I stand in astonishment and wonder at the revelation of Russia
that has come to me. I may be partially deceived and half-informed.
But if what I have seen with my eyes and heard with my ears in
Russia is Bolshevism, I am a Bolshevik.*
W.E.B. Du Bois, 1926

*The Negroes have slept too long. But beware! Who has slept
too long will not go to sleep again when he wakes.*
Lamine Senghor, 1927

The air was thick with tension. By the time the policeman had broken up the
protest in front of City Hall in New York City on December 14, 1929, at least 18
people—black, white and Chinese—had been arrested. Five hundred people
(according to a *New York Times* estimate) had been assembled at the protest,
and the crowd of onlookers were thought to be at least three thousand. The
recent onset of the Great Depression in October 1929 would suggest that this was
an angry "bread and butter" protest for New York's unemployed residents, but
it was not. Rather, the topic of the day was "Yankee imperialism," particularly
"the sending of marines and warships to Haiti." Banners at the demonstration
conjoined a defense of the Haitian movement against the occupation of the
republic by US Marines with a call for workers in the United States to protect
from western aggression both the sovereignty of the Soviet Union and the anti-
imperialist Chinese liberation movement. But why did the demands at this
protest in Manhattan link Haiti with China and the Soviet Union? Moreover,

why did the crowd of arrested and beaten protesters, male and female, reflect an ethnic spectrum as diverse as the places in question?[1]

The solidarity movement in defense of the rebellion of Haitian workers and students against the US Marines that culminated in the December 1929 protest was based out of New York City and led by two of the CPUSA's mass organizations: the Anti-Imperialist League (AIL) and the American Negro Labor Congress (ANLC). Both of these organizations were founded in 1925 in Chicago where the WP—later named the CPUSA in 1929—was headquartered at the time.

The ANLC and also the AIL to a lesser degree placed Haiti at the center of their movement to advance the fight against US capitalists' economic and political super-exploitation of black labor in the United States and Caribbean in the years 1925–29.

The goal for Communists at that time was to strengthen the sense of unity and common cause between white workers and workers of color, and thus developing the anti-racist "Negro question" within a framework that linked the Caribbean and United States became the main way to achieve this goal. Here, an analysis of the organizational activity of the ANLC and the AIL from their inception in 1925 until the climax of the ANLC's work in 1929 lays the groundwork for exploring the reciprocal nature of the movements that emerged in New York and Port Au Prince well into the 1930s, when the labor movement was expanding locally and globally. As we will see, the uprising of Haitian students and laborers who challenged both domestic and American ruling interests was a critical element of the unity forged between the CPUSA and the Communist Party of Haiti (CPH) that would ensue in the 1930s for such campaigns as the Scottsboro case and later the freeing of Jacques Roumain, founding member of the CPH, from prison.

The recently reorganized CPUSA had led this mass protest in support of the Haitian uprisings of December 1929 as a means of advancing the doctrine of the Moscow-based Communist International (Comintern) during the "Third Period." This Third Period doctrine, which was officially codified in 1928 at the Sixth World Congress of the Comintern after the end of the New Economic Policy era of socialist reconstruction, determined that Communists must forge a militant and independent role in the class struggle around the world, separate from and against more moderate political movements that involved considerable collusion with elected officials of the bourgeois state and nationalist forces who were more aligned with imperialists than the workers of their own lands. In part, this shift in Comintern strategy was derived from the fact that by the year of 1928, the Kuo Min Tang's (KMT) nationalist leadership in China had waged a bloody counter-attack against their former Communist allies in China. Tens of thousands of Chinese members of the Communist Party, among them the emergent Communist leader Mao Tze Tung, were forced into secrecy, hiding and general tactical political retreat under General Chang Kai Shek's military regime.

For Communists around the world, the Third Period was seen as the time for ceasing to collaborate with self-purportedly radical national bourgeoisies. In short, by 1929, Communists were dedicated to preparing workers around the world to directly seize state power in the interests of distributing resources and political authority under the auspices of Communist Party leadership. Hence, the Haitian uprising of 1929 provided an important opportunity for challenging US hegemony by following the lead of black working-class students and laborers in Haiti, just as enslaved Africans across the hemisphere had taken inspiration from the Haitian revolution over a hundred years before. Haitian workers led the charge against the US Marines, and Communists in the US followed through with calls for revolution and solidarity.[2]

When we look at the entire timeframe from 1925 until the Haitian uprising of 1929, we see that Haitian workers in particular, and Caribbean workers in general, played a critical though under-recognized role in the Third Period's progressive turn toward international anti-racism under the banner of the Communist International. While betrayals towards the Communists by Chinese nationalist forces was part of the shift in policy, so too was this shift encouraged by evidence that black and other people-of-color workers were already ready and willing to challenge their local national bourgeoisies and band together around class unity. Therefore, the Third Period beginning in 1928 is demonstrative, but not derivative, of the radical turn on the racism question through Communist-led organizations; rather, the origin is in 1925 when the ANLC was first formed— and the Caribbean was always a part of this process. This is why the history of the Communist International must be understood as a global process in which colonized regions and semi-colonized nations like Haiti, where black workers were the dominant majority, both impacted revolutionary strategy coming from Moscow and, in turn, were affected by decisions from the Communist global headquarters. The periphery—in this place, Haiti—was indeed an important if not leading site in the international working-class imaginary about revolution and radical praxis in the year of 1929.

This chapter focuses primarily on the US end of this axis, raising questions about the degree to which Communist mass organizations actually functioned at once as a medium and bulwark of Communist efforts toward building a workers' movement to overthrow capitalism and tear down the linguistic, cultural and geographical barriers separating their class. First, we assess the internal factors in Haiti in 1929 which suggest that Haitian students, workers and intellectuals were frustrated across the board with US military occupation. Communists in New York and beyond, in turn declared that Haitian rulers were complicit in the oppression on the island. Second, we trace the development of the Workers Party's internal evolution in the US toward a more openly anti-racist, pro-worker political strategy between 1925 and 1929 by way of the ANLC and the AIL. Third, we outline the convergence of Haitian nationalist and WP forces with the introduction of the Haiti Patriotic Union (HPU) in the US, and from this, Henri Rosemund's ascendancy as a black Communist Haitian in New York, whose activism in Communist organizations reflected the Third Period left turn in its purest form. Finally, we return to the 1929 climax of events with respect to Haiti to evaluate the extent of Communist solidarity at its peak.

INTERNAL CONTRADICTIONS IN HAITI AND THE 1929 UPRISING

Local students at the Damien Agricultural Institute in Haiti were incensed with a man named (ironically) Mr. Freeman, an instructor from the United States who had remained in charge of the college for what the students considered far too long. In spite of Mr. Freeman's long record of graft and political corruption, he had kept hold of his position at Haiti's foremost national institution of vocational agrarian training. Finally, in early November of 1929, the students led a "splendid" protest, explicitly denouncing the fact that Mr. Freeman earned "$833.33 a month whereas no Haitian in Public education [was] getting over $250 a month, and Mr. Freeman [was] earning more than the secretary of State who earn[ed] $500 a month. The students also protested against so many American experts." The students' aversion to the dictates of "American experts" who, with the support of Haiti's president and the US Marines, were depriving local residents of what little revenue the island generated, led to this protest which resulted in the "jailing of the students and the leaders, and attempts to take the 215 strike leaders that have presented themselves in Damien and some elsewhere." But even in the face of this fierce government repression, the students declared that "they [would] not go back unless their conditions [were] accepted."[3]

Alas, the students' demands were not accepted. In response to this blatant disregard on the part of the Damien school and government officials, the protests during these final days of 1929 in Haiti augmented, spreading at first from Damien to other sectors of the islands' working population in both town and country. Just as Jamaica exactly one decade earlier had experienced spontaneous strike waves that developed into an organized general strike, Haiti's student-led protests took on a similar form. But on this particular Francophone island in the West Indies, challenges to American empire were central to the resistance struggles of the black masses:

> The strike took a general political face against the present administration and the US occupation and was favored by 98% of the Haitian population, and as proof

of solidarity the employees of the National Bank of Haiti struck for 24 hours, the dock workers for 36 hours and the custom house employees who were replaced by strikebreakers within 48 hours. The high school young fellows and girls are yet on strike with the Damien students and they say that they will not go back to school until each and every Damien student is put back in their places and parents are taken back to the Custom House ... As proof of solidarity every business place except the Americans were closed for 24 hours including ... garages, and automobile workers under Freeman's administration ....[4]

This series of student-led protests against the "present administration and the US occupation" brought forth the leadership of the radical Roumain family on the island. Namely, there was word that one "Mr. Paul Roumain, the invariable 22 year old leader of the young workers and students and editor of the new paper 'La Presse,'" was implicated in this Haitian uprising. Spearheaded in part by Paul Roumain's brother, Haitian writer and activist Jacques Roumain, the CPH would eventually be formed in 1930 and Jacques Roumain would also have direct communication with the very same New York-based Communist organizations that would come out in support of the Haitian uprising in December of 1929.

As word reached newspapers in New York, ranging from the *New York Times* to the *Daily Worker*, that Haitian peasants and workers had been shot and killed in the melee ensuing from the student protestors, local CPUSA members— particularly the black Communists who had transitioned from the African Blood Brotherhood into the WP/CPUSA—led a campaign to challenge the US Marines' aggression on the island. The outcome of the Communist-led protests in New York City did not immediately lead to death at the hands of the state as it had in Haiti. But Rose Pastor Stokes, mentioned in the previous chapter, eventually succumbed months later to the brain injuries that she had sustained as a result of being beaten by the New York Police Department while protesting in defense of the "Haitian Revolution" that was then underway.

Weeks before this very mass protest in New York where Stokes had been clubbed and arrested, Otto Huiswoud, one of the original ABB members of Harlem who then joined the Workers (Communist) Party turned CPUSA, and was currently the head of the Negro Department of the CPUSA, sent a letter to all party district organizers instructing them that everyone start an ANLC chapter immediately, especially in light of the contemporaneous Haitian protests and the need to expand the solidarity campaign past New York City:

You have, no doubt, paid attention to the recent developments in Haiti. The situation is a very important one and at the same time a very critical one. We are doing everything possible in order to arouse the Negro workers to protest against the action of the American government in the sending of marines to Haiti, in the quelling of the strike of the Haitian workers and actually killing unarmed Haitian peasants and workers ... Every district should immediately mobilize the party membership in order to hold Mass Protest Meetings and also to demonstrate against the action taken by the Hoover Administration in Haiti. I want to call your attention to the fact that the New York comrades are already mobilizing the force of both the Party membership and sympathizers in order to hold demonstrations and mass meetings for this purpose. You should immediately arrange such Mass Meetings, but this should be done under the Auspices of the ANLC ....[5]

That Huiswoud insisted upon the foregrounding of the ANLC in the Communist-led, nationwide campaign to address the "critical" situation underway in Haiti points to the tremendous weight placed upon the Comintern mass organizations—namely the ANLC—in leading the fight against racism across the hemisphere.

INTERNAL DEVELOPMENTS WITHIN THE WP AND THE FORMATION OF MASS ORGANIZATIONS

As early as 1925, it was the political strategy of the Comintern to create a series of mass organizations that were seen as revolutionary tools to bring workers around the world toward Communism in a series of preliminary stages. The AIL and the ANLC, two US-based mass organizations under the direct leadership of the WP, were the primary political bodies through which anti-imperialist and anti-racist politics were propagated by Communists during the years 1925–29 leading up to the Great Depression. The ANLC, designed precisely to deal with the "Negro Question" of organizing black workers and headquartered in Chicago's South Side "Black Belt," had decided by May of 1925 that it "must be made a broad mass organization and must not be narrowed down by incorrect tactics merely to communists and their class sympathizers." In this critical evaluation of their organization's lack of mass support, ANLC leaders—Huiswood among them—concluded that they were failing to build a mass influence among black workers in the United States because the pro-Communist political thrust of the ANLC did not appeal to them. They believed that black workers had a pervasive "trade union consciousness" that was open to engaging in economic and political struggles for benefits like better wages, increased political representation in government, desegregated schools etc., and, therefore, that this demographic remained averse to moving beyond the realm of immediate socio-economic reform into a transformative politics advocating the overthrow of capitalism and creation of a workers' state.[6]

Concurrent with this assessment of black workers as incrementally inclined toward radicalism, the WP leadership made its first substantive though still relatively weak headway into exposing the linkages between the fight against American imperial expansion overseas and the struggle against racist oppression in the US. Invoking Haiti as a site of resistance was strategically necessary precisely because it doubly exposed the harsh realities of American empire overseas and racist super-exploitation of black laborers in the US itself. Even before the ANLC had been formed, in 1924 the *Daily Worker* reported that American military injustices in Haiti were so infamous that even an "unnamed union leader from the Pan-American Federation of Labor" had witnessed first-hand, "an American marine dragging two boys to jail. He inquired as to their crime, and found they were 'suspected' of petty theft, but that they would be given 18 months at hard labor, anyhow." His attempts to "secure the boys' release" had "failed." Since the general strike of 1919, "United States marines killed more than 3,000 peaceful Haitians, often by bombs dropped from airplanes upon villages where women and children perished," according to Dantes Bellegarde, Haitian delegate in the League of Nations. Even political moderates such as Dr. Leo S. Rowe who had "served in official dealings with Pan-American affairs since 1900 and until recently was chief of the State Department's Latin American Division had admitted that the native Haitian 'Government'…[had] been reduced to a shell." For any serious radical who purported to oppose American imperial rule and racial domination, the obvious question posed by Haiti at the moment was, What is to be done?[7]

In many ways, the Communist-led ANLC was the first significant radical attempt for workers in the US to seriously address the question of US imperialism in Haiti. In July of 1925, the WP distributed 8,000 flyers to invite black workers on Chicago's South Side to a mass meeting advocating "Africa for the Africans, China for the Chinese and Haiti for Haitians" as the key slogans. With the goal of uniting black workers in Chicago with exploited workers of color abroad, Communists Robert Minor and Lovett Fort-Whiteman, both leading Communist members of the ANLC in the mid-1920s, placed Haiti and Africa at the center of their political critique of capitalism.[8]

At the first annual conference of the ANLC in October 1925 in Chicago, the constitution and program also advocated the need for international solidarity of the workers in the US with workers of the Philippines, Haiti and Santo Domingo.[9] Additionally, in its November 1925 "Special Supplement" on "Imperialism and the Negro," the ANLC passed a resolution indicting imperialism, or "the enslavement of the entire world by capitalist nations," effectively "bringing under their oppressive rule the 1,100,000,000 darker colored peoples in Asia, Africa, the Philippines, Mexico, Haiti, Porto Rico, Central and North America." The ANLC in particular and the WP in general were making modest attempts to unite workers in the United States, particularly black workers, with workers around the world. But as the ANLC looked increasingly toward the possibilities of transformative political developments emerging in geographical spaces dominated by black workers, the organization remained clear that advocating for Communist revolution was to remain outside of its political program as a mass organization. Even after the radicalization of the Third International during the 1928 congress, the ANLC—or CPUSA for that matter—fell short of calling upon the workers of either Haiti or the US to overthrow the ruling classes and establish Communism.[10]

Another organizational entrée for Haiti into the Communist mass organizations was through the all-American Anti-Imperialist League (AIL). The AIL had begun the process of building solidarity between movements in the US and the Caribbean primarily because of its ties to the Communist Party of Mexico and also its incipient party outposts beginning to emerge in Cuba and Puerto Rico, as we will see subsequently. The AIL placed the fight against American "Wall Street" control over land, commerce and production, reinforced by the Marines' military occupation, at the center of a political strategy to unite workers in the Western Hemisphere under Communist leadership. When national headquarters of the WP shifted from Chicago to New York City in roughly 1926, so too did the headquarters of its mass organizations. The decision to move the ANLC headquarters to New York from Chicago was partially though not entirely a result of the mass Caribbean immigration to cities along the East Coast of the United States; indeed, several of the leading members of the ANLC—Richard B. Moore, Otto Huiswoud, Cyril Briggs and Grace Campbell—were all immigrants from the West Indies. Maintaining the headquarters in the US laid the basis for organization collaboration of the political forces drawn from the AIL, the ANLC and later the International Labor Defense—all of which would play significant roles in championing the causes of black workers in Port-au-Prince from their bases of operation in New York.

Although the ANLC leadership's decision to remove itself to New York seems to have unfairly implied that African Americans on Chicago's South Side were politically less diasporic in their outlook than what were perceived as the more cosmopolitan black leaders—both West Indian and non—in New York, it was also understandably based on the calculations of leading ANLC members that West Indian Communists in New York had a political base in the population that would be more open to anti-imperialist, internationalist politics than their counterparts in Chicago. By the beginning of 1927, the ANLC was headquartered in Harlem and its leadership was instrumental in strengthening ties between Communists in New York and anti-colonialists from all over the world, including Haiti.[11]

As an immigrant from Barbados and leading member of both the ANLC and the Negro Committee of the WP who lived in New York, Richard Moore attended two landmark congresses in 1927 that allowed the organization to make important headway in building anti-imperialist solidarity with people in Haiti. First, at an April 1927 congress of the League Against Imperialism in Brussels, Moore met with delegates from the French Caribbean and Africa. Second, at the Fourth Pan-African Congress at the Abyssinian Baptist Church in Harlem led by the prominent African American intellectual and co-founder of the National Association for the Advancement of Colored People (NAACP), W.E.B. Du Bois, Moore attended as a representative of the ANLC along with delegates from 13 countries. Resolutions from the congress demanded the US Marines' withdrawal from Haiti along with the abrogation of European rule over China and Egypt, criticized the US-owned Firestone Rubber Company for its maltreatment of workers in Liberia and advocated for black workers in the US to join trade unions.[12]

These resolutions demonstrate the appeal of anti-imperialist, internationalist politics from a broad political spectrum within the black intelligentsia that attended the Pan-African Congress in 1927 in New York City. But Moore was instrumental in pushing further the notion that the power to enforce these resolutions lay in the hands of everyday people rather than an elite minority. The *Daily Worker* reported that despite Du Bois's efforts to prevent the "session from acting on resolutions proposing to place the congress on a broader mass basis," Moore "had made a motion that all resolutions be reported back at the end of the conference so that delegates could decide whether it expressed their views or not.'" The motion passed. Ironically, the Du Bois who had visited Russia in 1926 and declared that he, too, was "Bolshevik," was the same Du Bois who, in the context of mass organizing in the United States, attempted to impede Communist advancement among black workers in his earlier years as a Pan-Africanist—though in his later years he himself joined the CPUSA and became an avowed Communist. With an eye toward mobilizing people from the ground up, the ANLC by the close of 1927 was in the process of strengthening its base among black workers and intellectuals. The ANLC was demonstrating an ability to lead an anti-imperialist movement based out of New York in support for oppressed black people across the globe in general and Haiti in particular.[13]

Haiti was also becoming increasingly important in the global political campaign of the AIL in this same period. On December 21, 1927, the central organizing body of the WP reported that motions had been passed regarding the anti-imperialist work of the AIL under the leadership of an important Communist organizer of the time whose alias was Manuel Gomez. At the upcoming conference of the Pan American Union in Havana, Cuba, the "central feature" in the AIL's propaganda "in connection with the Havana Conference" was

> … insistence upon the position that withdrawal of all US naval and military forces from Nicaragua, Haiti, etc. constitutes a prerequisite for any co-operation between Latin America and the US government, and that this must be put at the Conference as a dilemma.

The goal of the AIL in attending this Havana conference was to foment conflict between the US and pro-American nations in Latin America on one hand and on the other hand regimes that were less receptive toward US influence. In this way, the AIL was attempting to implement the Leninist strategy of building independent, self-determined regimes united in a common struggle against an imperialist foe—in this case, the US—and to "call upon the Latin-Americans to withdraw from the Pan-American Union and form their own federation."[14]

Apparently, the AIL was beginning to make some headway as a Comintern organization with international representation if not influence since, by the end of 1927, it had established chapters throughout the Latin Caribbean, namely in Cuba, Puerto Rico, Mexico, Colombia and Venezuela, as we will discuss later. But Haiti and other islands in the West Indies where black laborers were numerically predominant did not yet have chapters. Therefore, this Havana conference statement in opposition to US military aggression in Haiti and Nicaragua was a progressive step forward in intertwining the fights against imperialism and racism, yet at the time it was primarily a gesture toward imagining this unity of multiracial forces rather than a concrete organizational struggle, particularly in relationship to Haiti. That is, blood had yet to be shed in the US for this cause. The practical manifestations of this commitment to internationalist solidarity from the AIL and other Comintern organizations in New York City would emerge most fundamentally as a result of the radical uprising of Haitians during the 1929 "Haitian Revolution."

FROM CLASS COLLABORATION TO WORKERS' UNITY: ENTER HENRI ROSEMUND

As US-based Communist mass organizations began positioning themselves as champions of the cause for Haitian self-determination, they were doing so in collaboration with Haitian patriots—some of them from the bourgeoisie and others from the working class—who also believed that the immediate and most pressing cause was that of eliminating the US's military and economic grip on the island nation. Out of this political convergence of forces would emerge one Haitian patriot-turned-Communist, Henri Rosemund, whose role in the imminent Needle Trades strike and the ANLC would, as we will see, thrust him into the forefront of anti-racist and anti-imperialist work linking New York and Haiti, and beyond.

At the 1928 Pan American Congress in Havana, a delegation under the leadership of Haitian nationalist Pierre Hudicourt representing the *Union Patriotique*, or Haiti Patriotic Union (HPU), "was arrested by the Wall Street-owned Cuban government and sent home, without being allowed to go near the conference hall," reported Manuel Gomez at a meeting of the AIL in New York. Back in New York, the *Union Patriotique* was reported to have read a message at a conference on the Nicaraguan situation called by the AIL. The AIL returned the gesture several months later with a cable to the White House and President Coolidge demanding an end to the occupation of Haiti and aggression in Nicaragua, declaring that certain Latin American countries too were opposed to US intervention in the region.[15]

The manner in which the AIL and the HPU worked together for a single campaign against US intervention in Nicaragua and Haiti is a feeble yet significant example of how racial and linguistic differences were being challenged—at the prodding of the Third International. Here were activists representing English, Spanish and Creole-speaking demographics coming together during an era of Jim Crow segregation in the US and the US Marines' military aggression in the hemisphere. But they were still doing so within a paradigm that suggested "lesser evil" politicians could in fact support the cause of workers' emancipation. In May of 1928, the AIL featured Senator William H. King, Democrat from Utah, as the keynote speaker at a meeting in the New Harlem Casino on 116th St. where he spoke on the need for "full and complete freedom" from US Marine control in both Nicaragua and Haiti. Also there was William Pickens of the NAACP, Manuel Gomez of the AIL, Robert Minor of the WP, and Henri C. Rosemund of the HPU. King argued that despite the genuine efforts on the part of the US government to democratize and improve the political and social institutions in Haiti, it was now time for the Marines to leave the island and give Haitians free rein over their own development.

Rather than challenging King's paternalistic notion of humanitarian imperialism, the AIL, along with Haitian residents in New York who attended the meeting, backed King's resolution for the Marines' withdrawal. Although they represented different mass organizations, Gomez, Minor and Rosemund were all members of the WP—i.e., they were Communists—yet all were backing King in 1928, a representative of the very American ruling government apparatus the WP sought to eventually overthrow. This "class-collaborationist" approach of Communists to challenging American empire in Haiti in 1928, however, was part of a strategy that was quickly being rejected by the Comintern and represented the waning of the old approach rather than the rising tide of the new. Indeed, in the wake of the Damien students' protest of 1929. Responding to the militant direct action of the Haitian students, Communists in New York would soon challenge the US military occupation at the grassroots level rather than alongside elected officials of the American state like Senator King.[16]

Even more significant than collusion with US politicians was the unity that Communists appeared to be enjoying with local Haitian laborers in New York. This was evident in the recruitment of one leading Haitian patriot and labor activist into the ranks of the WP, Henri Rosemund. Not only was Rosemund a member of the HPU, but he was also a member of the General Executive Board of the Needle Trade Industrial Union based in New York, a "long time" member of the ANLC and even a leading member of the WP in 1928. At the height of the Haitian uprising in December of 1929, Rosemund seems to have returned to

Haiti to help build a Communist party in the context of this fierce uprising. The development of his own political activism is a testament to the mutual growth of the radicalization process between Haiti and New York during the interwar period.[17]

By August 1928, the Communist strategy of placing black and white workers into separate branches of political organization based on race and perceived differences in class interest was beginning to contradict the actual multiracial solidarity that was necessary to successfully challenge racist exploitation in the United States. ANLC leaders Huiswoud, Rosemund and Moore, all of whom were black and also prominent in the ranks of the Negro Committee for the WP, found themselves in an untenable political contradiction because the WP played down the issue of fighting racism in its political platform, such that the ANLC was increasingly called upon to initiate more direct actions against racism. A sort of bifurcation of political aspirations was therefore called into question by these leaders because they understood that the anti-racist struggle had to be embraced by all Communists and radical workers and not just relegated to the activities of the ANLC. In this way, the minutes of the first meeting of the WP's reorganized national Negro Committee revealed that the leadership—namely Gomez, Rosemund, Minor and Moore, along with Otto Huiswoud, George Padmore and Mary King—all felt that the Negro Committee was disconnected from the general WP apparatus and the political campaigns that lay therein. Rosemund observed critically how "speakers at negro street meetings," did not "explain the negro planks in the platform or appeal to those things in which negroes [were] especially interested as for instance: lynching; discrimination; segregation," such that the "negro plank in the platform [was] the last in the whole party platform." This political frustration was significant because on one hand, black Communists themselves had helped the WP come to the conclusion that a special, separate organization was needed to focus on anti-racism. And yet, these same Communists found themselves frustrated that the party was not itself more openly committed to advocating for an immediate end to racist terror as part of the vision for a Communist revolution.[18]

It was fast becoming critical that the WP determine how best to shuffle their few yet valuable cadres, both black and white. Tensions in one meeting arose when Rosemund motioned that George Padmore (alias for Malcolm Nurse, a young Communist from Trinidad who made his way to New York after dropping out of Howard University in the 1920s and would soon become a leading figure in the Hamburg, Germany-based International Trade Union Committee of Negro Workers) lead the ANLC, while another motion suggested that Padmore become a black editor for the *Daily Worker*, thus insuring that the party's official newspaper itself remained committed to reporting on and addressing issues with respect to the "Negro question." Finally, in the first September 1928 meeting of the Committee, it was decided that Padmore would become assistant editor to the ANLC's *Negro Champion*; Rosemund abstained. When in this same meeting, a motion was made that the *Negro Champion* "not make as its official policy the publication of party statements and propaganda, yet such statement of the party should continue to be published as from a friendly and sympathetic organization," Padmore and Moore were among the members who agreed, but Rosemund, again, abstained. It would seem that a very critical moment when New York-based leaders could have infused openly pro-Communist sympathies into anti-racist political activity, they demurred for fear that black workers would reject Communism, though it does not appear that this concern can be substantiated by evidence available at that time or even in hindsight. These political tensions notwithstanding, a flyer for an August 24th meeting of the ANLC in Brooklyn announced that Moore, Padmore and Rosemund were among the speakers.[19]

Although the ANLC leadership did not all agree on the question of openly merging Communist politics with the ANLC, they did agree that American workers in the US suffering from unemployment and poor living conditions were victims of the greed of the same rulers imposing military control over Haiti. Far away from New York, in the sprawling, impoverished communities of Cleveland, Ohio, a WP flyer called for all unemployed workers to attend a mass demonstration "on the public square to demand full wages for the unemployed, work or food" and "protest against American marines strikebreaking against workers in Haiti." Clearly, then, efforts to build an anti-imperialist movement within the US, particularly in defense of Haitian workers, were not solely relegated to the AIL and ANLC in New York.[20]

In the closing weeks of 1928, Rosemund featured an editorial in the *Negro Champion* criticizing the Republican Party in New York and endorsing instead the WP, "the only party that the workers of America and Negro workers should support and help because it has been militantly fighting for their improvement and will protect their interests in each and every point of view." As Haiti would take center stage in the anti-imperialist work of the WP in the ensuing months—culminating in the December 1929 mass protests—Rosemund's activities as a Haitian worker in the United States openly vying within the class struggle for Communist Party leadership, as the best defenders of the interests of the oppressed, were invaluable to the international unity that was emerging. Not only was Rosemund a leading member of Haitian workers in Brooklyn through both the ANLC and the Haiti Patriotic League, but he was also the single most important political figure to emerge from the tremendous strike of the Needle Trade Workers Industrial Union in the early months of 1929.[21]

As a member of the Executive Board of the union, Rosemund called upon black workers in the garment industry, "one of the industries in which a great number of [his] people" were involved, to join white workers in the planned strike for February 6th. He declared himself to be "taking the initiative to make an appeal to all of [the black workers] to support this strike which will be the first attack upon the needle trades bosses to obtain human condition," except that "[t]his time it will not be a strike, I hope, merely of white workers for white workers," but rather, "a blow against the bosses to secure the same advances for all workers regardless of color, creed and race...." To make such an uncompromisingly anti-racist position in regard to multiracial trade union solidarity, and to do so as a Haitian immigrant in New York when no other Haitians were evidently showing an affinity with the Communist base in the city, showed a commitment to internationalist, class-based unity on the part of Rosemund that was singular for his time.[22] And yet Rosemund's name is not a common reference for historians of US labor history, Communist history, or Caribbean labor history. Such historiographies must indeed grapple with the complexities—if rare—of figures like Rosemund if they seek to objectively lay bare the possibilities of emancipatory politics in the twentieth century.

The *Daily Worker* reported on February 7th that, while 12,000 workers participated in the first day of the general strike, "[the police] showed their true form when, together with a number of thugs, they beat unconscious Henry Rosemund, Negro fur worker ... while he was calling out the workers of one of the shops." Though he regained consciousness and was arrested and taken to court, so "serious were Rosemund's injuries that he collapsed while in the courtroom and had to be taken to Bellevue Hospital." Within weeks of the strike, the *Daily Worker* hailed it as a tremendous success and reported that the strike committee had arranged for scholarships for both black and white strikers to attend courses at the WP Workers School on the "History and Problems of the American Negro." Rosemund went even further months later to publicly claim that "[u]nder the leadership of the left wingers, race prejudice [had been] completely abolished in the Needle Trades Industrial Union which includes in its membership hundreds of colored workers of various nationalities."[23] Nothing caused more fear for the local barons of capitalist wealth and government than the idea of black workers leading the militant Communist fight for workers' rights. As such, the retribution on the part of local government and business leaders against the Communists in the needle trade movement was severe, for not only the WP leaders in general but even more specifically for Rosemund, causing New York-based party members to force their hand on the ethics within their organization in regards to defending black comrades who were being brutally singled out by attacks from the state—in this case the cops, courts and business. In short, the WP's potential to combat the ensuing repression against Rosemund was hampered by its own political weaknesses; some of these obstacles were overcome but others were not.

Notes from minutes of the meetings of the Negro Department in the WP reveal a negative assessment on the part of several black Communists of the union's and the WP's genuine effort to combat racism and defend Rosemund in the aftermath of his beating. The extent to which the WP was able to rally its own party members to come to the aid of Rosemund in terms of his physical recovery, emotional stability and political reinforcement thus served as an important litmus test for its commitment to fighting for black and white class unity in the labor movement. Fellow comrade Richard B. Moore made two motions relative to Rosemund that were critical of both the dressmakers union and the party: first, that Rosemund had a fighting record in the union and ought to be defended by his fellow unionists unconditionally in the face of intrigue from union leadership who considered him an overly zealous and radical troublemaker; second, that the party had been insensitive to the gravity of Rosemund's physical and financial needs in the aftermath of the police beating. Rosemund intervened with a motion that all party groups be instructed to mobilize for Toussaint L'Overture (TLO) Memorial Meetings, since the overall commitment to placing the fight against racism at the center of party work seemed wanting in his estimation.[24]

In the coming weeks, the *Negro Champion* did successfully carry out propaganda campaigns for groups to hold TLO meetings, and the results indicated that over sixty meetings were under way in various locales under the leadership of the ANLC nationwide. Certainly the decision to push for these TLO meetings, coupled with the fact that they were named in honor of the esteemed Haitian revolutionary leader, indicates that the ANLC was convinced that Haiti both historically and at present was pivotal to the fight against racism in both the United States and around the world. Yet it was the ANLC rather than the party that was more prominent in carrying out this effort. Therefore, the struggle to integrate the fight against racism—much less the international fight against imperialism—into the overall strategy of building a Communist party remained uneven precisely because mass organizations like the ANLC functioned at once to leverage the ties between black and white workers while simultaneously separating the cause of seizing state power as a platform position for the WP.

FROM HAITI TO LONDON VIA NEW YORK: THE THIRD PERIOD IN CARIBBEAN CONTEXT

These shortcomings in the way New York-based comrades collectively rallied to the defense of Rosemund notwithstanding, the WP-turned-CPUSA continued to push forward in its anti-imperialist campaign, climaxing in December 1929 to take the broadest, most militant stand against American empire as yet in its short history. An August 1929 directive from the national office of the CPUSA in New York to all department heads asked that they coordinate their work to support the upcoming tour of the AIL across the country. Several months later, when Haiti's President Borno announced that he would not run for office again, the *Daily Worker* seized the opportunity to declare "that US imperialism is thinking of changing its agent there" and that "[i]t now appears that American imperialism has some new lackey that would serve the same purpose while not being burdened by the public odium [that] Borno's long term of servility to the Yankee" had fostered. This editorial analysis launched a direct attack against the US capitalist class and its attendant political ties in Haiti insofar as it asserted not only the instability of the Haitian ruling elite but also its subordinate relationship to the US economic and political forces. Protests led by Haitian workers, peasants and students against the US Marines began only days after this editorial was published.[25]

What began as a militant strike of Haitian workers stoning the Marines outside of the US customs office led to a bloody, multi-day battle in which five peasants were shot and killed. The *Daily Worker* quickly rushed to the defense of the Haitian strikers, calling upon its audience in the US to "Stand by the Haitian Revolution!" Not only did the article's reference to this rebellion as the "Haitian Revolution" evoke memories of the revolutionary history of Toussaint and the slaves' overthrow of the French in the eighteenth century, but it also placed support for the Haitian workers on a par with defending both the Soviet Union and the Chinese nationalist movement against British imperialism. The association of Haiti with China and the Soviet Union was significant precisely because this was the basis for the multiracial collaboration referenced earlier that defended the Haitian workers outside of City Hall in Manhattan in December of 1929. As Communists in New York began to organize meetings and protests focusing on the Haitian uprising, the cohort that gave leadership to this movement included many Chinese and European immigrants: "Hands off China" and the defense of the Soviet Union were demands alongside "Hands off Haiti,"[26] given the politics of working-class militant solidarity that predominated in the Third Period.

Meetings were called for December 12th and 13th by the ANLC at St. Marks Hall in Harlem. Moore, representing another Communist-led group neighborhood association called the Harlem Tenants League, met along with Albert Moreau of the AIL, Otto Huiswoud of the ANLC, and Jean Lamonthe of the Haiti Patriotic League (also called the Haiti Patriotic Union); all spoke on the need for black workers to support the Haitian movement. In Chicago, a mass meeting "in support of the Haitian revolution" occurred several days after the New York demonstration. In addition, Japanese workers in San Francisco defied a police order and held a mass meeting in the Japanese section of town against western aggression toward the Soviet Union and to support the Haitian movement; six of these workers were arrested and three were threatened with deportation back to Japan. And in perhaps the most astonishing show of anti-racist solidarity, white workers from North Carolina, organized under the CPUSA-backed International Labor Defense and Trade Union Unity League, held a convention in which they demanded US forces to be removed from both Haiti and Nicaragua.[27]

This impressive nationwide show of support for the Haitian rebellion under the leadership of the CPUSA indicates that certain activists in the United States could and did make efforts to take leadership from the militant movement in Haiti to sharpen their own struggles against the US ruling elite. Furthermore, the CPUSA's membership base was boosted in both Chicago and Detroit when black and white workers, drawn into CPUSA circles because of the campaign to support the movement in Haiti, joined the party. But this movement not only impressed US-born workers; the *Negro Champion* reported in early January 1930 that as a result of the ANLC-led movement in defense of Haiti throughout 1929, over a hundred Haitian immigrants in Manhattan and Brooklyn had joined the organization.[28]

Communist-led support for the "Haitian revolution" had reverberations far beyond New York and the US in general. In the midst of this militant "Hands off Haiti" movement which continued throughout December of 1929, the *Daily Worker* announced that an international conference of "Negro Toilers" was to be held in London on July 1, 1930, under the auspices of the International Negro Unionist Committee—later named the International Trade Union Committee of Negro Workers (ITUCNW)—which was largely organized by black Communists. The purpose of the meeting was to "unite the race on a working class basis" in light of the "revolt of oppressed Negroes in Haiti, Africa and other lands." The ITUCNW would soon become the leading Anglophone, Communist-led organization through which black workers in the Caribbean and Africa were introduced to class-based ideas, and, at times, openly pro-Communist politics. Indeed, one of the most prominent Pan Africanists in the world to emerge post-WWII, George Padmore, was briefly in charge of this organization, and much of his later political training emerged as a result of his earlier involvement in the US—in New York's ANLC and in Washington, DC's AIL chapter—and later Hamburg, Germany, where he edited the ITUCNW's journal *The Negro Worker* and organized black mariners who were docked in Germany.[29]

Reports of this London conference, therefore, appeared in the pages of the *Daily Worker* precisely at the moment when defense of the Haitian revolt was sharpest, thus demonstrating how an international movement for black labor solidarity was at least partially propelled forward through the militant struggles of black workers in Haiti. Moreover, Communist defense of Haiti was part and parcel of an anti-imperialist movement that, under the leadership of the AIL and the ANLC, brought together a multiracial group of American workers who challenged imperial aggression not only in Haiti, but the world over. Haiti served as a "motherland" that represented workers' power in its own right. The Communist movement's support for the Haitian uprising of

1929 was integral to this process. Discussions of the African Diaspora and Pan-Africanism, therefore, would be remiss not to consider the ways in which a multiracial group of Communists in New York contributed to building—albeit unevenly—a mass movement that challenged US racism both in the United States and abroad; Haiti was central to this process.

* * *

It was primarily under the leadership of black Communists in the CPUSA who were organized in the ANLC that attempts were made to enter into regions where there were no parties yet established. The Communist-led movement in support of Haiti really represented the first major attempt to bring about a coordinated effort on the part of Comintern organizations that existed within this New York-Caribbean space. The radical upsurge in Haiti conjoined the different Comintern groups, namely the AIL, the ANLC and the CPUSA, into one struggle in defense of Haiti, the Soviet Union and China, as evinced in the December 1929 protest out front of City Hall in New York City. As the Workers (Communist) Party began to strategically address the "Negro question" by way of the fight against racism in the United States around 1925, it also started a campaign of unity with oppressed black people around the world, and the workers in Haiti were a chief but not the sole demographic that was part of this campaign against the American ruling elite. The CPUSA was simultaneously making attempts—indeed much more successfully—in the period from 1925 to 1929 to establish networks of communication in Mexico, Cuba and Puerto Rico, where Communist parties or nuclei had been established prior to or in 1925. At times, leading members of the CPUSA who were organizing the AIL were integral to fomenting Communist movements in these regions—particularly in Mexico, Cuba and Puerto Rico.

EL LIBERTADOR

ORGANO DE LA LIGA ANTI-IMPERIALISTA PANAMERICANA

Dibujo INDIO

10   CENTAVOS   ORO   AMERICANO

1 Front page of the first issue of *El Libertador*, literary organ of the All-American Anti-Imperialist League. (Courtesy of US National Archives, Washington, DC)

AMERICAN NEGRO LABOR CONGRESS

Provisional Committee for Organizing American Negro Labor Congress

WILLIAM BRYANT, Business Manager of Asphalt Workers' Union, Milwaukee, Wis.

EDWARD L. DOTY, Organizer of Negro Plumbers, Chicago.

H. V. PHILLIPS, Organizer of Negro Working-Class Youth, Chicago.

ELIZABETH GRIFFIN, President of Chicago Negro Women's Household League.

EVERETT GREENE, Chicago Correspondent of "Afro-American," Baltimore, Md.

WILLIAM SCARVILLE, of the Pittsburgh-American.

CHARLES HENRY, Representative of Unorganized Negro Steel Workers, Chicago.

OTTO HALL, Waiters and Cooks Association, Chicago.

LOUIS HUNTER, Longshoremen's Protective and Benevolent Union, New Orleans, La.

OTTO HUISWOOD, African Blood Brotherhood, New York City.

LOVETT FORT-WHITEMAN, Organizer of Congress.

AARON DAVIS, Neighborhood Protective Association, Toomsuba, Miss.

JOHN OWENS, Organizer of Negro Agricultural Workers, Ripley, Cal.

ROSINA DAVIS, Secretary of Chicago Negro Women's Household League.

E. A. LYNCH, Fraternal Delegate from West African Seamen's Union, Liverpool.

JACK EDWARDS, Representative Negro Pullman Car Workers, Chicago.

SAHIR KARIMIJI, Fraternal Delegate from Natal Agricultural Workers, South Africa.

Send all inquiries to Lovett Fort-Whiteman, 19 S. Lincoln St. Chicago. Ill.
Tel. Seeley 356?

The American Negro Labor Congress to Fight

All Racial Prejudice.

Jim-Crowism

For Equal Pay for Black and White Workers.

Against Discrimination in Labor Unions.

Against Lynching.

For a United American Workingclass.

-2-

5. To evolve more definite and concrete plans of making the American Negro Labor Congress an integral part of the militant movements of the oppressed peoples of the world.

6. To examine what progress has been made by our Negro students at the University for Far Eastern Peoples in view of throwing some light on the manner of selection of Negro students in the future.

7. To get further material on the subject of national and racial problems in the Soviet Union as treated by Bolshevik Policy for my yet unfinished book, entitled "Bolshevik Policy and Racial Problems"

8. To insist before the Comintern for the publication of a quarterly magazine for colonial peoples; a magazine that would develop an understanding of the class-struggle and capitalist-imperialism, rather than an approach which would assume a knowledge of these phenomena on the part of reader.

9. To deal with the matter of a commercial treaty between the Soviet Union and the Negro Republic of Liberia, West Africa, toward a concession of agricultural land for the cultivation of coffee, rubber, cocoa, spices, drug, etc. This matter had been taken-up before my-leaving Moscow. Our aim in the Comintern being of course, to get established Soviet Political influence on the African Continent.

10. To get instructions and formulate definite plans of conduct to be followed within the coming Conference of Colonial and Semi-Colonial Peoples to be held in Brussels in August.

The Future of the World is in the Hands of the Working Class, Black and White.

2 Part of the platform of the American Negro Labor Congress. (Courtesy of US National Archives, Washington, DC)

CHAPTER 3

El Dorado Sees Red

*Empires always involve a mixture of direct and indirect rule.
The central power has ultimate sovereignty, and exercises some
direct control, especially over military force and money-raising powers, in
all parts of its domain … The key to understanding empire lies
in the bargains struck between imperial centre and local "collaborators".
No empire could last for long if it depended entirely on
naked power exerted from the centre outwards.*
Steven Howe, *Empire: A Very Short Introduction*, 2002

*Colonies, we call them, these places where "niggers" are cheap
and the earth is rich; they are those outlands where like a swarm of
hungry locusts white masters may settle to be served as kings, wield
the lash of slave-drivers, rape girls and wives, grow as rich as
Croesus and send homeward a golden stream. They belt the earth,
these places, but they cluster in the tropics, with its darkened
peoples: in Hong Kong and Anam, in Borneo and Rhodesia, in
Sierra Leone and Nigeria, in Panama and Havana—these are the
El Dorados toward which the world powers stretch itching palms.*
W.E.B. Du Bois, *Darkwater*, 1920

Days before the Communist leader Rose Pastor Stokes had been clubbed and arrested by the NY Police Department (NYPD) in December of 1929 at a protest against the execution of Haitian dissidents by American Marines, Assistant Secretary of State J.P. Cotton was notified about a police raid in Havana of the Communist Party of Cuba's headquarters. This raid turned up names of Communists in New York City who were in contact with their Havana-based counterparts. At the very moment when New York-based Communists were demanding "Hands off Haiti", the CPUSA—mainly by way of their mass organizations the Anti-Imperialist League (AIL) and the International Labor Defense (ILD)—had begun to protest the crackdown on Communists in Cuba which resulted in mass arrests and even deportation of Chinese radicals who had been branded "foreign agents."[1]

In January, months before the Cuban police raid on Communist headquarters, just across the Gulf of Mexico in Mexico City, Julio Antonio Mella, founding member of the CPC, was gunned down by Mexican authorities while in exile from the Machado regime in Cuba. Haitian students killed by US Marines, Cuban Communists killed by Mexican police, Chinese Communists deported by the Cuban state all in 1929: national bourgeoisies in Mexico, Cuba and Haiti—with the tacit or direct support of American military power—were enacting desperate measures of repression against radicals in their respective jurisdictions as the walls were caving in on Wall Street.

But by 1929 the specter of Communism was also haunting the Caribbean in a region whose jurisdiction was more directly controlled by the US than all of these other nations: Puerto Rico. In the interim between the assassination of Mella in Mexico in January and crackdowns in Cuba and Haiti at year's end, General Palmer C. Pierce, a hired gun of the Standard Oil Company (progenitor of today's J.P Morgan Chase billion-dollar conglomerate), rang the alarm on May Day, the international workers' holiday, for Puerto Rico. Pierce called on the Secretary of State to seek immediate assistance in thwarting the "Red menace" after "Confidential agents of the Standard Oil Company" had contacted General Pierce with alleged reports that "Soviet agencies had been withdrawn from Mexico and Cuba and had now established headquarters at San Juan, Puerto Rico" with intentions to "stir up trouble in Venezuela." It did not assuage Palmer's fears to know furthermore that "elements in Mexico were supporting the revolutionary movements in Venezuela" insofar as "he understood that Mexico was preparing to send arms" there. The apparent propinquity of this Communist movement to the oil-rich basin posed problems for an important US financial sector concentrated in Venezuela. US government and military authorities faced increasing pressure to ward off against any threat against profits for finance capitalists such as the Rockefeller-owned Standard Oil Company in the months leading up to Wall Street's crash, much the way today a workers', pro-Communist uprising in the oil-rich Middle East would terrify the Pentagon. And this pressure, compounded by the fact that the Communist International had been gaining political momentum since 1925 across the hemisphere, was perceived as an Achilles heel to their incipient empire.[2]

But why Puerto Rico? General Pierce had clearly received faulty reconnaissance, since no Communist revolutionary overthrow staged from Puerto Rico ever came about. Pierce's alarmist response could have been attributed to his status as a veteran of both the Spanish–American War and World War I, and the idea that he had helped wrestle Puerto Rico from Spain in the 1890s only to possibly lose it to Bolsheviks a few decades later was unfathomable. All the same, it was indeed the case that, beginning in

1926, Communists from the United States had made conscious strides toward creating a party on the island, though only a "group" rather than a formally recognized party would emerge in this interval.

More to the point, if Communists in the United States were seeking to grant any weight to Leninism as praxis, then they would be compelled to support the anti-"Yankee" movements in the countries, republics and territories where US economic, military and political influence was most acutely concentrated. In short, they would have to act in genuine solidarity with their comrades who had formed Communist hubs of operation—in the form of parties, groups and mass organizations (AIL and ILD) in these locales. By 1929, Cuba was such a locale. So, too, were Mexico and Puerto Rico. And the manner in which this international movement was constructed in many ways helps inform our understanding of how and why the struggle against racial oppression was the determining factor for Communist expansion into the Black Caribbean.[3]

The interplay between anti-racism and Bolshevism in the hemisphere did not just take form in terms of how the CPUSA grappled with the "Negro question" relative to Haiti from 1925 to 1929. The genesis of Communist movements in Latino regions was a concrete process in which the Communist International worked through questions of anti-imperialism and the struggle against racial super-exploitation of workers of color. As we have seen, the physical shift in the location of WP's headquarters from Chicago to New York between 1925 and 1927 forced into existence a politically motivated New York-Caribbean aperture for black working-class militancy, at once rupturing with and building on the current Communist project at the hemispheric and global scales.

As a point of contrast to developments in Haiti and the British West Indies (BWI), however, the budding Communist movements in Puerto Rico, Cuba and Mexico rendered it difficult for US Communists to assume without question that the headquarters of Comintern organizations like the All-American Anti-Imperialist League (AAAIL) would be housed in the United States. Essentially, Communists in the US could not avoid addressing what were fundamentally problematic assumptions that they held when it came to entrusting the leadership of the global drive for socialism in the hands of laborers of color outside of the hemispheric metropolitan centers of finance capital.

Attendant with the consolidation of the AIL and ANLC in 1925 was a general consensus within the Comintern that the "Peasant Question" was central to the overall strategy of achieving socialism. In a speech delivered by leading Communist Nicolai Bukharin on April 2, 1925, the situation presented before the Communist International was articulated as follows:

> We all know that the colonial question will play a great role in the process of the world revolution. We know that from a certain standpoint the antagonism between capital in the highly developed metropolis and the backward colonies is one of the chief contradictions of capitalism, that these contradictions are nothing else

but—figuratively speaking—the contradiction between the world city, the centres of present industry and world economy, and the world village, that is the colonial periphery of the centres.[4]

It is notable that the peasant question and colonial question were seen by the Comintern very early on as related if not even interchangeable, and especially by 1925. In the metropolis of Chicago where the ANLC began and the AIL shortly beforehand, it was necessary to address the "peasant" and "colonial" dimensions of the struggles in which these organizations were expected to have the broadest political influence. Haiti in many ways fit the description as a largely peasant and semi-colonial republic. Moreover, many of the black laborers then living in northern industrial centers like Chicago had recently moved from southern parts of the United States during World War I in a mass movement referred to as the "Great Migration," thus leaving behind essentially peasant roots in the agrarian South to work in the factories of the industrial North. But Mexico, Cuba and Puerto Rico laid bare, even more than Haiti, the challenges associated with organizing largely agrarian populations. In this chapter, our attention therefore shifts to the Latino—i.e., "brown"—Communists who were engaged in this transnational process because the struggle against racism in the hemisphere remained an integral factor of this Communist International circuit, not simply in regards to explicitly black laborers but also in Spanish-speaking regions which, while significantly populated with laborers of African descent, were recognized racially as non-black but rather "brown."

In this way, what follows is an attempt to outline some of the limits and possibilities that the Comintern confronted in the years from 1925 to 1929 as Communist-led organizations and parties sprang into motion in Mexico, Cuba and Puerto Rico. The WP-turned-CPUSA faced an important historical conjuncture in the rise of "American" Bolshevism with the birth of Communist movements in the Spanish-speaking West Indies in 1925—first with a party in Cuba and later a "group" in Puerto Rico shortly thereafter. The vision and manifestation of the Communist International would objectively take on a more global form once Communists in Moscow, Chicago and New York in the years from 1925 through 1929 had to work alongside Communist parties and small cells of operation in subaltern epicenters such as Havana and Ponce. Notably, Communists based in New York and Chicago played active—though not unproblematic—roles in the formation of these Communist epicenters in the Spanish-speaking Caribbean. Without a doubt, linguistic and racial chauvinisms that served the interests of ruling elites were significantly challenged, though not without tremendous internal struggle and self-criticism by a largely white, Anglophone party in the US that helped to foment this process of Leninist strategic development among Spanish-speaking Communist groups of Latinos in Cuba, Mexico and Puerto Rico. Newspapers, namely *Daily Worker* and

El Machete, were not only the propaganda tools for promoting the work of these parties and the AIL; they were essential in themselves as ideological weapons that forged greater working-class unity across national borders within North America.

That US-based Communists had been charged by the Communist International out of Moscow with directing the political work in these Spanish-speaking regions of the hemisphere, however, was complicated by the fact that the struggles in Mexico, Cuba and Puerto Rico generated a set of radical confrontations with the local and American capitalist forces that were more intense if not more revolutionary than the class struggles led by Communists in the US. Therefore, the tensions between "center" and "periphery" that arose over the questions of how to grow the Communist International in the hemisphere, such as questions like where the headquarters of the mass organizations would be situated, manifested most sharply between the US and Mexican comrades, precisely because of the force and magnitude of the movement then underway in Mexico.

CENTERING THE PERIPHERY: COMMUNISM IN MEXICO AND THE UNITED STATES

Origins of the AAAIL in Hemispheric Context

The Bolshevik movement in Mexico is an important entry point for this historical inquiry of organized Communist activity in the Spanish-speaking regions of the hemisphere. Like China, already by 1925 Mexico had a sizeable militant base for Communist Party activity, which was developing among industrial workers as well as radical peasants in the campo. As we have noted, the global strategy for the Comintern in 1925 was to align Communists with the nationalist and, they believed, more progressive elements of the domestic rulers that they believed could be steered away from partnership with imperialists as a phase toward an eventual workers' overthrow of the state. But Mexican Communists who were not hostile toward President Calles in 1925 began to challenge the Comintern strategy of aligning with domestic rulers, precisely because they could see how reactionary and anti-worker their own elites had become.

Mexican Communists had begun, before the official leadership headquarters in the US and Moscow, to put forward political positions that pointed toward the need for more direct challenges to capitalism led by the party. Prior to the KMT betrayal in China and subsequent "Third Period" turn toward strategic advocacy of building independent workers' power, Mexican Communists had begun to point toward more radical shifts that would soon become part of the international Communist strategy. And this is not a minor point by any measure. Geographically unlike China, however, Mexico was not separated from the United States by a vast Pacific; rather, it was adjacent to the US and therefore the fates of both the Mexican and US Communists movements were closely intertwined. Therefore, attention to the relationship between the Communist Party of Mexico (CPM) and WP helps illuminate the role that people of color outside of the Chicago/ New York metropoles played in pioneering the strides toward greater and more entrenched Communist leadership within the working class on a global level.

Interaction between Communist organizers in the US and Mexico also meant that the strongest linkages between US Communists and their counterparts in the hemisphere involved one of the least representative areas in the region with a substantial demographic of black inhabitants. Although the particular form of anti-racism in the US-Mexico solidarity movement did not directly address the issue of anti-black racism, the cross-border Communist alliance cemented in this post-WWI period did, as we will see, help to lay the basis for the 1930s movement in Mexico to defend the African American "Scottsboro Boys" against execution under the racially segregated and discriminatory courts of the southern United States. Again, however, the primary manifestation of anti-racist solidarity between Mexican and US Communists in the period from 1925 to 1929 did not revolve directly around the defense of black workers in the region; rather, the question of the solidarity with the historically oppressed Indian peasants in Mexico was the chief issue that placed race at the center of US-Mexican Communist radicalism.

Within weeks after the peasant population in the Mexican state of Vera Cruz had established a self-proclaimed Soviet-style outpost at the end of 1924, a solidarity movement between Mexico and the United States had begun in the pages of the *Daily Worker* in 1925. In February, the *Daily Worker* announced that it had been "greeted" by the CPM as represented by one Comrade Ursula Galvan of the League of Agrarian Communes of the State of Vera Cruz. Speaking at an event held in a facility with "communist publications of the *Daily Worker* and *El Machete* shown from the schoolhouse walls," Galvan was described as having given a keynote address in which he

> ... held the crowd breathless as he developed his theme, "Lenin and the Peasant Problem." He compared Russian peasant life to the present peasants' existence in Mexico, told of what he saw during his visit in Russia ... [and] received thunderous applause and many vivas for the Soviet of workers and peasants.[5]

On one end, it is clear that as early as 1925 the *Daily Worker* had not only been circulated within Mexico but more importantly was met with some degree of support by the peasants of Vera Cruz for whom Soviet Russia stood as a beacon of "viva" or "cheers" for their own local struggles. Bringing this set of ideas as part of a comprehensive party program to Mexico was one of the chief assets of the US-based party. On the other end, *Daily Worker* readers in the United States were receiving from Mexico the news of actively engaged peasants for whom the Soviet agricultural experiment of collectivization had become not just an idea, but a praxis. Indeed, the AIL was just beginning to gain organizational traction in the United States and Mexican headquarters in Tampico. Hence, self-governing peasant councils were springing up in Mexico's countryside and challenging Mexican elites and American empire alike while radicals in the North were just beginning to coalesce. This unevenness of political development of radical forces suggests that the Mexican peasantry and left movement south of the border was more advanced and forward thinking at least with respect to militant direct action than the movement in the US in this period from 1925 to 1929. Such a premise implies, then, that logically it would be appropriate for the AIL to be led at least in part from a headquarters in Mexico. Instead, the decision was made for it to be housed in the US.

Close attention to the development of the AIL in the US and in Mexico demonstrates the ways in which Mexican Communists often laid the practical groundwork for the struggle against US imperialism that Communists in the US then supported. For example, the US branch of the AIL's "Anti-Imperialist Week" in the first week of July 1925—a week-long campaign that announced the formal introduction of the AIL to American workers in neighborhoods like Chicago's South Side—went to great lengths to connect up local struggles for bread with broader challenges to racial oppression by supporting Communist-led struggles in China and Latin America. The political collaboration that united the CPM and the WP had begun, importantly, in Mexico rather than Chicago. In point of fact, the very idea for the AIL's US-based anti-imperialist week was born on Mexican soil— advocated at the third annual convention of the CPM in the spring of 1925 and placed into effect in the US in the summer. Hence, from its inception, the relations of Communists operating in organizations like the AIL between Mexico and the United States were always already those of reciprocal activity and leadership; that is, the very nature of the process that generated these organizations was one of mutual growth and exchange of ideas and tactics for a common strategy. But the reciprocal nature of this process was not always sufficiently recognized or even understood by WP members in the United States, some of whom—even among the most committed—suffered from the political limitations of their own nationally parochial and possibly racially prejudiced beliefs that they were the predisposed leaders of the proletarian movement in the hemisphere. Close attention to meeting notes and political propaganda of the AIL in this period is critical to uncovering and analyzing this complex transnational political process.[6]

Leninism and the Mexican Peasantry

"Un peligro amenaza a la America Latina," or "a specter is haunting Latin America," announced the editors of *El Libertador*, the official literary organ of the Pan-American Anti-Imperialist League based in Mexico, in its first issue, released in March of 1925. Notably, this "Pan-American" League was the exact same "All-American" league, or AAAIL, that Communists in the continental United States had translated into the name of its sister organization.[7] The pages of *El Libertador* in its first issue reflected the manner in which the editorial staff remained committed to demonstrating its class solidarity with laborers in the United States over and above any national- or race-based allegiance to the Mexican republican government. Interestingly, it is quite possible that the editors of the Mexican paper could have been both US and Mexican-based comrades, since both Gomez and Ruthenberg's names appeared as authors in several of the paper's articles. This was a significant contrast from the post-WWI period when Mexican Communists were not so openly hostile to the government. While waving "adios" to the "'Socialismo'" of the Mexican government under President Calles in *El Libertador*, this AAAIL newspaper in Mexico greeted US workers, proclaiming an "End to the 'Races,'" since "'the Anglo Saxon' race is not our enemy. Our enemy is the North American banker." The political justification for unified organization between the AAAILs in both countries was provided as follows: "The Morgan camp that sent troops to Central America to smash the resistance and increase the exploitation here, sent troops to the state of West Virginia to smash the strikes and increase the exploitation of the miners there." Explicitly, the AAAIL saw *El Libertador* as a mechanism for the expression of a multiracial campaign to contest American capitalist investment within the US and in Mexico, particularly that of energy, whether it be in the form of US coal or Mexican oil.[8]

Such rhetorical solidarity as expressed on paper, however, was not fully reflective of the conflicts and internal struggles among Communists in the United States and Mexico at this time. Political correspondence between leading party members—Manuel Gomez chief among them—in the United States who had directly engaged with the Mexican Communist struggle, particularly by way of the AAAIL, shows signs of a much more tense and fractured solidarity campaign than *El Libertado* suggested. From a report of the Third Congress of the CPM held in the second week of April in 1925 as seen through the eyes of an American delegate who drafted the report, presumably Gomez, what becomes glaringly apparent is that there were real political limitations on the extent to which racial chauvinisms would be eliminated from the process of inter-party political collusion between Mexico and the United States.

An assessment by Gomez of the CPM revealed that its political influence within both the trade union and peasant quarters was limited, particularly in the latter sector. The pro-Soviet sentiment among the largely Indian-based peasantry in Vera Cruz was not actually led by the CPM, according to this analyst and, therefore, the decision at this convention was made to place the headquarters of the CPM in the industrially concentrated city of Tampico, where it was reported that "great headway has been made in the organization of the oil workers during the past two years." The Communists' perceived concentration of proletarian support in the oil sector, combined with the fact that "the railroads, the harbor workers, and the mines" were all seen as "strategic positions in the Mexican industry" for seizing control of the means of production, led to the decision that Tampico would serve as the "point of departure for all of our work in Mexico" rather than peasant-dominated regions like Vera Cruz.

Communists in the Mexican and US parties decided together at the April convention that it was best to initiate the geographic "point of departure" for radical movement from Tampico and organize outward toward the rest of the country. At stake in the decision to base the CPM in Tampico rather than Vera Cruz was the perpetuation of a persistent formulation in Marxist theory which *a priori* relegated the revolutionary vanguard struggle to more industrialized proletarian sectors that were concentrated in cities in contradistinction to the less industrialized peasantry, even in moments when peasants were showing a greater mass outpouring of allegiance to the politics of socialist internationalism than their urban counterparts. Although workers' control requires leverage over industrial production, revolution also requires pervasive class consciousness—and this ideological force can be based outside of the urban core. Therefore, Communists based in the United States were also implicated in this partial bias against the peasantry which had the potential to spiral into a chauvinism between center and periphery on myriad levels. For example, while the *Daily Worker* had welcomed the "greetings" of "Comrade Galvan" based out of Vera Cruz in February of 1925, only months later Gomez had essentially determined at the Third Congress of the CPM that this very same Galvan's leadership and the movement as a whole in Vera Cruz was not authentically Communist. That is, despite the fact that

> … in the state of Vera Comrade Ursulo Galvan is followed unquestionably by some twenty to twenty-four thousand organized peasants, whose organization is known as the "Liga de Comunidades Agrarios de Vera Cruz," and which is affiliated with the Peasants International of Moscow

… the general consensus—or at least this delegate's perception of the consensus—was that this apparent "Communist influence" was insufficient for making it a genuinely Communist struggle. Rather, the "actual fact," according to Gomez, was that "these peasants do not follow the CP and most of them do not know of the existence of the CP. The Central Committee of the party has no contact with the peasant masses."[9]

Instead of seeing the disinclination of the "peasant masses" in Vera Cruz to "follow the CP" as a weakness on the part of the central committee which could, by all accounts, have placed itself in closer proximity to the peasantry, the weaknesses were attributed to the personal flaws of Comrade Galvan and his leadership, claiming that

> ... Galvan is a natural born leader who has lived the life of the peons since childhood and has won their confidence. He is not a Communist, however, in the sense of one who understands the Communist position and has a real Communist ideology.

In essence, Galvan's perceived lack of a "real Communist ideology" was reflected in a more general assessment that the "Congress was practically an organization congress" in which "delegates themselves were for the most part inexperienced and uncertain"; uncertain, that is, of their historic mission as prescribed by comrades in the center—e.g., Tampico and Chicago.[10]

Hence the "Soviet of Mexican Peasants" which had been established in Vera Cruz and lauded in the pages of the *Daily Worker* was at once unified with and alienated from the very Communist International to which it was aligned, even at the local level of Communist leadership that was represented within Mexico. The leadership of the CPM, several years prior to that of the United States, began undergoing a "Bolshevization" campaign in 1925 which was defined by the commitment to "centralization and discipline." Delegates representing the peasants of Vera Cruz decried this "discipline" as a standard for Bolshevik loyalty. One delegate from Vera Cruz called "Bolio" stated that "'Of course I am not a member of the party, and I am not bound by any discipline, but you can decide what you want here, and I will go back and tell them about it.'" "Them" in this case presumably meant the tens of thousands of Mexican peasants of Vera Cruz to whom this Mr. Bolio was expected to answer. There was an error in the peasants' rejection of "discipline" and party membership. Workers' power requires individual allegiance to the collective strategy. But central leadership did not see their own alienation from this huge political base. In this way, the divisions between center and periphery persisted on even greater levels, taking on ever more distinctly national and racial forms. Clearly, Mr. Bolio felt as though the urban Communists in Mexico wanted to "centralize" leadership in a manner that was not representative of the decision-making process then underway for their comrades in Vera Cruz. The racial, or ethnic, character of this tension was inescapable, since the peasants were largely of Indian extraction, whereas the city dwellers and Communist leaders were likely to be less directly descended from this same Indian demographic.[11]

The Communist Headquarters for the AAAIL

Just as assessing the weight of the radical movement among the peasantry was in question by Mexico's urban comrades, so to was determining whether to establish the headquarters of the All-American Anti-Imperialist League in the United States or Mexico an item of debate within the CPM and also between Mexican and US leaders. The tensions seem to have arisen within the CPM at this same Third Party Congress of 1925 in the context of a larger political disagreement about how radical the CPM should be in relationship to the Calles government. Whereas some Mexican comrades and the WP agreed that the AAAIL's headquarters should be in the US, other Mexican comrades felt that it should be in Mexico. Delegates from Mexico City initiated the campaign to place the headquarters in Mexico City, an endeavor which was dismissed sardonically by the US delegate as blindly "obeying instructions received in a meeting of the [Mexico City] local." But the proposal was turned down by the CPM's leadership

> … unanimously, it being expressed that the prestige of the American Party as against the Mexican Party, its maturity and experience, and its position in the home country of American imperialism made it necessary that the effective direction of the Pan-American Anti-Imperialist League should be in the United States.

This assertion on the part of leading Mexican Communists that their comrades in Mexico represented a less politically mature outpost of the Comintern than their counterparts in the US is significant because the argument for the WP's maturity stemmed from its commitment to supporting the Calles regime while the CPM had a sizeable contingent that was not won to this position and felt a third candidate for presidency would create better conditions for Communist agitation and success in the country.[12]

It is clear that Communists in Mexico and their US counterparts were serious about the work of building Communist Party centers in Mexico and also linking the struggle for workers' power to the global strategy of the Communist International. But the decision at this Third Congress in 1925 to base the anti-imperialist movement in the United States rather than Mexico on account of the "prestige" and "maturity" of the American party was by no means an unproblematic gesture of international solidarity. Both the WP and CPM had been formed at about the same time, roughly in 1921, so (leaving aside the fact that some of the WP's members were immigrants from Europe who had history already with Marxism there) the only basis for this assertion lay in differences over the parties' approach to Calles. And since the Mexican comrades would come much more quickly to the conclusion that supporting the president was a faulty move, if anything, they were politically more astute than the US-based comrades. An aspect of this belief in WP "maturity," therefore, would seem to stem more so from the conclusion that those movements and parties thriving in less economically developed regions of the world were not prepared to lead the struggle for working-class emancipation in this context was certainly a blow to the very political process they were seeking to generate.

Instead of possessing more political "maturity," the WP seems to have had more mature revenue streams than its Mexican counterpart. The WP offered money—the American dollar—to the cause of thwarting Yankee rule in Mexico by helping to finance the AAAIL's activities therein. The US delegate's inclination toward retaining the AAAIL's headquarters in the United States for fiduciary purposes was expressed as follows:

> As you know, our party has undertaken to contribute $150.00 a month toward the upkeep and operation of the Mexican Secretariat of the PAAIL, and $100.00 to go to pay Wolfe's salary and $50.00 to pay for the publication and distribution of "El Libertador."

Certainly it had been the case that WP members such as Jay Lovestone were responsible for contributing to the monetary and also editorial production of *El Libertador*, as evidenced in an October issue of the magazine. And certainly one of the deepest acts of Communist solidarity then or at any moment in history is the sharing of finances and resources with those who have less means.

But finances aside, it was reported that the CPM's actual composition of party members was very low in 1925, numbering only in the dozens, even in the so-called "epicenters of support" based in Tampico, Vera Cruz and Mexico City; therefore, the party to the north almost certainly had a more robust numerical representation of members which could and did inspire and directly support the organizational development for the party to the south. Still, notions of "prestige" revealed how the disproportionate concentration of workers' income in the US was a factor in determining—problematically—from where to anchor the radical struggle against American empire in the hemisphere in 1925. If greater financial security was to be a measuring stick for leadership in the hemisphere, then the US Communists could become the *de facto* political leaders for reasons that were not necessarily proven by theoretical or practical strength in the battlefield against the capitalist class.[13]

As time progressed, tensions began to mount between the US and Mexican comrades over how to manage the organizational development of the AAAIL and also the CPM in general. When the CPM—in spite of tremendous internal dissent—nominally determined to stand behind the nation's current leader, President Calles, in the coming national elections, which had been the strategy of the entire Comintern since the 1921 decision during the New Economic Policy, some members of the CPM appear to have wanted overwhelmingly to pose a third-party political candidate for the coming elections. State Department officials noted that the WP leadership in Chicago expressed its unequivocal approval of Calles's leadership in 1926, even cabling to the Mexican president a note of "Congratulations on [your] firm stand American imperialist demands. Mexico's Land Petroleum Laws are vital to your independence. You have support of important section of the American workers against Wall Street." But this statement of proclaimed solidarity with President Calles by the WP on the part of an "important section of the American workers," was by no means a representation of the sentiments of a "section of workers" to whom President Calles's leadership was more accountable: Mexicans Communists who were contesting for state power themselves.[14]

At times, these tensions were exacerbated by the personal prejudices of such exemplary WP leaders as Manual Gomez, who was also then the General Secretary of the AAAIL in this period. Gomez's trip to Mexico in May of 1926 was purportedly in order to bring Bolshevik "unity" to what he considered an essentially "disorganized" Mexican party. While reporting to the WP General Secretary Ruthenberg in Chicago from Mexico in early May, Gomez said that pro-Calles support from the CPM was lacking, if not non-existent. Gomez reminded the CPM members that in the interests of unity—in this case meaning unity with the messaging of the WP which had chosen to support President Calles—that "under no circumstances could we put a third candidate in the field if this might mean the victory of the imperialist candidate." But in the eyes of some of the Mexican comrades, according to Gomez, the "general conclusion" instead was that there was no possible "victory" when choosing between the lesser of two pro-American evils. The "Calles government," claimed these Mexican party members, "represents an alliance between petty bourgeois and working class elements [to] build up a national capitalism," which was then "prepared to compromise systematically with American imperialism" because it could not get along without "Wall Street" capital.[15]

This is an important political struggle when taken into the global context of the Communist International because years before the "left turn" of 1928, when at the Third Congress of the Comintern it was determined the Communist movement would no longer align itself with national bourgeoisies of any stripe—including figures like Calles, the Mexican Communists had begun to move in this direction. While they had not fully developed the concept of "class against class" insofar as they still sought a candidate for the bourgeois state, they were able to see the fallacy of the "lesser evils" approach that the Comintern was still propagating. Therefore, in a sense, the "periphery" of the Communist International appears, in the case of Mexico at least, to have anticipated the political development of the center—based in Moscow and, in the case of the western hemisphere, Chicago and then New York.

Gomez's "doubts" about what was then characterized as leftist isolationism on the part of Mexican Communists soon magnified into open hostility and outright contempt for efforts made on the part of some Mexican members to give leadership to two fundamental concerns: how best to wage the anti-imperialist struggle by way of the AAAIL and how best to develop and lead the Bolshevik movement within the peasantry of Vera Cruz. In the case of the latter issue, Gomez observed that despite the fact that "several leading comrades are very active among the peasants ... and some have big personal followings crystallized in the various Ligas de Comunidades Agrarias," the problem was that "I do not know of a single case where a peasant has been brought into the party through these comrades." Rather than offering a rationale for how and why a party was the ultimate standard of revolutionary progress for these "leading members" who were very "active among the peasants," Gomez launched an even greater assault on the integrity of the entire organization in Mexico. Any "little group," he claimed, "like the Mexican Party," was fundamentally plagued with "no real organization hold, woefully weak theoretical equipment, confused ideology, no consistent attitude toward the trends of events in Mexico and distinct opportunist tendencies." Such "opportunist tendencies," Gomez claimed, were evidenced by the fact that "a number of comrades are tied up with administrative jobs secured by tacit bargaining with state governors," with the striking instance of "one comrade [who] is chief of mounted police of the State of Michoacan." In short, Gomez, stationed from on high in his northern Chicago headquarters, had inserted himself in this subaltern epicenter of Mexico City, placed himself directly in the Mexican context of political affairs, and concluded, essentially, that there was a theoretically and practically inferior structure embedded in the Communist International project underway that necessitated the active guidance and patronage of the WP. The point here is not to discount what could have been fairly valid concerns on the part of Gomez—such as police chiefs claiming to be Communists—if one evaluates the nature of the critique within the confines of Communist dominant praxis in this era. Still, one must recognize how Gomez's observations seem to reveal to some extent his own chauvinistic weaknesses.[16] The weight of Gomez's critique from a truly internationalist standpoint should instead have reflected a stronger articulation of how to overcome weaknesses of isolation and lack of political education since the potential benefits of such a strategy far outweighed the current weaknesses in Mexican communism.

Hence there was a political contradiction inherent in Gomez's US solidarity campaign with Communists in Mexico: his efforts were at times rebuked by Mexican counterparts as controlling and domineering, rather than unifying and mutually beneficial. In fact, tensions mounted to one point in which Mexican comrades who were working directly in the AAAIL movement based out of Mexico responded to such internationalist gestures on the part of their comrades like Gomez with a call for the WP to keep its "hands off the affairs of Latin American parties." During the very days when the AAAIL headquarters in Chicago was issuing leaflets and proclamations for an international proletarian campaign to demand that American rulers keep their own "Hands off" of China, Morocco, Haiti, the Philippines and other regions, Mexican Communists were calling upon their US counterparts to do the same. In regards to the headquarters of the AAAIL, the CPM's leading body, or "central committee," had determined that "the center must be in Mexico" predicting that based from therein, "the Mexican party shall oversee the Cuban and Central American Communist movements and direct them."[17]

On one hand, the Mexican Communists seemed to re-inscribe certain power dynamics of empire and control insofar as they sought to "oversee" the work in the region, probably revealing centuries-old biases toward the Indian descendents of the Mayans. On the other hand, the more obvious manifestation of unequal power dynamics was revealed by Gomez's response to the Mexican proposal for the AAAIL headquarters to be located in Mexico rather than the United States. Gomez averred in his letter to Ruthenberg that "in view of the present condition of the Mexican Party ... this latter proposition is a grim joke." The "joke," however, was on Gomez, who days later came under attack for refusing to consider the need to place the center of this movement in Mexico.[18]

The debate was heated and tensions ran high in the room; the comrades were exhausted physically if not ideologically. "Lasting until 3 am," recalled Gomez in a second letter to General Secretary Ruthenberg, "it was decided to go on record for the immediate transfer of the League headquarters to Mexico City, at the same time asking the US party to furnish a comrade for the work, and also funds to finance it." This decision was arrived at apparently due to some sort of compromise that resulted from political challenges to the assumed "prestige" and "experience" emanating from a headquarters in the United States. Mexican comrades purportedly "admitted" to the "superior experience, organization and resources of the US party, but [declared] that some of these resources should be made available to Mexico." Hence, for many Mexican Communists, the problem was not any inherent lack of experience on the part of their own organizational work and leadership that accounted for acts of opportunism or inexperience but, rather, financial insecurity.[19]

For some Mexican Communists, the tendency to determine the program for Communist organizational development in Mexico from the Chicago headquarters of the WP was seen as coercion by way of the Yankee dollar—a trend that was all too familiar in capitalist relations between the United States and other republics in the hemisphere. According to Gomez, the Mexicans were "very bitter at us for not having kept our promises regarding money and, in view of this fact, it is almost impossible to convince them that we are sincerely interested in anti-imperialist work." It posed quite an impossible political conundrum if Mexican Communists were not convinced that their counterparts in the continental United States were truly committed to building the anti-imperialist work in the AAAIL, much less in the WP itself. All the same, Gomez persisted in asserting the Mexican party's weaknesses by furthering his argument for maintaining the Communist center in Chicago:

> I took the position that Mexico was undoubtedly the strategic place for such a center, but maintained that the Mexican comrades were incapable of directing the work. I proposed that we declare in principle for Mexico as the center, with the understanding that until it is possible for the US party to send comrades here for the work, the actual directing center must remain in the US. This was substantially the resolution as finally adopted … Mexico is to continue as the apparent ("open") headquarters … a Mexican function as General Secretary (I myself suggested this) … To trust this committee (which thinks the Philippine Islands are near Alaska) with the direction of all the anti-imperialist work would be disastrous.[20]

Indeed, Gomez was absolutely right to conclude that any group in one nation alone should have been entrusted to lead internationalist, cross-border alliances on its own. And yet his critique was more condescending than political. That is, he had not even considered the possibility that what looked like the ignorance of Mexican comrades who thought the "Philippines Islands are near Alaska" might well have reflected the transnational migrant labor connection between Mexican laborers in the hemisphere and Filipino laborers who often worked alongside them in the industrial and agricultural bases across California and the Pacific Northwest more generally. Indeed, it was the case that Filipinos were heavily concentrated along the US mainland and islands in the Pacific Rim extending from Hawaii to California up through Seattle and into Alaska, often intermingling, politicking, and struggling alongside Mexican and other migrant laborers from Latin America. The Mexican comrades' familiarity with this historical circumstance of migrant Filipino laborers on the West Coast was not properly considered by US-based Communists such as Gomez. Hence, Gomez himself had set a very "disastrous" precedent in terms of how organizational work between the United States and Mexico would shape the course of history for the relationship between Communists in New York City and other radical and Communist-affiliated movements in the Caribbean, namely Cuba, Puerto Rico, Haiti and subsequently in the British West Indies.

In response to Gomez's series of reports on the Mexican situation, Ruthenberg concluded to Gomez that "it is not likely that we will be able to finance any considerable amount of work in Mexico or South America. Our own Party needs are more important to us and we have hardly the means to take care of." His reference to a collective "us" or "we" in reference to the work of the American party and AAAIL also connoted an "other," or Mexican counterpart, that was outside of the immediate collective. He concluded that "if the Latin

Department can relieve us of our duties and burdens in this respect, we will not object." What the WP considered the organizational "burden" of running the AAAIL itself reflected a theoretical shortcoming in understanding just how deeply internationalist unity had to be woven into an effort toward empowering workers in the US.[21]

In short, after a year of intense collaboration beginning in 1925, Mexican and US Communists who were actively engaged with steering the AAAIL appear to have presented starkly contrasting conceptions of where the center and fringes of the hemispheric movement of the Communist International were based. Mexican comrades were demanding that politically and operationally they would prefer to retain control over the means of AAAIL's influence by maintaining its headquarters in Mexico rather than in metropoles such as New York and Chicago. Or maybe this is only one aspect of the political development that was unfolding in transnational context between Communists in the United States and Mexico, largely under Gomez's leadership. It was also true that the WP had ensured that radical movements underway in Mexico were amply covered and supported in the pages of the *Daily Worker*, and Gomez's name was affixed to these articles. There was clearly a propoganda-based effort being made to politically educate US workers about the Communist International's anti-imperialist work by leaders such as Gomez in the pages of its leading political organ.

For Gomez, the ramifications of his dual role as an AIL and WP leader were profound. He was at once anxious over the extent to which his political leadership as an anti-imperialist should be colored Communist. Flyers by the WP with his name were being disseminated during his nationwide tour on behalf of the AIL in the latter months of 1926—a tour which purportedly ended up being cancelled for lack of mass appeal, patronage and funds. Gomez's role as leading AAAIL and WP member in relationship to Mexican Communist politics had a historical parallel to how New York-based black Communists such as Richard Moore, Otto Huiswoud and others operated relative to the ANLC and places like Haiti. As we saw with respect to Haiti, some of the leading black Communists were waging a struggle to keep the ANLC a separate mass organization from the WP, for a perceived lack of Communist popularity among black workers, just as Gomez was torn over the degree to which the AIL, operating within the United States, ought to be publically identified with the WP and particularly his own leadership. In the years leading up to the Third Period, these Communists who were essentially in charge of mass organizations like the ANLC and AIL were opposed to making plain the connection between the WP and the mass groups. In retrospect, however, it is not apparent at all that the workers in the bases of these mass groups rejected more overtly revolutionary sentiments. But Gomez—perhaps unlike the ANLC comrades who did not yet have parties among black workers in the Caribbean with which to correspond—was promoting a double standard: though he sought to disaffiliate the WP from the AIL in the United States with the estimation that this would make the former more popular, he was a chief critic of the programmatic distance between the CPM and the peasants in the "Ligas de comunidades" in Vera Cruz.

But even as the WP was at times operating against some of the most positive opportunities to strengthen proletarian internationalism with respect to Mexico, the more dominant political trend was still shifting—as was the Comintern as a whole—toward an increased focus on challenging the bourgeois state through international united action.

The Sixth World Congress in US-Mexican Context

Events at the international level in the years of 1927 and 1928—namely the Shanghai Massacre of Chinese Communists at the hands of the nationalist KMT—must have quickly motivated Gomez and the WP more broadly to shift an understanding of the world historic role of Mexico's Communist movement as well as its hemispheric significance. At the same time, both the US and Mexican governments were increasing their persecution of radicals. In August of 1927, Mexican radicals such as Diego Rivera seized the struggling AAAIL apparatus by its horns and began mass protests, numbering from thousands in places such as Tampico, against the imminent execution of Sacco and Vanzetti, two Italian-born American anarcho-syndicalist labor leaders who had been accused of a murder in 1921 and sentenced to execution. Months after Rivera's decision as an official of the AAAIL in Mexico to support these political prisoners in August, the WP in the United States established an actual Anti-Imperialist Department within the party in order to more directly bring the struggle against American imperial expansion and strengthen the fight between increasing domestic and foreign repression of workers' movements. The Anti-Imperialist Department's main mission was expressly to place the WP in charge of building Communist parties in the "American colonies," placing leaders like Gomez in the forefront of this department. The WP had figured that the best way to challenge imperialism in the hemisphere was to build independent parties in regions where American empire—or the British Empire in the case of the BWI—was preponderant.

At the Sixth World Congress of the Comintern in 1928, Gomez submitted a report on the "Colonial Question" in the United States which charged US Communists with the task of being "able to find the point of intersection of all these diverse movements" as were emanating from Mexico and places like Nicaragua at this time. Gomez had now surmised that the "'form of the All-American Anti-Imperialist League is well suited to this purpose.'" In the United States, the *Daily Worker* followed suit with Gomez's AAAIL mandates regarding the Western Hemisphere. One article connected the international and hemispheric dots by publishing an open letter from the AAAIL declaring that

> ... the same marines who are making your country safer for Wall Street are helping to drown in a sea of blood the revolution of the workers and peasants of China; these same marines are in Haiti, the Philippines, Santo Domingo, and Puerto Rico.[22]

It seems that the new political strategy provided by the Sixth World Congress helped to lay the basis for fortifying the reciprocal, comradely collusion of forces between Communists in the US and other parts of the hemisphere, namely in Mexico. Gomez's role at the congress elucidates this change. Conducting an almost complete about-face from his decisions on the "center" of the AAAIL from several years before, Gomez went against his own prior arguments and declared before the delegates at the Sixth World Congress that "'many reasons combine to make Mexico the traditional territorial centre of Latin American resistance to American imperialism, and it is in Mexico that the centre of our anti-imperialist movement throughout the Americas must be established.'" Mexico would increasingly function as a center for the "anti-imperialist movement," though there was nothing at all "traditional" about Gomez's quite timely and politically strategic decision. The world situation had drastically changed in the period from 1925 to 1928, and the need to concentrate more radical energy in building the movements in non-western regions was seen as a paramount task for international Communist victory.[23]

But just as Communists increased their concentration of political forces outside of the US, so too did ruling elites in the region who were opposed to this burgeoning Soviet network of parties and organizations rally around the cause to thwart this activity. Hence, in 1929, while Rose Pastor Stokes was being beaten and clubbed in New York City, a native rather than "foreign" Cuban Communist named Julio Mella had been banished to Mexico by Cuban authorities, only to be assassinated in the streets of Mexico City by presumably Mexican—and more than likely co-signed by Cuban and American—authorities. Thus begins another episode of the Communist International and black workers in the Caribbean relative to political developments on the island of Cuba.

Cuban ruling elites—whether maneuvering at the dictates of Spanish or later American financial interests—had a long history of blaming non-Cubans for radical developments on the island, going back to the days of independence struggles and slave uprisings. The racially prejudiced and politically repressive deportations of Chinese "foreign agitators" in Cuba depicted at the outset of this chapter was only one manifestation of the mass forced repatriation scheme of suspected anti-Cuban dissidents that culminated in the 1929 raid by the Cuban police against the Communist Party headquarters in Havana and the execution of Mella in Mexico. This act of essentially proto-fascist aggression against suspected Communists on the island and, indirectly, in the hemisphere as a whole, was an important feather in the cap of American imperial expansion in the region, precisely because the Cuban ruling factions were all vying for their place as chief executors and middlemen for US economic and military interests on the island and beyond. But the list of Communists based from New York City who were actively supporting radicalism in Haiti and Cuba and also Cuba's burgeoning Communist movement as 1929 drew to a close was only the beginnings of a unity that would intensify in the ensuing years.[24]

COMMUNISM IN CUBAN-US CONTEXT: 1925–29

When the Communist Party of Cuba and its branch of the AIL were officially formed the summer of 1925, they were almost immediately forced into illegality by the Cuban government. Operating under conditions of severe repression since its infancy, the CPC would have only roughly eight years before its first opportunity would arise to try to seize state power during the *coup d'état* in 1933. An organized socialist state would not take hold in Cuba until the 1960s under the leadership of Fidel Castro, but the political headway made by Cuban Communists beginning in 1925 was critical to the eventual revolution of 1959.

The pendulum swing of US imperialist rule over Cuba meant that the economic depression had begun there years before the 1929 crash on Wall Street. As such, the sharp intensification of US socio-economic and military domination over this small Spanish-speaking West Indian island in the years leading up to the Great Depression laid the foundation for the fierce political repression exhibited upon Cuban Communists and labor organizers in groups like the AIL and the National Cuban Confederation of Laborers (NCCL) (*Confederación Nacional de Obreros Cubanos*, or CNOC), or the Cuban united front labor union at the hands of the Cuban state. The Cuban Communist movement initially developed a foundation for solidarity with the WP/CPUSA cemented in this context. Indeed, the particular threat that Cuban radicals posed within the anti-American mass movement in Cuba not only placed them on the defense against the Cuban and US ruling elites but also in a position of militant leadership—however feeble—relative to the Communist movement in the United States.

So a politically combustible situation in Cuba began to emerge between 1925 and 1929 and finally exploded in 1933, as we shall see. Physical coercion of radical dissidents on the part of the Cuban government with the tacit consent of US authorities existed on one end; on the other end there was an increasing rage and resistance emanating from radical intellectual circles, combined with the increasingly organized labor movement, just as black labor unrest was spreading in Oriente province—the site of longstanding challenges to Cuba's racist socio-economic disenfranchisement of black laborers after the victory of independence. Ultimately, the budding network of organizations that emerged in 1925 linking Communists in Mexico, Cuba and the United States helped to bring about the single most important historical conjuncture of Communist and black forces in the Caribbean during the interwar period: Cuba's "September 4th Revolution" of 1933 and attendant rise of the Afro-Cuban "Soviet" of Realengo 18 in Oriente province. And the story begins with the leadership of Julio Mella, radical intellectual and co-founder of the CPC.

Julio Antonio Mella provides an important point of entry into the origins of the Cuban radical movement. Mella was a leading figure going back to 1925, if not several years before. He was assassinated before the age of 30, and in his death, he remained a martyred radical figure and part of Communist history whose vision and influence lived on among radicals from Cuba to New York City and beyond.

Origins of the AIL and the CPC in 1925

In early August of 1925, Mella greeted the Executive Committee of the WP on the front page of the *Daily Worker* which, in turn, placed his article alongside pieces that decried the contemporary Ku Klux Klan attacks on black laborers in the United States. At the level of propaganda at least, the WP in 1925 was beginning to link the domestic struggle against racist violence toward African Americans with the growing Communist movement in Cuba. For reasons that are not entirely clear, the WP also seems to have taken a more congenial, even-handed approach to its relationship with its Cuban Communist counterparts compared to those in Mexico during this period.[25]

Just as in Mexico, the Communist movement in Cuba from 1925 to 1929 was much more militant than that which was under way in the United States. In Mella's article, *Daily Worker* readers were informed that

> … the first Communist Congress today has resolved to organize the Communist Party of Cuba (CPC). We send to the Workers Communist Party of America, and to all the sections of the Communist International, revolutionary greetings, as comrades in arms of the proletarian revolution.

While readers of the *Daily Worker* and US Communists in general were presumably proud to receive "revolutionary greetings" from Cuba, they probably had little knowledge of how deeply felt and accurate the phrase, "comrades in arms of the proletarian revolution" was for their Cuban counterparts. In contradistinction to the formation in 1925 of the US-based AIL and ANLC, the CPC's branch of the AIL, and even the pro-Soviet labor union the NCCL, were born in a context of intense government repression that took the form of mass arrests and the kidnapping of some radical leaders so comrades in "arms" had both a literal and figurative meaning.

An important historical summary of "Communism in Cuba" which was released in 1934 and submitted to then Secretary of State Sumner Welles, who considered it "historically interesting" but "practically" of "no value," discussed the origins of the CPC and the Cuban AIL in a way that the *Daily Worker* did not—or perhaps could not for reasons of political expediency—in 1925. The Cuban branch of the AIL was officially formed in July of 1925 while US-based Communists were celebrating "Anti-Imperialist Week" only weeks before the CPC was formed. Both the AIL and the CPC were formed by the same coterie of campus-based intellectuals that included Mella. This intellectual cohort, which dubbed itself the "Universidad Popular 'Jose Marti,'" was instituted in November of that same year. The founding board of directors of the AIL included Mella and one Jose Acosta as well as "others in the working class," including even "one member of the 'Kuomintang.'" The references to "Jose Marti" and the KMT suggest that from inception the Cuban Communist movement was always a fusion of forces both "foreign" and "domestic," at once representing a nationalist movement for Cuban independence from US influence and also transcending boundaries of nation toward a larger goal of proletarian internationalism which included Chinese labor radicals from the KMT and Cubans from academic circles.[26]

Above and beyond activism among intellectuals and radical immigrants, the Cuban labor movement, led by the newly formed NCCL and representing supposedly 200,000 Cuban laborers, also evinced sympathies toward the Comintern. This sentiment within the labor movement laid a critical foundation for the rise of the CPC and AIL, just as Mexican peasants in Vera Cruz had shared common sentiment with though never officially joined the Kresintern. The NCCL "did not join any trade union international, though it sympathized with the Communist International of Labour Unions." Added to this mix of forces in the creation of the CPC, "in 1925 there had taken place two trade union congresses," recalled an article in the Communist-run *International Press Correspondences* (*Inprecorr*), "which had exercised strong influence upon the Labour movement of the country. The trade union congress of February 1925 had resolved in principle to create a National Trade Union Federation, the foundation congress of which took place in August" of 1925. Almost immediately thereafter, and concurrent with the formation of the AIL and CPC in the summer of 1925, the "persecution very soon began." *Inprecorr*'s description went on as follows:

> Trade union leaders were arrested, the textile-workers union and other organizations were dissolved. The activity of the sections of the Anti-Imperialist League and of

the Communist Party, both of which were also founded in the year 1925 and a big strike formed the pretext for strengthening the offensive. The Communist Party of Cuba was forced into illegality. The leader of the railwaymen of the northern province, Eurico Verona, and other active labour leaders were assassinated.[27]

Or at least this was the narrative according to Moscow's main international theoretical political organ, *Inprecorr*. Literature disseminated at the same time by the AAAIL based in Chicago and written by Manuel Gomez corroborated this same description from *Inprecorr* though it emphasized—perhaps over-emphasized—the role of Cuba's AIL in bringing forth this radical movement and ensuing persecution.

While the US branches of the ILD and AIL were making small yet significant inroads toward solidarity with their counterparts in Cuba in 1925, Julio Mella had been arrested, labor leaders had been executed or "disappeared," and "foreign" agents were deported all by the fall of that same year. A circular from the Cuban section of the AAAIL—with a masthead entitled "All-American Anti-Imperialist League" whose headquarters was on Washington Boulevard in Chicago—indicated that "Mella and twelve labor leaders were imprisoned. Undoubtedly a contributing cause of the arrest of Mella was his activity against American imperialism among the students of the National University … whose strong stand had 'embarrassed' the President in his relations with Crowder." Cuba's anti-government dissidents, especially those aligned with the Communists, had been brought under a long-term state of siege declared by President Machado in the name of "law and order." The AAAIL circular described the situation as follows:

> "Law and Order" for Machado, just as for President Chiari of Panama, signifies security and development of American interests at the sacrifice of the native victims, at the sacrifice of the economic independence of the state. If in Panama a simple rent strike of the workers-tenants could bring about the intervention of Yankee soldiers, we can expect that in the present situation in Cuba the bloodlust of Wall Street will not be satisfied with the indictments and arrests so far undertaken by the Cuban government but will insist upon still greater outrages. In spite of its reprisals, the Cuban section of the All-America Anti-Imperialist League will continue its activity in the National University (as long as the university is allowed to remain open), in the labor organizations, etc. It will give full voice to its program: Abolition of the Platt Amendment which makes Cuba a mere protectorate of the United States, abolition of the American naval base at Guantanamo, campaign against the forced loans of Wall Street.[28]

The AIL in Cuba was born of armed struggle and its demands were directly targeted against the US's military, economic and political influence over the island. But each of these demands—i.e., abolishing the Platt Amendment, etc.—were reform demands that the CPC itself placed in the hands of its mass organization rather than in those of the party. In this way, the AIL in the US began to support the specific demands emanating from each Caribbean region, while connecting the dots in US rulers' complicity in workers' oppression across the hemisphere. The ILD based in Chicago was fast on the scene, if feebly, by October of 1925. A translated letter from the ILD headquarters in Chicago indicated that 80 organizations representing 18,000 workers had devised resolutions on the Cuban arrests that were passed "unanimously" at the ILD conference held in the middle of September.[29]

From New York City, the ILD in December of 1925 paraded before the offices of the American Sugar Refining Company at 117 Wall Street, according to a *New York Times* article, and reported that part of the protest was due to the fact that "Mella, who is General Secretary of the Communist Party in Cuba, has been on a hunger strike for fourteen days" after having been "sentenced for having created dissension between students and Faculty in the University of Havana." "Dissension," of course, was a *New York Times* editorial euphemism for deep-seeded, anti-"Yankee" and anti-government sentiment as well as working-class rebellion that linked the Cuban academy to the sugar plantation. Quite fittingly, the New York City branch of the ILD had elected to stage its protest in support of the Cuban radicals outside of the American Sugar Refining Company housed on Wall Street in order to lay bare the connection between the profits enjoyed by American capitalists extracted from Cuban land and labor, and the American political support for Cuban repression of revolutionary leadership on the island. The AIL in New York seems also to have claimed representation at this same protest outside of the American Sugar Refining Company on Wall Street, specifying that the rally only attracted 150 supporters with banners such as "'Wall Street is Stifling Cuban Labor Movement'" and "'If Mella Dies on Wall Street Lies the Guilt.'" The Communist-led solidarity which was often manifested in the streets of New York tended to draw numerically small crowds in the years from 1925 and 1929, but this does not mean that the political significance of these campaigns was equally inconsequential.[30]

In 1926, despite the overall quiet of the Communist movement in Cuba and the United States at that time, General Enoch Crowder, the first US Ambassador to Cuba, informed the State Department that the "President of Cuba about three months ago … asserted he was satisfied that Soviet agents are operating in both the United States and Cuba in antagonism to organized government." Moreover, he added, President Machado had made arrangements for a spy called Sr. Miguel Stein to "obtain and discover every communication which exists between the Communistic organizations and the Soviet in New York with the organizations of that category which exist in Cuba, determining what persons in Cuba direct and labor in behalf of said organization." This transnational circuit between New York and Cuba had apparently become a thorn in the side of the US ruling elite during the years leading up to the Great Depression in 1929.[31]

But leadership of Communists in the Cuban labor and political movements was still quite weak and they had been essentially driven underground upon inception. Hence, the dominant attitude among US officials like Crowder was quite smug. In response to a *New York Times* article that warned of "imminent sabotage" that might well be visited upon American financiers in Cuba, Crowder averred that "it should be observed that there is no well developed racial party in Cuba, and that the character of the people does not make the island fertile field for the advancement of Communist ideas." Since a "racial party," meaning in this instance an *anti*-racist or multiracial group, would be the only force truly "fertile" and capable enough of bringing about a challenge to American empire, he concluded that "Cubans are easily led on political issues and may even resort to the violence of revolution on those grounds" yet "such issues are, however, local ones and generally speaking, the people do not think in terms of internationalism." Crowder was projecting his own American exceptionalist visions of a radical-proof empire onto a neocolonial outpost that had disproved and would continue to disprove his narrow vision time and again. Still, Crowder's ideological shortcomings were not entirely flawed. What he had correctly if unknowingly insinuated was that internationalism void of a truly "racial" core boiled down to little more than a "local" movement that could not provide a truly formidable threat to an American empire whose wealth is partially predicated upon the super-exploitation of darker-skinned laborers in the hemisphere.[32]

In spite of lacking a strong base in the black masses in Cuba at the time, the Comintern had still identified Cuba as a potentially leading hub for Communist revolution in the hemisphere. In 1927, however, the radical labor movement in Cuba was under even more severe attack by the Cuban government than in 1925, with "a large number of trade-union leaders, of whom the majority were not Communists, [immediately] arrested" such that the "trade unions were made impossible and the Labor journals were suppressed" while the NCCL's general secretary as well as "numerous other trade-union functionaries" were left, according to an *Inprecorr* article, to "languish in jail."[33]

As Cuba's labor leaders were languishing in jail, the US-based American Federation of Labor (AFL) was, while under William Greene's leadership, apparently unwilling to mount any serious challenge to the brutal labor conditions visited upon their ostensible Cuban brothers in the struggle. Decrying Greene as an "agent of National City Bank," the *Daily Worker* reported—though somewhat overstating the case—that "American workers in the beginning of the American imperialist epoch wrested Cuba from Spain believing that they were freeing her people," only to be misled in the present period by figures such as Greene. *Daily Worker* editors had inaccurately put forward the claim that workers in the US had "wrested Cuba from Spain" during the Cuban independence struggle in decades past. But the key point was that the WP could use the failures of the racist, nationalist AFL to demonstrate how Communists and their internationalist politics would better serve in uniting workers than any other group.

In 1928, the nationalist revolution then taking place in Nicaragua under General Sandino, coupled with the Comintern's left turn during the Third Period, offered an important context for the marked increase of attention in the pages of the *Daily Worker* to revolutionary upheaval in the Latino world. The paper noted that in the aftermath of the Pan-American Peace Conference in 1928 where Haiti's prominent League of Nations representative Dante Bellegarde was denied participation by the other Latino and US delegates, "several hundred Latin-American students at a protest meeting [in Cuba] denounced U.S. imperialism and urged a united Latin American struggle against the 'Colossus of the North.'"

But in spite of the *Daily Worker*'s efforts to support the militant movements against US economic and military power in Nicaragua and to a lesser degree in Cuba, these were ultimately only feeble attempts to mitigate the deepening and widening of American political, economic and military authority across the region in the 1920s. The *Evening News* and *Havana Post* lauded efforts currently underway to "intensify the economic relations between Cuba and the United States" at the initiative of National City Bank and Chase National Bank. Also, an increase in direct US military influence over the Cuban Merchant Marine was noted in these papers. General Electric, among other American pre-WWII industrial giants, reigned supreme—if temporarily—in this process.[34]

Enter Sandalio Junco: ANLC and Afro-Cuban Labor in Context

Albeit minimally, the role of black laborers in Cuba was critical to challenging American empire and destabilizing Cuban reactionary rulers in the years leading up to the October crash of 1929. One of Cuba's greatest Communist figures arose from the black labor force on the island, a trade unionist named Sandalio Junco. In January of 1929, only weeks after Mella had been murdered, Junco was among the speakers at the National Assembly for the Unification of Workers and Peasants in Mexico, alongside a New Jersey leader of the CPUSA named Albert Weisbord, who spoke on behalf of the textile workers then striking in Passaic, NJ. The US-Caribbean circuit was intensifying on all accounts since, by the end of 1929, leading CPUSA members in New York would also orchestrate an outpouring in the streets to defend the "Haitian Revolution." Clearly, the CPUSA's attention to developments within the black population in the Caribbean was intensifying in the very time when American capitalism was entering a period of crisis.[35]

But there was also a distinctly race-based network within this circuit, linking black workers from Cuba to New York and Haiti. In this vein, black Communist leaders of the American Negro Labor Congress such as Otto Huiswoud and Richard Moore who were then based in Harlem helped lead this process, openly defending the rights of Cuba's black laborers being led by Junco, describing him in the *Negro Champion* as a "Black Cuban Labor leader of the Latin American Confederation of Labor" and also the Provisional Secretary of the Executive Committee of the AAAIL. Junco was effectively a Communist labor agitator whose political ascendancy marked the onset of a Communist-led wave connecting Mexico, the United States and Cuba in 1929, with the explicit support of the ANLC and AAAIL and implicit support of Moscow itself. Historically obscure figures like Junco of Cuba and Henri Rosemund of Haiti were indicative of a larger hemispheric struggle that linked Communism and black workers in a manner that was quite uncanny for its time—or any time since for that matter.[36]

Though Crowder and Guggenheim basked in the glory of Cuba's ostensibly resilient capitalist democracy, the effects of the Wall Street collapse of 1929 gave rise to imminent dangers for American empire in Cuba, mainly in the form of anti-American sentiment on the island that held the "Yankee" rule responsible for Cuba's plight. Even though Cuba would eventually pose the most formidable, though unsuccessful, challenge to Wall Street in the Caribbean Basin with the 1933 Revolution, Standard Oil executives in 1929 had mistakenly identified as the chief menace to American empire the radical community of another West Indian island: Puerto Rico.

ORIGINS OF COMMUNISM IN US-PUERTO RICAN CONTEXT

As early as 1929, these oil executives were calculating frantically, albeit mistakenly, that Puerto Rico had now become the Soviet headquarters in the hemisphere. Indeed, Communists in the United States—some of whom were also active in the Communist movement in Mexico—had been consciously attempting since 1926 to build a Communist party, and they did so by attaching themselves to the already existing movement for the political independence of Puerto Rico. For the most part, however, the Communists—more than likely under the theoretical guidance of Moscow and directed from Chicago, then later New York—acted as the left wing of the pre-existing movement that was led predominantly by the Nationalist Party.

Their inroads in the period from 1925 to 1929 were made by creating an AIL chapter on the island and also a Communist "group," rather than a party based in Ponce. The work started during this period was part of what paved the way for larger struggles during the "Popular Front" against fascism, in which Puerto Rican Harlem played a central role. Concurrent with the beginnings of active work led by Communists in Puerto Rico was a legislative bill introduced on April 23, 1926, by Senator Millard E. Tydings of Maryland, calling for a "commonwealth" on the island. This same Senator Tydings would introduce a bill in 1936 calling for independence, which would be overturned, and in the process cause the death of dozens of Puerto Rican nationalists and radicals. Puerto Rico was a valuable military outpost, finance center and tourism playground for US capitalists and their minions, and imminent threats of Communist political infiltration merited swift and repressive measures by the state. Therefore, least welcome for commonwealth overseers was the idea that Communists were literally seeking to take that *wealth* from the hands of US corporations and place it in the *common* hands of everyday Puerto Rican laborers by advocating for socialist revolution.

Within Puerto Rico itself, there was an apparent increase in activism between 1925 and 1927 that was characterized largely by parliamentary political proceedings and legislative campaigns against American rule. The Nationalist Party led by Albizu Campos was only one among several branches of this larger political process. Communists from the United States made a decision during this period to begin the work of establishing a Communist base on the island. Small inroads were made in the form of "un grupo Comunista" which was "admitted" into the Comintern by the members in the United States, particularly due to the political work of another obscure yet indispensable figure named Navares Sager.

Internal Dynamics of Puerto Rican Independence and Strategy of the WP

Herein lay a recurring challenge in the pioneering process in 1925. With respect to Puerto Rico, and even more profoundly than in the case of Mexico, there were US Communists offering necessary support to the strategic and tactical growth of Communists based in Puerto Rico. But the Caribbean-based organizers on this island seemed to be more enlightened as to the complexities and nuances of the local conditions in which they were organizing than their allies in the US. This difference in what was the actual versus perceived nature of the political situation in Puerto Rico, and therefore how Communists should go about building and expanding the organizational bodies that would anchor their work, is an important recurring theme in the history of international labor and social justice collaboration for at least the past century. A comradely mix of unity and opposition was at the root of how the local and hemispheric forces pioneered the inroads of Bolshevism in Caribbean islands like Puerto Rico.

As early as 1925, both Cuba and Puerto Rico had begun the process of consolidating a radical nucleus, or critical mass, though the outcomes of their work in these incipient years was fairly different. Chapters for the AIL had been established on both islands roughly between 1925 and 1926. Possibly on account of the fact that Communist roots in Puerto Rican soil were initially planted by members of the WP in the United States, the Communist Party of Puerto Rico (CPPR) was not founded until 1935 in contradistinction to its Cuban counterpart, which was formed by a group whose leading members were themselves the products of more organic (meaning locally derived in this case) conditions one decade beforehand. When the CPPR did come to fruition in 1935, it was immediately acknowledged and supported by its "sister" party in Cuba. Ultimately, the key point to recognize is that the uneven development of Communist parties on the two islands did not negate the eventual growth of mutual solidarity efforts under the banner of the Comintern.

The wretched conditions of poverty borne out by pervasive disease and starvation would give the impression that revolutionary upsurge was imminent. Hookworm had been rampant in Puerto Rico since the US occupation at the turn of the century, intensifying after WWI, and carrying with it all of the attendant pain and suffering that this twentieth-century tropical "Black Death" inflicted on the impoverished, usually brown and black, peoples of the world. The *Daily Worker* captured the plight of the Puerto Rican masses in 1926: "most of the workers live in dirty hovels, the toilets are holes made in the streets, children always naked, unemployment always present, diseases like hookworm, anemia and under nourishment killing them off in large numbers." But while oppressive circumstances were a condition for revolution, they were not sufficient. Concerted and correct action rather than rhetoric, in the form of Communist political organization, was a necessity.[37]

Insofar as the organized strength of political resistance in Puerto Rico in 1925 was derived from anti-government nationalists, the bulk of whom were openly hostile to Bolshevism in any form, Communists in the US—in line with the Comintern's general decision prior to the Third Period to support bourgeois nationalist struggles against western imperialism—saw this nationalist movement as an opportunity for collusion against a common foe. In spite of Washington's admonitions to Moscow regarding Communist influence among the disenchanted masses in the US possessions of the Philippines and Puerto Rico, the *Daily Worker* had already begun to weigh in on the revolutionary potential of the latter island's political independence movement against the American empire. For example, in late December of 1925, the paper noted that in spite of the fact that the "protest of the Puerto Ricans still takes the form of petitions to Washington D.C.," the paper invoked the radical potential of the movement which was "in great part inspired by the organized industrial workers of the island." The paper also noted a recent "petition of redress of grievances signed by 13,000 Puerto Ricans [which had] just been handed to President Coolidge, coming from the Free Federation of Workingmen." Evidently the Puerto Rican laborers were astir, and notions of "freedom" for the "workingmen" were seen optimistically as harbingers by the WP of greater radical campaigns to come.[38]

US-based Communists were not only evaluating the socio-economic climate of Puerto Rico but then trying to imagine a revolutionary alternative and vision for the island's struggling masses. This was quite consciously an approach that Communists knew would not be supported by nationalist groups in Puerto Rico in 1925. While the current leadership of the Puerto Rican mass movement had apparently requested to be "'considered as a part of the United States with the full rights of national life,'" the *Daily Worker* reproached this use of petitions that "will not free them from their misery" and prescribed instead that Puerto Ricans "must cast in their lot with the workers in the states; for the complete abolition of the profit system." But the newspaper's criticism that the movement had failed to advance theoretically the notion of the "complete abolition" of capitalism did not prevent the editorial board at the *Daily Worker* from entirely dismissing the merits of the independence struggle as a site for Communist infiltration and influence. At least posing a certain degree of resistance to the barefaced presence of US profiteers on the island, still, the nationalist-led movement was then considered as having made "greater progress than the masses of workers in the United States" according to the paper.

Navares Sager and the AIL in Puerto Rico

As had been the case in Cuba, Mexico and Haiti, the resistance—whether in the form of protests, strikes, petitions, or other means—of Puerto Rican activists to US rulers carried with it repercussions that were more harsh and repressive than in the US. In this context of upheaval in the country, Navares Sager, the Communist representative in Puerto Rico at this time, began a correspondence series with comrades based in Chicago, primarily General Secretary Ruthenberg of the WP.[39]

The first in a series of exchanges between Sager and Ruthenberg expressed the fact that the socialist and the nationalist parties had a much sounder base of support on the island than did the Comintern, one that had roots in the struggle for independence that was stripped from the island during the Spanish–American War a few decades before. But even more important was Sager's criticism of the WP insofar as "in spite of the fact that we have here in Puerto Rico a considerable labor movement ... our Party ... has thus far hardly paid the attention that this colony of the Wall St. empire deserves." Notably Sager's reference to "our Party" revealed the manner in which his status as an organizer in the AAAIL concealed a much more fundamental mission of posing an aggressive Soviet challenge to "this colony of the Wall St. empire" by way of the US-based Communist movement.[40]

Sager as an individual was therefore integral to building a support apparatus to develop and grow the move toward independence and, eventually, socialist seizure of state power in Puerto Rico. He began petitioning to the very same General Secretary Ruthenberg who had all too recently dismissed the CPM as a "loose gathering" of radicals in his private letters with Manuel Gomez. While it may indeed have been the case that the Mexican collectives were not as organized or disciplined as their US counterparts, it was significant that Ruthenberg during these years was to some degree negatively judgmental toward comrades who were embarking on this process overseas. We have observed how the essence of the comradely struggle underway in Mexico at this time was premised upon international solidarity, and yet this solidarity was inescapably racialized and subjective. This same dynamic is evident upon close scrutiny of the correspondence between Sager in Puerto Rico and Ruthenberg in the United States, though the primary aspect of the relationship was one that strengthened the working classes' capacity for challenging racist super-exploitation and increasing workers' power.

The main point of conflict for Ruthenberg and Sager revolved around the question of the strategic collusion with nationalist forces on the island. Ruthenberg expressed to Sager a general disinclination toward making too quick of a break between the nationalist forces and Puerto Rico's incipient Communist movement. Sager, however, was convinced instead that a better approach was to spend less time enmeshed in the details of independence campaigns led by bourgeois nationalists and advocate instead for workers' power under the leadership of Communists. In turn, while ceding Sager's ultimate assertion that the Nationalist Party "cannot really represent the interests of the Puerto Rican masses—except in a temporary and partial way," Ruthenberg insisted that Sager follow the program of action set forth by the Comintern at the time:

> ... in Puerto Rico, we must remember, the next point on the order of business is national revolution. It is ridiculous to presume otherwise. There can be no proletarian revolution in Puerto Rico while American imperialism reigns and American troops are there to suppress all disturbances.

Certainly the process of building a global, semi-clandestine Communist movement was taken seriously by all involved—including Sager and Ruthenberg.

If Sager's disagreement with Ruthenberg over the issue of coalition support for the nationalist regime was one of substance, then the very question of self determination was in jeopardy of being overlooked. Communists like Sager brought to bear important observations about the potential for proletarian revolution in Puerto Rico—observations which did not always fit smoothly into the imagined socialist projects articulated by central leadership. A close examination of the choices made and issues addressed demonstrates the intricacies of organizational development, in this case with the AIL in Puerto Rico. Small inroads were made during this period through the mutual cooperation of US and Puerto Rican-based Communists as personified by Ruthenberg, Sager and Gomez.[41]

In a two-month timeframe, and with only partial adherence to the program for national liberation as set forth by Ruthenberg, Sager set himself to the work of organizing a Communist group—not to be mistaken for a party. On his account, Sager was able to rally the support of disaffected former Socialists and members of the AFL-led labor movement on the island, giving rise to a nucleus of Communists under the direct influence of the WP. Notably, however, this process of early Communist formation in an American neo-colony began without the expressed consent of Ruthenberg even though he later made arrangements for the WP to support Sager's efforts. Sager noted to Manuel Gomez, leading representative of the AAAIL who was currently embroiled in Mexican-US relations, that "these comrades feel that the present situation demands a Communist program and Communist Party; the time is now ... for the formation of the CP, and action is already being taken." Sager was apparently conscious of the fact that his desire to establish a party might have been considered premature by his counterparts in the US. He assured Ruthenberg of the relative authenticity of the WP's new comrades in Puerto Rico, stating they were "proletarian in character" and "sincere militants." But these Puerto Rican radicals were "proletarian" in not only form but also substance, since they had chosen to take the Leninist call for self-determination to its logical conclusion by determining rather than requesting the criteria for forming a party on the island.[42]

The overwhelming economic impoverishment and political repression in Puerto Rico was such that it was incumbent upon US-based Communists to offer much-needed fiduciary support to their Puerto Rican counterparts in order for this movement to gain traction. Sager presented before Gomez in very dire terms the financial constraints of his comrades. As was the case in Mexico and Cuba, Puerto Rican Communists were operating under conditions of impoverishment and political repression that comrades based in Chicago were not directly and immediately grappling with. Sager described the present situation as one in which

> Unless we have means to cover necessary expenses we will be handicapped, lack of travelling expenses will localize our movement to San Juan only. But it is a problem which we in Puerto Rico cannot solve for most of our comrades suffer poverty; either we are not working or are receiving starvation wages. We will appeal to the American Party to advice [sic] us on this matter.[43]

It was "advice," not mandates, Sager requested from the WP. Unfortunately, and as is the case in many social justice movements, control over money and operational matters became the Achilles heel of this transnational solidarity as expressed between Communists in the US and Puerto Rico.

Comrade Ruthenberg, who was the current general secretary of the Workers (Communist) Party, approached the question of financial support problematically, to say the least. Ruthenberg's response revealed just how pervasive the grip of neocolonial ideology was on the American population, even as reflected in the WP leadership. Directly following his letter to Gomez dismissing the "loose organization" of Mexican comrades, Ruthenberg wrote to Sager indicating that any semblance of party formation in Puerto Rico would, quite naturally, have to function as a branch of the WP since Puerto Rico was essentially a US colony. "The Communist organization in Porto Rico," claimed Ruthenberg to Sager, "in view of the fact that Porto Rico is under American control, would necessarily become a part of the Workers (Communist) Party and would be given the position of a district organization of the Party" while reminding Sager that it was "only the most trustworthy elements who can become a nucleus of a Communist Party." Prefiguring a contradiction that would arise on a greater scale in 1930, Ruthenberg's rationalization of US-led Communist organization in relationship to Puerto Rico was based on the fact of US financial hegemony over the Puerto Rican economy. A concern for the Puerto Rican comrades, however, was identifying whether or not political guidance from the US was *a priori* justified due to economic preponderance of the Yankee dollar. Certainly Ruthenberg understood that the realities of political repression necessitated the securing of "trustworthy elements" critical for the origins of a party on the island; however, the assertion that the US was overseeing this "nucleus" itself implied a paternalistic bias that slighted the ideological maturity and leadership of these Caribbean counterparts.[44]

No doubt Ruthenberg was satisfied that his own "trustworthiness" had been proven as a leader. But the irony of his inattention to the language barrier indicated that while trustworthy, he might indeed have not been fully competent in understanding the nuances of just how multifaceted and laborious a successful campaign for international solidarity really was. Ruthenberg indicated to Sager that he had already arranged to "send you under separate cover a number of charter applications together with copies of the program of the Party in English" along with an "enclosed money order for $25, so that you can meet the travelling expenses which you indicated in your letter are necessary." Inevitably, the conflict of an internationalism that re-inscribed neocolonial chauvinisms regarding how language would articulate mass ideas to foment mass change would pose a problem for said movement. How could a Puerto Rican outpost adhere to the Comintern if its leading party representatives could not reciprocate such gestures of solidarity at the level of language translation and inclusion? Ruthenberg must not have spoken Spanish, and yet he had been considered "trustworthy" enough to help lead the Communist International in a primarily Spanish-speaking hemisphere. More than likely, nationalist leaders such as Albizu Campos would have noticed these tensions around language in the Communist movement and looked on with cynical disapproval.[45]

Nevertheless Sager continued in his efforts of building a Communist party, adhering to the orders of the Chicago headquarters of the WP. But in his attempts to extend the AIL more deeply into the political inner workings of the nationalist independence movement, Sager found that Campos was not only politically but even personally averse to active collusion with "Yankee" forces—Communist or otherwise. When Sager extended an invitation for Campos to meet with members of the US branch of the AAAIL, Sager reported that

> ... in reply to my inquiry if he would extend his anti-imperialist lecture tour to the U.S. ... he stated that being an avowed enemy of the U.S. it would not be consistent for and ethical for him to set foot in the United States.

One decade later, as Campos languished in an Atlanta penitentiary, he would openly welcome the support of Communist-led groups like the International Labor Defense (ILD) as they fought to secure his release during the era of the Popular Front. In 1926, though, Campos's deep skepticism if not outright dismissal of the possibility for multiracial, cross-border progressive politics emerging out of the United States itself was at least partially the response to a racially biased national chauvinism even among Communist leaders like Ruthenberg and Gomez, who did not question their formulas for proletarian internationalism even when variables like language, culture and industrial development posed obvious challenges to Communist strategies of the time.[46]

Sager, unlike Campos, was committed to building the Communist International in spite of such weaknesses; therefore, he pushed forward in the campaign to construct a Communist "grupo" in Puerto Rico that seems to have fit the categorization standard as set forth by Ruthenberg. Invoking the Declaration of Independence of the United States, the Puerto Rican Communist group created its own charter in Spanish and sent it to Ruthenberg, stating that "We the undersigned believe that the moment has arrived for the class-conscious workers who struggle in the vanguard of the workers' movement" to overthrow the "exploiters" of labor, both foreign and domestic. The "destruction of the system of Capitalism and establishment of a Dictatorship of the Proletariat" was seen as the "only force or power that can definitively redeem the workers and the rest of enslaved and exploited humanity." Apparently, this group of Communists concentrated in the subaltern epicenter of Ponce, Puerto Rico, was concerned with the question of human redemption from slavery and exploitation, and this was the meaning behind their urgent call for a "dictatorship of the proletariat" on the island and around the world.[47]

The daily activity of this group was apparently much more mundane and local than the grandiose rhetorical gestures toward militant seizure of state power in the name of proletarian internationalism. The Puerto Rican incipient Communist movement appears to have been functionally a wing of the larger, Campos-led nationalist movement, a movement that did not advocate for the overthrow of capitalism—much less the "dictatorship of the proletariat." This did not mean, however, that the Communist group was ineffectual in terms of the island's internal politics. In fact, Sager reported that by way of the AAAIL there was a marked change in the labor movement, especially among Puerto Rican tobacco workers, due largely to Communist influence. A labor leader called Barcelo, Sager noted cynically, "but yesterday an open enemy of labor and 'bolshevik' baiter, is now turned 'bolshevik.'" A "close understanding" between the nationalist and Communist forces, claimed Sager, was emerging. But this was not to be mistaken, however, with a class understanding.[48]

Even a "close understanding" was beginning to emerge in terms of the WP's approach to the Puerto Rican Communist movement. It had come to pass after months of activity and leadership emanating from the island that General Secretary Ruthenberg admitted to Sager the WP's own shortcomings relative to the language barrier. Speaking on behalf of the WP as a whole, Ruthenberg expressed that:

> We realize the need of some simple statement of the Communist principles in the Spanish language and we have given to Comrade Gomez the work of immediately translating into Spanish my pamphlet on the Workers (Communist Party) ... [we] will add ... a general statement in regard to the Porto Rican situation ... If you wish to draft the addition in relation to Porto Rico, we will be glad to have you do so with the collaboration of the comrades who have organized the League.[49]

Ruthenberg had even more to offer. He was "glad to ship to [Sager] 100 books immediately (membership books) together with a supply of stamps," all complete with the title "'Communist League of Porto Rico.'" In this way, and on Ruthenberg's account, the Puerto Rican comrades had arrived into Communist history with a written record, and as such their political situation would receive a "general statement" in WP literature henceforth. But having been supplied with membership cards, Spanish translations, and general statements, the movement in Puerto Rico was still not in a position to flourish substantially, much less act as a base for Soviet seizure of Rockefeller's oil wells in Venezuela.

* * *

The Puerto Rican Communist movement that Navares Sager spearheaded with the Anti-Imperialist League appears to have disappeared from the scene of transnational Communist activity just as the Great Depression struck toward the end of 1929. This movement did not re-emerge—or at least does not appear to have done so—until 1935. In its place, Communism in Mexico and even more so in Cuba began in 1930 to take on increasingly prominent roles in the mass movements then underway in both regions and also in New York. Moreover, the arrest and expected execution of nine innocent African American young men from Scottsboro, Alabama, in 1931, opened the door to greater activity around the anti-racist struggle in the United States and in Mexico and Cuba. The CPUSA's leadership of the New York-based AIL and the ILD would be critical to conjoining the Communist and anti-racist dimensions of this Bolshevik network between the US, Mexico and Cuba. In the process, many of the linguistic and racial boundaries that had challenged the Communist International in its early period of solidarity work began to dissolve. At the root of this transnational solidarity was the fact that the "Negro question" took on a much more prominent role in Communist circuits of organization in the years from 1930 to 1934 when Communist ascendency enjoyed some of its most explicitly proletarian influence among black workers in the hemisphere, as we will see in the case of Cuba's Realengo 18.

PART II

TWO STEPS FORWARD

CHAPTER 4

Every Country Has a Scottsboro

The chief interest and ultimate security of the United States lies in the loyal friendship of the Western Hemisphere.
Sumner Welles, Former Assistant Secretary of State for
Latin American Affairs and Special Envoy to Cuba, 1934

There is a Scottsboro in every country.
Diego Rivera, 1933

"On the earthen floor of the house of the poet of Realengo 18," reported Josephine Herbst in 1935

> … one man draws with a stick a map of Cuba. He shapes the island and we stare at its smallness that is now being related to the world. Outlines of the United States take shape roughly. There is an ocean, Europe and a sudden great bulge of the stick moved by an inspired curve makes the Soviet Union. Everyone in the room smiles.

Herbst was a writer and a member of the Communist Party of the United States (CPUSA). She was herself inspired by these black Cuban peasants:

> We are very high on top of the world in Realengo. We are in the midst of steep cultivated mountains with banana and tobacco growing in regular rows. Around these cultivated patches virgin forest bristles in tough area … its difficult trails are too narrow for the artillery of an army.

Realengo 18—or Commune 18—was the Cuban Soviet.[1]

Realengo 18 was formed in 1926, when the peasants of the eastern Oriente province created their own constitution. By 1934, the state's attempt to dislodge the realengo had been futile. In August, airplanes "whirled overhead looking for places to drop bombs" on the "squatters," as they were referred to by the US

State Department. In the meantime, Communist-led workers in surrounding districts of the realengo and also in Havana staged protests explicitly in support of the peasants' struggle to retain their land. Hence, in the daily lives of these guerilla warriors of all ages in Realengo 18, the necessity for class warfare was always already present. "Agents from the big sugar mills below penetrate Realengo 18 on horseback wearing very white starched clothes, riding haughtily with whips in their hands and guns on their hips," wrote Herbst, bringing about an atmosphere wherein "contempt is thick in the air as the invader disappears." Cuban peasants and proletarians in town and country, alongside and sometimes under the banner of the Communist International, were determined not to cower before the government-sponsored repression in the aftermath of Cuba's "September 4th Revolution" of 1933.[2]

The peasants' "own struggle to hold the land to which they have given so much labor," Herbst wrote, had laid the basis for their "fight for freedom." This local struggle for freedom was organically rooted in the long history of the nineteenth-century Cuban struggle for independence from Spanish colonial domination. Then in 1912, the Afro-Cuban movement for civil and economic rights in the eastern Oriente province heightened the level of militancy within the peasantry in this part of the island against both native Cuban and foreign American ruling elites. Rising Communism found fertile soil in this region, as Herbst found:

> The district of Realengo is small in comparison to Cuba and Cuba is only a tiny island but no one in Realengo feels alone in the fight for freedom. They talk too much of what is going on in the world ... Soon it was too dark to make maps and we began singing, first the *Marseillaise* and then the *Internationale*. Everyone knows that since that time much blood has been shed in Cuba; the iron military rule has tried to crush strikes, stifle protests. Neither jail nor guns can completely silence such singing.[3]

The peasants' ended their evening singing the Communist *Internationale* and began their day with the struggle to keep Canadian bankers off their land. What, then, did it mean for these peasants to defend the Soviet Union while based in the "Black Belt of Oriente" in 1934? Reciprocally, what did it mean for Reds elsewhere to defend the cause of these black peasants in Realengo 18?[4] The origin of Cuba's peasant Soviet in the "Black Belt" of Oriente was complex. The struggle underway at Realengo 18 should not only be seen as an isolated tradition of black radicalism that began during the 1912 peasants' uprising against Cuban racial exploitation, which was bitterly repressed. Rather, it must be understood more proximately as a tradition that was mediated by a surge in Communist activity led by the Comintern in 1930 with a mandate for "Colonial parties" to establish and strengthen Communist movements in the colonies and semi-colonies, with Cuba at the helm. This policy objectively forced the convergence of anti-colonialism and anti-racism, characterized as the "Negro question," since racist super-exploitation of people of color in the US and across the hemisphere had been the cornerstone of capitalist profits and political power since the days of slavery.

This chapter focuses on the relationship between the Comintern mandate in 1930 and the actual work of the CPUSA, Communist Party of Cuba (CPC) and Communist Party of Mexico (CPM). Up through the year 1934, their attendant organizations—particularly the Anti-Imperialist League (AIL) and International Labor Defense (ILD)—in the US, Mexico and Cuba that put this anti-colonialist and anti-racist objective into practice. Advocating for workers' right to self-determination in the "Black Belt" of the US and Cuba formed a critical component of Communist praxis against American imperial power and Cuban native elites during the "Third Period" of Communist policy, beginning in 1928 and ending in 1934.

Communists in New York City—black and white alike—such as leading figure James Ford, had been instrumental in laying the practical and ideological groundwork to make such militant challenges to capitalist rule a historical reality in Cuba. The Communist movement in Cuba that was then unfolding under intense conditions of tyranny at the hands of President Carlos Mendieta, who replaced President Gerardo Machado in the aftermath of the 1933 *coup d'état*, reinforced the necessity for revolutionary change for Communists like Ford.

THE 1930 COMINTERN ANTI-COLONIAL MANDATE IN NEW YORK-CUBAN-MEXICAN CONTEXT

During the years from 1930 to 1934, states of emergency became the modus operandi for self-purported democratic governments in the western hemisphere, namely in semi-colonies of the United States like Mexico and Cuba where Communist parties were fast growing. The assassination of the Cuban Communist Julio Antonio Mella in Mexico by local authorities in collusion with the United States in 1929 opened the door to a new wave of hostility, terror, and repression in the region. The repressive and pro-US Mexican government formally severed ties with the Soviet Union in 1930—earning what Assistant Secretary of State Welles would later consider the "loyal friendship" of the US—while being castigated by the Comintern as an example of "social fascism." But this repression only worked to strengthen a Communist militant base for class struggle around the "Colonial question" and the "Negro question" for one reason: there was a party and global infrastructure that was determined to sharpen iron with iron, meet repression with resistance.[5] The Communist International had determined in 1928 that the African American workers of the US South formed a demographic "Black Belt" that created a geopolitical nation within a nation, which had the right to essentially fight for its own self-government. But this strategy was also extended to the "Black Belt" of Cuba's eastern province of Oriente and, while articulated in a different manner, to the Black Caribbean islands and regions where people of African descent were the clear majority. Hence, when in 1931, nine innocent young black men in Scottsboro, Alabama, affably referred to as the "Scottsboro Boys", were falsely accused of raping two white girls and summarily condemned to execution, this brash act of racist terror fomented a movement against Jim Crow racism in not just the US, but worldwide, forcing a unity of interests in the plight of black and Latino workers in the US, Cuba and Mexico—and beyond. Therefore, the Mexican revolutionary Diego Rivera's notion that "there is a Scottsboro in every country" was born in this historical matrix of political tyranny and economic depression wherein Communists were a leading force in challenging outright the brutal super-exploitation and degradation of working-class people of color not only in the US South but also, as we will see, in Mexico and Cuba.

Four years before, when the pinnacle of multiracial class solidarity embodied by Realengo 18 had been realized, Communists at the local and global levels had begun a focused, deliberate and coordinated campaign to organize movements between parties in the "colonial countries" like the US and those in the colonies and semi-colonies like Cuba. After several revisions, the Comintern in Moscow submitted in March 1930 a mandate to the Communist parties of the United States, France, Great Britain, and Holland, with special instructions on how to build working-class-led parties in the Caribbean. Notably, this mandate was submitted as a result of "recent mass movements which have taken place in the principal islands of the Antilles," namely in "Haiti, Santo Domingo, Guadeloupe [and] Cuba." Such rebellions as were under way in the republics and colonies of the Western Hemisphere—particularly in the West Indies—had motivated Communists to harness that energy and engage these workers around the politics of "class against class." The significance of this observation lies in the fact that laborers in the so-called "periphery" were often in the leadership, or vanguard, of class struggle in the hemisphere and particularly in relationship to the parties such as the CPUSA.

The Comintern noted that such revolutionary fervor had been first evinced in Central America with the "resistance of the Sandino supporters in Nicaragua." Moreover, the strategic importance of the Caribbean Basin and Central America was seen by the Comintern to lie in its abundance of oil, a natural resource that was not only the lifeblood of contemporary capitalism but also a necessary geopolitical leveraging force for aspiring Communist states as well. The geopolitical importance of the oil wealth based in Venezuela, Colombia, Mexico and Trinidad meant that

... one of the essential tasks of the Communist Parties and revolutionary trade unions in imperialist countries is to devote greater attention than in the past to the colonial and semi-colonial countries and work effectively to bring together the revolutionary elements, to organize them and to educate them.

In this context, the Comintern offered an important self-criticism that Communists in the "imperialist countries" had been hitherto inattentive to and therefore remiss in carrying out such internationalist praxis.[6]

Without a doubt, this mandate issued by the Politburo was an indispensable component of the radical upsurge that the Comintern helped to foment in the Caribbean for the duration of the Third Period. The AIL and ILD came together to help put this directive into practice, and their corresponding literature reflected this emphasis on the question. Communist direct or indirect influence was critical to the force behind much of the class uprisings and struggles that black workers led and participated in across the hemisphere over the next few years. At the same time, however, this advance in the commitment to international antiracism which was being directed from metropolises including New York, carried with it at times remnants of the very elitism and tendencies toward paternalism that capitalism promoted in the most industrialized regions around the world. The Comintern headquarters in Moscow had charged the Communist parties in western metropolises with the task of selecting from "among the best, most active and most devoted workers ... the elements to form the nucleus of the Communist movement." The mandate was mechanical in its expectation of how the "best" workers would be "selected." The process of identifying and recruiting itself required that current parties have a level of intimacy with and knowledge of local conditions which was not yet there; moreover, recruitment was predicated above all on the affinity for Communism that colonized workers themselves had to become convinced of embracing.[7]

While the primary achievement of this mandate was its insistence upon cross-border, truly international solidarity led by the Comintern, the mandate then went on to re-inscribe colonial boundaries in terms of its decision for which parties were assigned to their corresponding colonies:

It is up to the Communist Party of the United States to develop the work already begun in Jamaica, and to take the initiative of this work in Porto Rico, Santo Domingo and Haiti. For Martinique, Guadeloupe and French Guiana, it is up to the French Communist Party to carry on this work and to assist in the work in Haiti where the population speaks French. The Dutch Party must take over the work in Curacao and Dutch Guiana. It is up to the British Party first of all to carry on the work in Trinidad, British Guiana and British Honduras, and come to an agreement with the US Party regarding work in Jamaica.[8]

The Politburo had not unproblematically formulated out a political program in a spatial pattern that re-inscribed the colonial boundaries of language and geography that were maintained by the rulers to whom Communists were opposed. In order to see how Communists carried out this mandate, it is necessary to focus attention on the specific context of Communist organizations and parties in Cuba and Mexico relative to developments in New York, the metropole of the "Wall Street" empire and the contemporaneous headquarters of Comintern political organization in the hemisphere.

COMMUNIST REORGANIZATION AND THE BIRTH OF THE NEW YORK-BASED ORGANIZATION

The intensification of Comintern activity in the Caribbean beginning in 1930 was accompanied by shifts in the organizational structure and objectives of CPUSA mass organizations, changes that were seen as more conducive to promoting this new initiative of party-building in the Caribbean. The All-American Anti-Imperialist League (AAAIL) and International Labor Defense (ILD) underwent significant restructuring to position themselves more squarely in the work of challenging colonialism in the hemisphere—particularly in the Caribbean "Black Belt" islands of the Antilles. In addition, the American Negro Labor Congress (ANLC) was disbanded in 1930 and replaced by the League of Struggle for Negro Rights (LSNR) which in turn paved the way for certain new initiatives in the Caribbean. Most relevant to radical activity in the British West Indies, the West Indies Sub-Committee of the International Trade Union Committee of Negro Workers was formed in 1933 and headquartered in Harlem.

As the global depression intensified and unemployment mounted in the United States, the CPUSA embarked on a massive campaign to place the struggle for jobs more centrally in the struggle against the capitalist class. In February 1930, it was announced that the "immediate issue before the Party is to mobilize all its forces for the broadest possible unemployment campaign, culminating in the International Unemployment Day, February 26." Subsequent reports in 1930 indicated that there were at the time 14,000 members of the CPUSA with over 1,250,000 laborers in the country marching under its leadership at the Unemployment Day parade in March. Moreover, as a result of a recent recruiting drive, 900 of the new members were black. On August 1, the Comintern-initiated annual holiday called "International Red Day," the *Daily Worker* reported that Communists in New York led a protest of over 30,000 laborers and unemployed from the metropolitan area

> ... under a sea of banners pledging defense of the Soviet Union and Soviet China, war on imperialist war, demanding that all war funds be given to unemployed relief, calling on workers to join the CP, the YCL [Young Communist League], the revolutionary unions of the TUUL [Trade Union Unity League].[9]

The International Labor Defense's self-assessment in 1930 was that while Haiti and Mexico were its present areas of concentration, there was a need to expand into the rest of the West Indies and Caribbean. This decision on the part of ILD leadership converged with an increasing emphasis on struggling against the lynch law and anti-black racism that were especially prevalent in the "Black Belt" of the US South. Therefore, beginning in 1930, the ILD became another important conduit whereby the struggles of African Americans in the United States were ideologically linked with radical anti-colonial struggles in the even deeper South, based in the Caribbean and, in this instance, Cuba.

Following the movement to defend the Haitian uprising in December 1929, a memorandum in January 1930 mandated that "every district of the ILD must immediately begin a campaign for popularizing the revolutionary traditions of the Negroes among the Negro workers." The ILD instructed that

> the birthday or the anniversary of the death of such Negro revolutionists as Nat Turner, Denmark Vesey, Toussaint L'Ouverture, etc. must be used for holding large mass meetings among the Negro workers, and for organizational purposes. A list of names and dates of Negro revolutionists will be sent to all districts.

No extant records reveal the intellectual substance or demographic composition of these meetings—assuming that they even took place. Yet it was significant that the ILD had chosen to take such a cross-border, cross-linguistic approach to conjoining the history of anti-colonial and anti-racist struggles led by black workers in the hemisphere. Moreover, the use of grassroots, intimate gatherings to cultivate the political consciousness "among the Negro workers" who were affiliated with the ILD in the United States—particularly in an era of wider rebellions emanating from the periphery in the Antilles—was singular for its time.[10]

Concurrent with the ideological lessons in black revolutionary traditions in the United States and the Caribbean, the ILD formed a Caribbean Secretariat that—at the behest of the Mexican comrades based in Mexico City—was removed from Mexico and headquartered in New York. The intense political repression in Mexico had forced the Mexicans to make the decision that such a shift in organizational headquarters was necessary. By 1930, New York officially had become what Communists themselves described as the "imperial metropole" from which to guide the Communist parties and their affiliates in the Caribbean:

> The Caribbean Secretariat has been the object of persecution especially for the last few months in Mexico City … In view of the jailings, deportations and assassinations of workers in Mexico by the Mexican government, and especially against the leading comrades in the Caribbean Secretariat, the work of the ILD almost came to a standstill and for the last few months the Caribbean Secretariat

has been working illegally and this was one of the reasons for the decision asking the MOPR [*Mezhdunarodnoye Obshtchestvo Pomoshtchi Revolutzioneram* (International Red Aid—IRA)] to give its approval for bringing the Secretariat to New York.[11]

The ILD Secretariat in New York was to give support to work in Cuba. They would publish *Mella*, the newspaper of the Defensa Obrera Internacional [DOI], its Cuban section. This paper would then be sent to Cuba. The Caribbean Secretariat was to work in New York and help to "organize the Anti-Fascist Alliance in Caribbean countries." Toward the end of 1930, it became clear that the New York district of the ILD had "adopted Cuba for patronage," whereas Chicago had done the same for combating "white terror" in Mexico.[12] Cuba—not Mexico—became the focus of the ILD's Caribbean activity.[13]

The US section of the Anti-Imperialist League (AIL) also went through reorganization in 1930. The CPUSA pushed the AIL to increase its focus on militant class uprisings in Haiti, Nicaragua and the Philippines. In an attempt to get financial and political support from longtime "friends" of the AIL, leaders such as Earl Browder, Albert Moreau and Roger Baldwin—the former two being leading members of the CPUSA—found a new set of difficulties—namely, the intense militancy emanating from the Caribbean. One obscure fellow traveler, Wilbur Thomas, opposed the militancy:

> As you know I am deeply in sympathy with the AIL in practically all of its work. I am however quite out of sympathy with the thoughts expressed in the recent news release and in the resolutions concerning Haiti and the Philippines. This sentiment finds expression in such statements as "by any means at hand to the point of armed revolution." ... I am sorry if this puts me out of the fellowship of the League, but I cannot be party to revolution "by any means."

Clearly, US Communists would have to seek allies outside of the country if they sought support for militant, direct action. Cuba and Mexico were indeed sources of such an alliance rather than liberal American whites. People like Wilbur felt uncomfortable with the Communist view that revolutionary change would occur by "any means at hand"—including violence.[14]

Militant struggles in the Caribbean and developments in Mexico pushed the Communists based in New York to restructure their organization. Center to all this was Sandalio Junco, black Cuban labor leader and Communist.

MEXICO: ON THE FOREFRONT OF THE COMMUNIST THIRD PERIOD SHIFT LEFTWARD

The convergence of the fight against racism and US imperialism is demonstrated in the Mexican Communist experiment in this period. Early in 1930, Sandalio

Junco was apparently about to meet a fate similar to that which befell his radical compatriot Antonio Mella. After fleeing to Mexico from Cuba, he was apprehended. Mexico was going to extradite him to the hands of President Machado's executioners. Unlike Mella, Junco had organized a defense network across the hemisphere, according to *Negro Champion*, the primary voice for anti-racist, pro-Communist advocacy buttressed by the ANLC, ILD and AAAIL. Together, these groups with their attendant newspaper sparked a regional campaign to defend Junco, the Afro-Cuban labor leader. In the face of such international opposition, the Mexican government demurred. Junco fled. However, this tactical retreat was followed by much more aggressive political mobilization and unity among Mexican Communists who only faced increasing repression in the coming period.[15]

Several major schisms and realignments took place within the Mexican Communist movement and with respect to Moscow, Nicaragua and the US in 1930. Early in the year, the Mexican government formally ruptured its long-held ties to the Soviet Union. This diplomatic initiative was purportedly based on claims from General Enrique Estrada of the Mexican government that "'pernicious elements of Russian origin'" were found in Mexico. Communists went on the offensive in the streets of Tampico and New York and also in the pages of the *Daily Worker*. A February article in the newspaper decried the accusations on the part of General Estrada, with counter-evidence coming from one leader named Jorge Paz (he seems to have been a Cuban Communist who was deported to Mexico and later moved to New York):

> … in raiding their houses documents have been found proving that they were directed from Moscow! I am one of those politicals deported from Mexico. Upon me they have found no documents from the Soviet Union, neither from the Red International of Labor Unions. But on the other hand the Mexican police have robbed $275,000 from me that belonged to the periodical *The Latin-American Worker*, organ of the Latin-American Trade Union Confederation in its Mexican branch.[16]

At the hemispheric level, Communists used newspapers like the *Daily Worker* to argue that the repressive house raids and deportations visited upon labor leaders like Jorge Paz were far from neighborly or peaceful gestures toward radical dissidents on the part of Mexican rulers. At the international level, Communists even more aggressively mounted an attack in the pages of *International Press Correspondence*, charging the "Portes Oil government" with underhanded attempts to further the interests of America's Standard Oil Company, which also had outposts in Mexico, by blunting the force of the mounting labor movement led, in part, by radicals like Jorge Paz.

The CPUSA's political orientation toward geopolitical boundaries shifted to some degree, became more porous, and the support for workers in the hemisphere more visible in its own newspaper as well as to the eyes of US officials. The *Daily Worker* reflected a shifting notion of "America" within the paper itself. Demonstrations of the "American proletariat" referenced places as geographically disparate as Rio de Janeiro, Buenos Aires, Los Angeles, Cleveland, Detroit, and Washington, DC, where workers were challenging US oil conglomerates in Mexico. For example, a Mexican official named Senor Rubio who had reported ties to American oil wealth received the "horrified apologies of Detroit authorities" after he was met with hundreds of angry protesters in this city. Days later, he found that in "New York some 3,000 workers protesting against the crimes of Yankee imperialism both in Mexico and Hayti, fought the police for two hours under the slogan 'Down with the white terror in Mexico!'" Purportedly, within 24 hours of his return to Mexico, the Mexican government had severed ties with Soviet Russia.[17]

Efforts to reorganize the CPM, the AIL and the ILD brought about an explicit recognition on the part of Communists in the United States that both US and Mexican parties had suffered from a political problem of "provincialism." The US branch of the ILD helped to pave the way for correcting this problem. Leaflets in both Spanish and English would be created for dissemination within the US to mount a propaganda campaign against "white terror" in Cuba and Mexico. While this might have been only a minor advance in overcoming the language barriers that the CPUSA had acknowledged earlier in the year, it was important nonetheless and part of a much larger process of combating barriers of nation, race and culture that the criticism of "provincialism" was supposed to address.[18]

The clearest breakthroughs in the battle against narrow subjectivity between Communists in Mexico and the United States manifested in an adjustment to the prior dismissal of peasant radicalism that the CPM's industrial-based leadership had put forward since the party's founding. In 1930, the Mexican Reds, who were generally concentrated in the cities, began to soften their own ethnic and political prejudices toward the Indian peasantry in places like Vera Cruz. They now saw in the objective weaknesses of the peasants' movement the potential for workers' power that could be derived from the peasants' militancy. Copies of a report from the Comintern that were reviewed in the US State Department pointed to this development in relationship to the Mexican peasants of Vera Cruz:

> Here we can observe some success won by the Communist Party in establishing contact with the Indian masses through the regional peasant organizations which it has created (one of these, in the State of Vera Cruz, has 3,000 Indian peasants). This success serves as a pledge of the actual about-face of the Communist Party toward the nationally oppressed Indian masses. Nevertheless, the revolutionary movement of the Indians which took place this year, passed by the Communist

Party, without its participation and leadership, spontaneously. Such was the revolt of the survivors of the Hucheticos tribe in the state of Oaxaca, in April-May, 1931, occasioned by the refusal of the state authorities to confirm the election by the Indians of their municipal council, and by the attempt to impose upon them the henchmen of the local landlords.[19]

Gone were the days, it would seem, of referring to these agricultural-based workers as disorganized "peons" lacking in Bolshevik consciousness. Communists who were reporting on these events under way in Mexico were also seeing through a new lens the importance of the uprisings led by Indians in Mexico. In fact, Communists in Mexico and the US now admitted to negligence in not following the lead of the peasants' militant challenge to the government. While the Comintern had commissioned Communists in 1930 in countries like the US to oversee and "educate" the masses in regions such as Vera Cruz, the political conditions were such that "tribes" like the Hucheticos were presently giving leadership to the parties in Mexico and the US alike. They led militant direct action against eviction from their homes and lands. Certainly the US State Department felt their wrath. Indeed, the much-lauded anti-eviction campaigns from Harlem to Trinidad throughout the 1930s were not the first or most radical signs of resistance to brutal landlords in the region. Mexico set forth a most militant viable template in this regard.

In this internationalist spirit, the militancy from these peasants was acknowledged and reciprocated, and Communists in the US were indeed critical to helping push forward the movement in Mexico. The Mexican AIL, "which had ceased to exist, has again revived" and organized a meeting in Mexico City subsequent to the peasant rebellion in Oaxaca, "at which 1,000 persons were present." "In recent months, local organizations of the League have been established, and groups of students, professors at universities, and others have founded the League." The AIL's recent progress in the academic community of Mexico City which was in turn motivated by a peasant rebellion in Oaxaca was seen by Communists in the US and Mexico as an important advance in the struggle against American imperialism and Mexico's plutocratic elite.[20]

As the Communists struggled against "provincialism" with respect to Mexican/US radical solidarity, a greater hemispheric interest in the fight against Jim Crow racism in the US was manifesting in Mexico. Mexican support for the "9 Jovenes Negros," or the Scottsboro Boys, began in this context. One petition submitted to US authorities in Mexico to protest the execution of the Scottsboro Boys came from Tampico, the same city where only several years before there had been a protest of over a thousand people in defense of Italian-born American anarchists Sacco and Vanzetti who were later executed. Another report from J. Reuben Clark to the Secretary of State also indicated that the "'Syndicate of Workers in Tile and Other Similar Factories of Monterrey, Nuevo Leon,

Mexico'" were incensed at having "'learned of the cruel and infamous execution which the Supreme Court of America proposes to carry out on May 13th [of 1932] next.'" There is no evidence that the AIL or ILD gave direct leadership to either of the protests emerging from Tampico and Nuevo Leon respectively; however, the boundaries of nation and culture were being overcome in an attempt to thwart Jim Crow injustices in the US South. Such solidarity, clearly in line with Comintern strategy around the "Negro Question," raised concern about an incipient civil rights movement for US officials at the time.[21]

Diego Rivera made a landmark trip to a Harlem headquarters of the Urban League in 1933 to make one point clear: "There is a Scottsboro in every country." In Rivera's view, the same systematic denial of basic liberties and exploitation that was carried out by the government of Mexico was also proven to exist in the US South where the African American population was most densely concentrated. The *Chicago Defender* covered the story of Diego Rivera's trip to New York during which time he stopped in Harlem. While the article in the paper played down the class content of Rivera's provocative statement, regarding him as a famed artist with a "pretty little wife, wearing her native costume," it described how Rivera had descended on the Harlem political scene at a local branch of the Urban League to demonstrate that the "race problem" was "universal." The article offered a timely interpretation of Rivera's linkage of racist oppression in Mexico and the United States. It stated that Rivera "feels that the Caribbean Race man and the American Race man should unite not as unto themselves, but in the world movement against capitalistic abuses." Rivera and his "pretty little wife"—that is, the formidable Frida Kahlo—were hardly the quintessential "race" couple that abided by traditional gender roles characterized by a strong husband and trophy wife. However, the overall summation of the racial plight that linked Caribbean—presumably meant to include Mexico in this article—with African American people was profound and accurate. Still, Rivera's own words were indeed much more solidly anti-capitalist than was the article's analysis: "The Race problem was never solved by a capitalistic nation ... The true persecution is economic as well as social. It is indeed, fundamentally economic." It might have been more accurate for the *Chicago Defender*'s headline to read, "Racist Economic Problem is Universal." Radical, intermittently Communist, artists like Diego Rivera helped to bring the anti-racist movement embodied by the Scottsboro case into international popular consciousness.[22]

Nearly one year subsequent to Rivera's visit to Harlem, the Black and Brown Movements linking the American "Negro question" with the plight of Mexican laborers had become even more interpenetrated, paving the way for a greater convergence of forces between the Afro and Latin Movements in Mexico, the Caribbean and the United States. A new organization with significant Communist influence in the United States, one that eventually functioned to eclipse the political activism of the AAAIL, emerged in 1934 called the American League Against War and Fascism. It sponsored a Paris conference in which four African American women delegates were described as having put forward an analysis that represented their class solidarity with laborers in Mexico who were then suffering in the throes of the global depression. Similar cross-border, cross-race, intra-class solidarity was reciprocated several months later in 1934 when the US Consulate in Tampico received local petitions from the ILD in Mexico against the latest measures to execute the Scottsboro boys. In this way, the same anti-racist "specter" that haunted the Jim Crow South was also apparently haunting the US Consul at Tampico, Mexico, owing in no small part to the conscientious efforts of Communists in the days, months, and years past.

BLACK WORKERS IN CUBA: A VANGUARD IN THE CLASS STRUGGLE

But if the specter of anti-racist unity in defense of the Scottsboro boys had disturbed Tampico in November 1934, then it had outright haunted Cuba by November 30 of this same year, to the point where young white Communists in the Cuban Young Communist League were being murdered in cold blood for defending the Scottsboro Nine. Radical Cubans in the Communist-led YCL, ILD and Committee for Negro Rights (presumably a Cuban offshoot of the American branch of the League of Struggle for Negro Rights) were assembled in Havana at a protest in which police had fired on and successfully executed one brave YCL youth—a white 23-year-old named Domingo Ferrer. Even more notably, at least to Communists at the time, "many prominent persons" such as the proud nephew and namesake of Antonio Maceo, the seminal black Cuban independence leader, also addressed the crowd at this protest. Indeed, the convergence of the Communist-led slogan in defense of the "Scottsboro Boys" with the decades-old, Cuban independence symbol of Antonio Maceo, personified by Maceo's nephew, crystallized the best of Cuba's radical experiment of the 1930s. As we have seen, by the close of 1934, black peasants in Realengo 18, who were also the descendants of veterans for Cuban independence, were running a peasant commune on the other side of the island in the hills of Oriente province outside of Guantanamo Bay with the active support of Communists.[23]

The national office of the ILD in the United States, then located in lower Manhattan's East Village, immediately issued a cable to US Secretary of State Cordell Hull in response to Ferrer's death. Anna Damon, acting leader of the ILD at the time, presumably knew that no cable could begin to express in practical terms the level of militant solidarity that would indeed be necessary to bridge the political movements under way in Cuba and United States.

However, the cable aggressively denounced the "murderous assault of the Cuban government on workers peacefully demonstrating their protests against … nine innocent Scottsboro boys," which "resulted in the wounding of scores and the death of at least one worker"—attributing Ferrer's death to the "direct outcome of the intervention policy of the American Government in Cuba." Moreover, the "latest act of terror of the Mendieta Government," said to have been "installed and manipulated by the US State Department" in order to "protect Wall Street investment in Cuba and preserve the island as an integral part of US imperialism's war machine" was then conjoined with the struggles of African Americans.[24]

The ILD's cable asserted that the intensified "oppression of the Negro people in the US" made them "victims of the same imperialism that enslaves Cuba," all of which was "symbolized by the Scottsboro case." Insisting upon the "immediate evacuation of Guantanamo Naval Base," which hunkered down ominously below the mountain-based peasant commune at Realengo 18, was therefore a practical demand that demonstrated the manner in which the Comintern was attempting to overturn geographic boundaries of nation in the common struggle against the American empire's racially prejudiced core. There was an origin to this anti-racist solidarity that extended roughly back to the year 1930.[25]

The New Year of 1930 caused a certain degree of consternation for US and Cuban authorities alike as the question arose; where in the world is Sandalio Junco? While Junco's fate and exact whereabouts were unknown, as he fled imminent repatriation back to Cuba at the hands of the Mexican government, Cuban authorities were much more squarely positioned to contain—or at least attempt to contain—the political influence that the Jamaican pan-Africanist Marcus Garvey was also having on black laborers in the island at the onset of 1930, which coincided with the onset, more importantly, of the sugar harvesting season. Black unrest in Cuba was incited by renegade leaders both foreign and domestic, and Garvey's power lay in the fact that his mass base was both foreign and domestic—not unlike Communists in this same period.

Garvey was ideally positioned to connect with everyday black people, unlike almost any other radical figure in the Diaspora in 1930, perhaps even more so than the Afro-Cuban labor leader Junco himself. Garvey's work in the United Negro Improvement Association (UNIA), based in Jamaica, put him front and center as labor's representative in the islands. He had maintained a political base of influence among not only black laborers who identified with the context of Anglophone British West Indian affairs, many of whom were migrants in Cuba at the time, but also in Cuba's Afro-Latin population, many of whom found themselves working alongside migrant Jamaican and Haitian laborers in gruesome labor conditions. Garvey rallied these laborers around the common goal of race unity in opposition to white-owned private enterprise in the sugar industry in 1930. The cane fields on the island quickly went up in smoke, quite literally, in a manner reminiscent of the slave rebellions that ripped through the Caribbean in the days of colonial enslavement. It was in this context that Communist—and even nationalist—forces became more aggressive, indirectly taking leadership from the black sugar workers' uprising that Garvey had inspired. Garvey's deportation from the island of Cuba by President Machado in early 1930 was characterized by the US authorities as a political phenomenon falling under the category of "miscellaneous Communist activities." The Cuban Secretary of the Interior had blurred the distinctions between Garveyism and Bolshevism for what seem to have been quite understandable reasons.[26]

Garvey and the Communists were deemed "unpatriotic," foreign menaces in the eyes of Cuba's Secretary of the Interior. A US official at the time said, "the deportation of Marcus Garvey, therefore, has been a measure taken by the Government for the general benefit of Cuban society and in accordance with ideals of patriotism." Days later, the *Liberator* reported that President Machado had banned the right of all workers to meet during the sugar-grinding season:

> Acting more and more openly as the bloody agent of US imperialism in its virtual exploitation of the Cuban masses, dictator Machado, president of Cuba, issued an order yesterday through his Secretary of the Interior, prohibiting all workers meetings and affairs during the sugar manufacturing and sugar cane harvesting season. The measure is taken to stifle any efforts of the workers for better conditions and wages and has roused the workers to a high state of resentment. Many Cuban Negroes and Haitians are involved.[27]

Inspired presumably by two forces—Garvey's calls for race unity against oppressive white sugar oligarchs, and Communist agitation for the overthrow of Machado—black laborers in Cuba, both foreign and domestic, rose up in January 1930.

THE ANATOMY OF A COUP—COMMUNISM AT THE HEART

On the heels of the island's deportation of Garvey and crackdown on black sugar workers' organization, Communists increased their lead in workers' general strikes and uprisings across the island. In turn, this radical upsurge drew increased repression at the hands of the fast-toppling Cuban state, then headed by President Machado. That is, black Cuban workers' radical protest, and its attendant repression, propelled forward the spread of labor rebellion on the island and, in turn, violent suppression. Furthermore, class struggle in Cuba forced to a head Communist international support—albeit flawed in many instances—from the United States.

A fundamental measure of revolutionary success is the extent of political backlash that revolutionaries face at the hands of the state. The Cuban AIL and ILD were declared illegal—again—in 1930, just as Communists in New York were reorganizing the official headquarters of these Comintern organizations in the hemisphere. At the level of appearance, this would suggest that in Cuba both the AIL and ILD were in political retreat, given their decisions to operate clandestinely rather than openly. In essence, however, these Cuban Communists were helping to lay the basis for a massive workers' counter-offensive only several years later that would culminate in the Revolution of September 4, 1933, which, tragically, would ultimately play into the hands of proto-fascist forces of a new, social-democratic stripe.

There is support for the case that Communists played a considerable role in the mounting protest movement against Machado's government and "Yankee imperialism" in 1930 during the general strike that began on March 20, 1930, the Comintern's International Unemployment Day. On this day in New York City, thousands had gathered in the streets for the general cause of combating unemployment under the banner of proletarian internationalism. On the eve of the corresponding protest in Cuba, US Ambassador Harry Guggenheim (1929–33), a pivotal figure in the formulation of US foreign policy relative to Cuba during the years leading up to the 1933 Revolution, noted that President Machado was "somewhat concerned" about this strike. For not only had it been "ordered" by the "Third International," but it was expected to receive support from several labor unions along with the non-Communist *Union Nacionalista*.

Not only had the Comintern helped to initiate this strike from points far to the north and east, but black Reds like James Ford were also on the scene from the "Colossus to the North" as early as 1930 and poised to promote greater support from the United States for the movement led by their Cuban counterparts. The "Negro question," on Ford's account, was a fundamental basis for building this transnational Red solidarity. He used the pages of the *Daily Worker* to initiate an intense campaign of political education about the history of black laborers on the island, noting that the "influx of Haitians and Jamaican Negroes has increased considerably since the inception of this slave traffic in 1912. In 1912 there were 700 Jamaicans and 233 Haitians in Cuba; the number rose to 27,088 Jamaicans and 35,971 Haitians in 1921." Fast-forwarding to the uprising under way in Haiti by 1929 and attendant popular support generated by the CPUSA for this rebellion, particularly in New York, Ford noted that in Cuba, "Only a few months ago Junco, a native Negro labor leader, barely escaped from the country with his life." Ford was attempting to broaden the anti-racist struggle and appreciation for the militancy of black workers' unrest by creating narratives that located the struggles of Haitian militants and black Cuban leaders like Junco at the heart of his articles about world socialist revolution in the wake of the global depression.[28]

There was a discrepancy between the rhetorical politics of solidarity represented in the pages of *Daily Worker* and the actual organizational support that materialized. In May 1930, as the AIL in lower Manhattan began the process of headquartering the entire AAAIL in the city, the Cuban leaders of the AIL petitioned the League Against Imperialism's center in Berlin, Germany for additional funds and political support. The reason for their operational and logistical problems was, on their account, due to the fact that their more affluent US comrades were in dereliction of their fiduciary duty. While it is not entirely clear why the US AIL headquarters had not been generating adequate funds and support for the Cuban branch, we can assume that such monetary problems were only secondary causes for the Cuban AIL.[29]

In 1930, Cuban AIL members were still dealing with the effects of heightened political repression under President Machado that resulted in the aftermath of the March general strike. On one hand, the March 20 strike had increased the radical fervor on the island and, in turn, quickened the pulse of the rulers, causing "uneasiness among the small bourgeoisie." The strike foreboded the "prospect of a railroad strike against the United Railways Enterprise ... [and] Cuban Telephone Company," which were run by British and US finance capital on the island, respectively. On the other hand, this strike also formed the pretext for the Cuban government's crackdown on Communism such that the AIL was declared illegal by the Machado government. Luigi Viondi of the Cuban AIL petitioned the Berlin headquarters, suggesting, "we will have to give it another name in order to legalize it." No amount of money from the AIL in the US could eliminate the Cuban AIL's fundamentally political problems associated with having been driven into illegality under a proto-fascist regime backed by US and British imperial interests. But a firm commitment to internationalism would mean consistent financial support, the best possible political line with respect to workers' power, and boots on the ground from fellow Communists and their working-class allies from near and far, particularly from the US.[30]

In the face of being driven underground, leading AIL member Viondi petitioned the Berlin headquarters of the AAAIL, charging that the US counterparts were providing insufficient support. According to Viondi, having "established contact with the organization in the United States, which has sent us a copy of its by-laws and some theses or resolutions of the Congress of Frankfurt," it remained problematic to Viondi that "it is not sufficient for us." On Viondi's account, formalities and procedural matters like by-laws and conference reports would not pass muster. Due to these apparent weaknesses of the US affiliate, Berlin became the focus of Cuba's "orientation of the Anti-Imperialistic work." It would appear that the AIL headquarters in New York evinced traces of the same insufficient support for their counterparts in the Caribbean that characterized Workers [Communist] Party relations with the Communist nucleus in Puerto Rico several years before—i.e., sending start-up materials to their Caribbean affiliates with the expectation that such support was a sufficient show of internationalism.[31]

Even though support from the US in 1930 was uneven, the number of Communists in Cuba continued to increase in the face of heightened repression under President Machado. This fact suggests that while support from external parties was significant to development of Communism, the primary factor was the internal commitment to developing the movement. August 1930 brought another government raid similar to that carried out in 1925 on the Communist office headquarters of the CPC. The more recent raid, though, had purportedly turned out a list of over two thousand Communists in Cuba in contradistinction to the list of two hundred names only several years before.

In due course, a large section of anti-government forces, led in part by Cuban military leaders Carlos Mendieta and Fulgencio Batista, would ultimately seize the reins of the larger mass movement on the island directed against President Machado that Communists and militant black workers had indeed initiated. That is, the road to this revolutionary *coup d'état* was paved by the efforts of singular Communist leaders like Viondi in the AIL and long-time African diasporic radicals like Marcus Garvey who helped incite workers' uprisings at the point of production. The list of two thousand names in Cuba also implicated US comrades based in New York, with government agents purporting to find "receipts for remittances of money sent to Communists here from New York." In short, Communist influence in Cuba was giving rise to a "Red menace" on the island, which, in turn, augured a new era of coercive US foreign policy to thwart this movement under the auspices of Ambassador Guggenheim.[32]

In the period from 1930 to 1934, the foreign hand of US military and economic rule played an increasingly direct role in the fascistic repression of workers' resistance under way in Cuba—though this was not often acknowledged in the public discourse of purportedly progressive "New Deal" civil society in the United States itself under President Franklin Delano Roosevelt. Ambassador Guggenheim was well aware of the importance of maintaining a liberal appearance of US diplomacy in Cuba, even though in private consort with the Secretary of State he frankly acknowledged the need to assist Cuban authorities in their suppression of Communism when the threat of radical upheaval directly infringed upon US business interests on the island. In response to intelligence relayed by one Cuban official relative to the recent raid on the CPC office in August, Guggenheim wrote:

> I said I thought he could count on our cooperation in carrying out any investigations which circumstances might indicate as being in the interests of both countries …
> I did not know how real or extensive the Communist menace in Cuba might be, but that arrests on a large scale would be likely to cause a good deal of uneasiness and might provoke unfavorable comment in the foreign labor press. Unless actual

danger to life and property would result from allowing the suspected persons to remain at large, it might be preferable to keep them under close surveillance.[33]

That only the infringement on "life and property" of US businessmen would warrant direct American military intervention in Cuba's affairs uncovers the deep-seated roots of economic interest embedded in pre-World War II US imperialism. The Cuban authorities under President Machado were much more apprehensive about the precarious nature of their own control of the state and therefore sought US support where they felt it was wanting. Once US enterprises came under direct attack from labor and political unrest, led in large part by Communists, US warships were fast on the scene.

The *New York Times* opportunistically seized the situation of mounting unrest and repression in Cuba to contrast the Cuban dictatorship with the supposed tolerant, democratic civil society in the United States. In mid-August 1930, days after the raid on Communist offices in Cuba, the *Times* announced that Communists in the US freely expressed their radicalism by publicly "cheering Seven Spanish Communists, deported from Cuba because of their activities." These seven Spanish Communists arrived at the port of Manhattan on a steamship named, quite appropriately, *Cristobol Colon* (Christopher Colombus). While "no arrests were made" at this protest of less than a hundred people in New York, speeches delivered in both Spanish and English demonstrate the manner in which linguistic boundaries did not hinder this solidarity protest. The US branch of the ILD based in New York was a leading voice at this rally to defend the seven deportees who were supposedly members of the National Cuban Confederation of Labor, or NCCL. Such demonstrations of internationalist unity as this one helped to lay the basis for a greater network of collusion of Communist forces with the larger masses of workers in the labor movement, despite the challenges that Viondi had outlined with respect to the AIL's support for Cuban political work.[34]

Just as the US section of the ILD was edging toward increasing its support for the labor struggles of NCCL in Cuba, the CPUSA had begun to offer what it considered "fraternal counsel" rather than paternalistic dicta to the CPC. An open letter from the CPUSA to the CPC in the pages of *The Communist* published in November 1930 was very telling. It stated that the

> … CPUSA by no means intends to substitute for the directives of the CI [Comintern], but only to give what assistance our opinions may be to you in concretizing the CI directives, and to carry out the tasks of fraternal counsel which are the duty of one brother Party to another.

The fundamental basis of this unity, then, was a shared sense of brotherhood. But this fraternal relationship notwithstanding, the CPUSA seems at times to have perceived itself as the "big brother" to the Cuban section.[35]

The open letter quickly degenerated, however, into an open indictment of the CPC's leadership during the March 20th protest. It asserted that

... the Communist Party of Cuba failed at that time to fully understand the fact that although 200,000 workers had answered its call to strike on March 20, this was only because the March 20 movement was for the masses a struggle for bread for the unemployed.

The CPUSA report continued its criticism with the observation that "for the masses the question of legality of the trade unions did not represent that burning, immediate issue of daily life which the most backward workers could understand." This might well have been the case, and perhaps the Cuban Communists were more concerned with legality and financial support than pushing the workers' demands to the forefront—but the US counterparts were not exactly in an equivalent position. Their offices were functional and their operation was, for all intents and purposes, legal. What is more, these "forward" thinking US Communists had also retained the controversial notion of "backward" masses in the Caribbean periphery.[36]

The CPUSA charged the CPC with the task to "energetically penetrate the masses with its own slogans and demands, expressing the immediate needs of these masses." The US Communists were obviously attempting to offer what they considered to have been honest leadership in bringing about socially, politically and economically fundamental change in Cuba. And if Cuban comrades were chagrined, President Machado was panicked. He interpreted this solidarity as expressed in *The Communist*—however flawed—as an affront to his leadership, which it was. He answered the CPUSA's call for concrete "slogans and demands" at the end of 1930 with a direct, nationwide attack on Communism in a speech delivered in January 1931. Months later, he followed this public statement with an official presidential declaration of a state of siege on the island. *Agrecion comunista implacable*, or implacable communist aggression, was the ideological rationale for President Machado's declaration of a state of siege in Spring 1931.[37]

While Machado was quite opportunistically ringing the anti-Communist alarm in order to better fortify US direct military muscle on his behalf, the truth was that Communists had dismissed much of the anti-Machado movement as riddled with petit-bourgeois students and intellectuals and, even worse, reactionary elites who wanted Cuba under their own thumb. Therefore, in the months and years leading up to Machado's forced removal from office, Communists in Cuba were not content to surrender the revolutionary impulse of the working masses to the leadership of bourgeois Cuban opposition forces like Mendieta and Fulgencio Batista. Even though mass uprisings in districts like Santa Clara were partially under the leadership of renegade military forces,

Communists noted that there was also evidence of independent radical struggle from below, led, notably, by courageous working-class women who needed to feed their shoeless children. For example, in 1931

> ... a hunger revolt took place. 3,000 people, the majority of them women, stormed the offices of the Minister of the Interior in order to demand food for their starving families. The police were unable to hold the crowds in check. The nervousness of the Cuban authorities spread quickly to the United States Department of Justice.

The "nervousness" also spread quickly to the State Department.[38]

The class struggle then underway in Cuba during the months leading up to the revolt of 1933, led in part by the CPC, was significant on a local and even on a global scale. "Up with Communism" was the slogan at the May Day celebration in Havana in 1931. Weeks later, "Down with America" was the heading of Albert Einstein's cable to the US president upon word of the imminent "execution of the eight negroes of Scottsboro." The US rulers had multiple reasons for nervousness, caused not only by radical uprisings in Cuba but also by the growing anti-racist solidarity for the Scottsboro case that took on global proportions.[39]

Above and beyond Einstein's cable "in the name of humanity and justice" sent from Berlin, Germany, it was also reported by US Consulate officials in Berlin that "during the night June 30 one plate glass window of the Consulate General and glass panel of entrance as well as two windows Wetheim tea room right of entrance broken by stones thrown by group young men." This same tactic of defacing the US Consulate would be a preferred protest tactic for incensed Cuban radicals on a number of important questions implicating US socio-economic control in the Caribbean for the duration of the interwar period. In the case of Germany, however, these young men had apparently wrapped the stones in paper that "contained protest of young Communist organization against condemnation of eight negroes Alabama." From Calcutta, India to Rio de Janeiro, Brazil, to Cologne, Germany, there were people storming US Consulate headquarters located quite literally only a stone's throw away from their protests against the arrest and expected execution of the "nine Negro boys."[40]

In this global context, the Scottsboro campaign arrived on the scene in Cuba and the Cuban CP declared its allegiance to this cause on the Fourth of July in 1931, the day that the US celebrates its independence from British rule. The historical conjuncture of massive unemployment in Santa Clara along with the global opposition to the imminent execution in Scottsboro gave rise to a reinvigorated ILD in Cuba; quite appropriately, it based itself in the "Black Belt" of Oriente. In short, the Communist movement in Cuba was strongest in terms of class struggle and working-class leverage over the bourgeois state where its organization alongside and among black workers—both Cuban and non-Cuban—was strongest. And the Scottsboro case helped bring about this upsurge in strength. Maintaining an ILD headquarters in what was most likely Santiago was presumably quite different from one based in the west of the island, toward the more industrialized center in Havana. Again, the Scottsboro case offered a convenient yet potent trope through which to enact this process.[41]

Yet the IRA's struggle to defend the Scottsboro boys, which had reverberations in the "Black Belt" of Oriente, was only one aspect of the way racial politics played into the Red International's circuit between the US and Cuba. The other aspect of the circuit was the relatively negligent manner in which the Caribbean Bureau of the Comintern addressed the concrete matter of consolidating a large base of black laborers in Cuba to actually join and take leadership within the burgeoning Communist movement on the island. That is, the Caribbean Bureau of the Comintern did not offer any practical solutions for how the CPC could augment its demographic representation among people of African origin, even as the Scottsboro campaign became more popular within the Cuban movement. "While the Party membership is growing (500 members at present compared with about 300 a year ago)," noted one report, it also stated that "the composition of the membership continues to suffer in three essential respects." Among the "essential respects" was the lack of "native-born Cubans" and "very few Negro workers, though one-third of the population is Negro," defects which were "especially strong in the Havana organization." The CPC was in a difficult position precisely because the epicenter of Communist organization remained in Havana even though the anti-racist struggle, if it sought to be successful on a large scale, would necessarily have to include and even base itself in the eastern portion of the island—the portion considered by Communists to have been more "backward" than the proletarian base in Havana. Ironically, or perhaps to the point, by 1934, the peasants of Realengo 18 were indeed in the forefront of Cuba's Soviet movement even though party headquarters was on the other side of the island.[42]

In spite of the relatively weak base of leadership within the black population in Cuba in 1932, Communists in New York, and Harlem in particular, were indeed instrumental in helping to bridge the gaps between Black and Red in Cuba. When a Cuban labor leader in the Cuban National Confederation of Labor named Ermando Grau disappeared in August of 1932, marking only the most recent in a rash of strange "disappearances" of radical—often Red— Cuban native leaders, the ILD based from its headquarters in lower Manhattan was the first organization on the scene, issuing a resolution against this labor and political persecution. The resolution notably conjoined the demand for Grau's release with the freedom for the Scottsboro young men as well as US-based Communist labor leader Tom Mooney. Days later, an alliance of forces in Harlem including a local branch of the Cuban YCL, a local Puerto Rican branch of the AIL, and the local Harlem branch of the CP, united for a protest of over a thousand people through Harlem on behalf of Grau San Martin and persecuted radicals in Cuba.[43]

In order to garner local support for the rally, Communists announced in the *Daily Worker* the route of the protest:

> The demonstration will start at 4pm at 124th Street and Lenox Ave and proceed along the following route: Down Lenox to 116th St, east to Madison Ave, down Madison to 114th St, west through 114th St, past the Porto Rican Anti-Imperialist Association headquarters to Lenox Ave, down to 110th St where a meeting will take place ....

Among the scheduled speakers was "Sanchez for the Anti-Imperialist League, Carl Hecker for the International Labor Defense, and Shepard for the Communist Party." The route and the speakers tell us a great deal about the politics of the period and place. Harlem was much more than a "Negro Mecca" and cultural "renaissance" capital for the duration of the interwar period. Even though in 1934 James Ford determined that Harlem was a "petit-bourgeois" center of black leadership rather than a "Negro Mecca," the CPUSA leadership in Harlem in 1932 was helping to bring about the collusion of black, Latino and white workers in the myriad communities of Harlem—many from the US, and many from the British West Indies, Haiti, Cuba and Puerto Rico. In turn, this circuit of leadership coming from upper Manhattan gave rise to an ever-expanding network of people and organizations to include Puerto Rican radicals in lower Harlem.[44]

Albert Sanchez and Henry Shepard were Communists of Puerto Rican and African American origin, respectively, whose Red political activism in Harlem would physically lead them to building the Communist movement on distant shores in the islands of Puerto Rico and Cuba. That the protest ended on 110th Street precisely where the Park Palace Casino was located, the premier Communist hub in the ensuing period for Cuban and Puerto Rican solidarity campaigns, only demonstrates further the degree to which the circuit taken reflected a hemispheric strategy toward building multiracial, cross-border solidarity under the leadership of Communists.

THE SOVIET OF REALENGO 18: COMMUNISM'S CARIBBEAN CLIMAX

Cuba's "September 4th Revolution" which began in August of 1933, fundamentally heightened the material significance of the "Negro Question" in the hemisphere for Communists as disparate as Cuba and New York. "Negroes with guns" had become a real problem again for US and Cuban rulers whose political and economic wealth was concentrated in the "Black Belt" of Oriente, especially once these diasporic laborers in town and country began to speak of Soviets and to act as Red guards. The period of militant and political upheaval from August 1933 through the rise of Realengo 18 in late 1934 marks a phenomenal if brief era of progress for the Communist movement within Cuba and beyond, with the leadership of black laborers loosely or directly affiliated with Communists being at the core of this progression. In addition, the movement under way in Cuba strengthened and intensified the commitment of Communists in the United States—and particularly in New York—to the movement under way in Cuba.

The manner in which US Communists responded to the Cuban revolt is similar to how they reacted upon word of the Haitian uprising in 1929. As soon as news spread to Communists in New York that their fellow class brethren in Cuba had been shot down at a protest in early August of 1933 by President Machado's fast-eroding state apparatus, a demonstration called jointly by the LSNR, ILD and AIL was scheduled to take place in Harlem. President Machado's days were numbered, as were the days of Welles—President Roosevelt switched Welles's appointment from Assistant Secretary of State to diplomatic envoy to Cuba in the midst of the 1933 coup, after being charged by Machado with acting as if the United States were a colonial superpower unduly commanding affairs on the island. But the implications of this instability within the bourgeois forces only meant greater repression for the masses of radicalized workers. While the numbers of unknown deaths at the hands of Cuban police mounted, the *Daily Worker* offered an exposé of the plight of Cuban laborers implicated in this massive general strike and the ensuing coup which was then under way, particularly highlighting the growth of the Communist movement led by the CPC and YCL and based in the industrial region surrounding Havana. Even before the seizure of power from the Grau regime on September 4, 1933, the *Daily Worker* reported:

> The decision to go to work was reached last night … at a packed meeting of over 700 bus workers in the Trade Union Center of the Confederacion Nacional Obrera de Cuba [CNOC]. The attitude of the workers was clearly shown when after a speech by one of the active strikers, a member of the Young Communist League, over 50 young bus workers signed application cards for the YCL … Many sections of the Communist Party and Young Communist League opened legal headquarters yesterday. In the central section, the police arrested all comrades but later released them. The police said they would inquire whether the Communists were legal or not, since they hear that "this government was a government of all save the Communists."[45]

That "'this government was a government of all save the Communists'" could not have been a more profoundly accurate understanding on the part of Cuban police—at least until Fidel Castro's successful revolution in 1959, which, even then, was not explicitly linked with Communism per se at the outset of seizing power. However, the presence of such proletarian support for the CPC and YCL, primarily through the active organization of the NCCL and based among such critical sectors like transportation workers, demonstrates the degree to which the "Red menace" was indeed poised to help cripple if not entirely shut down the socio-economic apparatus of Cuba at the onset of the general strike.

A question is raised as to how "advanced" the Communists were during the initial days of the strike. That is, it was based in the industrial districts closer to Havana rather than on the opposite side of the island to the east where there were more sugar-based laborers. This problem had remained the Achilles heel of the Communists. Very quickly, the United Fruit Company suffered the blows of a fierce backlash within the sugar sector, once over two thousand of its employees went on strike. Upon hearing of "rumors of an uprising, the manager demanded protection," and the government was forced to meet with eight strikers who put forward such demands as "recognition of labor unions; eight-hour day with double pay for overtime; one dollar a day for unskilled labor." Behind the strike was not only the NCCL, predictably, but also the entire Latin American radical labor community that united under the banner of the NCCL. A protest held on August 27, 1933, involving over two thousand laborers at one Macabi sugar mill left the mill "paralyzed," since laborers shut down the electric lights and telephone systems. Only 17 Cuban soldiers were reportedly on the scene. Clearly, the laborers were in control, the soldiers in retreat—or else strategically re-routed.[46]

As Grau San Martin prepared to seize the reins of the movement on September 4 through popular approval from the laboring sectors, intellectuals, students and military junta forces, it became clear that he, too, would have to willingly promote the use of military force against the inimitable Communists whose "class against class" approach was a threat to all but the workers. Indeed, Cuban Communists had gone so far as to challenge the liberal policies of the San Martin forces contending for power. In short, in the days and weeks ahead, radical laborers, often led by Communists, became increasingly engaged in sit-down strikes and political agitation as evinced in Macabi, entirely undermining the conciliatory efforts of San Martin to increase workers' rights without granting full ownership of production to the workers themselves. Hence, the revolutionary process that Communists were attempting to establish was considered too much of a menace for the self-proclaimed radical forces that were temporarily at the helm of the *coup d'état*, i.e. San Martin.

Partially motivated by the desire to appease US businessmen such as those managing United Fruit, the various parties and organizations then contending for state power—excepting Communists—made a tacit recognition of the fact that the Cuban military would, in any case, be used to thwart labor uprisings that could not be contained by the political movements controlled by the competing elite forces—left or right. Communists and black laborers—only a small fraction of whom were Red—suffered the brunt of this political concession. In other words, there was a consensus among the leading sectors of the movement—as Communists were still a minority, though a powerful one— that the goal of ousting Machado and later the interim President Cespedes was not to implement a system of socialism from below. Such a system would inevitably require that Cuban and American capitalists would be entirely expropriated, placing control of the means of production in the hands of the state which, in turn, would then supposedly lay the basis for the "dictatorship of the proletariat" like the striking bus workers in Havana.

Days after Grau San Martin took leadership of the republic on September 4, Ambassador Welles, in the final days of his office, began a series of almost daily correspondences with President Roosevelt in order to determine the extent to which the US ought to intervene directly since the military overthrow of the pro-American Cespedes Government. Insofar as Welles had surmised— perhaps apocryphally—that "the army mutiny was originally engineered by a few Communist leaders in Habana under the guidance of Martinez Villena," Welles concluded that the "secretly semi-Communist program" of even the Grau regime was too close to Moscow for America's comfort. Hence, he calculated:

> If this government continues much longer and no counter revolt is successfully staged by the conservative groups it will be replaced by a soldier workman which will last until a concerted revolt of the majority takes place ... we should take no action which would permit the creation of the belief that any Cuban Government was installed by us ... we would not be "favoring one faction out of many," but lending friendly assistance.[47]

"Friendly assistance" to whom, one might wonder. Surely no friendly assistance was granted to the Communists in Santiago. There, in the heart of Cuba's black majority, the situation was considered "grave" for the rulers but an opportunity for Communists—in spite of the blood they were shedding in order to attack "members of the present revolutionary group in control" and also the recent arrival of America's naval destroyer *Sturtevart* which was stationed in Guantanamo Bay.

In Santiago, the heart of the Oriente "Black Belt," for the days and weeks after the purportedly progressive San Martin's seizure of power, Communists were astir. Reports to Welles from the US Consul stationed therein indicated "five persons having been killed in the city jail with crowds running through the streets and considerable shooting." Moreover, it did not help that Communists were "meeting before the army barracks and Communist speeches over the radio" were heard across the island, calling the American military's bluff, only kilometers from the naval destroyer called the *McFarland* which was anchored directly outside of Santiago. Though the "commanding officer [did] not come ashore" initially, Welles noted with some assurance that the presence of destroyers on both sides of the islands had indeed helped to intimidate this most radical wing of opposition. But Welles's confidence was only partially well-founded, as the recent death of one Cuban YCL member named August Torre in Oriente had led to a protest of 15,000 Cubans who in turn stormed the American garrison at Guantanamo Bay and demanded to no avail the immediate ouster of the officer responsible for Torre's untimely demise.[48]

Bourgeois American newspapers such as the *Daily News* and *Chicago Tribune*, in contradistinction to the *Daily Worker*, cast the September events in Cuba and particularly in the black stronghold based in Santiago, in terms of anarchy that necessitated America's intervention. The trepidation evinced by US media was certainly understandable insofar as the Communists in Cuba had maintained their uncompromising anti-collaborationist slogan of "Down with San Martin," despite the fact that he had proclaimed to represent a political agenda that was sympathetic to workers' empowerment. What is more, they had conjoined this demand with the slogan "Down with the United States." Ignoring totally the violent aggression against radical protesters primarily at the hands of Cuban police and military authorities—probably with US assistance—the *Daily News* was aghast at the militancy of the workers, noting "machine guns were fired over the heads of the crowds while the cavalry attacked the communists with their machetes. Later communists swarmed through the streets screaming that Sergeant Hernandez Soler, who commanded the soldiers, would be executed." Panic in the US most assuredly mounted once the *Chicago Tribune* corroborated such news toward the end of September, reporting that in Santiago, "sugar laborers, now syndicalized, are offering strong resistance, with the threats to kill managers and their families now prisoners in the mills they have taken" such that "sugar laborers and communists are running wild." But what was developing in Oriente province and throughout Cuba for that matter was hardly anarchy led by aimless "sugar laborers and communists" who were "running wild."[49]

Actually, Communists *had* gone on the political offensive for the time being, buttressed by the valiant efforts of laborers concentrated in the sugar sector, many of whom were black. However, the arms of the state were much more violent and deadly than the arms of the radicals. In the heat of the September 1933 insurrections across Oriente, with US warships in clear view of Santiago, Communists had gone so far as to physically present the remains of slain martyr and Communist hero Julio Antonio Mella to remind one another that the lives of those lost had remained the lifeblood of the present struggle. While US officials ordered more warships to intimidate the seemingly fearless rebels based in Oriente, deemed too physically proximate to Guantanamo and too politically loyal to "'Viva, Moscow,'" Cuban Reds evoked the symbolic representation of leaders like Mella to further their cause of workers' power on the island and beyond.[50]

Though the CPC was cabling Comintern headquarters in Moscow with a "request" for the "international support of the proletariat," their proletarian international muscle was not to be found in Moscow, or New York for that matter, but rather was actually hidden in plain sight, in the form of the black migrant laborers amassed in the "Black Belt." One report to the State Department noted that in the district of La Gloria outside of Santiago, Communists had gained sufficient strength in the interior such that self-determined Jamaican migrant laborers were acting as Red guards to prevent the US fruit owners from entering their—i.e., the laborers'—mills. In this way, at that time, insurrection in Cuba took the form of inter-Caribbean solidarity incorporating into its network such obscure Jamaican laborers as these, "patrolling all the roads and refusing to permit the owners to work on their own properties." The report from La Gloria went on to say that "an American woman was prevented from milking a cow on her own farm by a group of five laborers who insulted her and wrenched her arm." Old racial tropes of black men threatening white women saturated the coverage. It was the pretext for US intervention.[51]

In response to the mounting revolutionary unrest emanating from Oriente province, the Cuban government, which by October of 1933 had successfully all but removed the San Martin regime, was under the leadership of military commander Fulgencio Batista. Batista had pledged to protect US enterprise at all costs, while San Martin waffled on the subject, and Batista enacted a most vicious backlash against the migrant laborers on the island, such as those Jamaican Red guards in La Gloria. Beginning in November of 1933, mass deportations of Jamaican and Haitian laborers concentrated in the sugar sector of Oriente—the very demographic that had helped to lay the foundation for Communist aggression on the island in 1930—marked the beginning of a long period of intensified political and economic repression under Batista, as Communists would indeed attest. Moreover, he had the explicit though underhanded approval of the US State Department and, by extension, President Roosevelt.[52]

Not only did President Batista's "counter-revolutionary" Cuban government which was established after the 1933 coup have the consent of US rulers in their extreme and racially prejudiced repression of the laboring population, but also, they had the support of proto-fascist Dominican President Rafael Trujillo, the single most racist dictator in the Caribbean, in carrying out their military intervention in Cuba. Many Haitian migrant laborers who faced deportation from Cuba in a series of concentration-camp-style detentions subsequently left to work in places like the Dominican Republic. History records their fate:

30,000 slaughtered by machete in 1937. As early as September 11, 1933, Trujillo had offered his assistance to the US military in thwarting the Cuban uprising. One representative of the US Legation in Santo Domingo relayed a message to US Secretary of State Hull that the Dominican Minister of Foreign Affairs

> ... called on me this morning by direction of the President of the Republic, to inform me that in view of the confidence of the Dominican Government in the "purity and justice" of the policy of the President of the United States with regard to the Cuban Situation

the Dominican Republic would readily offer its "loyal friendship."[53]

Though the US declined the offer of support from proto-fascist President Trujillo of the Dominican Republic, the US-originated Ku Klux Klan was already on the scene in Cuba and enacting fascist terror that made Trujillo unnecessary. By March 1934, the Cuban KKK strengthened itself and became openly violent, lynching one young black Cuban named Jose M. Proveyor, a "Negro student [who] was lynched in one of the main streets of Trinidad [Cuba]."[54] The point is plain: when the political fate of Cuba was up in the air, Communists were too politically and militarily weak to seize power. The military was not under their control; the party was under-represented among black workers and industrial workers; the forces of reaction took hold. As a result, the backlash from the new Batista regime was even more fierce and repressive than that of Cespedes, Machado and the previous regimes. In this way, Communists and black workers would be forced to suffer the brunt of this reaction.

Even though the Communist movement in Cuba faced increased repression, and black workers were being terrorized on the island, New York-based Communists did not altogether fail to defend their class brothers and sisters. In an effort to consolidate the political gains that had been made among black laborers in Cuba's "Black Belt" of Oriente, Ford attended a labor congress in Cuba in February of 1934 to promote the cause of Communist-led "revolutionary" trade unions rather than "counter-revolutionary" unions that were aligned with various branches of Cuba's ruling elite parties. On Cuban soil, Ford vowed, "The Congress pledges to develop further the activities of the youth" and "to develop the movement for the special demands of the Negroes for the right of self-determination for the Negroes of the Black Belt of Oriente." Weeks later, Ford returned to his New York political nest where he was currently heading the Harlem Section of the CPUSA, only to declare that Harlem, the so-called "Negro Mecca," was in fact the center of international and national reformism. That is, Ford had presumably seen in Cuba a level of black working-class militancy that actually displaced Harlem as the symbolic "Mecca" of anti-racist activism for black people around the world—or at least in the hemisphere.

Still, Harlem's Communists were there to defend Cuba's anti-racist struggle. Henry Shepard responded to the racist upsurge in the aftermath of Cuba's September 4th *coup d'état*. Shepard was on the scene formally representing the League of Struggle for Negro Rights only months after James Ford's monumental trip to Cuba. Shepard's visit was not simply in response to Proveyor's death; rather, a rash of lynchings, presumably enacted by the Cuban KKK, had recently taken place in the context of "skirmishes between the Negro workers and white lynch gangs … in Trinidad, Manzanilla, Aliquizar, Kuira de Milaro, and other parts of the island." To underscore the point, the "Negro question" was not simply a US domestic matter for the Red International, and particularly not where lynch law was concerned.[55]

Above and beyond the explicit presence of anti-black racism as represented by the lynch-happy Cuban Klansmen, proof of anti-black aggression in Cuba that ensued after the Batista-Mendieta regime seized power at the tail end of 1933 into 1934 was found in the wave of beatings and gang violence that were documented in the *Harlem Liberator*. This newspaper, having been resurrected after a publication hiatus, noted the following occurrences relative to Cuba's black population:

> A lynch gang composed of members of the ABC [a Cuban secret society] and the police force marched through the streets shouting "Down with Negroes." They raided and destroyed many shops and stores owned by Negroes. The Wall Street puppet government, the Mendieta regime, appears to have extensively prepared these brutal attacks against the Negro masses. Before the lynch drive opened, many Negroes were discharged from the police force and militant Negro leaders were arrested on orders of the military officials and threatened with death if they did not cease their activity. The lynch wave indicates the growing fear of the Wall Street Cuban government of the increasing militancy of the Negro and white workers and is an attempt on the part of the lackey government to smash the unity of the Negro and white toilers of Cuba.[56]

Indeed it was the case that the class unity of "Negro and white workers" as evidenced in Oriente only months before was a formidable threat to Cuba's stability in the wake of the 1933 coup. Moreover, the leadership given to this multiracial unity could only have arisen from class-conscious organizers like Communists who had proven, time and again, that the "Negro question" would not simply be relegated to a concern for black laborers alone. The *Harlem Liberator*'s analysis—and Comintern's response—was valid yet far from sufficient. The call for black and white unity alone could never cure the illnesses of decades, if not centuries, old racial systems of domination to which Cuba had never been immune.

It was true that open racists in the Cuban KKK, military and police force had led the charge against black people on the island, making no distinctions in class or ethnic origin. Even more dangerously, however, they had paved the way for a popular and indeed pervasive sense of nativist *Cubanismo*, which, in turn, relegated the interests of the non-native black laborers—or "foreigners"—to the periphery. Cuban radicals—black and white—might have been able to unify for common economic interests, but if pro-Cuban nationalism remained a core principle in their unity, even if class based, it left them open to castigating their migrant laboring allies to the periphery for a common Cuban patriotic agenda.

* * *

Essentially, black laborers such as the valiant Jamaican Red Guards who seized control of US sugar estates would inevitably have been derided as foreigners in this context of reactionary provincialism. Moreover, the Communist movement's advances during this period of upheaval from 1933 to 1934 were still relatively weak in terms of consolidating a long-term commitment to anti-racism in the Cuban progressive movement. Therefore, the relationship between the Red International and Black Caribbean relative to Cuba would soon meet new challenges. Grau San Martin, the deposed leader of the 1933 coup who would soon join forces with the Comintern for a "Popular Front" against what was called the "fascist" Mendieta regime, had propagated a racially prejudiced "fifty percent" law, which mandated that fifty percent of all jobs be reserved for native Cubans rather than a majority of immigrant (i.e., black West Indian) workers. Alas, Communists themselves would support it (if critically) by 1935.

NO MORE COMMUNIST MEETINGS IN THIS PLACE

The KLAN IS WATCHING

NEGROES BE CAREFUL

Don't get in trouble by joining the COMMUNISTS.

KU KLUX KLAN, P. O. Box 651, Birmingham, Ala.

3 Ku Klux Klan terrorist flyer circulated in black working-class community, linking Communist influence with the fight against racism, no date (courtesy of US National Archives, Washington, DC).

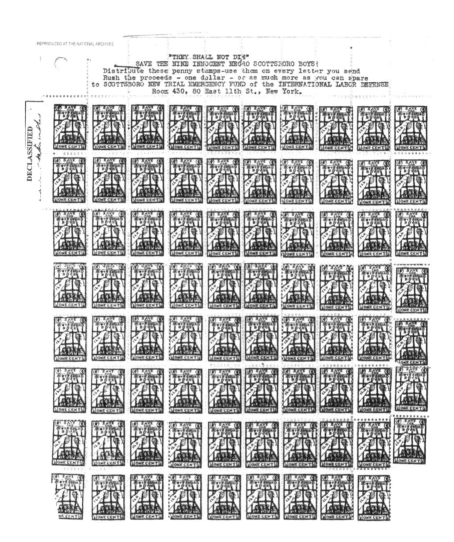

4 Penny Stamps created to raise money and political consciousness for the defense of the Scottsboro boys (courtesy of US National Archives, Washington, DC).

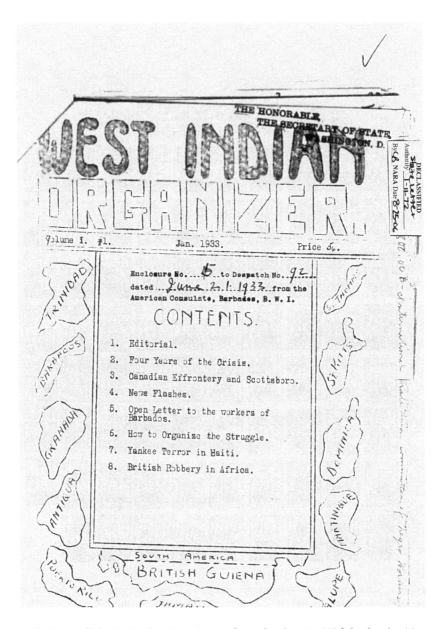

THE HONORABLE
THE SECRETARY OF STATE
WASHINGTON, D.

WEST INDIAN

ORGANIZER

Volume I. #1.   Jan. 1933.   Price 5¢.

Enclosure No.....5...to Despatch No...92...
dated ...June 21. 1933...from the
American Consulate, Barbados, B. W. I.

CONTENTS.

1. Editorial.
2. Four Years of the Crisis.
3. Canadian Effrontery and Scottsboro.
4. News Flashes.
5. Open Letter to the workers of Barbados.
6. How to Organize the Struggle.
7. Yankee Terror in Haiti.
8. British Robbery in Africa.

SOUTH AMERICA
BRITISH GUIENA

5 First issue of *The West Indian Organizer* confiscated and sent to US federal authorities, 1933 (courtesy of United States National Archives, Washington, DC).

Enclosure No. 3 to Despatch No. 1937
of November 19, 1934, from the Embassy at Habana

RIOS DE TODOS LOS PAISES UNIOS

Bandera Roja

Organo Central — Parti... ...munista de Cuba
(Seccion de la I.C.)

| AÑO II — NUM. 29 | HABANA, 12 DE NOVIEMBRE DE 1934. | PRECIO: UN CENTAV |

¡IMPIDAMOS LUCHANDO EL ATAQUE A LOS CAMPESINOS DEL REALENGO 18

¡DEMOSTREMOS QUE SABEMOS BATIRNOS POR LOS NUESTROS!

— (EDITORIAL) —

Despachos se la Agencia Havas, informan que en las lomas próximas al Realengo 18 ha habido un levantamiento de campesinos en actitud de bélica protesta. Han partido tropas para aquel lugar y un corsario del ejército evoluciona sobre las lomas.

En las últimas semanas hemos informados sobre el problema de los campesinos de aquella región. La huelga general del 8 de Octubre llevó como consigna la solidaridad con esos campesinos. Hemos informado constantemente sobre la preparación secreta que realiza el Cuartel General del Ejército y la inminencia de un ataque armado contra las 5.000 familias campesinas de Realengo 18. El despacho actual justifica plenamente el alerta que lanzamos y demuestra cuan necesario es que el proletariado y campesinado de todo el país intensifique de una manera urgente sus actos de solidaridad con los 30.000 pobladores de aquel territorio.

¿En favor de quién es enviada la artillería del ejército y los aviones militares?
(Pasa a la 3)

LAS MASAS CELEBRARON REVOLUCIONARIAMENTE EL SIETE DE NOVIEMBRE

La conmemoración del XVII Aniversario de la Revolución Rusa ha sido una jornada de acción y de lucha.

Apesar del salvaje terror que desarrolla la Dictadura Militar, el pueblo trabajador ha demostrado con huelgas, demostraciones, veladas y mítines realizados el días 7 de Noviembre, su firme decisión de derribar el régimen de hambre, terror y explotación en que vivimos, y sus crecientes simpatías por la obra gloriosa de nuestros hermanos, los obreros y campesinos de la Unión Soviética.

Toda la prensa burguesa, con Pepín Rivero y "Acción" a la cabeza, se esforzó por silenciar los preparativos de la campaña del 7 de Noviembre, mes en los últimos días, tuvo que romper muy a su pesar, su silencio ante la agitación y movilización de las masas. Cayetano Fraga y Pedraza quisieron también restar importancia a la campaña, pero sin poder ocultar la enorme movilización de policías, soldados y porristas que realizaban, quisieron justificarla con provocaciones y ridiculas "des
(Pasa a la pág. 2.)

EL PROLETARIADO RESPONDE CON SUS LUCHAS AL ATAQUE DEL REALENGO 18

Apenas los obreros han conocido las noticias del movimiento de tropas del Ejército para atacar a los campesinos del Realengo 18, han empezado a formular sus protestas. El Gobierno, como no ha podido quitarles las tierras a más de 5.000 familias, por medio de sus falsos ofrecimientos, ha emprendido el ataque armado, el despojo a mano armada, esto demuestra que el proletariado, que Mendieta que el proletariado, se defender a sus hermanos los campesinos del Realengo 18, amenazados a
(Pasa para la pág. 3.)

De Ultima Hora

Los últimos despachos recibidos informan que las fuerzas del Ejército acampadas en La Lima en actitud para atacar a los campesinos del Realengo 18 han sido retiradas para Guantánamo. La prensa trata de restarle importancia al movimiento después de haber publicado que más de 400 hombres bien armados se habían levantado contra el Gobierno. La respuesta rápida y enérgica del proletariado en todo el país detuvo por ahora la mano criminal de Batista y Mendieta en su intento de ahogar en sangre la protesta de más de 5.000 familias campesinas del Realengo 18.

Dice la prensa que el problema ha sido "definitivamente solucionado aceptando los campesinos un año de tregua".

Después de la protesta levantada por el proletariado en todo el país —las demostraciones frente al Royal Bank of Canadá en la Habana y Santiago de Cuba, los acuerdos de huelga en numerosas fábricas y la preparación a la huelga general en Santiago de Cuba—la prensa burguesa junto al gobierno, trata de reducir a la nada importancia de la lucha campesina con el fin de atenuar las acciones de solidaridad. Pero el peligro del despojo no ha disminuido. La última movilización de ejército demuestra que el ataque —por ahora refrenado por el brazo proletario— puede realizarse en cualquier otro momento.

He aquí por que las protestas y lucha de solidaridad deben ahora, más que antes, intensificarse y extenderse. Es solamente así como podremos evitar el despojo a los campesinos y el ataque armado del Ejército.

EL "CUBANISIMO" ABRAZO DE GRAU Y BATIST

Las anteriores gestiones de "mediación" entre los auténticos y el gobierno que fueron rotas bajo la presidencia de la huelga general del 8 de Octubre adquieren ahora, un mes después, un nuevo auge. Reorganizando el gabinete de Mendieta, el nuevo Secretario de Gobernación, Mazas, ha recibido el encargo de lograr la "cordialidad" entre su gobierno y los sectores de la "oposición" con el fin de celebrar las elecciones a la Constituyente. Alrededor de esta "cordialidad", se mueven en la traslación todos los politiqueros de las clases dominantes; con esta "cordialidad" llena la prensa sus columnas a su alrededor, se hacen mil especulaciones.
(Pasa a la pág. 2.)

Estudiantes Revolucionarios contra los "Pepillos" de la reacción burgués-imperialista

Un frente único de catedráticos espúreos, de líderes estudiantiles abecedarios y auténticos, ha logrado la triste y miserable satisfacción de destruir el local que el Ala Izquierda Estudiantil tenía en la Universidad. El objetivo perseguido es intimidar a la gran mayoría de estudiantes pobres, en la lucha por la matrícula, el transporte y la vivienda gratis.

Alentados por el apañipio Pepín y el provocador Mañach desde las columnas de sus respectivos periódicos, pretendidos por Batista y Pedraza; Chi...
(Pasa a la pág. 3)

¡DETENGAMOS A LOS VERDUGOS!

La burguesía y los terratenientes españoles, después de la momentánea victoria obtenida, tratan de estrangular el movimiento revolucionario. No les ha bastado el bombardeo e incendio de pueblos y regiones enteros—cuya destrucción tratan calumniosamente de achacar a los revolucionarios—sino que han henchido las cárceles y transformado los barcos en prisiones.

La ley de fuga, las torturas, las persecuciones más salvajes, son los recursos que ponen en juego las clases dominantes, traneidas de miedo cerbal, de que estalle nuevamente la insurrección. Las dos ejecuciones efectuadas en Gi...
(Pasa para la pág. 4.)

6 Front page of *Bandera Roja* (Red Flag), newspaper of the Communist Party of Cuba, agitating in defense of peasant commune called Realengo 18 (courtesy of US National Archives, Washington, DC).

7 Front page of *Bandera Roja*, calling for defense of Haitian workers being deported during the workers' coup of 1933–34 (courtesy of US National Archives, Washington, DC).

CHAPTER 5

The "Black Belt" Turned South and Eastward

Haiti is a country of people without shoes … The people without shoes do not know how to read or write. The greater part of them have never seen a motion picture nor a railway train. They live in huts constructed of mud and dung, or in tumbledown houses; they get up with the sun and go to sleep when night falls … On Saturday they dance to the beat of Congo drums and on Sunday they go to mass—because they believe equally in the saints and in the old African gods. Their worship is all mixed up. They get old, they die, and the following day are buried after an all night wake during which their friends drink, sing and play cards as if they were at a fiesta ….
Langston Hughes, *Daily Worker*, 1934

Yet in nature some time soon and in the fullness of days I shall die, quietly, I trust, with my face turned South and eastward; and, dreaming or dreamless, I shall, I am sure, enjoy death as I have enjoyed life.
W.E.B. Du Bois, *Darkwater*, 1920

The photograph from Cuba portrayed a black couple staring pensively into the camera. They stood proudly before a bayonet fence memorial to the independence struggle, erected in Santiago de Cuba. Photographs from Haiti included prisoners working on docks during the US Marines occupation, a passport-sized snapshot of the young but balding Jacques Roumain, and an image of the statue of Jean-Jacques Dessalines covered with banners denouncing the occupation while advocating for the election of legislative bodies. "Greetings from Jamaica" was the warm message imprinted on a postcard that pictured hospitable female agricultural laborers in the foreground while an imperial coaling steamer loomed large in the background. A sugar plantation in British

Guiana was the setting for a postcard collected from this South American colony of the British Empire in which black laborers were captured in their presumably daily work routines with the inscription, "waiting for paymaster." But "wait" for their "masters" some incensed rebels soon would not.[1]

Joined by his wife Hermina on several though not all of these ventures, Otto Huiswoud, a native of Dutch Guiana and prominent black figure in the world Communist movement, collected these images while on political assignment. He was seeking to draw black workers from these Caribbean basin into the American Negro Labor Congress (ANLC), based in New York, and also more specifically into the upcoming conference of the International Conference of Negro Workers to be held in the summer of 1930 in Hamburg, Germany. Concurrent with Huiswoud's trip, in April of 1930, the Politburo of the Communist International had sent a memorandum to the US, French, British and Dutch parties with instructions to heighten Communist influence in places like Haiti, Santo Domingo, Guadeloupe, Jamaica and Cuba in the wake of the social and political unrest triggered most recently by the world depression in 1929. And yet Huiswoud's camera lens and postcard collection captured images of objects that spoke a thousand words about the humans— the black humans—that the Comintern mandate on the "Colonial Question" could only begin to convey. It was incumbent upon dedicated, courageous and strategic organizers like Huiswoud and James Ford to bring such mandates to life through the parties and organizations that built the Communist presence in the Caribbean from the ground up.

THE "BLACK BELT" IN GLOBAL CONTEXT, CARIBBEAN FOCUS

Just as conditions in Cuba highlight the tremendous role of hemispheric Communism as a force for anti-racist unity, in the period from 1930 to 1934, socio-economic developments in the non-Spanish-speaking West Indies— namely in British Guiana, Jamaica, Trinidad, Guadeloupe and Haiti—also fundamentally shaped both the limits and possibilities of how the Communist International grappled with the "Negro question" in the Western Hemisphere. In the United States, the dismantling of the ANLC and its subsequent replacement with the League of Struggle for Negro Rights (LSNR) in 1930 marked the official beginning of a somewhat new crop of African American "Black Bolsheviks" such as Harry Haywood and James Ford. For these emerging leaders in the CPUSA and global Communist movement, their interpretation of the dimensions of the fight to overturn racism, as an outgrowth of the mandates of the "Black Belt thesis," caused a degree of tension with certain non-African American comrades from the Caribbean, namely Otto Huiswoud and, later, George Padmore, over how best to implement the Comintern strategy relative to this Afro-Caribbean region outside of the continental United States.

This chapter focuses on the political advances made in the relationship between the Comintern and the concurrent working-class unrest in Haiti and the Anglophone West Indies, demonstrating that these advances bore within them seeds of the very contradictions that were obstacles to the fight against racism that Communists sought to negate. On a global scale, the new hub of this anti-racist international movement was no longer based in New York, in spite of the reorganization of the ANLC to the LSNR and its headquarters which lay therein. Rather, the new international central organization location of radical black leadership in the class struggle under the banner of the Third International was based in Hamburg, Germany, under the leadership of another prominent Communist from the Caribbean: George Padmore. This new geographic delineation of the Comintern in relationship specifically to black workers in the Caribbean thus complicates present understandings of how Communists addressed the right to self-determination in the "Black Belt" of the deeper south and east based out of New York, now that Padmore's International Trade Union Committee of Negro Workers (ITUCNW) was a viable mass organization based out of Europe. Just as the post-WWI *Crusader* of Cyril Briggs's African Blood Brotherhood had been instrumental in sparking Bolshevik sympathies in the region, so too would the *Negro Worker*, literary organ of the ITUCNW, play an important role in shaping the praxis of the Comintern with respect to the Anglophone and Francophone Caribbean. Close examination of the periodical reveals the early inroads that the ITUCNW made in the West Indies between 1930 and 1934 and, more relevant for our purposes, the sustained role of New York comrades in carrying out this project.

As was demonstrated in the previous chapter on Cuba and Mexico, the Communist International's proclamation that a "Black Belt" of laborers must be recognized as critical to the overthrow of capitalist oppression was not confined strictly to US geopolitical borders. Communists purported that the task was to lead a movement of self-determined liberation within the black laboring mass populations throughout the hemisphere and integrate these struggles into the broader anti-capitalist campaigns such as unemployment relief, anti-eviction, factory sit-down strikes, etc., and the release of the Scottsboro Nine. But the "Black Belt" thesis itself was never uncontested political strategic terrain. Just as 1930 opened a new wave of organization building and class struggle for Communists in Mexico, Cuba and the US, so too did there arise a heated controversy and debate reflected in Communist presses regarding the complex nature of the "Negro question" from a hemispheric rather than a simply US perspective. Therefore longtime black Communists such as Huiswoud who had been involved with the Comintern dating back to the post-WWI period in New York and also newer recruits such as Harry Haywood, a Midwest/Down South

Communist, were responsible for giving substance to the meaning of the "Black Belt"—even if their methods or understandings were not entirely in sync at the internal party level or even with one another. Even George Padmore's break with the Comintern in roughly 1933 to 1934 cannot be fully explored without considering the position at that time relative to black laborers in the West Indies. At a minimum, the Black Caribbean factored quite prominently into the ways in which the anti-racist struggle was strategically organized for the Comintern at an international level.

Across the Caribbean, a more concretely organized labor movement was beginning to materialize. While such regions as British Guiana, discussed in Chapter 1, had roots in the labor movement going back to the pre-WWI period, the fact remains that part of the impetus behind the advance in labor organizing which began in the wake of the world depression was the support and leadership generated by the Comintern. One of the most significant advances made by the Comintern in the Black Caribbean in this early period of labor organization was through the active collaboration—if not recruitment— of West Indian labor leaders. In the years from 1930 to 1934, Communists explicitly collaborated with black labor leaders to include two radicals from the Caribbean, Henry Critchlow and Vivian Henry, placing British Guiana and Trinidad, respectively, on the map of Soviet influence and, in turn, on the map of working-class militancy from which Communists must take heed. The pages of *Negro Worker* tell the tale. The open affiliation of black labor leaders such as Critchlow and Henry in the Caribbean with Communists in New York, Germany and even Moscow in the years leading up to the oft-discussed labor rebellions of 1937 provided an important ideological and material pretext for the climax of uprisings that materialized and the independence and federation movements that ensued across the Caribbean.

Even though the Comintern was largely unsuccessful in bringing about substantially sized vanguard party organization among black laborers across vast swaths of the Caribbean, small-scale yet historically significant headway was made in places like British Guiana and Trinidad; moreover, Haiti actually founded a Communist party in 1930. Comintern organizations based in New York headed an intense though hardly unproblematic campaign to support the rising proletarian movement underway in Haiti, bringing together transnational Communist leaders like Henry Rosemund and prominent domestic Haitian intellectuals like Jacques Roumain. But by 1934, while the Cuban Communists were mounting a massive attempt to seize state power and support the land confiscation of black peasants in Realengo 18, Roumain and other Haitian radicals had been driven into prison for their articulations of the "Negro Question" and proletarian solidarity in such cases as the Scottsboro campaign. Vast chasms of linguistic, cultural, political and national difference must account for the varying outcomes in how the Comintern manifested itself in the short 90-mile distance separating Haiti and Cuba. So Haiti is the most fitting point of entry into our discussion.[2]

FOUNDING THE COMMUNIST PARTY OF HAITI: ENTER JACQUES ROUMAIN, HENRI ROSEMUND AND THE AIL

The start of the New Year in 1930 brought over a hundred Haitians living in Brooklyn into membership in the American Negro Labor Congress (ANLC) at a meeting in the home of a local Haitian resident. It is not certain what these Haitians talked about in their ANLC meetings in Brooklyn nor how they might have impacted the dynamics of the ANLC by broadening its immigrant base among Francophone West Indians. But Rothschild Francis, the AIL member and longtime socialist from the Virgin Islands, was present at the meeting where a hundred Haitians joined the ANLC. The political network linking islanders in the Black Caribbean by way of the New York-based ANLC and AIL was critical to Francis's presence at this meeting. In turn, it is certain that contemporaneous radical struggles underway in Haiti were critical to the process of ANLC growth within this immigrant Haitian community in New York.[3]

Just as developments in Haiti had pushed Haitians in Brooklyn toward the anti-racist struggle in the United States then being waged by the ANLC, so too did it appear that Communists in New York—particularly the Haitian comrade Henry Rosemond—were important for the founding of the Communist Party of Haiti (CPH) and the mass protests in the island during the early 1930s. The *Daily Worker* reported in February of 1930 that the "workers and peasants of Haiti are not going to stand this tyranny much longer. They recently revolted, and they will soon revolt again. There is a Communist Party starting in Haiti (CPH) and this will be our leader." In this way, the CPH began during this period and its founding was broadcast in the pages of the *Daily Worker*, as the founding of the Mexican and Cuban Communist parties had been announced in this same paper in the 1920s.[4]

Henri Rosemund's role in the development of the Communist network linking New York and Haiti was key. He had been at the front of the militant anti-racist struggle in New York while leading the needle trades strike in which he nearly died from a police beating, and in the process he learned about pushing the limits of multiracial solidarity both within the WP and in the larger labor movement. Given his recent history, Rosemund was the best candidate for pursuing a political connection between the two regions, so returning to Haiti to pioneer this process was necessarily his next endeavor. Hence, in 1930, he played an active role in disseminating literature in Haiti from the Crusader News Service, the publication house that had sponsored the *Crusader* after World War I and presently the *Liberator*, primarily under the auspices of the editor Cyril Briggs. In 1930, when President Hoover was still running the country, there was a wave of protest across Haiti which ensued after the rebellion in late 1929. Thus the year 1930 began with a collision of forces in which radicalized local Haitian laborers were apparently aligned against both Haitian authorities and also President Hoover's "Commission."

President Hoover had sent a commission to inquire into the disturbances of 1929 surrounding the US Marines in particular and the exploitation more broadly by US businesses and officials in the country. Rosemund was purportedly found to have been circulating literature from the Crusader News Service and the AIL in Haiti during Hoover's investigation. It was reported that he had "already organized a section of the Anti-Imperialist League" which was "composed exclusively of the intellectuals and upper class groups of Haiti." At one protest, over five thousand Haitians led by women amassed in the republic's capital in opposition to the arrival of this Hoover Commission. At one point, there were said to have been over 30,000 Haitians who had turned out in protest against the Hoover Commission. Undoubtedly, the Communist agitation that Rosemund had led in New York in the months leading up to this rebellion in Haiti had been an indispensable training ground for his present activity which appears to have taken place in Haiti itself.[5]

By August of 1932 the Haitian government had officially declared martial law across the island only months after President Machado had declared a state of siege in Cuba. Just as the political repression in Cuba only deepened the frustration among dissidents on the island, so too did President Vincent's declaration of martial law push Haitian workers, peasants and journalists to act in greater rebellion. In this context, a *Ligue des Curriers General de Haiti*, or General Haitian Workers League, was formed in 1932 and immediately the leading members of this labor organization were arrested and jailed in both Haiti and neighboring Santo Domingo. Reciprocally, in New York, a Haitian Sub-Committee of the AIL was formed in 1932. In this way, the interim period from 1932 through 1934 was ripe with local black labor and political militancy in Haiti, such as the organization of the Workers League which championed the cause of the Scottsboro Boys among its constituents. In this way, Comintern organizations headquartered in New York and radical developments in Haiti intensified and increasingly coordinated their activities, or so it seems, during the years when politically the Comintern had placed the anti-racist struggle at the forefront of its strategy for international working-class solidarity.[6]

When labor leaders from the Dominican Republic were arrested in Haiti toward the end of 1932, followed by the arrest of Jacques Roumain and other Haitian dissidents in early 1933, these radicals received support from the CPUSA and also the ILD and AIL. All of this political turmoil would climax in 1934 when the Haitian United Front Scottsboro Committee was banned from holding meetings and public assemblies, trumped only by the arrest in October of Jacques Roumain, head of the CPH. In the interim, ironically, the US Marines withdrew from the island in August of 1934. In this manner, the "Negro question" had hardly become a matter that was distinct to the CPUSA, Cuba, or even Mexico, for that matter. The unique history of Haiti as the first African republic in the Western Hemisphere in which enslaved peoples rose up, created their own independent nation state, and asserted their humanity alongside other nations during the era of modern capitalist formation, makes its relationship to the budding Communist International in the interwar period that much more profound for several reasons. First, it was not compelled by the delimitation, according to Communist praxis, of first resolving the colonial problems and fighting for self-determination, because it was already an independent nation. Second, and connected to the first point, black radicals were by necessity placed in an adversarial position with their native black bourgeoisie precisely because it was the literal black face of the forces behind the oppression of the everyday people on the island.[7]

THE "BLACK BELT" THESIS IN CARIBBEAN CONTEXT: HEMISPHERIC ASPECTS OF THE "NEGRO QUESTION"

Outside of Haiti, the Comintern's most notable mass organization campaign among black workers in the Caribbean was the outcome of conscious efforts on the part of Communists directed out of Hamburg rather than New York—some black and others not—who were involved in the International Trade Union of Negro Workers, a subsidiary of the Profintern, or Red International of Labor Unions (RILU). The ITUCNW, under George Padmore's lead, laid the basis for an expanded network of political agitation and literary propaganda that undoubtedly had an impact on the political consciousness of laborers in the Antilles—particularly the Anglophone Caribbean—during the years from 1930 to 1934. Critically to this process, politicized black seamen from the West Indies and US—many of whom were willing to take a risk, willing to put their lives on the line to bring "foreign agitator" ideas such as Communist ideas back home, knowing they might forever remain nameless and obscure—acted as couriers of seditious literature in the Western Hemisphere. While the seeds of propaganda that were spread by these couriers did not take root in the form of Communist parties during the interwar period in this region, they did in part nourish the groundswell of subsequent labor uprisings of the late 1930s and the later rise of the federation and independence movements that ensued.

As the effects of the world depression began to magnify, Communists were agreed on the fact that the super-exploitation of the darker races across the globe—and black laborers especially—had laid the foundation of capitalist imperial enterprise leading up to and during this period. Reaching further back in history, the shedding of black blood in World War I—though hardly without some level of resistance on the part of radicalized African peoples—had also proven that at the global scale, people of the African Diaspora were useful cannon fodder in the wars of inter-imperialist, western rivalry. Therefore, maintaining black workers in relative marginality in terms of social and economic elevation was a dominant consensus—both spoken or not—among leading western powers including the United States, Britain, Germany and colonial authorities in the Caribbean. Communists in the Western Hemisphere were therefore positioning themselves, as they saw it, to bring to the point of production the political tools for waging organized campaigns against colonial rulers and, ultimately, do so through unity with the growing Communist forces around the world. Political education—i.e., literature and propaganda—was therefore a key tactic for this. *Negro Worker* was the weapon, and ITUCNW, the organizing mechanism.

In early 1930, *The Communist* outlined a strategy of political organization for the emergent ITUCNW that would presumably guide radicals such as Huiswood in the process of recruiting for and establishing a base of support among black laborers all over the world for the coming London conference. While the "Black Belt" thesis that put forward the right to self-determination was among the ITUCNW's trade-union points of unity, the January article in *The Communist* indicated this thesis's relatively minor weight as a point of unity for the ITUCNW. "Equal pay for equal work" was the first point of unity in the ITUCNW's early program; point sixteen was "Self-Determination of Negroes: In South Africa, in the West Indies, and in the Southern part of the USA," such that "the trade unions of the Negro workers must become the central organs and transform the economic struggles of the Negro workers into political struggles, into a combined economic and political struggle for power and self-determination." Moreover, point seventeen charged Communists with "Fighting the Influence of the Church and Bourgeois and Petty-Bourgeois Ideas and Movements" to include "Garveyism, etc., [which] detract the Negro workers from their fight hand in hand with the international working class." In this way, the ITUCNW's program of action—at least as articulated in the US-based *Communist* magazine months before the actual delegates from across the Diaspora were selected—laid the basis for how Communists would then carry out this praxis, though several years later during the Popular Front period Communists would reject this political strategy as "isolationist" and "left sectarian."[8]

In the immediate context, however, Huiswoud's "World Aspects of the Negro Question" had become the center of a controversial debate over how to understand as well as carry out the work of the ITUCNW in particular and anti-racist praxis in both the US and Caribbean. Huiswoud, a Caribbean native and pioneering veteran of the movement under way in the US and Caribbean since the post-WWI era of New Negro radicalism, would soon embark on his second major trip into the tropical basin—the trip from which the photographs described at the outset of this chapter were derived. He considered it an elided contradiction to suggest simplistically that black laborers in the United States faced the same colonial oppression as those across the Diaspora in the colonies and semi-colonies on account of the common struggle all black workers faced as super-exploited labor. He asserted instead that it was "essential that we distinguish the situation of the Negro masses in the colonies" from the situation in the United States since "we must take into consideration the National-colonial character of the Negro question in Africa and the West Indies and the racial character of this question in the United States."[9]

At stake theoretically for Communists organizing in various regions across the US and Caribbean was the question of whether the particular historical and cultural differences across the hemisphere in which black workers toiled could be subsumed into a broad political thesis that the "Black Belt" theory was meant to address. Boundaries of nation, language, race and culture were far from overcome in contemporaneous Communist debates about the "Black Belt" thesis. Whereas "a common language and culture" were seen by Huiswoud as distinguishing factors in the colonial and semi-colonial context of "national oppression," he argued that "in contrast to this the Negro in America has … no distinct language and culture from the dominant racial group; it is a minority of the population; its only distinguishing feature is its racial origin." In this way, Huiswoud was articulating what he considered the unavoidable divergences in nation, culture and language that complicated the application of Leninist approaches to the "Black Belt" in the Western Hemisphere. It was such activity pioneered by Huiswoud, and later followed through by figures like Ford and Padmore, that laid the basis for bridging the struggles in the US Deep South and the deeper South for the ensuing period. Ultimately, the "Black Belt" theory was more of a trope than a substantive political strategy for self-determination, when taken in hemispheric context.[10]

Huiswoud's position, however, did not emerge victorious in terms of official doctrine recognized by the Communist International on the "Negro question." Rather, Harry Haywood and James Ford led the way in attacking Huiswoud indirectly and "Bourgeois-Liberal Distortions of Leninism on the Negro Question in the United States" directly. This was probably due in no small part to the fact that Haywood and Ford were both the sons of African American laborers rather than being born of Caribbean heritage like their fellow CPUSA members Moore, Huiswoud and Rosemund. In Haywood's account, it was fallacious to assume that racism against black people in the United States took on a qualitatively different character from colonial oppression in places like Trinidad or Jamaica. In his critical analysis of such "distortions" of the common core of racism coming from his comrades, he argued that the false conclusion being put forward was as follows: capitalist super-exploitation of African American citizens of the US in the fields and mines of Alabama is qualitatively distinct from the colonial exploitation of Jamaican sugar workers in Cuba. If Huiswoud represented a Caribbean-derived experience such that his own understanding of racism and anti-racist unity was fused into a long history with New York City Communists dating back to the post-WWI period, then such "new guard" figures as Haywood grew more directly out of the US-based phenomenon of Jim Crow racism. Ultimately, for Haywood, Huiswoud's position was not grounded in a sound reflection of the lived experiences of people of the African Diaspora in the US and Caribbean and that, instead, an insufficiently radical and, ultimately, "bourgeois distortionist" perspective was at the root of this analysis precisely because it falsely considered what were superficial differences in the character of black oppression to be fundamental.

Haywood rebuked what he considered Huiswoud's "confused" arguments directly in the pages of *The Communist* soon after the appearance of his comrade's piece on the "World Aspects," and his position won official recognition by the Comintern. He argued that "Comrade Huiswood ... attempts to substantiate his position by creating non-existent differences between the position of Negroes in Africa and the West Indies on one hand and those of the US on the other." In 1932, a restatement of the Comintern's position on the "Black Belt" reaffirmed Haywood's point, asserting that:

> It is not correct to consider the Negro zone of the South as a colony of the United States ... however, it should not be overlooked that it would be none the less false to try to make a fundamental distinction between the character of national oppression to which the colonial peoples are subjected and the yoke of other oppressed nations. Fundamentally, national oppression in both cases is of the same character, and is in the Black Belt in many respects worse than in a number of actual colonies.[11]

But an important question would be why was "national oppression," or racism, being articulated in competitive terms of better versus "worse"? It would seem that the point should not have been to indicate where conditions were definitively "worse" but rather to understand the real factors that would inevitably come into play relative to questions of language, culture and nation in determining the meaning and applicability of Leninism throughout the African diaspora. In other words, the particular conditions in each locale for black workers and the general conditions of racist superexploitation were always both present, and Communists at the time had no choice but to grapple with both aspects in order to build a sound international united infrastructure. While this debate was raging, contemporaneous developments across the Atlantic in Germany helped to synthesize these leaders' positions through the concrete lessons that the work of the ITUCNW was bringing to bear.

THE ITUCNW AND THE *NEGRO WORKER*: PINNACLE OF COMMUNIST INFLUENCE IN THE ANGLO-CARIBBEAN

The founding convention of the ITUCNW in Germany brought many of the questions surrounding self-determination and the "Black Belt" thesis to the surface. Ford summarized the generally repressive political conditions faced by black delegates, especially in the United States and Caribbean, which thwarted the Comintern's attempts to gain the attendance, representation and participation necessary for this conference to be as successful as possible. He described how:

> At Chicago, in the United States, when meetings were called for the election of delegates, the meetings were raided … [At] Nearly every meeting held in the United States for the election of delegates, police and spies were there either to intimidate the workers or to try to get names … In Haiti, in the face of the unrest of the workers, passport difficulties were encountered. In Trinidad, meetings were prohibited by the police. In Cuba, because of the terror carried on against the workers by the American puppet, Machado, the delegate elected had great difficulties and did not arrive for the Conference. The delegate in Panama was arrested and after some delay, was released, but did not arrive.[12]

This common experience of "difficulties" and prohibitions visited upon black delegates from Chicago to Panama seems offhand to validate what was then Haywood's claims to the universality of "National oppression" across the Diaspora, stretching the "Black Belt" from the United States to the Caribbean Basin. And yet, the reality is that the main way that Ford was able to gather this intelligence and data about the hardships in each case was by means of Huiswoud's personal visits to these regions—at least relative to the Caribbean. In other words, the comrades were collectively building the movement even though they had political differences, and this was the essence of what centralism and Communist discipline entailed.

Huiswoud's experience indicated that the colonial boundaries of empire acted as a common impediment to recruiting delegates for the conference. But it was clear that the conditions of repression were especially pronounced in the context of the British Empire's Anglophone Caribbean. Notwithstanding their political differences over how to formulate the nature of racial oppression in the national versus colonial context, western ruling classes in Europe and the US alike were all united around the principle of full repression of Communist efforts aimed at black working-class mobilization and organization on an international basis.

Political and economic conditions within the British West Indies posed a distinct set of tactical challenges given the nature of colonial rule in the British Empire. In Jamaica, Huiswoud was able to build off of the support he had garnered from his successful struggle waged in August 1929 at the UNIA convention as a representative of the ANLC. On Ford's account, in

> ... Jamaica Comrade Huiswoud has been successful in getting a delegate for the London Conference. This delegate is a Negro Railroad worker ... From the reports of Comrade Huiswood, it was stated that this delegate was elected by a committee ... of the Jamaica Labor and Trades Union.

Selecting a delegate was only half of the battle, since the next factor that was particularly relevant for British colonial subjects was the fact that due to "certain passport regulations with regards to these West Indian British subjects [it] is better for them to go to a port in England." In Trinidad, also a part of the British Empire but operating under different conditions of Crown rule, the issues were "slightly different because from there it appears the government political repression [made the] holding of meetings and Huiswoud's plans more difficult to implement" on account of the "vigilance of the British authorities and the Trade Union bureaucracy, who are under the control of the British Labor Party." This was only the British rulers' method of overseeing a colonial challenge to the Comintern in the Antilles.[13]

Conditions in the French imperial outpost of Guadeloupe did not present barriers of language so much as those of fiduciary constraints, at least according to James Ford and also as discussed in the letters published in the *Negro Worker*. The deep impoverishment of potential delegates who were involved in labor unrest on the island of Guadeloupe hindered their ability to garner funds for attendance. One "comrade" from Guadeloupe sent a letter directly to Ford indicating "a few facts about the situation there and expressing a desire to attend the London Conference; also telling of the response of the workers in the Island to newspaper publicity carried on some months back with regards to our Conference." However, owing to a lack of funds incurred by legal fees from proletarian strikes in Guadeloupe, it would seem that such comrades were prematurely cut off from a possible new inroad of recruiting and consolidating black working-class leadership of the labor movement from around the world.[14]

In an otherwise obscure locale such as Guadeloupe for the budding of a Bolshevik movement—remote, that is, from Moscow—the necessity for reserving funds to send for a delegate from this outpost of the French Empire was a challenge that Communists were still learning to prepare for as they began to embark on building the ITUCNW. However, Ford quickly took leadership from the Guadeloupe radicals and wrote: "I told Huiswoud, if possible, he should get a delegate there and bring him to America, providing he had the funds, and that we would try to get him across to the conference." Notably, it was "America" rather than France where it was suggested that funds and support be garnered for this obscure black radical figure in Guadeloupe. In spite of the fact that the colonial mandate from the Politburo of the Comintern had charged French comrades with organizing in Guadeloupe, it so happened that, according to James Ford, Communists in the US were better positioned to actually offer the material assistance to radical laborers in the Francophone Caribbean—or at least in Guadeloupe—in spite of linguistic differences. Therefore, Ford helped to ensure that the Politburo's mandate was carried out in spirit though not precisely as articulated in the mandate's written form.[15]

FROM ANLC TO LSNR: TWO STEPS FORWARD, ONE STEP BACK

Ford's ascendency as a leading Communist in regards to the organization of black laborers in the US and Caribbean laid part of the basis for the liquidation of the ANLC—a group which had been led for the most part by longstanding black Communists like Cyril Briggs and Richard Moore—and its replacement with the League of Struggle for Negro Rights (LSNR). Much related to the obvious question of what would happen to the one hundred Haitians having just been recruited to the ANLC in the wake of the "Haitian Revolution" in 1929, whose organization had been liquidated, there was also the question now of how building a new group, the LSNR, would be able to maintain the connections and campaigns that the ANLC had begun to forge in places like Jamaica.

In March of 1930, Briggs had written to his comrade George Padmore, indicating that he and others such as Huiswoud and Moore were having a "helluva time getting the committee to function." Referring to the Negro Committee of the CPUSA which, in turn, was renegotiating the structure of its organizations including the AIL and ILD at this time, it was stated to Padmore that "[e]ven the Negro Department does not function properly because of the failure of most of its members to attend its meetings. I am raising hell over it ... Even our friend Ford does not seem to take the department seriously." While one might retrospectively dismiss this internal exchange between Briggs and Padmore as trivial gossip emerging from self-centered leaders, it was actually the case that the present leadership of the Negro Department was adamant about pursuing the policy of building Communist organizational influence in the Caribbean and concerned that new organizations might lose sight of this core goal. Therefore, the push to liquidate the ANLC and reconfigure the Negro Department without an attendant commitment to building Communist cells in the Caribbean temporarily hindered the potential for greater collusion of forces between the United States and the Caribbean in 1930 when the AIL, ILD and ANLC were all undergoing considerable organizational restructuring. Hence, much of this work was redirected to what would be the ITUCNW.[16]

Still, the Negro Department of the CPUSA while under the leadership of Moore and Briggs made important advances in the West Indies in the short time period from 1930 to 1931. In 1930, at a July meeting of the Negro Department, the minutes reflected a proposal that "several comrades be sent as agitators and organizers to the West Indies, with particular emphasis to Jamaica, where a start has already been made." While Huiswoud would obviously have been the most likely candidate, a personal statement on his own behalf noted that this was impossible since, on his account:

> ... "when I was removed as the candidate to the Central Committee, I was never told I was removed from the Negro Department ... One day when I walked into the Central Office I was notified by Comrade Williamson that the Secretariat decided I was to go to the district and work there."

Days later, another meeting of the Negro Department noted that the "political assassination of Comrade Moore, and the removal of Huiswoud" had deeply impacted the morale and activity of these leaders such that another representative, one Harold Williams, was necessary to send to the West Indies at that time. Ultimately, in spite of their efforts to engage the West Indies through their roles in the Negro Department, leading black Communists such as Briggs, Moore, Huiswoud and Harold Williams were enmeshed in internal leadership disputes that resulted in a lack of communication about such dire matters as the "Negro question."[17]

Notwithstanding the criticisms on the part of members of the Negro Department based in New York, there was still a general consensus among all leading Communists at this time that the Comintern alone was positioned to best engage with black laborers around the world and in the West Indies particularly. Given the preponderance of "Third Period" politics in 1930 that advocated the independent revolutionary movement of workers under the leadership of Communist parties and mass organizations, any form of unity with nationalists or "petit-bourgeois" liberals was decried as an aberration of Leninism, as had been reflected in the Cuban and Mexican movements. Comrades in the Negro Department of the CPUSA would soon sever ties with a sector of leadership in the Black Caribbean, namely Rothschild Francis, the Virgin Islander who had for so long acted in friendly collaboration with Communists since the post-WWI period. An article from the *Liberator* in

September of 1930 indicated that Francis had now become an arch-enemy of the Comintern.[18]

With the denunciation of such former allies as Francis, Communists believed they were positioning themselves to build more independent, class-conscious tools of emancipation for black working people. But this political shift did not accompany sufficient political contacts in places like the Virgin Islands to buttress an independent campaign of Communist organization and alliances. Therefore, to a certain degree, the ideological critique of leaders like Francis and even Garvey, as we have mentioned in the case of Cuba in 1930, somewhat isolated New York-based Communists from contemporary leaders who had more of a mass following in the Caribbean than their Communist counterparts. Or at least this problem of political isolation from the largely Anglophone Caribbean population was evident until around 1933.

At the internal level of CPUSA activity beginning in 1930 and extending until 1933, divisions within the Negro Department over the fate of the ANLC inevitably led to larger schisms within the CPUSA over the particular manner in which the new LSNR would improve on the mistakes of the ANLC. One result of this political tension was that the struggle against Jim Crow racism became a much more US-focused endeavor for the ensuing period of LSNR activity. This was in contrast to the more regional—rather than national—methods implemented by the ANLC in the years before. For example, an early program of the LSNR as articulated in November of 1930 indicated nothing about affairs in the Caribbean at that time, and affiliated organizations that were at the founding convention in St. Louis included representatives from Latin American trade union organizations but none from the more recognizably Black Caribbean. In contrast, the ANLC's founding program was much more internationalist and incorporated the Caribbean into its political program.

In New York, the "Negro question" also took on a distinctly more local air, with the exception of solidarity efforts in support of movements then underway in Cuba and Haiti. Not only did the *Liberator* become the *Harlem Liberator* by 1933, but upon its inception in 1930 the LSNR based in New York was immediately swept into the fierce and important political struggle associated with the Yokinen trial, that incriminated Finnish Communists in Harlem in "white chauvinist" behavior. The struggle around determining the fate of August Yokinen, a janitor at the Finnish Workers Club in Harlem, who had been proven guilty by local Communists, was carried out in the streets and parks of Harlem during the early months of 1931. Moreover, the Yokinen affair was compounded by the arrest and false accusation of the Scottsboro Boys in Spring 1931. These two cases of racism against black people in the United States focused the brunt of anti-racist activity at the time toward domestic struggles. Therefore, it actually fell on the New York-based AIL and ILD and, more than any organization, the Germany-based ITUCNW to proceed more deeply in expanding the "Black Belt" thesis past the continental borders of the United States.

INTERNATIONAL LABOR DEFENSE AND THE CHALLENGES TO ORGANIZING IN THE CARIBBEAN

In 1931, the ILD established a series of "Patronati committees", modeled after the Italian Patronati committees beginning in 1927, in an effort to consciously build what it considered to be anti-fascist support across the West Indies and especially in Haiti, Santo Domingo and Puerto Rico. The mission statement of the ILD Patronati committees for the Caribbean proclaimed:

> With the increasing terror of American imperialism and its puppet governments in the Caribbean countries, which assumes a fascist nature in some countries ... the International Red Aid and the organization in the imperialist country dominating these colonies, should conduct energetic work to develop the widest mass support [for what were termed the] victims of imperialism.

This endeavor, while focused in the "American colonies," gave rise to an "English section" of the Caribbean committee also headquartered at the East 11th St address in lower Manhattan. As such, ideological entrée to the Anglophone Caribbean was generated in part by way of an ILD publication called the *Caribbean Defender*, paving the way for a series of directives from the New York headquarters offering instructions for how best to carry out the struggle against empire among these Caribbean "victims of imperialism."[19]

The ILD's Patronati committees, with the attendant publication of *Caribbean Defender*, were significant internationalist endeavors on the part of the Comintern. But the ILD had something of a patronizing approach toward the business of actually establishing such committees in the Anglophone Caribbean among black laborers. In the hemispheric struggle against colonialism, surely it was monumental for this demographic to be introduced to literature from US-based Communists, which outlined what was happening with movements then under way in the US, Caribbean and other parts of the world against colonial rule and economic exploitation. All the same, the political instructions of the ILD's English section on how to establish "branches and locals" in the Anglophone Caribbean, though offered in a language of counsel rather than dicta, were somewhat unrealistic. Moreover, they did not take fully into account the intellectual, cultural and linguistic specificities of the very people they were honestly attempting to reach out to and impact:

At the branch meeting the following matters should be taken up: reading of minutes of previous meeting; organizational matters; reports of committees; educational work. At each branch meeting there should be a discussion of some important issue confronting the workers (as, the white terror etc.) We recommend articles in the Labor Defender for this purpose. One comrade should be appointed at the previous meeting to lead the discussion. He should make a brief report to the membership ....[20]

In an effort to cultivate a much-needed sense of class consciousness in the Caribbean, Communists in lower Manhattan did not seem entirely sensitive to the difficulties that would likely be associated with attempting to meet on a monthly schedule when transportation and financial resources to attend meetings had proven to be a challenge to this point. No doubt part of the nature of organization-building was predicated upon the need for members to make time for such matters. There was also a presumption that Caribbean members could read the *Labor Defender*. And even if they could read it, there stood the possibility that the *Labor Defender* was not entirely interesting to read and without the collaboration of local writers in the Caribbean, such a possibility was more than slight. Hence, from these instructions we can glean how the ILD based in the US perceived the promulgation of anti-imperialist organization in the Caribbean in these early years, and while each of these efforts was valid on some level, they reflected many of the same insufficiencies that were evident in the AIL's work in Puerto Rico a few years before.

Above all, arriving at a common political language was much more complex than simply the creation of an "English section" of the Patronati committees which could then communicate with laborers in the Anglophone Caribbean. As an example, the notion of "white terror" which was articulated in ILD publications at the time was common in left-wing, western circles but possibly misleading in the Antilles of 1931. "White terror" correctly denoted the process of anti-Communist backlash during the phase of "war communism" in Russia of 1920 and also referred to subsequent periods of proto-fascist repression of Communists around the world, as we discussed in the case of Mexico. The notion of "white terror," therefore, was a common expression in places like Mexico where Communists were well aware of the political rather than phenotypic associations that the color white evoked. But there remained the chance that this term would be interpreted by Trinidadians who were not familiar with Soviet history to mean literally terror of, or by, white people as a race. After all, such an interpretation would probably have reconciled quite accurately with their lived experiences as beasts of burden caught in the matrix of British colonial rule and American military might—with white workers unleashed to repress black militants.

This slight observation on the business of "white terror" is by no means sufficient for leveling a case that Communists were unable to articulate their politics in a manner that inevitably and/or repeatedly failed to ground itself in an international language of class warfare. Rather, the very act of attempting such a publication at this rabidly racist moment in world history was a victory of great measure. And yet, there arose—and surely continues to arise—a problem of language in relationship to revolutionary political organization that probably was not readily apparent at that time. Consider the fact that directives for ILD Patronati committees were generated from lower Manhattan without the input of the actual subjects who would be expected to interpret and carry out such instructions for organizational activity. In the end, the purpose of evaluating the implicit contradictions of the ILD's praxis during this period is not to denounce the pioneering efforts in the construction of organized anti-imperialism in the Anglophone Caribbean; rather, it is to understand the real historical limitations and possibilities associated with the Comintern given the uneven weight of imperial domination concentrated most heavily against black workers in the hemisphere and not to mention the sustained imprint of centuries of racial ideological oppression and cultural expression. No one, no matter how radical, was able to escape this most concrete of historical realities.

But possibilities for international organization dedicated to challenging racial exploitation were still on the horizon due in small part to these minor yet historically significant efforts. The *Caribbean Defender* was a unique endeavor at this moment in history. The first issue of this bulletin might not have been so encouraging for its readers, however, since it noted that "due to financial difficulties" it was "up to you," the readers, to "succeed in building a real organization among the English speaking workers in your country," a notion that while accurate with respect to the need for people within a location to be the primary force of the class struggle under way, was problematically promoting the notion that workers in one region had more claim to a nation than others. Still, the bulletin put forward a very detailed and profound history of Hindu workers in the Caribbean, presumably to encourage a target audience in islands like Trinidad and mainland colonies like British Guiana of the need for integrated class struggle against the British Empire—and this was decades before Cheddi Jagan led a similar campaign in the 1950s and '60s.

The *Caribbean Defender* was open, though not entirely self-critical, about the feeble transnational circulation of this bulletin, charging the Caribbean readership as follows: "Although it has a daily growing circulation in the United States its representation in the Caribbean and South American countries still leaves much to be desired. There are at present just 15 subscriptions and bundle orders amounting to 183 copies" of which only "25%" were paid. Perhaps it was the ILD's organizational strategy that left "much to be desired."[21]

How could "black and white" unity be the supreme strategy and "immediate task" of the ILD in places like British Guiana where black and Hindu laborers were the bulk of the population? A September issue of the *ILD Builder* placed the Scottsboro case at the center of anti-racist unity in the hemisphere rather than simply in Alabama, stating that:

> The terror with which the capitalist oppressors seek to crush the struggle of the workers against the increasing starvation and misery strikes hardest against the most exploited section of the working class—the Negro masses; Scottsboro is followed by the Camp Hill, Chicago[,] Birmingham massacres and throughout the country a wave of discrimination, lynching and terror rises. In Cuba and other Latin American countries deportations and brutal persecutions are increasing against the Negro toilers. To unite the white and Negro toilers to meet this terror is one of the most important and immediate tasks of the International Labor Defense.[22]

Certainly the ILD was making an attempt to universalize the struggle against racism, taking the seemingly local cases of anti-black persecution in places like Scottsboro and correlating these attacks with the plight of laborers in the "Black Belt" of Oriente. Such political leadership indeed paved the way for subsequent movements to defend Scottsboro in islands like Haiti in the months and years ahead. All the same, there was not a substantial class of white laborers in the region who functioned—even economically speaking—in a capacity analogous to those of their African-derived counterparts in the Anglophone Caribbean. Hence, the call for multiracial solidarity in this bulletin should have acknowledged the black-Indian socio-economic divide as the central point of unity for the anti-racist struggle. This would have been more relevant to the ILD's prospective work in this region, if it hoped to trigger a united response from the most broad yet forceful cross-section of the working class. Clearly, the writers of these various ILD bulletins were themselves more attuned to the conditions of racism as manifested in the United States rather than in the Anglophone Caribbean where their bulletins were meant to be circulated.

Still, the ILD was a leading voice in the struggle against Jim Crow lynching in the US during the post-1930 period of reorganization for Comintern mass organizations. In this way, the conjoining of the ILD with the ITUCNW—guided by the deeply internationalist and politically nuanced praxis of George Padmore—laid the basis for increased Comintern influence in the Black Caribbean. As a result of this organizational collusion between the ILD and ITUCNW, there was an increase in government repression toward black radicals implicated in these organizations in the Caribbean at the hands of the British and American Empires. Just as the ILD was assessing its work at the close of 1931, the US Embassy in London was recognizing the degree to which "[t]here are strong indications that [the ITUCNW] is being brought into close relations with the sections of the International Labor Defence throughout the world" and beginning to "establish Red Aid organizations in Africa and other negro countries." "Negro countries" not only referred to places like Haiti but also presumably colonies such as those in the Anglophone Caribbean—to include even the US Virgin Islands. And indeed this was the case.[23]

INTERNATIONAL TRADE UNION OF NEGRO WORKERS: GEORGE PADMORE AND THE WEST INDIES, 1931–34

During the period from 1931 through roughly mid-1933 under the leadership of Padmore, the International Trade Union Committee of Negro Workers and its various publications—including books, pamphlets and the seminal newspaper *Negro Worker*—were the primary determining factors in the Comintern's relationship to the Caribbean. In 1931 alone Padmore released two landmark texts, the *Negro Workers and the Imperialist War Intervention of the Soviet Union* and more notably *Life and Struggles of Negro Toilers*, both of which placed the question of the West Indies squarely before readers of the "Negro question" on an international scale.

Internationalism was hardly an easy political commitment to maintain in a world of competing nations and "fatherlands," the Soviet Union chief among them. *Negro Workers and the Imperialist War Intervention in the Soviet Union* stated plainly that the Soviet Union's progress was a necessary precondition for furthering the self-determination of black workers around the world. Above and beyond defense of the geopolitical integrity of the Soviet Union, the main purpose of the political education put forward in this book was to motivate "black toilers" themselves to engage in class struggles in their local spheres of influence. And "socialism" was not necessarily the stated goal; rather, "freedom" was:

> It is very important for the Negro Workers to get a clear understanding of what is going on in the Soviet Union ... in building up socialism. This is very important for the black toilers in the United States, Africa and the West Indies in their emancipatory struggles for freedom and self-determination.

No doubt this document testified to a high level of commitment to the vanguard program of the Comintern on the part of Padmore, linking the struggles of everyday laborers in the African Diaspora to the Soviet socialist project. But Padmore's valorization of black workers' independent "emancipatory struggles for freedom and self-determination" carried within it the seeds of major contradictions for the "Negro question" precisely because the Soviet Union had already begun the process of brokering political foreign policy and economic concessions in the early 1930s with the British Empire—concessions that ultimately would help lead to major schisms between such black internationalist figures like Padmore and the very Comintern he had elected to defend.[24]

In the meantime, however, Padmore's role in furthering—no matter how shallow—Communist influence, particularly relative to the Caribbean, remained pivotal for the success of the ITUCNW in that region. The release of his second text, *Life and Struggles of Negro Toilers,* penetrated much more deeply into the past and present history of black labor rebellion without asserting that Africa alone was the *a priori* source of, or future for, black peoples' emancipation. As such, his material experience organizing alongside Communists of various racial hues in the common movement to throw off the yoke of colonial and neocolonial inflicted rule informed his vision of what was possible through multiracial, international collaboration. He formulated these early analyses as a young, militant radical who had committed to the socialist project, and done so after having organized alongside Henri Rosemund, the ANLC and the Negro Department in New York in the years just before. One cannot retrospectively bifurcate or negate entirely the actual conditions informing the consciousness of those leaders such as Padmore, whose role in advocacy of black workers' empowerment was deeply embedded within the inner workings of the Comintern. That is, the Comintern was not an external influence; ITUCNW was part of the Comintern, and the Comintern part of the ITUCNW.

In contradistinction to what he termed the "domestic slavery" of Haile Selassie's leadership as a "new emperor" of Abyssinia, Padmore portrayed the "life and struggles of Negro toilers" from below, detailing the self-activity of the "toiling masses" as a basis for realizing a world view that, in turn, could bring about freedom for black laborers around the world, while dismissing rulers of the status quo. In this world view, the Caribbean loomed large though it was geographically and demographically relatively small. He referenced "signs of unrest among the natives in the British West Indian colonies of Trinidad, Jamaica, Barbados, Grenada and British Guiana, the United States Virgin Islands and the French colonies of Martinique and Guadeloupe." Moreover, he pinpointed the "monster mass meetings [that] are being held throughout the islands, rallying together the workers and poor farmers under the slogan of 'The West Indies for the West Indians!'" But his point was that struggles such as those under way at Felicity Estates in Trinidad were ripe for development of a larger class unity through the leadership of the Red International of Labor Unions (RILU), since it was the Comintern-led umbrella organization that supported the ITUCNW.[25]

Padmore's promotion of the RILU, however, was propaganda that could only be sound if the RILU was politically committed to same. That is, if the Comintern was vying for leadership of black workers' militancy, then the current leaders of this movement had to either sign on or prepare for being pushed out. Therefore, Padmore clearly incurred the wrath of social democratic labor leaders such as Captain Cipriani heading the Trinidad Workingmen's Association since he asserted in the pages of *Negro Worker* that the RILU must be placed on the map as the single most important union in defense of black laborers across the globe. For example, he stated that it was the "first" labor body that

> ... furthered the development of the trade union movement among the colonial peoples, and succeeded in rallying a great part of them to its banner. It is the only international which conducts a consistent and permanent struggle against white chauvinism ... for the correct solution of the national-race problem.

Clearly he had situated the "Black Belt" thesis's seemingly irreconcilable distinction made by Huiswoud and Haywood between the race and the national problem; he labeled it a "national-race problem," demonstrating some level of ideological commitment to bridging rather than dividing his fellow comrades' Huiswoud and Haywood political debate outlined beforehand. All the same, it was hardly accurate to state, as he had, that a permanent commitment to anti-racism had been fostered by the RILU. In point of fact, the RILU magazine hardly made mention of any class struggles taking place in the West Indies in 1931, even though rebellion was pronounced; rather, the RILU generally relegated such matters to the work of the ITUCNW, its "Negro" labor organization. In short, the RILU's commitment to combating racism was partial rather than complete, and it unduly placed what was necessarily an international commitment to solidarity around anti-racism onto the shoulders of black comrades in particular.[26]

Therefore, where the RILU's own agitation failed to take on the "Negro question" aggressively, the *Negro Worker* addressed this issue in plain talk yet still "theoretically," and the subject of the Caribbean was introduced upon inception of the paper's publication. The first official issue noted that

> ... it is our aim to discuss and analyze the day to day problems of the Negro toilers and connect those up with the international struggles and problems of the workers. It is therefore necessary that we receive the fullest cooperation of Negro workers. This means that articles, letters, points of view and pictures of your daily life must be sent to us.

The *Negro Worker* was therefore a sort of Anglophone political bridge linking the "New Negro" periodicals of the post-WWI era and such home-grown, local presses like Jamaica's *Plain Talk* that would arise in the years from 1935 to 1939, except that the *Negro Worker* was the only periodical explicitly funded and politically directed by the Comintern.[27]

In a somewhat more rhetorically inviting manner than what was presented in the *Caribbean Defender*, the editors of *Negro Worker* openly welcomed the "fullest cooperation of Negro workers," drawing them into a reciprocal process of give and take, participation and education. An editorial by Padmore on

"Imperialism in the West Indies" advised, in turn, that the ITUCNW "should render all aid and assistance possible to the struggling West Indian workers, and to support the economic and political demands of the toiling population of the West Indies." With the focus on "economic and political demands," it was clear that the "fullest cooperation" that the *Negro Worker* sought was actually geared to rooting this discussion in questions of a socio-economic and political nature, and this request for articles and letters was honored already by the first issue itself.[28]

A portion of the *Negro Worker* was dedicated to printing "Workers Correspondence," carefully edited and selected by Communist staff writers whose political agenda was far from objective. This section offered a very important and singular vantage point for understanding the impact of the Comintern on black laborers in the Caribbean and vice versa. Even though the "comrade" from Guadeloupe failed to make it to the founding 1930 conference of the ITUCNW, the *Negro Worker*'s editors ensured that the voice of French-speaking laborers from Guadeloupe was heard from the onset, printing the following message from presumably the very "comrade" who could not attend:

> The call to the International Conference of Negro workers did not leave the workers of Guadeloupe indifferent. The papers spoke a lot about it. Due to the cyclone of September 12th, 1928, our resources came to an end. At the time when we had started to recover, a strike of agricultural workers took place, the results of which are the following: Dead—2, wounded—4, jailed—5. This is the capitalist procedure! ... and above all the French Government whose slogans are: Liberty, Equality, Fraternity! Let me tell you about the meaning of this trinity. These three words have been separated by three periods. We should read: Liberty, none, equitability, none, fraternity, none! This is the slogan of the capitalists![29]

Rejecting the false "slogan of the capitalists!," or French government, this comrade from Guadeloupe had implicitly adopted the slogan of the socialists in the Soviet Union, even admitting several issues later that the laborers of Guadeloupe had chosen to take up the struggle of "class against class" and therefore requesting of the ITUCNW that "[y]ou should help us by means of concretely pointing out to us how we are to set about work." In directly calling upon the ITUCNW to help them engage in better forms of class struggle against French capitalists, these workers of Guadeloupe were undeniably reflecting a sense of solidarity and trust during a very opportune moment in history. Still it is not clear that this assistance ever materialized.[30]

One at least semi-successful yet still significant instance of an ITUCNW network that was established with the assistance of LSNR and ILD headquarters in New York was Padmore's direct correspondence linking Communists in the Deep South of the US with laborers and agitators in the West Indian colonies.

A letter from Jim Allen, a preeminent Communist theorist of the "Negro Question" in his own right who wrote for the Red bulletin entitled the *Southern Worker*, communicated greetings to the *Negro Worker* staff:

> Comrades: I think we can be of great aid to each other. Our paper can furnish you with a weekly digest of Southern conditions and you in turn can give us great aid by supplying us with information about the movement and conditions of the Negro masses in colonial countries ....

In short, comrades in the southern US were also looking to their counterparts who were centered in the anti-colonial struggle for inspiration and the *Negro Worker* was an important conduit for expressing this cross-border solidarity.[31]

At the organizational level, however, the RILU was reporting very different results about the impact of the ITUCNW within black working-class communities globally, and in the US and Caribbean regionally. A "Special Resolution on Work among Negroes in the United States and Colonies" released in March of 1931 indicated that "the weaknesses of our work in the USA can be proved by the still insignificant number of Negro workers to leading trade union work. These weaknesses can particularly be felt in the South of the USA." Moreover, it was stated that "In the West-Indies and in the Latin-American countries the organization of Negro workers into the class trade unions has practically not been started even ...."[32] But rather than being content to maintain black working-class unity at the level of agitation and propaganda through papers like the *Negro Worker*, the CPUSA began to make more significant headway in the planning of Communist organizational penetration into the West Indies. This decision correlates precisely with the work of the ILD Patronati committees referenced previously in this chapter.

Though these plans on the part of the CPUSA were only met with modest degrees of success, they demonstrate the efforts toward solidarity that were made by Communists in the hemisphere during the period from 1930 to 1934. The opening of 1932 brought forth two sets of resolutions. First, the Negro Department devised a four-month plan, the goal of which was to establish a progressive West Indian group based in New York with the mission of giving "maximum support in the form of political guidance and moral and material assistance in the development of the revolutionary movement in the Negro colonies concentrating upon the Negro West Indies." The "main task" of this West Indian committee was to "prepare the launching of a paper in one of the West Indian Islands." Second, the creation of a "Negro Trade Union Committee" other than the ITUCNW was suggested alongside a four-month period in which a particular emphasis would be placed on Scottsboro and the plight of the "Sugar Industry in Guadeloupe." The sustained commitment to focusing on conditions in Guadeloupe, considering the fact that as early as 1930

James Ford had been in correspondence with French-speaking Guadeloupe "comrades," indicates that linguistic boundaries had not been entirely obstructive toward the CPUSA's goals of organizing in the "Negro West Indies." Even the LSNR had ventured away from its primarily US-focused approach to the "Negro question" to instruct, from its lower Manhattan headquarters on 13th St., "All Groups and Affiliated Organizations of the League of Struggle for Negro Rights" about the literature of Padmore and the ITUCNW.[33]

Perhaps this incremental effort toward establishing a base among black workers in the Caribbean helped to precipitate another important political development at the opening of 1932 relative to the ITUCNW: its main headquarters in Hamburg, Germany, was raided—again. But the reasons for this raid by German authorities were much more attributable to the work led by Communists in Hamburg itself than to the plans emanating from New York's CPUSA organizations, though US officials were hardly pleased to know that such plans were under way from New York. Black colonial sailors were fast becoming the tools of agitprop and political education for a transnational circuit that made British colonial authorities and US officials increasingly uncomfortable—not to mention the disapproval met by Germany's rising fascist star, Hitler. Among the documents confiscated during the raid was one exposé of the Jim Crow conditions endured by African American dock workers, stating that "the Negro longshoremen of the United States are the victims of the worst forms of discrimination on the job."[34]

Not only was literature found in the ITUCNW headquarters that attacked US capitalism, but also there was explicit denunciation of maltreatment of black laborers—seamen in particular—who were subjects of colonies under the control of European empires, namely Britain: "The conditions among the Negro Seamen and dockers in the African colonies and the West-Indies are even worse than those in America ...." But rather than cowering in the face of such inhumane conditions, the ITUCNW advocated:

> Equal pay for equal work of colonial and white seamen; 3 watches of deck and 4 in the stoke hold; 7 hour working day while in port; One free day in port for every Sunday at sea; Double pay for overtime ... Negro workers! Defend the Soviet Russia, the Fatherland of the Working class!

In spite of the raid on the ITUCNW, the political commitment of Padmore and the *Negro Worker* endured, embracing the Soviet Union ever more fiercely as the British, US and German authorities increased their political repression and economic exploitation during the years of the global depression.[35]

Just as the ITUCNW was being attacked by the fledgling, proto-Nazi state at its German headquarters, so too did it come under persecution from the British colonial state in the West Indies. In 1932, several days after May Day,

the Executive Governor of Trinidad issued a decree in the spring banning the
Negro Worker and all literature of the ITUCNW from the island. Months later,
another ban was extended to include any literature from the CPUSA. One
correspondent from the US Consul, Alfredo Demarest, conveyed the news to
the State Department:

> His Excellency the Governor of the Crown Colony of Trinidad and Tobago has by
> proclamation dated April 21, 1932, banned two series of publications as seditious.
> The first is the "bulletins" issued by James E. Welch of Washington, D.C. In this
> regard I beg to refer the Department to my confidential dispatch no. 2374 dated
> December 8, 1931. [i.e. of Labor defender or Colonial News "bulletins"] ... The
> second series of publications banned by the Trinidad Government is "The Negro
> Worker," and all other publications issued by the International Trade Union
> Committee of Negro Workers of Hamburg, Germany.[36]

Initially, it was ITUCNW literature coming from Hamburg that was banned,
not that of the CPUSA, which was also presumably making its way into the
island by way of organizations like the ILD's Patronati committees and the
Caribbean Defender. Even though the more geographically proximate CPUSA
was seen as a threat to the consciousness of black people in the Caribbean,
British colonial authorities had determined that the ITUCNW's agitation
had caused more political damage to the colonial apparatus. Comparatively
speaking, the ITUCNW, even more than the ILD, LSNR or AIL (the latter
three being based in the US), presented a clear and present danger to empire
in the hemisphere where the exploitation of black laborers was the most
concentrated. And Trinidad's Governor could with one fell swoop choose to
ban, raid, or kill at his discretion since he both ran the state and essentially
regulated the economy. As mentioned earlier in our analysis of the ILD's
Caribbean Defender, the term "white terror" in the case of Trinidad was just as
much a phenotypic as it was a political description of the fierce repression—
and permanent state of exception—that black laborers experienced in this
"Black Belt" island beyond the continental United States. The challenge
remained, therefore, for the Comintern to demonstrate through practice that
white workers in Britain and beyond were equally committed to smashing this
proto-fascist aggression against their class counterparts in Germany, Trinidad
and elsewhere.

But as was the case of Communist activity in Cuba and Mexico during the
period from 1930 to 1934, radicalism in the Anglophone Caribbean intensified
rather than retreated in the face of repression such as Trinidad's sedition acts
of 1932. Those radicals who were engaged in organizational and labor activism
in their respective colonies were objectively in the forefront of the battles
against empire and racial discrimination in the hemisphere, because they were
operating out of locales where socio-economic conditions of oppression had

taken their most vicious form. Two important figures that emerged in the circuit of Red and Black organization during this period of Depression-era crisis in the Caribbean were Vivian Henry of Trinidad and Henry Critchlow of British Guiana.

Vivian Henry, a member of the ILD in the Caribbean who was a Communist sympathizer and important leading black labor activist in Trinidad, offered a first-hand account of the anti-Communist ban in Trinidad in the pages of the *Harlem Liberator* in the spring of 1933. Only months before, he and Critchlow had ventured into Moscow by way of Germany while attending a conference of the International Labor Defense along with their comrade George Padmore. A February--March issue of the *Negro Worker* proudly announced that "Negro Toilers Speak at World Congress of ILD," reprinting in full the long speech from Padmore that outlined the dangers and possibilities associated with the Comintern's organizational influence—and lack thereof—among black laborers around the world, and particularly in the colonies, including the West Indies. This same issue of *Negro Worker* also recorded a speech presented by "Comrade Henry," a formal "delegate from the West Indies Labour Movement," who noted that the specter of Haitian radicalism in 1929 had haunted the entire Antilles; language was not a barrier in this case. Scottsboro and the attendant counter-attack waged by the ILD were significant according to Henry, who proclaimed:

> Thus have the British imperialists joined bands with the white oppressors and capitalist exploiters of the United States in the latter's attempt to legally murder nine Negro boys in Scottsboro, Alabama. This shows that no matter what differences exist between the British and American imperialists, they are prepared to bury their differences and to crush every expression for freedom on the part of the Negroes and other oppressed colonial peoples. We are glad to be at this World Congress of the International Labour Defence. We are glad to see the Negroes from every part of the world collaborating in the Congress .... Our fight is a fight for elementary rights of freedom of speech, and press, and assembly. We want the right to organise, to publish and distribute literature which furthers the cause of the Negro masses ....[37]

Henry Critchlow simply wrote into the *Negro Worker* to let readers know that he arrived "home," to British Guiana "safely."

But "home" was British Guiana only to a certain degree. For both Critchlow and Henry had found during their travels as delegates to the ILD convention that Communist outposts in Germany and the Soviet Union also made them feel at home and, to the point, more comfortable as radical labor organizers than in their Caribbean communities. One issue of the *Negro Worker* pictured Henry and Critchlow laying flowers before the graves of German labor organizers and radicals—presumably Communists—who had been killed at the hands of

Hitler's Gestapo police force. This was the same police force that with US and British consent had raided the ITUCNW headquarters in Germany time and again; therefore, the common allegiance to proletarian internationalism and the struggle against empire—whether in British, German, or American form— laid the basis for their solidarity with the Comintern.[38]

After chronicling his experiences in Germany and Russia before crowds in British Guiana, Critchlow informed readers of the *Negro Worker* that the leadership of the British Guiana Labour Union (BGLU) resolved the following: "Be it resolved that this meeting of workers having listened to the new methods of organization of the British Guiana Labour Union pledges itself to give the Union its numerical and financial support." Just at the moment when the BGLU had resolved to take up "new methods" that had a distinctly Communist character, "fascist terror against Negroes in Germany" became the rule rather than the exception. Hence, there was a confluence of political forces in the Caribbean taking shape by way of the BGLU, to some degree, while Communists such as Padmore were being relentlessly hounded and driven into secrecy by fascists in Germany. Such a merging indicates that on some ideological level a vision of emancipatory politics that was being enacted in British Guiana was one that attempted to reconcile the needs and demands of laborers in the colony with those of active Communists around the world.[39]

The year 1933 was striking precisely because important political breakthroughs, while minor, were made relative to Communism and the West Indies just as Padmore, a leading member of the ITUCNW circuit, departed from the scene. Partially due to the increased police raids on the ITUCNW headquarters in Hamburg, Germany, which forced the reassignment of its headquarters and leaders to places like Copenhagen, a West Indies Subcommittee of the ITUCNW was established in New York. The Comintern did not entirely relinquish its commitment to pursuing the "Negro question" and trade unionism by way of the ITUCNW, even though "fascist terror against Negroes in Germany" and indeed around the world was on the rise. The choice of establishing a West Indies Subcommittee of the ITUCNW in New York was also based on the historic matrix of Communist-West Indian organization that began in Harlem as early as the post-WWI period of 1919. Moreover, the CPUSA's aforementioned "draft four-month plans" for work in the West Indies in 1932, which outlined plans to base the work in New York, had surely played a role in establishing a local outpost therein. This West Indian Subcommittee of the ITUCNW was possibly interchangeable with the West Indian Workers Progressive Society. The significance of the West Indies Subcommittee of the ITUCNW also lies in the fact that it helps to pioneer the form of labor and social equality-oriented mass organizations linking the West Indies and New York during World War II, federation and independence years in islands like Jamaica.

The *West Indian Organizer*, published by the West Indian Workers Progressive Society with its headquarters at 135th Street in Harlem, made its debut in the West Indies in January of 1933. Failing to cross the desk of the US Consulate in Barbados for nearly six months, this transnational West Indian contraband left British and American authorities in a tailspin to uncover the precise nature of its political agenda and grassroots support. Take note of several "tasks and aims" of the paper:

> To relentlessly expose the deception of Cipriani in Trinidad, and other West Indian reformist misleaders; to popularise the work of the Latin American Confederation of Labor and the International Trade Union Committee of Negro Workers, Hamburg, Germany; to spread the "Negro Worker" among West Indians, here and at home; to fight against Imperialist War; to defend the Soviet Union and the Chinese Masses.[40]

In June of 1933, the *Haiti*, a US-owned Ocean Dominion Steamship Company vessel that was due to arrive in New York, charged a member of the ship with distributing "internationally seditious literature and communistic pamphlets advocating the overthrow of all West Indian governments and seizing their control by the workers and organizing against the capitalist government of the United States." One of the specific documents in question, entitled "Resist War Plans of the McDonald Government," demanded "freedom from colonial tyranny, better living conditions, down with all imperialism, defend the Soviet Union, and defend the cause of workers and oppressed peoples." It was signed by the West Indian Subcommittee of the ITUCNW, headquartered out of the Communist base in lower Manhattan on 10th Street.[41]

This current project does not reveal information on the alleged crew member whose literature was confiscated, nor any evidence that much more agitation was generated, at least from this headquarters. But the very proof of this organization's existence with its accompanying literature suggests that the ITUCNW's influence in the West Indies was not insignificant for the revolutionary movement, or for the British and US authorities. The specific circuit between ports in New York and in Barbados is evidence of the use of black seamen as couriers of this transnational network. In point of fact, the labor rebellions on St. Kitts several years later in 1935, discussed in the next chapter, implicated Communist seditious literature which, in turn, directed British and US colonial authorities back to this fleeting yet significant organization of West Indian progressives spread across New York, from the Communist headquarters of lower Manhattan up to Harlem.

But State Department surveillance of this organization in 1934, based on information handed over by agents of the New York Division of the Post Office, noted that "no Negroes have ever been seen around the premises" of the lower Manhattan headquarters where the *West Indian Organizer* was nominally published. It probably was the case that the *West Indian Organizer* in particular and WIPA generally were not solely organized by or composed of solely black radicals, much less black Communists. In other words, it was quite likely that white Communists had also been producing this material as well, which in turn demonstrates that it was not necessary for the racial identity to be black in order to, on some level, advance the struggle of black workers. This does not minimize the significance of this fleeting organization and its praxis; indeed it is a testament to the anti-racist commitment on the part of Communists in the United States to building a movement against "all imperialists" and for socialism.[42]

Many black Communists at the time were conscious of this anti-racist commitment within what was largely a Euro-American driven movement—at least in the US. But not all black Communists were convinced that white comrades were truly anti-racist in practice. By 1934, the Comintern had lost—or expelled, depending on which version is taken up—one very important and unmistakable black Communist who was searched for on any premises where he might be found from Germany to Uganda: George Padmore. And to Padmore, the "white man," including white Reds, became understood as inseparable from empire. But while Padmore declared "Au Revoir" to the *Negro Worker* in August 1933, the editors of this magazine declared "Bravo, British Guiana!," demonstrating the resilience of this Communist movement in the face of its own internal contradictions as well as external pressures of increasing fascist repression.[43]

In spite of the obvious blow that the ITUCNW suffered as a result of losing Padmore's leadership, it is still possible to trace the continued significance of the ITUCNW and Communist-led organizational networks between New York and the West Indies through the duration of the period leading up to the Comintern shift out of "Third Period" into "Popular Front" strategy in 1935. In turn, this shift ushered in a new stage in this historical process. And in order to understand this process in its complexity, it is important to recognize that by 1934 London was in many ways the headquarters of Communist political activity associated with the British West Indies, hence leading to another layer of historical investigation altogether—only part of which will be addressed subsequently.

By August of 1934, the LSNR had made political connections between London and Africa. New York was chiefly the intermediary for developments in Cuba while London—presumably by way of the Negro Welfare Association and attendant AIL organizations—was the same for developments in the British West Indies and Africa. The colonial parties had considerably carried out the Politburo mandates of 1930, though no parties emerged in the British West Indies. But one important question is whether or not this international circuit of metropole-colonial organizations was more a newspaper circuit than an actual organizational network with significant political and labor influence.

Also by August of 1934, British fascists by way of the United States had consolidated a transnational political circuit based in Trinidad. That is, at the very moment when Pepin Rivero was advocating for the extermination of Realengo 18-style black peasant communes in Cuba, Sir Oswald Mosely of the British Union of Fascists had created a "Black Shirts" branch in Trinidad. Hence the Comintern would have to reckon with fascist aggression in the Caribbean not only on Cuban soil but on Trinidadian soil also. Reportage from Trinidad indicates that Edward York, a former American citizen, helped start this circuit:

> Object of Mr. York's tour is to study and make plans for the formation of Fascist nuclei in Bermuda, British Honduras, the British West Indies and British Guiana. "Our Colonial policy," he stated, "is an Imperial one. When our party is in power, we intend to pay particular attention to the development of the Colonies, so that they can sell more to Great Britain, and thus be able to produce more British goods. Benefits must be reciprocal."

Following the example of the British Labor Party, the Trinidad Labor Party would energetically oppose an attempt to introduce fascism in Trinidad. Similar action would be taken by the British Guiana Labor Party.[44]

York's plans for the "reciprocal" exchange of goods and services between Britain and the British Empire in the Caribbean under a fascist regime was far from welcomed by traditional parties in the colonies that—though far from Communist—were even more averse to fascist dictatorship. The year of 1934 foreshadowed the rise in "white terror" clothed in "Black Shirts" in Trinidad which, would meet the resistance of a whole new circle of radicals that were circulating between New York and the West Indies in the years to come. Communists were not entirely in sync with the other actors in this anti-fascist movement for reasons that can only be partially accounted for with the current archival research. One important link to the broader anti-fascist struggle that Communists maintained as the "Popular Front against Fascism" arrived on the scene in 1935 was through the political leadership of Henry Critchlow and the BGLU.

In June 1934, the *Negro Worker* printed an article, presumably from Critchlow, announcing "British Guiana Labour Union Reports," in which the writer expressed sympathy with the *Negro Worker* editors who were suffering from setbacks in the newspaper's publication. But the writer also wished to inform readers about recent setbacks in the labor movement then underway in British Guiana, due to the ever-mounting political repression at the hands of colonial authorities. Upon asserting that conditions in British Guiana had gone from "bad to worse" after the militant labor uprising articulated in one successful "Down Tools Day" led by the BGLU, the writer concluded that the BGLU would have to wait until conditions were more than laborers "could bear" before their influence would once again mount on the island. But rather than considering the strengths and weaknesses of this decision from the BGLU to wait for a more opportune and indeed popular moment for political resistance, the *Negro Worker* editors rejected in a comradely manner any attempts to retreat in the face of political repression:

> This is a wrong idea comrades. Of course, it is true that the more workers are oppressed, the readier they are to struggle against this oppression, but you must continue as you are doing, with doubled efforts, exposing daily the imperialist oppression, guiding and teaching the workers, how, through small, but militant actions, they can finally throw off the yoke of oppression.[45]

Less than a year later, the Comintern would be advising against its own advice, admonishing isolated and "small but militant actions" as the global threat of fascism mounted and was drawing the Soviet Union closer into a long-term struggle with "imperialist" enemies, most recognizably Nazi Germany. The Comintern's usage of the *Negro Worker* to act as a voice box for class struggle remained present—faithfully printing black workers' correspondence from around the world for the duration of the paper's publication. All the same, editors at the newspaper's headquarters had the tendency to weigh in rather one-sidedly, placing the local perspectives of comrades in places like British Guiana on a lower level of political prestige than those which had been officially recognized in Moscow.

Here we return to Otto Huiswoud, whose journeys internationally kept him promoting the Communist cause of black working-class struggle. One State Department report on the "Activities of Crusader News Agency in Antwerp" covered the short time-span from late November to late December of 1934 during which period Huiswoud was arrested while editing and circulating the *Negro Worker*; the report uncovered the "complete dossier relating to activities in Belgium of the Crusader News Agency and of its director Otto E. Huiswoud" which included the following contacts:

> Patterson, William 80 E. 11th St Room 430 NYC; Critchlow, Hubert, Regent Wellington Street Georgetown; Henry Barbusse rue Lafayette in Paris; League of Struggle for Negro Rights, 2162 Fifth Ave, NYC; BGLU; Editor, Barbados Advocate, Bridgetown, Barbados; Editor, Barbados Herald, Bridgetown, Barbados; Editor, Listin Diario, San Domingo, Republica Dominicana; Mr. TA Marryshow, Editor, Grenadian Wes Indian, St. George, Grenada; Editor, L'Essor, Hence d'ossainville, Port-au-Prince, Haiti; Secretary, Barbados Workingmen's Association, Bridgetown, Barbados; Secretario, Liga Humanitaria, Santo Domingo; Secretary, Grenada Workingmen's Association, St. George, Grenada; Secretary, West Indian National Association, San Fernando, Trinidad[46]

The contact list on this dossier alone uncovers a whole new series of black radical networks of individuals, newspapers and organizations that brought together the Red International and the Black Caribbean. Noteworthy in this list of recipients of the *Negro Worker* is the editor of the *Barbados Advocate*, Algernon Crawford who, as we will see in the next chapter, became involved in the political organization of New York-based Communists during the period of labor rebellion on the island of Barbados in 1937–38. Like Barbados, nearly every island mentioned in this list of *Negro Worker* recipients with the possible exception of Haiti and the Dominican Republic experienced a series of strike waves that became pronounced in 1937. Clearly, each one of these islands was already involved in Communist circuits of newspaper propaganda, as exposed in this State Department dossier of Huiswoud's activities, before the 1937 rebellions. This indicates that the conjuncture of Caribbean labor uprisings Communist black militant forces by 1934 at least partially provided the historical context for the Caribbean labor uprisings that ensued, as we will see, several years later.

PART III

RACE, NATION AND THE UNEVEN DEVELOPMENT OF THE POPULAR FRONT

CHAPTER 6

The Temperament of the Age

*The World respects the strong and have very little sympathy for the
weak. You may say it is not the right thing to do, but to us it does not seem
material what you think or feel about the matter. It is the temperament of
the age that counts, and if you want to continue living and be regarded as
an active unit of the human family instead of a footpad, you will have to
adjust your philosophy to suit the temperament of the age.*
The African Nationalist, 1935

Go on and Up! Our souls and Eyes
Shall follow thy continuous rise;
Our ears shall list thy story
From bards who from thy root shall spring
And proudly tune their lyres to sing
Of Ethiopia's Glory
"Ode to Ethiopia," Paul L. Dunbar, 1915

The colonial dictum is to shoot first and find out later ...
Negro Worker, 1935

In January 1935, when news of a shooting of three unarmed protesters by British
colonial mercenaries at Buckley Estates in St. Kitts, British West Indies, hit the
New York offices of the International Labor Defense (ILD), the story did not
go unrecognized in the pages of the *Daily Worker.* Moreover, the *Negro Worker*
and the *Barbados Observer* covered this significant event. On March 4, 1935, the
Daily Worker released word that

... three strikers were murdered and nine persons seriously wounded when armed
police and soldiers of the Defense and Reserve Forces fired point blank into a
peaceful assembly of striking cane field laborers and sympathetic town workers on
January 30th at Buckley's Estate ....

The workers were struggling to receive more than the present pay which was then at "18 cents a ton for cutting and leading sugar cane." West Indian parents were struggling to work, children had to eat and rebellion was inevitable. But England, rather than utilizing its forces of "defense" to challenge imminent fascist aggression the world over—indeed haunting Abyssinia—had chosen to unleash its might against the unarmed protesters at Buckley's Estate with the tacit consent of the US authorities. This use of force resulted, predictably, in the deaths of unarmed laborers. It's in this context that the *Negro Worker* made the ubiquitous observation that the "colonial dictum is to shoot first and ask questions later," an assertion that remains true today.[1]

The British West Indies took leadership in a series of labor uprisings in the period from 1935 to 1939 that were in many ways the most radical social movements at the point of production then underway in the hemisphere. No Communist parties ever arose in this context. However, a group of half a dozen or so Jamaican labor activists formed an "Inner Circle" that was loosely aligned with Comintern policy and definitely with Marxist theories of class struggle, and Trinidad similarly formed mass organizations which collaborated with Communists of the time to organize workers on the island. But the fact that the Comintern did not establish any parties in this region of the Caribbean is a real and significant historical observation that bears weight in itself. Given the pervasive nature of working-class unrest in the hemisphere which in the United States had culminated in the rise of the Communist-led Committee for Industrial Organization (CIO), one must attempt to reconcile the phenomenon of massive sit-down protests of tens of thousands of laborers in automotive centers like Flint, Michigan in 1937 with the fact that black laborers in islands like Trinidad and Barbados were burning the oil fields and non-black-owned town shops—*and* having sit-down strikes on sugar and other plantations, engaging in direct action methods of their own.

Placing the militant workers' uprisings in the West Indies in the same geopolitical map as other regions where black workers were fighting against oppression means we cannot isolate struggles in islands like St. Kitts from developments in Harlem and, more important, from developments in relation to Abyssinia, or Ethiopia, in East Africa. Indeed, the year 1935 cemented an era of black labor and political unrest circuiting between Harlem and the British West Indies for the duration of the interwar period and climaxing in 1937. This chapter accounts primarily for those struggles that directly involved the Comintern on some level. The ILD and ITUCNW remained in contact for a few years, but the National Negro Congress (NNC), a new CPUSA mass organization that replaced the LSNR, as praxis shifted again during the "Popular Front against Fascism" (herein Popular Front) beginning in 1935, was the main conduit for these linkages. Beginning in St. Kitts and Jamaica, then in Harlem and later in St. Vincent among other islands, the "temperament of the age" had arrived with a vengeance.

In this context of fierce labor uprising in the British West Indies and beyond, a series of black radical newspapers—namely *The African Nationalist, Plain Talk* and the *Barbados Observer*—were published in the BWI. Along with the influence of Comintern literature that continued to be circulated in the BWI, primarily *Negro Worker,* these newspapers became an important component of the class struggle in the region and its ties to the Comintern. What follows is therefore also an investigation of the significance of radical newspaper history among black workers and intellectuals which linked New York and the West Indies during the era of the Popular Front.

ABYSSINIA, ANTI-FASCISM AND COMPETING "MOTHERLANDS"

Looming large for black radicals in the Caribbean and the US was the imminent invasion of Abyssinia by Italian fascists which took place in October of 1935. In point of fact, the Harlem Riot of 1935 was also part of this hemispheric uprising of black people in opposition to racist oppression and looming fascist aggression in the African kingdom of Abyssinia, long considered the aboriginal and metaphorical "motherland" and symbol of freedom from colonial rule, of descended slaves, of a pre-colonial and independent period that pre-dated the Middle Passage. Notably, this wave of rebellion on the part of black laborers since the beginning of 1935 pre-dated both the Seventh World Congress of the Communist International and its declared Popular Front, and also the Italian invasion of Abyssinia, demonstrating that black workers in the Caribbean had preexisting anger and reason for rebellion—and that the coming invasion of Abyssinia would simply exacerbate. Moreover, fears of an imminent invasion of Abyssinia were already evident and factored into the precipitation of a larger global Communist-led Popular Front that ensued in Spain, Germany and major metropoles across Europe.

Essentially, the British colonial ruling class had been utilizing its own fascist methods to stifle unrest among black laborers in the Caribbean and globally. Indeed, much like American rulers, they had been to this point much more concerned with thwarting anti-colonial and Communist threats than with the rise of Nazi Germany. Indeed, it was the manifest power of anti-black racism as the leading force in global exploitation that remained still the chief mission of western powers until the actual invasion of Poland in 1939. While revisionist history has portrayed the role of French, British and American militaries that valiantly united to fight the Germans, it is more accurate that their avowed enemy—since 1917—was the Soviet Union.

NATION OVER CLASS: THE NATIONAL NEGRO CONGRESS IN
HEMISPHERIC CONTEXT

In tandem with the momentum generated by support for Abyssinia, important organizational developments around the relationship between the "Negro question" and the larger anti-fascist struggle within the continental United States under the auspices of the CPUSA would have important implications for the nature of how Communist organizational activity—or lack thereof—ensued in relationship to black laborers in the Caribbean. Significantly, the replacement of the LSNR with the NNC marked a shift toward a more nation-based focus for the CPUSA in the struggle against racism. The dissolution of the LSNR undoubtedly laid the basis for not only a more nationalist approach to anti-racist activity for Communists in New York, but it also paved the way for greater collusion between Communists and their erstwhile "petit-bourgeois" black political activists in the US than did their previous emphasis on their class brothers and sisters in the Caribbean.

A debate held in January of 1935 under the Joint Committee on National Recovery and Social Science Division of Howard University was the pretext for a series of conversations between the black Communist James Ford and prominent contemporary race leaders Francis Crosswaith and Oscar De Priest, both of whom had been decried as enemies of the proletarian struggle in the years and even decades before by Communists like Ford himself. The idea was raised to hold a congress, perhaps in the spirit of the Pan African Congress in 1926 in Harlem that Richard Moore had attended on behalf of the American Negro Labor Congress (ANLC). This congress would act to coordinate black-led organizational activity and strategy. On one hand, this put Communists such as Ford in direct political collaboration with former arch-enemies within the black progressive community such as De Priest, Crosswaith and even A. Phillip Randolph, the latter of whom apparently wrote from his sickbed on news of the NNC's founding that "I shall cooperate with the Sponsoring Committee in every way I can to help toward the success of the Congress." The CPUSA's increasingly nationalist discourse and cross-class collaboration within the black population of the United States objectively complicated their ability to mount a truly internationalist response when, in the case of Haiti, over 30,000 Haitians were massacred by Dominican President Rafael Trujillo.[2]

On the other hand, the founding of the NNC also occasioned the direct support and sponsorship of R. Palme Dutt of the Communist movement in Great Britain, thus strengthening the axis of collaboration between London, New York and the Anglophone Caribbean. Dutt, leading member of the British Communist Party, editor of the *British Labour Monthly* and an Indian by birth, was also a member of the Executive Committee of the Communist International

(ECCI) and author of *Fascism and Social Revolution*, a foundational if controversial text which reflected the contemporary debate within the Communist movement over how to approach and abate the fascist onslaught in Europe. Upon news of the NNC's official commencement in the end of 1935 in Chicago, Dutt proclaimed, "There is no question that a really representative Negro Congress, based in the U.S. and with wide international connections, could exercise a big and badly needed influence in world opinion." Chief among Dutt's concerns was Abyssinia, "especially in the period now opening when the example of the struggles of the peoples of Ethiopia against the foreign invader is bound to lead to a new and upward movement throughout Africa." Indeed this was the case not only for Africa but also for sections of the British Empire in the British West Indies.[3]

Apart from the international solidarity exhibited by British comrades like Dutt, the NNC was the outgrowth of a broad and popular appeal within the progressive African American population across the US with more inclusion of intellectuals and professionals and less emphasis on industrial workers, under and unemployed. The class-collaborative basis of the NNC meant that this organization was born of a much more national political context than the ANLC and LSNR which, in contradistinction, were unilaterally under the political authority of the Moscow-based Comintern. While the NNC retained its core as a pro-workers' organization, chief among its campaigns to challenge the disproportionate rollback in federal financial relief to poor black workers, it also took up the question of Jim Crow segregation and civil rights for which all black people in the US were victim—even doctors, lawyers and celebrities. Harlem blocks teeming with black folks often crowded into apartments with overflow on the fire escapes outside was captured on camera by Jewish radicals participating in federally funded public arts projects. This context was also the Comintern's Popular Front strategy for addressing the "Negro question."

When direct federal relief to the unemployed was reported to have officially ended on December 1, 1935, and states were notified that they had received their last allotment under the Depression-era federal relief arrangement, the National Urban League was already taking up the campaign to challenge this plan in relationship to city dwellers in places like Chicago, New York, St. Louis and Detroit who were primarily trapped in the declining industrial North. A bulletin from the "Negro Workers' Councils" of the National Urban League from December of 1935 forewarned that the "Government is 'getting out of this business of relief,' but 3,000,000 Negro workers still remain unemployed, with no hope of steady jobs in the principal agencies," such as the National Reemployment Service and the Works Project Administration.[4]

Months prior to the NNC's founding, and in the wake of the 1935 Harlem Riot, a "Negro Workers' Council" Bulletin from April noted that "Seventeen cities have formed Negro Workers Councils since the last Bulletin was released, making 42 Councils now organized in 17 states," claiming a total of 30,000 members that stretched "from coast to coast and from North to South." In further evidence of the broad US-based collaborative efforts giving rise to the NNC, the *Negro Worker* attributed the following factors:

> ... the changing attitude of Negro middle class and its organizations; the growth of a broad progressive bloc in the official trade union movement pledged to industrial unionism; and the general united front from mass movement of the toilers against fascism and war ... The general united front movement has had the greatest influence among the Negro youth, who, almost everywhere in the country, are uniting their organizations to carry through progressive social activity directed against jim-crowism and segregation. A great upsurge has been seen among both white and Negro farmers and agricultural workers who have effected fighting organizations during the depression in the heart of the reaction-ridden "deep South."[5]

The NNC sought to capitalize on what Communists generally seem to have characterized as a mass upsurge in black militancy across the country that had transcended the CPUSA's own immediate leadership and reach. Hence, the geographical borders of the continental United States fundamentally shaped the political basis for the NNC's response to both labor and social conditions in the black community in the years from 1935 through 1939.

Despite this US-based emphasis, the NNC's organizational constituency remained at least somewhat committed to reaching into the Caribbean. According to one article in the *Negro Worker* entitled the "Fight for Civil Rights of the Negro People in America," it was noted that "[a]lready a National Negro Congress is under way in Cuba." What follows will illustrate how the NNC in New York played an active role in supporting the editor W. A. Crawford of the *Barbados Observer* after he faced political repression for propagating the insurrectionary movement underway in Barbados in 1937 and also for his coverage of Communist-led activity in the US, particularly that of the ILD. The NNC also responded to the massacre in the Dominican Republic of tens of thousands of Haitians in 1937, as we will see in the final chapter. But the alliances that the NNC made with political organizations and figures in the trade union and progressive communities in New York and overseas at once strengthened and challenged the traditional approaches to the fight against racism through Comintern mass organizations that up until then had linked the Red International and Black Caribbean. Much of the labor rebellion that ensued in the Caribbean during the Popular Front was, as in 1919, more militant than the politics being propagated by the NNC itself.[6]

ABYSSINIA, COMMUNISM AND THE WORKERS' UPRISINGS IN
THE BRITISH WEST INDIES, 1935–37

While Harlem tenants were disproportionately unemployed and forced to live within segregated housing conditions whereupon generations of family members from great-grands to infants were crowded into rows of tenements, made manifest in the May 1935 "race riot" of Harlem, black working-class unrest struck with force in 1935 on the tiny island of St. Kitts. The protest at Buckley Estates also marked the founding of the St. Kitts Defense League in Harlem. Harlem housed im/migrant laborers from across the British West Indies and the US South; the former had begun to create a network of popular organizations that were designed to address both their needs in New York and also the substandard conditions of their brethren in the Caribbean. Notably, rather than modeling the defense leagues for the popular labor rebellions in the BWI after the contemporary CPUSA-affiliated political defense leagues for Albizu Campos of Puerto Rico and Jacques Roumain of Haiti, the Harlem-based British West Indian leagues such as the St. Kitts Defense League appear to have sought to defend an entire island—and an incipient and would-be nation—of struggling political prisoners rather than just one or two pre-eminent figures.

Whoever Buckley was, the maintenance of business matters on his estate was by no means unimportant to the US Consulate then stationed in the British West Indies, especially since it was rumored that Communist agitation based out of New York had played a role in fomenting the rebellion. A report from one Perry N. Jester of the US Consul to the Department of Justice revealed that the recent demonstrations in St. Kitts were not entirely disconnected from the influx of radical literary agitation which had circulated through the hands of laborers on the island by way of the ITUCNW and its West Indian subcommittee which was based on Harlem's 135th St. While he had gleaned from the *Barbados Advocate* that the immediate context surrounding the strike in St. Kitts as well as an attendant protest in Martinique was "definitely attributable to wage reductions," Jester had surmised that these spontaneous protests were "undoubtedly of greater significance when taken in connection with certain other factors." The "other factors" connoted Communism.

In appearance, this protest-turned-uprising was spontaneous; in essence, there was a long history of political agitation on the island and Communist propaganda helped inspire an ideology of rebellion and class struggle within what seemed to have been a politically disinterested population of laborers. Jester's understanding was that "no definite cases of the dissemination of subversive communistic propaganda have come to the attention of this Consulate" in St. Kitts, and yet he also knew it was "well known" that "publications of this kind are still coming into the island." Jester then went on to describe how his (presumably wealthy and white) acquaintance had ventured into St. Kitts to discover what exactly had triggered the uprising among the laborers. According to this acquaintance:

> While riding through one of the most extensively cultivated agricultural sections of the Island [he] took advantage of the occasion to talk with various plantation overseers, and in connection with communistic propaganda was told that while pamphlets of various kinds had been coming into the Island for some years, up until very recently the negro workers paid no attention to them whatsoever, but that at the present time they were reading them.[7]

Notwithstanding the fact that this intelligence was derived from the perspectives of "various plantation overseers" of private finance capital, it still reveals how at the moment of insurrection workers on St. Kitts had clearly been reading and circulating Communist literature.

What impact that Communist propaganda might have made on laborers in St. Kitts appears to have been slowly materializing when taken from the perspective of British colonial authorities at the time. "Many people here," said Jester, "observed during the last two or three years a gradual but distinct change in the attitude of the negro population toward the white man, particularly in and near the City of Bridgetown and other thickly populated towns of the Island." Moreover, it was noted that "such a thing as an organized riot could not and would not have taken place several years ago." And it was precisely this radicalism, which had an active Communist influence traversing the boundaries of British West Indian plantations and defense committees in Harlem, that had such officials as Jester nervous about the future of American and British Empire in the region.[8]

Jester seems to have identified the political network of radical ideas that connected black workers in the Caribbean with Communist organizational activity in New York. Jester admitted that "all of these things are at the present time no more than straws in the wind, but they do indicate a trend in a certain direction which many people believe will become more and more apparent in the months ahead." Jester had conjectured quite correctly to the US Justice Department officials that the ensuing class uprisings which would climax in fierce labor rebellions in the British West Indies of 1937 would be sparked, in part, from Communist leadership in Harlem rather than strictly from within the islands themselves. And he cautioned his superiors accordingly.[9]

Jester had ascertained as early as 1935 that even Barbados was linked to the transnational circuit of black radical propaganda. His report on the St. Kitts uprising concluded with a reference to the March 30, 1935, issue of the *Barbados Observer*, an important newspaper edited by radical Black journalist W. A. Crawford, in regards to the "reported organization of West Indian Harlemites in New York City to protest the deaths at St. Kitts in connection with the strike" Jester advised that the Department of Justice draw special attention to the "names of the organizers of the St. Kitts-Nevis Labor Defense Committee in New York" which were given therein. But the coalition of black people in Harlem aligned with the St. Kitts-Nevis Labor Defense Committee was not only formed through these Harlem-based defense corps; the *Negro Worker* also championed the cause of the St. Kitts martyrs in the pages of its paper.[10]

Editors of the *Negro Worker* took the opportunity to expose this government crackdown in St. Kitts, documenting the manner in which the lives of these laborers were seen as dispensable by their rulers at the time. A "note and comment" from the September 1935 issue of the paper indicated that the colonial government in St. Kitts, namely in the personage of Chief Justice Sir James Rac, retrospectively determined that the shootings were justified on the premise that "'had the police and the Defence Forces not taken the action they did attempts would most likely have been made at burning the estate property.'" The *Negro Worker* lambasted the unjust defense of this "wanton killing" on the part of Royal troops, a defense which was premised upon what "'most likely'" would have happened. The editors noted the cynical decision for an "inquiry" on the part of British authorities which was "being made on the rates of pay of the workers over which the disturbance arose." But the "colonial dictum," concluded these editors, was "to shoot first and find out later.'" In St. Vincent, however, the rule was to shoot first and ban Communism later, placing a strategic barrier between the Red International and black working-class struggle at a very timely moment in radical history.[11]

Seemingly by osmosis, the wave of rebellion on the islands spread from St. Kitts into St. Vincent, but it was not until November of 1936 that the Trinidadian native and New York-based Communist, Charles Alexander, fully documented in the *Negro Worker* the monumental rebellion in St. Vincent and subsequent ban of Communism on the island. Alexander retrospectively proclaimed that "this day will go down in the history of St. Vincent as one not to be forgotten." After having been directly confronted with the

> … massing of the unemployed in the latter half of 1935 before the Court House in Kingstown, the capital of the Island, the barricading of the colonial secretary in his office and the refusal of the masses to disperse until they were granted relief from hunger

… the colonial governor did not hesitate to reach for a lifeline of "assistance" from the mother country's headquarters in London. The "Atlantic fleet" arrived on the scene.[12]

In one sense, the very act of recording this history and commemorating St. Vincent's day of rebellion in the pages of *Negro Worker* was a means by which Alexander at least in the realm of propaganda extended a fraternal arm of comradeship to his brethren in the Caribbean. At the height of the world depression, Alexander correctly proclaimed that "the West Indian masses are on the march," and he summoned the ITUCNW to play a direct role in the militant anti-colonial revolts of black islanders in St. Vincent and across the region. So as Communists whose main task was to remain vigilant for opportunities to heighten workers' militant rage and hone it into an organized political strategy for revolution, some level of political direction was a must. Alexander wrote: "Everything must be done to heighten this anger and increase this resistance. The International Trade Union Committee of Negro Workers has a tremendous role to play in this respect. It must not be found wanting." In another sense, the implicit criticism on the part of Alexander was that up to the present point, Communist presence by way of the ITUCNW had been fundamentally "wanting." Instead of the ITUCNW, the most direct assistance to the laborers in St. Vincent was found at the intra-Caribbean level within the BWI: "Defense committees sprang into action, lawyers were engaged from other islands, particularly from Grenada and Trinidad, to fight for the release of those arrested." In this way, the St. Vincent uprising sparked a transnational circuit of defense committees which was also a popular front of sorts implicating lawyer and unemployed, Trinidadian and Grenadian, in the common anti-colonial struggle at the point of production for better wages.[13]

The labor movement that arose in the Caribbean in the wake of Italy's invasion of Abyssinia had a distinctly racial character to it. And this phenomenon of racial nationalism, infused with anti-fascist support for Abyssinia, was an ideological grounding that emerged—unevenly and not uniformly—within the mounting resistance movement against colonial domination and exploitation that was rippling through the BWI in 1935. In the days and months leading up to Italy's fascist invasion of Abyssinia in October of 1935, the growing labor movement in the BWI was also openly proclaiming its allegiance to the Abyssinian state. The Comintern, too, was engaged in this pro-Abyssinia campaign, complicating any notion that race-unity alone was the motivating factor in the labor unrest across the British West Indies.

In September of 1935, the *Negro Worker* depicted on its cover the image of a multiracial "Hands off Abyssinia" protest in South Africa presumably led by the Communist Party of South Africa. Enclosed in the pages of this issue were also updates from the BWI where popular campaigns in defense of Abyssinia were simultaneously taking place:

> The British Guiana Labour Union held a huge protest meeting and sent the following cable to the Emperor of Abyssinia stating, "The Negroes of British Guiana hail your declaration that you will defend your Empire to the last man against foreign aggression." The Negro Progress Convention in session at Georgetown sent resolutions to the British Government and the Abyssinian

Emperor … In Trinidad Negro mass meetings have been held … The Italian consul has protested against our newspaper's description of Mussolini as "that mean scoundrel." … In St. Lucia meetings have been held and resolutions passed demanding that the British Government and the League preserve peace in Africa.[14]

Henry Critchlow, the British colonial subject from British Guiana whose engagement with the Comintern was inextricably linked to the growing labor movement in Guiana, was described hailing the Ethiopian king on behalf of the "Negroes of British Guiana" in the pages of a Soviet Union-backed international periodical for black workers. This was one form that the popular front in defense of Abyssinia took in the wake of its occupation.

In terms of the fledgling anti-fascist movement to defend Abyssinia, Communists were not necessarily the most aggressive actors in terms of militant direct action within the transnational circuit between Harlem and the British West Indies. On the docks of Trinidad and in the churches of Barbados, there appears to have been a much more "hands on" approach to the "Hands off Abyssinia" campaigns than struggles more directly led by Communists. In August 1935, the *Daily Worker* received word that "Negro stevedores of Port of Spain, Trinidad … recently refused to coal an Italian battleship, and forcibly prevented the crew from coaling it themselves." The article noted that

> … word was also received in New York yesterday that St. Michael's Episcopal Cathedral, St. Michael's Parish, Barbados, British West Indies, was burned to the ground several weeks ago by a crowd of workers protesting the defense by the white rector of Fascist Italy ….

These black Christians in Barbados had clearly oriented their racial and spiritual allegiance to the lost tribe of Solomon in Abyssinia and they would defend the integrity of this state with the centuries-old slave tactic of "burning to the ground" their sworn enemies; except in 1935, the enemy was Mussolini and his fascist supporters at the pulpit in "little England." Certainly, Communist propaganda had been a small yet formidable threat to British colonial domination in the West Indies as the case of St. Kitts illustrates. But for some black laborers, it seems that the front lines of the battle to defend Abyssinia began in the churches, such as in this case of Barbados.[15]

Though the sharpest manifestation of pro-Abyssinia sentiment was through militant direct action in the BWI, newspapers were important to both initiating and acting in conversation with the process of radicalization in the region. Hence, British colonial authorities ensured that continued if not heightened surveillance and, if need be, banning of anti-colonial literature was chief on of its list of things to do as global fascism mounted. The dissemination of propaganda like the *Negro Worker* was being consistently thwarted in both the London metropole and in the Caribbean for precisely this reason. In the meantime, black radicals in urban centers across the West Indies had become more vocal, and many of these radicals were not visibly involved with Comintern networks of anti-fascist activity in this period.

A new crop of black radical presses in the BWI that arose in this context is exemplified by two pivotal newspapers in Trinidad and Jamaica respectively: *The African Nationalist* and *Plain Talk*. A close examination of each paper offers a far from comprehensive perspective of the gamut of black radical presses that emerged in the remaining years before WWII; rather, it offers two examples of how international racial-national support for Abyssinia and Communist political developments were infused into the militant black socio-economic unrest of the moment.

ANGLOPHONE CARIBBEAN NEWSPAPERS IN POPULAR FRONT CONTEXT

Both *The African Nationalist* and *Plain Talk* appear to have been representative of the popular discourse shaping Caribbean-based anti-fascist thought relative to Abyssinia on the eve of invasion by Italy. These papers were much like the periodicals of the post-WWI "New Negro" period insofar as they were derived from and also cultivators of the critical thought and militancy of everyday black people in the Caribbean. But unlike the post-WWI periodicals headquartered in Harlem, newspapers published from within subaltern epicenters in the Caribbean in the mid-1930s were in the leadership of this transnational ideological process.

Haile Selassie's relationship with black workers in the Caribbean prior to and during the fascist onslaught was central to the message of *The African Nationalist*. He communicated directly with the Trinidadian supporters of his nation in 1935 by way of this monthly periodical, which was edited by one C. Francis Taylor who was also a leading member of an organization called the African Nationalist League. Through its pages, Selassie presented the basic justification for his defensive posture against Italy, and he did so utilizing entirely modern and contemporary standards of international law with respect to state sovereignty, independence and just war:

> As an independent sovereign Empire, we insist on preservation of our liberty, maintenance of our economic integrity and inviolability of our frontiers. We will defend our liberty to the last drop. We have committed no act which in law or morals justifies Italy to menace us with war. We have come before the bar of international justice with a clean conscience.[16]

Selassie's notion of a "clean conscience" was quite important for several reasons. First, it premised the moral law for defense of his state on the grounds that Abyssinia's "liberty" and "economic integrity" were unquestionably just and sound. Second, it set the "bar of international justice" for popular allies to include the Soviet Union and the League of Nations—essentially subverting the proletarian internationalism of the previous period and reinforcing instead the discourse of national self-defense and self-determination across class boundaries. In an age of emergent and dwindling empires, this empire—indeed the oldest of them all except arguably Japan—was asserting its place such that class antagonism was stifled rather than encouraged in perseveration of the national "frontier" and political status quo.

The third significant factor in Selassie's reference to a "clean conscience" was that it asserted a valiant triumph over "badmindedness," or ill-based human intentions. Such a communal assertion of ethical and moral cleanliness on the part of this African kingdom invoked principles of race-based redemption which in turn inspired the Diaspora to defend Abyssinia's "frontiers," even from the distant shores of Trinidad. In this way, the editorial commentary in the first issue of *The African Nationalist* was premised upon socio-biological and also metaphysical conceptions of the "African Family," proclaiming that "We are now faced with one of the greatest crises that has ever confronted the entire African family." The purpose of the article was to assert that this racial family had itself been reaffirmed in the face of the impending "crisis" wrought by fascist Mussolini, hence calling upon black brethren to "stand solidly behind his imperial majesty Selassie and defend the sovereignty of Ethiopia." Several prodigal sons in this African family apparently led the charge in Trinidad if we take, for example, the aforementioned stevedores who militantly refused to coal Italian ships in August 1935 as an act of solidarity with Abyssinia. Notably, however, these laborers reached out for publication of their anti-fascist activity to the Communist editors in New York at the *Daily Worker* rather than the locally based editors of *The African Nationalist*. All the same, *The African Nationalist* was foundational for reflecting the pro-Abyssinian "temperament of the age" which had recently been born in the British West Indies as well as across the waters in New York in the months leading up to Abyssinia's invasion by Italy.[17]

Another important periodical, *Plain Talk*, springs into being in Jamaica in this context of what appears to have been an emergent pro-Abyssinian defense network in the region. In the years of its existence from 1935 through 1937, *Plain Talk* was like a journalistic sponge, absorbing the various social and political dispositions of laborers, government workers, and the general population whose perspectives were not so prominently displayed in the pages of the island's mainstream, colonial-endorsed newspaper called the *Daily Gleaner*. Much like *Crusader* had done for black people across the Diaspora after WWI,

Plain Talk acted as a radical ear to, voice of, and lens for the struggles emerging from this epicenter at the parish level as well as documenting those experiences of migrant Jamaican laborers at sea or in Cuba.

Plain Talk was essentially taking the pulse of labor and political movements in the Caribbean and United States from 1935 to 1937. Notably, editorial staff at *Plain Talk* were keen on reporting news related to Communist organizations that addressed the "Negro question" in the United States. This newspaper is an important archive for assessing the extent to which the Comintern and its attendant organizations were integrated into other progressive forces emanating from Jamaica in particular and the Black Caribbean more generally. Moreover, *Plain Talk*'s abrogation in 1937 paved the way for other radical journalistic voices, namely the prominent Jamaican Marxists, Richard Hart and Wilfred A. Domingo, who contributed to a journal called *Public Opinion* from their radical hubs in Jamaica and Harlem respectively.

Plain Talk's historical significance as a partial conduit for Communist praxis in the hemisphere was evident from nearly its first appearance, though its message was far from pro-Communist. An early issue of this newspaper in mid-May 1935 yielded a fascinating hodgepodge of concerns at the local, hemispheric and international levels. The logo across the top of the paper revealed the non-confrontational politics of the editorial board by way of a quote from President Roosevelt: "The New Deal is a Square Deal." An editorial comment on the goal and mission of *Plain Talk* entitled "Glory of the British Crown" was hardly anti-Crown, advocating for the "contentment and harmony, yes, amity—between State and people" and for the "stability of Colonial Expansion and Imperialism." Another article presented a relatively objective and politically indifferent exposé of Hitler's rise post-WWI up to the contemporary period in the mid-1930s. This article was important because while hardly pro-Soviet in its interpretation of the rise and significance of fascism, it indicated that the *Plain Talk* editors were avid about functioning as a tool for the political education of their reading demographic on affairs of global fascism, paving the way for discussions of fascist aggression in Abyssinia in future issues of the paper.[18]

If the editors of *Plain Talk* consciously established themselves as not pro-Soviet, this did not mean that "American correspondents" for the paper were unsympathetic to the Communist question. Scottsboro had hit the West Indies in the pages of this same mid-May issue of *Plain Talk*. Coverage of the overturned verdict became another source of political education for black people in the Caribbean about their fellow workers in the US. But there was no reference made to any extant Scottsboro committees in Jamaica, as there were apparently none, nor to the history of those committees which had been established in other islands such as Haiti and Cuba. Rather, this piece simply demonstrated that the editors sought to objectively convey information about racial inequality and injustice in the US court systems such that the overturned verdict was a victory for racial justice in itself. This piece was one manifestation of how the Scottsboro movement manifested in the Black Caribbean during the Popular Front.[19]

The Scottsboro article did not make explicit references to work of the ILD nor implicit assumptions about Communist influence in this case, but another adjoining article in this mid-May issue discussed updates in the case of an incarcerated political prisoner, a young Communist named Angelo Herndon, in relationship to the ILD's struggle for "due process" while the case ascended to higher courts. In so doing, *Plain Talk* brought the civil rights struggle of the ILD for Herndon's freedom before the Jamaican reading audience:

> The rights of free speech, the right of white and negro to organize and meet together, and the right of the jobless and starving to demand relief, were defended by Seymour in his appeal for Herndon. The basic constitutional rights to speak, assemble and petition of redress of grievances, he insisted, are involved in the Herndon case.[20]

While the lawyer called "Seymour" was connecting the dots between free speech, black and white unity, unemployment, relief and the Angelo Herndon case, the editors at *Plain Talk* were inviting their readers to draw correlations between the struggle for "basic constitutional rights" of radicals and black laborers in the United States, Jamaica and the British West Indies over all. Again, if indirectly, the influence of developments in the Communist movement on the consciousness of progressives in the Caribbean was evident. But the influence of developments in Abyssinia on the consciousness of black progressives editing *Plain Talk* was even more pronounced.[21]

In subsequent issues of *Plain Talk*, the editors made a conscious decision to fully support Haile Selassie, and hence his empire, as he prepared for invasion from Italy. One of the first in-depth editorials of Abyssinia offered in May's last issue was clearly intended to indicate the formidable strength of the Ethiopian Army and preparedness to thwart an Italian intrusion, implying not only that Italian fascists ought to be wary but also that the newspaper editors were on the pro-Ethiopian front. Weeks later, Selassie was heralded in the paper as the "Man of the Hour" and "King of Kings," hence positioning *Plain Talk* as unequivocally pro-Abyssinian in a period when the British Crown was granting tacit consent to this fascist encroachment onto the Ethiopian Crown. An issue in early July presented the cartoon image of Ras Tafari, or Selassie, with the inscription of "Lion of the Tribe of Judah," giving a royal kicking, a literal boot, to Mussolini as the former stood proudly over Africa and the latter was catapulted back toward Italy. Such a cartoon reflected the popular support that anti-fascist discourse in support of Abyssinia enjoyed during this period in not only the Caribbean but in the US as well.[22]

Indeed, Judah's "tribe" had become a transnational army of frontier fighters that seemingly had no national borders, connecting Chicago with Kingston and placing Harlem's May 1935 riot at the center of the battalions of support for Abyssinia. In late June, *Plain Talk* reported that an "American Negro Organization" in Chicago pledged to help organize a Jamaican battalion of foot soldiers for the "Ethiopian Frontier" as follows: "We learn that a group of Jamaicans ... have decided to launch a series of Meetings throughout the entire Island, for the purpose of getting together a Battalion of stalwart men to defend the Ethiopian Frontier from the Italian Invaders." This "Battalion" would reportedly be "freely transported to Africa with the aid of American Negro Organization in Chicago" which, averred the Jamaican editors, "we understand, has already dispatched a large Battalion to the African Continent."[23]

It is not clear to what "American Negro Organization" this piece referred; however, the larger point is that a Chicago-Jamaican political network was then extant and premised upon race-based support for the nationalist project of defending Abyssinia. Perhaps there were other movements linking the US and Caribbean that were independent of and perhaps even an alternative to the more obvious Harlem-Caribbean connection which was often interpenetrated by Communist organizations like the LSNR, ANLC, NNC and ITUCNW.

Plain Talk also revealed to its Jamaican readers that in New York a "race-uniting cause" which had been derived from the Harlem Riot of 1935 against the "white man" had been consolidated into a pro-Abyssinian front of black organizations that were presumably independent of Communist leadership. That is, two groups called the Negro Industrial-Clerical Association and the International Congress for African Justice reportedly sponsored a meeting in the aftermath of the Harlem Riot because "an under-current of discontent over alleged discrimination in favour of white persons" had given rise to the "depth of emotion" made manifest in the desire to support Abyssinia. Like *The African Nationalist, Plain Talk* was concerned with presenting the image of a Pan-African frontier that had no geographical borders except those that surrounded the one legitimate, sovereign and black empire: Ethiopia. In the pages of this paper, the Communist movement was a faint shadow rather than a haunting specter over fascist Italy, even though its presence was acknowledged.[24]

Still, one barrier within the Pan-African movement for Abyssinia that *Plain Talk* was apparently either unable or unwilling to consider was that of language. For even in documenting the spread of this Abyssinian movement in the subaltern epicenter of Cuba, the newspaper gathered reportage from Anglophone—and primarily Jamaican migrant laborer—writers whose stories were mainly relevant to concerns surrounding the British Empire. Therefore, a huge racial demographic in Cuba, namely the Afro-Latin population based in the "Black Belt" of Oriente province, was not able to voice any relevant expression of pro-Abyssinian sentiment. Notwithstanding this limited linguistic approach to black laborers in Cuba, the paper documented amusing though profound cases of the Pan-Africanist fervor that was aroused within the migrant labor population in Cuba in the wake of Italy's invasion of Abyssinia.

Some Jamaicans living in Cuba who were subjects of the British Empire were also politicized around the movement in defense of Abyssinia, at times even to the point of petitioning to the British Empire for permission to fight on behalf of the "King of Kings." In one case, a man named A. Barkley was chairman and P. B. Phillips the secretary of an organization of presumably Jamaican migrant laborers living in Miranda, Oriente Province of Cuba, who had banned together for defending Abyssinia. When this group petitioned to the British Consul in Cuba by expressing a passionate outcry of support "For the cause that lacks assistance. For the wrong that needs reistance [*sic*]. For the future in the distance/ And the good that we can do," they were met with a harsh and dismissive response from the Acting British Consul who replied—and perhaps jokingly carbon-copied to the United States State Department—"Gentlemen, I beg to acknowledge receipt of your letter dated July 21st the contents of which have been carefully noted. I regret to have to state that I have no information on the subject about which you are enquiring." Their petitions for redress fell on deaf ears.[25]

In short, they were asking one of the most racially prejudiced imperial regimes in the world for permission to defend the only extant black monarchy in the world then suffering directly from fascist aggression. The politely dismissive response on the part of the British Consul was made plain before readers of *Plain Talk*. In a rhetorical spin much like the *Negro Worker*'s decision to publicize Sir James Rac's dehumanizing support for violence against striking laborers, *Plain Talk* exposed the open hostility as expressed by the intermediaries for the Royal Crown toward this incipient transnational Abyssinian brigade.

Above and beyond openly agitating on behalf of Abyssinia, *Plain Talk* was dedicated to voicing the everyday struggles, thoughts, hopes and grievances of local Jamaican islanders in, quite literally, "plain talk," in a year—1935—when class struggle was on a sharp rise across the island. In this year, there was a marked intensification of pro-direct action black radical sentiment within the "struggling mass" on the island, much like that underway in St. Kitts, and this feeling was reflected in the letters printed in the paper since practically its first issue. Notably, discussion of any relationship between these struggles and Communist organizations in New York, much less anywhere else, was conspicuously absent.

From its earliest issues in May and June, *Plain Talk* responded to the labor rebellion that was ensuing on the island. That is, letters to the editor documented and also encouraged a whole spectrum of Jamaican popular beliefs, rhetorical styles and political vantage points that emerged in the fervor of labor unrest on the island. One letter, published in late May, was an open statement to the Governor of Jamaica, gently cautioning him to

... seriously give the land and labour questions the greatest consideration ...
from all angles, some of which are a Minimum Wage, better pay as now prevails,
Working Mens Compensation Bill ... in order that there cannot be even the
thought of unrest anywhere in this Island under your administration.

Another letter to the editor in this same issue from one Edgar Smith noted
that Jamaican leaders have been derelict for over a decade in improving the
agricultural base of the economy, the Governor himself opting for foreign
imports and capital investments all to the detriment of the average independent
Jamaican peasant and farmhand. Mr. Smith used the examples of "the parishes
in Manchester, Clarendon and St. Elizabeth," where, he averred, "[f]ar more
agriculture could be carried on in these parishes if something could be done to
convert the dry areas into fertile ones." He therefore landed an attack on the
"idle" deliberations of those who obscured if not ignored the ever-sharpening
detrimental effects of absentee landlordism on the island: "it is useless to
idly talk of land being fertile, and the agricultural resources of the Island as
illimitable, when there are Proprietor Land Grabbers who possess hundreds
and thousands of acres of uncultivated land in wild waste and ruinate." Hence
his admonition to the Governor was that "the sooner the Legislature get
seriously to the consideration of the above Problems in all earnestness as their
command—the better it will be for the Governor and the Governed."[26] On one
level, Mr. Smith was giving voice to a virtual Jamaican popular front against
colonial oppression that had both local and global dimensions. Here in tiny
Jamaica, Mr. Smith was discussing a process wherein the people, or "governed,"
were essentially the entire struggling mass of toilers for whom resources should
be focused "locally." In other words, there was an insular inclination toward the
specifically and uniquely endowed qualities of the island's natural resources and
increasing urgency to begin the process of agricultural economic development
from there.

But on another level, the local focus of Jamaica's united mass struggle from
below in 1935 by no means failed to address the global aspects of this battle for
Jamaicans inland and at sea, particularly in relationship to the British Empire
and imminent war directly involving the European fascist dictatorships of
Germany and Italy. *Plain Talk* reported in June 1935 that a cable was sent to
the Secretary of the Colonies from, presumably, manual laborers and middle-
class Jamaicans, protesting the monopolies which were weakening the financial
base of the workers and advocating instead for Anti-Trust Laws—especially if
colonial authorities were banking on selecting from this very demographic a
faithful army for the all-too-imminent danger of fascist territorial aggression
onto "Mother" England, much less any liminal spaces in her empire.

One letter from a Jamaican mariner indicated the political tsunami
of devastation that the British rulers might soon face, given the rampant

discontent festering within the ranks of black colonial seamen for whom racial discrimination was the only standard labor practice they had known, especially on the Direct Fruit Line:

> After going on the ship and start to work one soon find out the true colour of the Steward towards us. We scrub on our knees all day, and clean brass until our fingers are bursted … We are called out of our beds at five o'clock in the morning, the white fellows don't sleep where we sleep; but they are always out long after we start our scrubbing work that they used to do we had to do it and the Chief Steward say nothing about it.[27]

The "true colour of the Steward towards" this mariner and other Jamaican workers was presumably "white." But the color was more so a marker of attitude and behavior than reference to the Steward's hue, for in this case it was the racist attitude toward the collective of black crewman that connoted his color, and this attitude subjected the islanders to scrubbing on their knees and cleaning brass as if they were in military basic training.

Such open exposure of the brutal conditions of dehumanization that had been wrought by the race-based project of colonial domination under the British Crown became increasingly commonplace in the pages of *Plain Talk*. And yet these relentless conditions suffered by Jamaican and other British West Indian laborers, particularly migrant laborers, laid the basis for "great men" who could both articulate and lead the ensuing anti-colonial labor and political struggles in Jamaica and across the West Indies. In this case, it was a man called Alexander Bustamante, who established himself in the pages of *Plain Talk* in the latter days of June 1935 as a "composed, fearless courageous" man who could not only expound upon, in the plainest of talk, the plight of migrant Jamaican workers in Cuba who were presently suffering from the brutal labor conditions buttressed by racially and ethnically discriminatory Cuban legislation such as the 50 percent law, but who could then castigate the British authorities in Cuba for their hypocrisy in abetting such dehumanization.[28]

And even dehumanization is a term that is too opaque, for according to Bustamante, the existential experience in Cuba was "always worse than they can paint," validating this claim with the evidence that, "I speak from experience as I have lived in Cuba," and was presumably returned to Jamaica where he was waging the transnational struggle from "home." For it had been his experience that, as he claimed, "Time and time again I have had to use every effort and courage, not only to defend Jamaicans, but West Indians on the whole, from unjust attacks of Police and Rural Guards." Given the "indifference" that his responses elicited from British Consul reps in Cuba, "very often" he averred satirically, "it would be just as well to appeal to the Chinese Consul for protection." Hence, he concluded:

> ... there is but one way of preventing the blasting of Jamaicans in Cuba, and that is
> to again send another commission to investigate. Such a commission would have
> to be composed of fearless, courageous men, for by virtue of the present condition
> in Cuba, they too might be blasted up.

Careful not to rudely stereotype all Cubans as foreigner-blasters, Bustamante
noted that "it would be silly to think that all Cubans are undesirable, for in
Cuba like Jamaica and in every other part of the world human hearts are alike."
Rather, it was simply the "savage authorities" that he felt the British government
should castigate rather than promulgate. Bustamante was indeed "blasting up"
the very government to whom he was petitioning, all the while utilizing the
natural language of the subjects on whose behalf this subaltern had spoken so
plainly.[29]

Plain Talk's discussion of Cuba remained delimited to those testimonies
offered by Jamaican laborers without documenting the Spanish-speaking or
Francophone perspectives of black Cubans and Haitians. Still, language—
especially the colloquial language of Anglophone Jamaicans as evidenced
in *Plain Talk*—functioned as a political tool for mobilizing cross-border
movements in the region, in this case between Cuba and Jamaica. For
example, Bustamante's call for a "new commission" to investigate the
"blasting up" of black laborers from the British West Indies on the island of
Cuba was indeed the same type of political mobilization that Communists in
New York had put forward for investigating labor conditions in the Caribbean
a few years before—but very problematically. As we will see in the next
chapter. During the Popular Front era in Cuba, Communists had agreed to
support Grau San Martin's 50 percent law in 1935, meaning 50 percent of all
jobs in Cuba—in each industry, plantation etc.—must be held for Cuban
natives.

By 1937, President Trujillo of the Dominican Republic was in the process
of orchestrating the slaughter of tens of thousands of Haitians. This flood of
Haitians into the Dominican Republic was the direct outcome of the forced
deportation of Haitians from Cuba in the aftermath of the 1933 coup. These
Haitians had been deported, as had many Jamaicans, during the period that
Bustamante was describing in the pages of *Plain Talk*. An article in early
February 1937 announced that as a means of forcibly repatriating over 40,000
Jamaicans back to their island

> ... it is reported here that the Cuban Government is constructing concentration
> camps in which to house these Jamaican labourers who had been working on
> Cuban plantations, and are now awaiting their return to their native home under
> the new labour laws of the Cuban Government.

In this way, Bustamante and the nationalist movement had become more militant in fighting racist policies in Cuba by 1935 than the Communists who had conceded to proto-fascist nativism in the name of Cuban unity.

That is, Communists in Cuba, in line with Comintern strategy, had considered it too controversial and therefore unpopular to stand unequivocally for defense of the im/migrant black laborers and hence risk losing the support of more "moderate", i.e. jingoist, Cubans who had at the time begun to gravitate toward Communist circles on the island. Such figures as Bustamante were indeed speaking a quite different message of tolerance and humanity when they encouraged readers not to look wholly negatively on all Cubans, even Communist Cubans, for surely Bustamante was aware of the Comintern's decision not to side with the non-Cuban black workers. It is only through such a comparative approach to archival evidence from sources in the Anglophone and Spanish Caribbean that we can even begin to see the complexities of these conflicting yet overlapping and inter-penetrating "radical" processes which were circuiting across the region, from the Caribbean through New York.

Ultimately, *Plain Talk* was important for cementing notions of home for a people with a large migrant population. In this way, Ethiopia became much more of a symbolic home, as the Italian invasion carried into 1936. Ethiopia, the "aboriginal home of Black people," as *Plain Talk* revealed in 1936, was not the Soviet Union; nor was the Soviet Union Ethiopia. *Plain Talk* had made a decision to establish itself as a "racial school master," implicitly rejecting a class-based—i.e., Marxist—analysis. For black migrant laborers in Cuba suffering under the super-exploitation of colonial rule at the hands of the "white man" and also being ostracized from the "progressive" campaign of the status quo law led by Grau San Martin and supported by Communists, Abyssinia truly had a meaning that challenged the "popular" discourse of the Communist front in this very period.[30]

While *Plain Talk* was ruminating about the glories of Ethiopia, the *Daily Worker* was calling upon black Harlemites suffering under the throes of Jim Crow racism in the Deep North to also defend their "home." But home explicated a very different space and incorporated a different race: the Soviet Union and its Communists. "Leave everything and come to the Soviet Union" was the message brought before black people who were *Daily Worker* readers and living in the New York tenements and across the United States in 1936 during the Italian occupation of Ethiopia. Since the Soviet Union had been the single most vocal and determined member of the League of Nations to challenge fascist aggression in Abyssinia in 1936, it is clear that for black anti-fascists of the era, political allegiances were often made to both Abyssinia and the Soviet Union.

NEGATION OF THE NEGATION: POPULAR FRONT RETREAT
OF WORKERS' ORGANIZATIONS IN THE NEW YORK-
ANGLOPHONE CARIBBEAN CIRCUIT

While close interrogation of *Plain Talk* reveals that the popular movement to
defend Abyssinia in Jamaica was not aligned per se with the Comintern, several
Jamaican migrants to the US who were then living in Harlem—even certain
members of Garvey's Universal Negro Improvement Association (UNIA)—
became part of the radical organization circuits that Communists were helping
to lead in 1935. With Padmore's defection from the Comintern, new coteries
of black Communists emerged, and their sympathetic allies in the British
West Indies worked in tandem to produce the last substantive endeavors of
Communist praxis linking New York and the Caribbean. Notably, Algernon
Crawford, editor of the *Barbados Observer*, worked alongside leading black
CPUSA member Charles Alexander, editor of the *Negro Worker*, among others.
In this context, the Garvey/Communist division over mobilizing black workers
climaxed in Harlem when a leading UNIA member broke with Garveyism and
aligned with the CPUSA. The political leadership of "Captain" Arthur L. King
of the Harlem UNIA branch helps to elucidate this anti-fascist Red and Black
matrix that arose in 1935, demonstrating the shared interest in anti-racism that,
just as in 1919, resulted in an open break between these two movements over
the question of multiracial unity and direct action against police terror. Because
Communists had a much stronger track record on leading militant direct action
against police terror, obscure radicals such as King broke with the latter to join
with the former.

Dating back to the Harlem Riot of March 19, 1935, political conditions which
grew out of the movement against a brutal police killing of an unarmed black
man had led to the consolidation of the All People's Party (APP) which "placed
the blame of the incident where it belonged, at the doors of the New York City
administration." King believed that multiracial alliances by way of the APP
were useful for garnering the mass support that was necessary to combat local
acts of racist aggression in Harlem and also global acts of fascist aggression in
Abyssinia. At the local level, these conflicts forced the abdication of Arthur King
from his "throne" of leadership in the New York branch of the UNIA—and
closer to the work of the Comintern.[31]

In a discussion of the All People's Party and the Popular Front movement
in Harlem, the *Negro Worker* reported in October of 1936 that fighting on this
front was the "outstanding" Captain Arthur L. King, "former City President
of the Universal Negro Improvement Association," who was considered by
Communists to have been "conservative in the extreme" before the March
1935 riot but most recently had been "ousted from the Association because
of his progressive stand towards the People's Party of Harlem." The internal

tensions within the UNIA leadership's center and periphery—i.e., Garvey based in Jamaica and King based in Harlem—in the aftermath of the Harlem Riot essentially revolved around disagreements over the extent to which Communist alliances were fruitful for the organizational strategy of the UNIA.[32]

Not only did the Harlem Riot bridge a former divide between certain local UNIA and Communist organizers, but the October 1935 invasion of Abyssinia had sharpened tremendously the internal divisions between King and Garvey over how to proceed in the anti-fascist movement. As early as November, Garvey in a private letter had instructed King not to associate with Communists. In a response dated late December of 1935, King averred that the factionalization prevalent in the current UNIA branch in Harlem was reminiscent of the detrimental in-fighting at the 1929 convention of the UNIA held in Jamaica where Otto Huiswoud attended on behalf of the American Negro Labor Congress and challenged directly what he considered to have been Garvey's "failed" leadership of black workers. Though King requested from Garvey more understanding and leniency for the alliances with Communists that had been built in Harlem, King's UNIA chapter had already agreed by policy vote to continue its alliance regardless of Garvey's approval. Months later, King's chapter of the UNIA openly endorsed a Scottsboro Defense Committee which had been formed by the joint unity of the American Civil Liberties Union (ACLU), CPUSA and NAACP despite Garvey's orders not to affiliate with Communists. As a result, King's dismissal from the UNIA was all but cemented by early 1936, and this opened the door to his more active collusion in the Communist-affiliated anti-fascist movement between Harlem and the British West Indies for the duration of the interwar period and beyond.[33]

King had become a member of a network of Communist and black radical organizations based out of Harlem that was dedicated to challenging fascism against Abyssinia and would make small yet significant advances in supporting the labor rebellions that rocked the British West Indies beginning in 1937. In the latter half of the 1930s, King would play a leading role in an organization called the West Indies National Emergency Committee and also the Jamaican Progressive League, both of which were based in Harlem and charged with the mission of supporting the labor and political movements of the West Indies. As such, this placed him in direct political contact with Wilfred A. Domingo, the "fellow traveler" of the Communist movement who began writing for *Public Opinion* in 1937 and whose ties to Communism dated back to the post-WWI New Negro days in Harlem.

But while the Popular Front was consolidating in Harlem by 1937, fascism was intensifying sharply across the Caribbean. A Nazi-style sterilization plan similar to projects which had been experimented upon Jews had been approved in Bermuda by island authorities purportedly to solve the unemployment problem. Though Haitian migrant laborers living in the Dominican Republic had suffered the worst setbacks from the fascist aggression in the Caribbean in this period, Jamaicans and other British West Indians were enduring hardship wrought by barefaced capitalist repression. The British colonial government had continually denied civil liberties and any pretense of peoples' rights was outright denied. And this was an important basis for the major class struggles across the BWI in 1937.

Communists and affiliated radical networks in the transnational circuits linking NYC and the Caribbean helped to promote this unrest.[34] Toward the end of 1936, Charles Alexander proclaimed in the *Negro Worker* that 1937 would be "A New Year of Struggle for the West Indies." His native Trinidad would indeed experience a strike wave concentrated in the oil sector that affirmed the conjecture he made months beforehand. Alexander had ascertained that "with the opening of the year 1937 in this vast colonial empire of British imperialism new vistas of struggle of the masses loom on the horizon." These "new vistas" were visible to Communists like Alexander who had concluded that the objective conditions of deepening economic impoverishment and social degradation would lead to more radical sentiment in the Caribbean: "there will be no general rising of wages, the hours of toil will not be shortened, no provision will be made for the unemployed" without the establishment of "new and larger struggles of the masses—broader and more systematic battles for the rights to live." Implicitly, Alexander's message was that "broader and more systematic battles for the rights to live" must conjoin the "broader and more systematic" objectives of the Communist International around campaigns for civil liberties and socio-economic reforms. Alexander had pinned his hopes on the ITUCNW, demanding that it provide "assistance" to the campaigns for locally based legislative and executive councils led by laborers in the British West Indies. But just as the West Indian "masses [had] come of age, so to speak," proclaimed Alexander, the ITUCNW was in the process of being disbanded and the *Negro Worker* discontinued.[35]

The oil field workers of San Fernando would indeed pave the way for a broad cross-section of the toiling population to participate in a multiracial, island-wide popular struggle. But this struggle received minimal coverage in the *Daily Worker.* Instead, the *Chicago Defender* had remained intact to cover the protest, though predictably the *Defender*'s reportage occluded the degree to which the Comintern factored into this radical movement. When it reported that "thirteen persons were killed and 44 wounded within four days of the opening of Trinidad's biggest oilfield strike," the *Chicago Defender* article concluded that the cause of this labor strife had been

> ... engendered by dissatisfied Race workers, led by a native of Grenada named Uriah Butler who is claimed to be the supreme chief servant of the British Empire Workers and Citizens Home Rule Party, and whose attempted arrest provided the

opening installment of a chapter of bloody battle between the strikers and the local forces, throughout the island.

This oil strike was then described as having given way to a situation that was

> … so tense … that not only did the fever affect the sugar estates in the central part of the island where laborers joined in another series of demonstrations resulting in the death of one and injury to three, but the peaceful capital city received such a touch of the infection that laborers in different avenues of activity also went on strike.

Though it was correct to assert that the ensuing general strike in Trinidad took place under the leadership of "race" leaders such as the prominent Uriah Butler, the *Chicago Defender*'s strictly race-based analysis of this labor movement only partially accounted for the complexity of the radical movement then underway in that country.[36]

While the black nationalist *Defender* had written Communist agitation out of the Trinidad uprising, the *Chicago Daily Tribune* went to the opposite extreme of the *Defender*'s insular analysis. The *Tribune* attributed the protest strictly to a foreign "Red" menace. According to an article in late July of 1937 which purported to "Link Red Agents with Trinidad's Oil Field Strike," recent information was reported to reveal that "Communist agents were behind the violent strike and riots which for a month tied up Trinidad's oil fields." In particular, it was noted that "Communism was tied to the strike when, during a dawn raid, police and blue jackets discovered a 'red book' containing carefully prepared plans for the spread of the strike throughout the British West Indies and British Guiana," and as such the government had narrowed down the Communist "agents" to "a dozen local men in public life who are known in London as being closely connected with communism." But surely those "dozen local men" could not have forced ordinary civilians, who chose to depart from their daily routines, to "spontaneously" rebel alongside their oilfield comrades.[37]

If the *Chicago Defender* had inaccurately attributed the strike to race "sympathy," then the *Tribune* article had just as inaccurately attributed the strike to other factors—namely foreign class allegiance to "communism." But the inaccuracy lay in the incompleteness of both perceptions which posed a false dichotomization between race and class, when the class system of exploitation was always already prefigured *through* racist super-exploitation. So it was never a question of either Red or Black, but how black oppression anchored the capitalist colonial structure and Communists, in turn, used anti-racism to overturn it. One leading East Indian Communist at the time, Adrian Cola Rienzi, seems to have been very important to the radical process under way in Trinidad. But so too did figures such as Elma Francois of the Negro

Welfare Association, which had for several years been in strategic contact with Communists in London and beyond. And such contact did not make Francois any less black; indeed, it directed the fight against black oppression in Trinidad against the most accurate target: racist colonial capitalism. Still the *Chicago Tribune*'s assessment of the "Red agents" in Trinidad did account for one important aspect of the protest movement: London was the much more probable source of Communist influence by 1937 on the island than New York.[38]

The New York-based *Daily Worker* made a modest attempt to give coverage to Trinidad's protest in the form of a small article featured not so prominently at the bottom of a page in late June, releasing a figure of 14 rather than 13 killed in the Trinidadian oil strike. Most significant here is the evidence revealed in the *Daily Worker* that in the aftermath of the summer protests of 1937, ties between Trinidadian protesters and Communists in New York developed by way of the WIDC based out of Harlem. And the form that this transnational network took reflected the Popular Front ethos led by Communists during this period.[39]

In November, months after the strike had passed, the WIDC requested the "undivided sympathy and support" of the "American people" in the form of sending communications to the Colonial Secretary at Trinidad and also by assisting the WIDC in raising funds "in defense of Butler and his fellows." Making these recommendations of support to Ben Davis, a leading black Communist leader at the time and also the author of this particular article, was one Anatole Mais, a representative of the WIDC, who had personally fought alongside Uriah Butler and others in the months prior in Trinidad. In the conclusion of his interview with Ben Davis, Mais encouraged US radical support to be generated from "those in America who recognize common cause with the exploited and oppressed wherever they may be." We will see how CPUSA support for Caribbean struggles during the era of the Popular Front had overwhelmingly veered toward the movements in Mexico, Cuba and Puerto Rico, strikingly under-emphasizing the urgent needs and goals of black laborers in the rest of this Caribbean region. Implicitly, Mais was calling upon the Comintern to reconsider the geopolitical configurations of the international movement that had manifested itself in the circuits connecting the CPUSA with the CPs in Mexico, Cuba and Puerto Rico. After all, defense committees and solidarity campaigns were needed for workers in Trinidad just as much as for Puerto Rican progressives in Ponce. But in contrast to the relatively minimal alliances that the CPUSA offered to the Trinidadian labor movement in 1937, Harlem-based support for the rebellions that rocked Barbados in 1937 was somewhat more pronounced.[40]

Prescott Childs of the American Consul at Barbados revealed to the Secretary of State several accounts of the Barbados uprising which appeared in local papers, the *Barbados Advocate* and the "colorful (and colored)" *Barbados Observer*. In the eyes of one writer for the *Barbados Advocate*, not to be mistaken for the more radical *Barbados Observer*, anarchy had indeed hit Barbados when "the ever loyal colony with its proverbial law abiding subjects" had become the object of a grave disaster in the last days of July 1937. Reportedly, "various mischievous bands operating in the scattered country districts caused trouble on Wednesday and Thursday the 28th and 29th stealing potatoes from the fields, cutting telephone wires, [and] raiding numerous cross road grocery stores." This was only the beginning of the rebellion. The devastation was even worse according to the *Barbados Advocate*, for the "mischievous bands" had descended from the mountainous countryside into the city of Bridgetown like the ghosts of escaped maroons. According to the *Barbados Advocate*, the rebellion was like receiving a visitation from a "Spanish insurgent" but "without the accompanying expression of grievances":

> "Serious rioting broke out in Bridgetown yesterday morning following disorders on Monday night." In one simple short sentence such as this the world learned yesterday that another far flung unit of the British Empire had gone wrong. A quiet and peaceloving community saw its masses suddenly flareup with all the venom worthy of a Spanish insurgent without the accompanying expression of grievances. Barbados the ever loyal colony with its proverbial law abiding subjects ... For three hours law and order was flouted, for three hours lawlessness prevailed, for three hours her pride and glory hung in the balances, and in the end she was found wanting. Death at length put an end to the wanton destruction of property.[41]

Colonial "justice" had prevailed in this otherwise "peaceloving community" only with the "death" of those responsible for the "wanton destruction of property." This journalist explicitly ascribed feminine gendered attributes and racialized conceptions of whiteness to the colony of Barbados as if the island and its wealth had been caught in the grips of a beastly black menace. But this characterization was more the result of ideological shortcomings on the part of this journalist rather than ignorance of the events at hand. For indeed the destruction had been vast.

Indeed, the *Barbados Advocate* neglected to uncover the most basic questions surrounding the causes that led to this rebellion. After all, the rebels had been searching for food—mainly potatoes and grocery-stand items. Starving people had been termed "mischievous" for attempting to feed their children. This "quiet and peaceloving community" of white colonists in Bridgetown and elsewhere felt "pride and glory" for a way of life that had been premised upon the disproportionate dearth of resources that were allocated to the vast majority of inhabitants on the island. The *Barbados Advocate* did not recognize these contradictions, as it was advocating clearly on behalf of the elite minority rather than the incensed majority.

So, too, were US Consul representatives like Childs then stationed in Barbados advocating on behalf of this elite in the aftermath of the summer rebellions of 1937. Childs updated the Secretary of State on "Negro Communist Activities" in the US and Barbados later on in 1937. According to Childs, the same West Indian Defense Committee (WIDC) that was concurrently providing support for Trinidadians was also supporting radicals in Barbados at this time. The Executive Board of the WIDC had invited two island men that factored prominently in the recent unrest, named G. H. Adams, "Member of the Colonial Parliament" and "Barrister at law" and Algernon Crawford, "Editor and Proprietor of the Barbados Observer" to come to the United States "for the purpose of bringing local conditions before the great American Public." Clearly, these professional men were implicated in the "mischievous bands" that the *Barbados Advocate* had denounced.[42]

Just as Jamaican radicals had begun to produce independent periodicals like *Plain Talk*, so too did Barbados have a newspaper that voiced the opinions of local residents who were not determined to "advocate" on behalf of the British Empire. The *Barbados Observer* was one such paper. Extracts of an article taken from a mid-September 1937 issue of the *Barbados Observer* revealed further that the WIDC from its Harlem base was "endeavoring to focus the spotlight of world attention upon the economic and social hardships under which the masses in these colonies labour. The International Labour Defense is lending the cause its support while the Nation, the Amsterdam News, the New Masses" and others were described as "taking active interest" in the campaign. It would be one-sided to conclude, therefore, that Communist organizations during this period were solely or narrowly concerned with the plight of people in Spain or the Soviet Union; rather, the popular sentiment had far-reaching and global appeal and was also manifested, if only temporarily and in a less pronounced manner, in relationship to the Black Caribbean.[43]

In this way, local yet prominent black professionals in Barbados had been thrust into a transnational campaign that was spearheaded by the ILD and WIDC based in Harlem. In turn, Crawford was promoting the work of these organizations in his paper. The US Consul noted that "'recent articles appearing in the Barbados Observer have been published by the International Labour Defense in pamphlet form and circulated from coast to coast of the American continent.'" Hence, Barbadian readers of Crawford's paper were being informed that their cries for justice had echoed from "sea to shining sea" in the continental United States by way of the ILD.[44]

To say the least, Childs was not pleased about this NY-based show of solidarity. He concluded that

> ... it is thought, therefore, that the American government may care to watch the activities of these men if they arrive in the United States and the organizations

listed … endeavor to collect funds in the United States for radical activities after their return to Barbados.

For in the event that any future "radical activities" in Barbados might ensue with Red aid provided in US dollars, "such donations, even if they should eventually get beyond the pockets of the collectors, would by no means be considered a neighborly and friendly act by the majority of the colored and white population of Barbados." In Barbados, implied Childs, the "majority" were co-signatories to the "good neighbor" dicta of the day; by default, the "mischievous bands" in the countryside and conniving Communists in the United States were not welcome neighbors in this community.[45]

But perhaps the reason behind Child's vigilance against any signs of Communist promulgation of the class struggle in Barbados was precisely because the current of radicalism and anti-colonial sentiment on the island was much more mainstream than he was willing to admit. Indeed, Childs had personally published in the September 1937 issue of *The Patriot* a fierce diatribe against "Negroes and the Comintern" written by the Acting Speaker of the House of Assembly at Barbados and also the Chief Justice on the island:

> It is not only in South Africa that the Comintern is trying to enlist the native races and stir up trouble … For this reason it is from America that the threads run to the North American negroes of the West Indies, to the natives on the east and west coasts of Africa … After the American negroes have received their finishing touches in the courses of the Moscow and Leningrad revolution schools, they are sent to their "districts of work." … They organise strikes and insurrection in the sugar-cane plantations of the West Indies and preach the Revolution in the ports along the east and west coasts of Africa … Wherever in the world negroes dwell the red emissaries from Harlem are to be found, a symbol, as it were, or the world-wide significance of the American negro question.[46]

Despite what was generally an accurate assessment of how Communists planted themselves in the transnational movement between the West Indies and New York during the interwar period, there are several historical facts that this characterization ignored.

First, it was rarely Communists themselves who organized the strikes as had emerged in St. Kitts, St. Vincent, Jamaica, Trinidad and Barbados. Rather, local labor leaders—none of whom seem to have been members of a Communist party—themselves waged these struggles to demand higher wages and better social conditions. Second, while some of the "emissaries" such as Huiswoud, Ford and Haywood were indeed Comintern-trained, many were not. The "emissaries" of the movement, especially in the most recent period of rebellion in the latter half of the 1930s, were also figures like A. G. Crawford.

At times, as we will see, the emissaries were Haitian migrant refugees who had fled to the churches of Brooklyn with grisly details of the Trujillo massacre, that Communists like Max Yergan would then address. At other times the emissaries were Jamaican mariners whose only natural recourse was to express their grievances in the pages of *Plain Talk* and *Daily Worker*. These caveats notwithstanding, the report that was submitted to the State Department on the Comintern and black radicals was generally reliable insofar as Harlem had indeed remained the "symbol, as it were, of the world-wide significance of the Negro question." More specifically, New York, from the piers of lower Manhattan to the Communist organizational headquarters in Harlem, was indeed to remain an active unit in the worldwide struggles for the civil rights of black people.

In early June of 1938, US Embassy representatives in London informed Washington that

> Our friends advise that they have gleaned from information through various communist sources here that the Comintern may be possibly sending funds for the purpose of exploiting the labor disputes which have recently occurred in Trinidad and Jamaica, via the Communist party of America's headquarters in New York City [to the amount of some] $50,000 to $75,000.

Moreover, there was even more direct concern about what was essentially a gathering of half a dozen "prominent Negro Communists" then living in the United States and believed to have been capable of organizing "support here for elements in the West Indies;" namely, "James W. Ford, William L. Patterson, Harry Haywood, Ben D. Amis, Manning Johnson, Richard B. Moore, and Cyril Briggs." The fact that "some of these persons came from the West Indies originally and any one of them is quite capable of directing a supporting movement in this country" only heightened this concern about the role of comrades in New York. Projecting that the aforementioned individuals would more than likely express their support by way of the National Negro Congress, he further surmised that "contacts would presumably be established through members of the National Maritime Union [NMU] acting as couriers" who would, in turn, "probably be members of the defunct Marine Workers Industrial Union who entered the National Maritime Union en masse and some of whom are probably on boats now plying between American and West Indian ports." The political career of Jamaican Communist Ferdinand Smith no doubt corroborates this projection about the NMU.[47]

Though this sum of Comintern funds to the West Indies was apocryphal, the *Daily Worker* corroborated the fact that financial support was being organized well into 1938. Activities of the NNC in Harlem that were in support of Crawford and the struggles under way in Barbados affirm the perception that Communists at the time were a far cry from advocating for workers' rule in colonies like Barbados. The *Daily Worker* began to publish in mid-June of 1938 a series of accounts of W. Algernon Crawford's successful reception in the Harlem circles of the NNC. At one NNC dinner to defend Crawford, who had been "arrested and charged with criminal libel" after the 1937 riots because he had "dared to print the facts as they truly existed," Crawford himself revealed before the supping journalists and supporters that the "standard of living in Barbados is almost primitive." Crawford considered this living not only "primitive" but moreover dehumanizing insofar as "conditions such as these were responsible for the so-called riot last July in which 14 workers were killed, 42 wounded and 500 jailed." "But the people are rising," he assured the crowd and, moreover, "they are demanding land—land which they didn't get after Emancipation."

Crawford's sentiments about the value of human life as revealed in the *Daily Worker* before this crowd of NNC supporters could not have been more diametrically opposed to those that had been expressed in the pages of the *Barbados Advocate*. "Peace" on the Crown's terms meant civil strife for the toiling mass. But such strife in turn only served to further promulgate the burgeoning civil rights movement that brought together Communist and black radical organizations in New York and the Caribbean. This civil rights movement in transnational context was expressing itself in places like Barbados and with the explicit support of Communists and their sympathizers in New York. An announcement was made on June 28, 1938, of a press rally and "united mass meeting" for Crawford which was "under the auspices of the West Indian Defense Committee," but it was actually sponsored by the "St. Ambrose P.E. Church, the New York Council of the National Negro Congress … the Sons and Daughters of Barbados and the International Labor Defense." Among those present were not only open Communists such as Max Yergan but also black radical leaders like A. P. Randolph and the writer Myra Page. Such a conglomerate of forces, it was proclaimed in the *Daily Worker*, would bring about "another mile post in the struggle for civil rights for Negroes in the West Indies."[48]

Ultimately, this Communist Popular Front support was not necessarily considered by US officials to be the most direct radical threat to American empire in the hemisphere. The reason was, as this one embassy official correctly averred after having studied the "principal report delivered by Earl Browder at the recent Tenth Convention of the Communist Party," that

> … the scope of party activities is so general and their ramifications so extensive that their activities on a given question can be carried out by a mass organization over which they exercise control, which on its surface shows little relation with communism.

Indeed, the "general ramifications" of this movement between Harlem and the BWI did not result in a politics that advocated for workers' rule over the means of production and seizing the state apparatus for socialist victory, as this was the era of the Popular Front rather than the Third Period.

TOWARDS THE LATIN CARIBBEAN

The relationship between the Comintern and British West Indies was not as established as that which existed in the Spanish-speaking matrix of forces. Circuits between Puerto Rico, Cuba, Mexico and the CPUSA in New York— particularly in "Spanish Harlem"—were much more closely identifiable as Communist-led during this same period from 1935 to 1939. One obvious reason for this difference is that Communist parties had officially been formed in all of these Latino locales, and Puerto Rico's party most belatedly in 1935, such that Communists based in New York had more direct affiliations with their "brother" parties in these regions to the south. But one more subtle difference, a difference that points toward the persistence of linguistic and cultural barriers that the Communist movement never truly supplanted, is that for the most part, black laborers in the Anglophone Caribbean seem to have been generally more loyal to the anti-fascist struggle that embraced Abyssinia while the Spanish-speaking radicals in Mexico, Cuba and Puerto Rico—and even the CPUSA—were more politically supportive of the anti-fascist movement in defense of Spain.

In spite of this frontal blow to "proletarian internationalism," which was manifested by differential support for anti-fascist movements in Abyssinia and Spain, one common thread that seems to have united radicals across the Caribbean was the mounting political repression that all radical laborers felt, beginning in 1935 at the hands of local government authorities as fascism intensified around the world. Concurrent with the brutal killing of black laborers in St. Kitts at the hands of British troops in 1935 was the mass arrest, deportation and execution of anti-government—and therefore anti-"Yankee"—dissidents in Puerto Rico and Cuba. Hence, Communists in both islands and also those based in New York played an important role in the popular movements against fascism that emerged on both islands and in Mexico, all of which were important Spanish-speaking hubs of activity by this time.

CHAPTER 7

Good Neighbors and Popular Fronts

The complete victory of the Socialist system in all spheres of our national economy is now a fact. This means that exploitation of man by man is abolished … I think that the constitution of the USSR is the only thoroughly democratic constitution in the world.
Joseph Stalin, *New Constitution of the USSR*, 1936

In Germany, they came first for the Communists, And I didn't speak up because I wasn't a Communist; And then they came for the trade unionists, And I didn't speak up because I wasn't a trade unionist; And then they came for the Jews, And I didn't speak up because I wasn't a Jew; And then … they came for me … And by that time there was no one left to speak up.
Pastor Martin Niemoller, no date

This property was opened and developed by private capital. It was not taken from the peons. Archeologists find no trace even of an ancient people having lived in this region.
Washington Daily News, Mexico, 1936

In July of 1939, a supposedly "Authentic Report from Mexico" was released to the US State Department which warned of imminent "Red Spanish Forces on the United States Border." It purported to offer evidence disclosing the fate of some 230,000 Spanish Civil War refugees currently in France for whom Mexican President Cardenas had apparently made arrangements with former Spanish Republican Premier Juan Negrin. The account also indicated that "among those arriving in the near future are 16,000 members of the former 'International Brigade'" and that, moreover, "contrary to the Mexican Constitution, the Cardenas-Negrin agreement provides that the Red soldiers may live in military colonies, under army discipline, and may possess arms." Tensions were apparently exacerbated by the fact that "the Red Spanish exiles talk openly of taking an active part in the forthcoming uprising in the United States."[1]

At the ideological level, this report anticipated the rhetoric of US "border control" aimed at combating foreign threats looming from the Mexican side of the Rio Bravo, setting the stage for ensuing decades of racially prejudiced anti-immigration protocol which would be directed largely against Mexican laborers attempting to enter the US. This "authentic report" reflected a very material fear that US authorities maintained of the Communist Party of Mexico (CPM) and its new "Popular Front" government during a period when "good neighbors" was the established rhetoric of the hemisphere. Moreover, an expectation that pro-Republican Spanish Civil War veterans would factor into the "forthcoming uprising in the United States" reveals that any trepidation over this international convergence of "popular" forces between the US and Mexico was perhaps justified—though a "forthcoming uprising" clearly never happened.

This chapter begins with an examination of the Mexican Communist movement that unfolded in the years from 1935 through 1939 as a point of entry into an analysis of how the Communist International addressed—or failed to address—the "Negro question" in particular and anti-racism more broadly, during the Comintern era of the Popular Front in New York, Mexico, Cuba and Puerto Rico. The consolidation of Communist forces in Mexico, which began after World War I had developed into a larger network of Latin-American parties which culminated in 1939 in the historic gathering of these parties, along with the CPUSA, in Argentina. The CPM appears to have been central to bringing about this international solidarity in the hemisphere. Once Mexico was pinpointed as the haven of anti-fascist veterans, Albert Gomes, a radical anti-colonialist from Trinidad, became directly linked to the Mexican-based network for smuggling these war veterans from Europe and through respective islands in the Caribbean such as Trinidad. But archival research indicates that Mexican Communists and also those in Cuba and Puerto Rico seem to have been nearly silent when tens of thousands of Haitian migrants were killed in the Dominican Republic. Moreover, as black laborers across the British West Indies rose up in fierce rebellion, climaxing in the protests of 1937, the progressive movement in Mexico and Communist hubs in Cuba and Puerto Rico did not make a concerted effort to support these resistance struggles.[2]

Indeed, a new coterie of Communists emerged such as Blas Roca, chairman of the Communist Party of Cuba (CPC), and Vito Marcantonio, a councilman in Spanish Harlem, and their attendant ties to the ILD, NMU and other various organizations. Above and beyond developments in Mexico, what follows is an attempt to shed some light on the ways that Spanish Harlem became a major hub of Communist operation, in certain cases conjoining the "Negro question" with the movements then underway to resist "Wall Street reaction" in Cuba and Puerto Rico. We have seen how the Harlem Riot of 1935 ushered in a new wave of black radicalism involving local New York-based Communists with movements underway in the British West Indies; this rebellion also helped bring together black and Latino radicals in Harlem by way of the All People's Party (APP). In this context, the struggle for Puerto Rican independence was taken up by leading black Communists like James Ford, who were organizing alongside anti-fascist progressives in the APP like Marcantonio.

However, Communist organizations in Spanish Harlem that directly engaged with their counterparts in Cuba and Puerto Rico around the "Negro question" did so in a manner that was fundamentally problematic. A Pan-Latino matrix of forces aligned with the Popular Front in many ways displaced the support for the "Black Belt" in the Caribbean that had been the stronghold of the Comintern only several years beforehand. Black migrant laborers who were in Cuba acting as "Red Guards" during the September 4th Revolution of 1933 were all but excluded—with the tacit consent of Communists in Cuba and the US alike—from Cuba's Popular Front beginning in 1935. The negative ramifications of such political maneuvering are therefore part of this Communist history, but they do not negate the significant headway against racism led by multiracial coalitions of Communists and workers linking Harlem and the Spanish-speaking Caribbean.

MORE FOR LESS: MEXICO'S POPULAR FRONT IN HEMISPHERIC CONTEXT

With President Cardenas at the helm of the campaign, Mexico emerged as the subaltern epicenter of the Popular Front in the hemisphere as early as 1935, much to the dismay of its "good neighbor" to the north. The alliance of labor and political forces in this popular milieu paved the way for an expansion of social and economic benefits for the general population in the country. It also laid the basis for greater political support for anti-fascist popular alliances around the world. Moreover, this mass movement provided support for the rapid acceleration of government confiscation of select German, US and European real estate enterprises that Indian peasants had been heretofore unable to harvest for their own gain. At the international level, the Comintern's more legalistic approach of advocating for reform-based bourgeois rights as a form of class struggle was reflected in the Popular Front policy that was adopted at the Seventh World Congress and elaborated on by the CPM's own leading representative, Hernan Laborde. In this way, the emergence of the Popular Front in Mexico was inextricably linked to the Comintern's shifting political orientation in the wake of fascist aggression.

In his speech, Laborde outlined the present tasks "of the oppressed masses of Mexico, under the leadership of the proletariat and its Communist vanguard." The primary task was "to put once more into motion the bourgeois-democratic revolution which was begun in 1910 and betrayed by its principal bourgeois leaders, and to carry it to its close," in the form of "primarily anti-imperialist tasks." Reflecting on the present state in which "Mexico continues to be a semi-colony, in mining, in oil, in the railroads, in the electrical industry, in agriculture, and in the small and weak light industries." Laborde's political point of reference was the Mexican Revolution of 1910 but the strategy that he was pursuing was to attempt what Bolsheviks had done in Russia during 1917. He proceeded to disclose how a "wrong line" of the CPM during the Third Period had inevitably "prevented us from seeing the favorable conditions" stemming from "the taking of power by President Cardenas to the end of 1934," conditions which were considered conducive now to fostering "a vast people's movement against imperialism." At the Seventh World Congress, Laborde had officially determined that erstwhile class enemies like President Cardenas had become allies in the more immediate global struggle against fascism and imperialist "reaction."[3]

The basis for political unification with President Cardenas—and therefore correcting the official political line of the CPM—was premised upon "one condition: that the Callista politicians and generals be expelled." Although the CPM had reluctantly supported President Calles in 1925 under the guidance of the Workers Party, along with the CPUSA during the Third Period of Comintern strategy the CPM had decried Calles and the Mexican government as "social fascist." Importantly, there were internal factors within the Mexican movement that were mentioned in detail by Laborde at the Seventh World Congress which led up to this adhesion of Mexican Communists to Popular Front policy rather than simply an acceptance of mandates from Moscow. As we will see in the cases of the contemporaneous unfolding of campaigns within Cuba and Puerto Rico, internal developments within these respective islands were also critical to the Popular Front turn that they followed beginning in 1935. This latter observation debunks the myth—as does most of the political upheaval discussed in this historical account—that Communists in the Caribbean were simply responding to a top-down Moscow directive for how to build socialism around the world.

More strikingly in Mexico than anywhere else in the hemisphere, it seems, by 1936 the effects of this Popular Front approach to Communist organizing meant that the CPM had increased its bargaining power within the labor movement, and even in the Mexican government. One "general strike of 50,000 workers of the entire system of the National Railways of Mexico" became effective "at 5p.m. when Mexican and red flags were raised over all stations and offices" to the disapproval of President Cardenas, who had apparently "threatened to declare the strike illegal" in "some quarters." The president's immediately antagonistic response, however, softened into an agreement on behalf of state representatives to meet in the same building—though not at the same table—

with the labor leaders: "General Vasquez, Secretary of Labor, and Eduardo Suarez, Finance Minister, conferred with Luis Rodriguez, private secretary to President Cardenas, while in another room in the National Palace the strike committee held a private session."[4]

But a strategic repositioning of the Mexican Cardenas regime from adversarial to progressive bourgeois also required a similar shift in position to the Roosevelt administration, since Communists had determined that he, too, was a lesser evil than certain reactionary sectors of finance capital in the US. That is, the CPM's optimism toward the Mexican government necessitated, on their account, that the party also strategically realign themselves with respect to President Roosevelt, evincing a more favorable position towards the president of their Yankee neighbor than ever before. In this way, Communists from the US to Puerto Rico and Cuba all began to reconsider the possible benefits of President Roosevelt's "Good Neighbor Policy" as a potential bulwark against fascist aggression and what it considered to be more oppressive factions of Wall Street's empire in the hemisphere. The CPM in fact prodded its US counterpart to participate in the coming Inter-American Peace Conference in December of 1936 in Buenos Aires that was to be chaired under the auspices of President Roosevelt as a means of building solidarity—from "below"—behind his "Good Neighbor Policy."

The *Communist* reported in September that Hernan Laborde, "of our brother Communist Party of Mexico, advanced the idea at the recent Ninth Convention of the Communist Party of the United States," that the "question of the Inter-American Peace Conference should not be separated from the discussion of the present and vital problems of the Communist Party of the United States." According to Laborde's rationale, Roosevelt's apparent "break from the Monroe Doctrine, the traditional policy of the reactionaries clustered around the Republican Party" ought to be considered an aspect of the larger progressive labor movement that was rising in the US. This softened—though Communists at the time considered it more nuanced—approach to Roosevelt was meant to build momentum for the global forces that were aligned against the fascist powers in Germany, Yugoslavia, Finland and Italy, and their proto-fascist counterparts in the US, France and beyond. Gone was the option of taking a "neutral attitude to the rest of the world."[5]

Mexican-based US business enterprise—considered by Communists to represent the more reactionary, fascistic branch of the capitalist class—inevitably suffered from Roosevelt's seeming "break from the Monroe Doctrine." The *Washington Daily News*, a chief media spokesman for hardline finance capitalist aggression, reported a "Revolutionary Agrarian Experiment Now Under Way in Mexico" with "Landowners in Despair" and "Peons" facing "Starvation as Government Seizes Land" and "Introduces Collectivism." What was characterized as a Cardenas-backed "bloodless" revolution (inspired at worst by the Soviet Union and at best by Roosevelt's leniency toward populist regimes) began in Laguna, "the richest irrigated farming district in the republic," in what was "probably, the most advanced social experiment in the Western Hemisphere." But rather than primarily attributing this phenomenon to the Communist movement based in Mexico or Moscow, the paper asserted that "sporadically since 1915 the government has announced land distribution policies" such that in Laguna, "overnight the 3000 hacendados who owned almost all the region have been dispossessed." Still, the role of Soviet Russia was not altogether dismissed as a foreign influence in this collectivization process: "As in Russia, the Mexico collectivization experiment is hard on the kulaks, who in Mexico are called hacendados, or latifundistas. The old plantation aristocracy has been torn up by the roots."[6]

Similar reports of "Mexican Collectivism" in the *Washington Daily News* from November of 1936 also declared that "Anglo-American Lands" had run "afoul" even though disproportionately more British rather than American absentee landlords in Tlahualilo suffered from land confiscation by the government. Tlahualilo, or "12 large haciendas rolled into one," was a "superplantation" in which "Britons own two-thirds of it, and Americans the other third," until the onset of the "expropriation program announced October 6" in which "all but 360 of the 135,000 acres" were seized and distributed "among the peons." This "superplantation"—or "Anglo-American" neo-colony—came fully equipped with "its own cotton seed mill ... police force, post office, company store, airport, golf course, tennis court ... a beautiful mansion for the manager ... its own agricultural experts, educated in the United States."[7]

Certain responses within the American public sphere to the collectivization program on the part of the Mexican government revealed the deep-seeded racism of the American landlord aristocracy in Mexico in the pages of the *Washington Daily News*. One landlord, Mr. Holby, expressed his perception of the confiscations as follows:

> "We believe that our workers received a better deal from us than they could have got anywhere else," said Manager Holby. "We give free medical service. For 30 years we have provided schools for our employees and paid the teachers ... We have always paid better wages than the average ... This property was opened and developed by private capital. It was not taken from the peons. Archeologists find no trace even of an ancient people having lived in this region.[8]

This passage demonstrates the ways in which US finance capitalists such as Mr. Holby backed their "patronage" settlements with racialized epistemologies from second-rate archeologists. Holby's lack of even the most basic historical understanding of Mayan and Aztec—i.e., pre-western—much less ancient Mesoamerican peoples, was revealed in his remark that there was "no trace even of an ancient people" who indeed had spanned the breadth of the region, even if they had not been concentrated in the precise locale of Holby's plantation. Surely British landlords were equally incensed about the abrogation of their prosperous land holdings in Mexico for the benefit of local "peons."

However, any shared Anglo cultural prejudices against the native Indians which arose in the face of their land expropriations did not override the most pressing economic and military needs on the part of US rulers to secure hegemony in the region. The *Washington Daily News* made an implicit commitment to sustaining the Monroe Doctrine with the promise that no British backlash in Tlahualilo would occur "without the United States' consent." Hence, Roosevelt's stated goals of scrapping the Monroe Doctrine for a policy of "good neighbors" could not belie America's sustained policy of racist imperial hegemony in land and factory across Mexico.[9]

The Mexican-based Popular Front therefore helped to position this republic as a Communist epicenter and inspiration for the international and hemispheric struggles directed against US capitalism on a rather tenuous political platform relative to the US ruling elite. US business enterprise and political domination in Mexico was far from overturned, even as progressives softened their line against the Roosevelt administration. At the same time, however, it was in this context of popular alliances that a leading labor representative in the US, John L. Lewis of the Committee for Industrial Organization, acted as a bridge for labor organizing between the United States and Mexico in 1937, fundamentally challenging the long tradition of racial segregation and jingoism in US-based labor union activity. Ultimately, Communists in the US found themselves willingly taking more leadership from their comrades in Mexico than they had been willing to consider a decade beforehand.[10]

This was the political context in which the CPM announced that the Mexican Republic under President Cardenas was on a "revolutionary path" in celebration of the twentieth anniversary of the 1917 October Revolution in Russia. Such an amalgamation of forces between the US and Mexico was no minor consideration for State Department officials, even if the solidarity accompanied a concession to President Roosevelt's policy of "good neighbors" and reframing of a Mexican president as now on the road to revolution. This purported "revolutionary path" not withstanding, none of the progressive change in Mexico seems to have resulted in response to the systemic slaughter of Haitians which had occurred only hundreds of miles away across the Gulf of Mexico that same year.[11]

By 1939, Communists were of the general consensus that Mexico ranked among the "most progressive" Popular Front governments in the hemisphere. The New Year was met with joint support from President Cardenas and also Vincent Lombardo of the Mexican Confederation of Labor—and presumably including the CPM—for some 3,600 Indians in the Union of Chamula

Day-Laborers and Peasants who had declared war against the "German coffee plantations in Chiapas state." Clearly this was seen as a blow to Nazi financial expansion in the hemisphere, and it was led, as had been so many militant movements in Mexico, by the peasants, who in this case were based in Chiapas. And in spite of the CPM's apparent lack of support for a movement to avenge the deaths of those Haitian migrants slaughtered in 1937, Haitian Communist Jacques Roumain decided to reside in Mexico in the later years of his life indicating that there was some basis for political affinity between this exiled Haitian Communist and the Mexican left. But the bulk of Mexico's Popular Front energy in the hemisphere undeniably focused on sections of the Spanish-speaking population that were not considerably represented by Afro-Latin laborers. Rather, it was through Communist Party developments in Spanish Harlem, Cuba and Puerto Rico where the convergence of Communist organization and anti-racist militancy illuminated most poignantly the strengths and weaknesses of the Popular Front.[12]

THE COMMUNIST PARTY OF CUBA AND THE "NEGRO QUESTION": THE POPULAR FRONT'S 50 PERCENT SETBACK

We remind you that the Cuban revolution depends more than that of any other country, on the support of the international proletariat, and we want to emphasize this requirement of the brother Parties. Cuba is a small country; but its revolution draws the attention of millions of the exploited of Latin America, who will greet it as their revolution, as an emancipating revolution from the fierce yoke of Yankee imperialism. The Cuban revolution has repercussions, not only in South and Caribbean America, but also has great influence on the Negroes in the United States, who watch it with great love. We are helping in the revolutionization of the masses of a whole continent; the Cuban revolution must be considered as a part of the international proletarian revolution, as a part of the struggle for Soviets throughout the whole world.
Blas Roca, Seventh World Congress of the Communist International, 1935

While Mexican Communists were supping with the president at the National Palace in 1936, progressives in Cuba of myriad stripes were facing considerable hardship under the repressive political regime of President Mendieta, which was fortified by the military dictatorship of General Fulgencio Batista. Even though the CPM was in a much less antagonistic position relative to the Cardenas regime than the CPC was to the Mendieta-Batista regime in 1935, by 1939 Communists in both locales were aggressively propagating the leadership of their respective governments. In short, by 1939, Cuban Communists and those in the US, Mexico and Puerto Rico were openly endorsing the leadership of General-turned-President Batista—the same Batista who only several years beforehand had orchestrated the deaths of radicals who sought to overturn his military dictatorship in the aftermath of the September 4th Revolution. Cuba was a small island with massive hemispheric weight in terms of militant challenges to US imperial power, but the Communist movement undoubtedly lost muscle and gained body mass when it sublimated the class-warfare stance to attain legal status.

Weeks after a general strike of laborers, professionals and peasants in March of 1935, Antonio Guiteras, a young Cuban revolutionary nationalist who was aligned with the exiled leader Grau San Martin, was assassinated by Batista's military. Hundreds of labor leaders who were implicated in organizing the strike had been jailed and some even disappeared, likely meeting a fate similar to that of Guiteras. In this sense, the adoption of a Popular Front policy on the part of the CPC was probably regarded by Communists on the island as a welcome concession to bourgeois democracy, given the months and even years of government-sponsored violence directed against all radicals and especially Communists.

In another sense, the adoption of Popular Front policy in Cuba resulted in an unwelcome backlash against black laborers on the island, foreign and domestic alike—therefore undermining much of the Communist base among laborers and peasants in the "Black Belt" of Oriente up through the March 1935 general strike, when this workers' movement was at a peak. As we have seen, deportation of Jamaican and Haitian migrant laborers that had already begun in the early 1930s had become even more intense in the context of Mendieta's political repression. But by mid-1935, Communists in Cuba had chosen to align themselves with Grau San Martin who supported a "status quo" law that demarcated "50 percent" of all jobs for strictly Cuban laborers, hence forcing black migrant laborers into a status of unemployment and almost certain deportation. Inevitably, Communists in Cuba who sought to form popular alliances with the Grau sector of anti-government forces were forced to succumb to nativist racism in Cuba that was directed in the main against black foreign laborers. In the face of this challenge, they initially demurred but eventually conceded. How did the Communists agree to not only collude with Grau San Martin and his racist 50 percent law, but also finally come to endorse Batista by 1939, when in 1934 they were attempting to mobilize workers against both?

Transition from General Strike to Popular Front, March–August 1935

The March 1935 general strike of the workers on the island, occurring months before the Comintern transitioned into the Popular Front period, was a masterpiece in coordination and a testament to the blood, sweat and tears of the class uprisings that had occurred since the post-WWI period. It demonstrated the relative strength and determination of an emboldened working class. Even more specifically, this general strike represented the final culmination of Cuban Communist activity as open advocates of a Soviet proletarian world order opposed to all elements of the capitalist class, still reflecting Third Period strategy. Ultimately, however, in terms of seizing state power in the fight against Wall St. imperialism and the native bourgeoisie and political leaders, the goal was lost. The working class was not solidly aligned behind the Communists by 1935, though the potential and energy had not been realized as yet. In part, Communists had not developed the capacity or strength to seize power because the military was under proto-fascist control and would not be won to their cause. So in the aftermath of their being forced back underground in the strike's suppression, Communists remained all the more antagonistic toward the Mendieta-Batista regime and instead sought the refuge of "lesser evil" elites such as Grau San Martin. Indeed, the general strike was the final hurrah of the working-class-oriented Third Period strategy for the international conglomerate of Comintern organizations that was then concentrated in Cuba.

An especially illuminating example of Cuban oil workers during the last days of the March 1935 general strike demonstrates the local and hemispheric network of working-class support just as the CPUSA, CPC and CPM began to soften their class against class and anti-racist praxis. The *Daily Worker*'s reportage of the International Federation of Petroleum Workers in Cuba was meant to rally the laborers in the US and Mexico in support of their class counterparts in Cuba precisely because oil was already considered the strategic lifeblood of capitalist industry and military power, especially that of the United States. Communist agitators and labor leaders were particularly anxious to cut this lifeline and therefore weaken American empire across the entire region.

Since the post-WWI period, radicalized oil workers had acted as an important bulwark to British and US economic and social control in the hemisphere. The support for Cuban petroleum workers from the "Regional Proletarian Defense Committee for a United Front of Workers and Peasants" in Oaxaca, Mexico, in September of 1935 was a direct outgrowth of this Cuban oil workers' strike during the general strike of March 1935. Moreover, the oil workers of Trinidad in 1937 who aggressively put forward direct action methods of protest in San Fernando were also part of this inter-Caribbean oil workers movement. But in Cuba as opposed to in Trinidad, Communists had made "further strides because of their activities in the general strike." These "strides" were primarily ideological insofar as widespread sentiment within the Cuban labor movement was that "politicians cannot solve our problems." Moreover, solidarity in the US was evident when radicals began to "mobilize rapidly a movement of protest through cables and air-mail letters" on their behalf. Similar support from US counterparts in the *Daily Worker* was nowhere near as visible when Trinidadian oil workers of 1937 rose up in retaliation against local authorities and foreign oil enterprises on the island. But an important precedent was set for proletarian internationalism by the petroleum workers in Cuba during the March 1935 strike with the support of local and transnational networks, particularly the CPUSA. Sadly, this class solidarity would be redirected in the months to come.[13]

In spite of the intense class struggle being led by these Cuban oil workers, ties between the CPUSA and CPC were insufficient for supporting such intense militancy. Fiduciary negligence on the part of the CPUSA, an evidently recurring problem throughout the past decade, was a key issue in CPC-CPUSA relations at the beginning of 1935, thus placing political focus on the most pragmatic of concerns. Letters from the CPC to the CPUSA, some of which were published as open letters in the *Daily Worker* from Blas Roca to Earl Browder, indicated that the Cubans had yet to receive the money or propaganda necessary to carry out work in Cuba. The outcome, warned Roca, would be that Cubans would shut down their newspaper circulation, causing grave consequences for their political work on the island, just as they were preparing for the March general strike.[14]

Leading up to the Seventh World Congress, there were vastly different national conditions in which the respective parties were operating. Cuban radicals were being shot and disappeared, while US counterparts were cabling telegrams and writing articles in the *Daily Worker* in their defense. In spite of this disproportionate political repression, reportage of events like the oil workers' strike in the *Daily Worker* set off a series of important solidarity endeavors on the part of the US-based ILD and AIL to form joint actions with both the CPC and CPM in defense of the strikers, particularly in the "Black Belt" of Oriente. For example, on March 12, the *Daily Worker* printed an article from the CPC calling upon the CPUSA to support the Cuban strike which was apparently already in motion. Only a day later, headlines followed up with a report that strike leaders had been killed. In this context, the CPUSA declared "All out to 55 Wall Street! ... Hands off Cuba! Join the march from there to the Cuban Consulate at 17 Battery place." According to Carlos Hevia of the NCCL who had recently "just fled from Cuba to the United States," not only had "more than 200 [strikers] already been killed" but also "the number of strike leaders whose dead bodies [had] been found in the streets of Havana with bullets in their back" had reached "officially to fourteen." After striking government workers "closed down all business and commercial activity throughout the island," President Mendieta apparently saw to it that "prison terms were prescribed for government employees" who persisted to strike. And the *Daily Worker* reported these events in detail.[15]

It was in this fierce phase of the general strike that the CPC then released in the pages of the *Daily Worker* on March 14 its official manifesto, declaring that the "toiling Cuban people" must form a "united front against Wall Street imperialism and Mendieta death squads." Exposing the "counter-revolutionary"

Mendieta regime as having taken the "path predicted by the Communist Party," the manifesto observed the rapid "spreading" and leadership within "the student movement" to include "teachers [and] even the children of the primary schools." Moreover the manifesto celebrated the "peasants of Realengo 18 and more recently the peasants of Realengo 3" who had continued their land confiscations within the "Black Belt" of Oriente, where "the whole population [was] rising up against the criminal abandonment of the most elementary matters of hygiene." Notable is the fact that the "whole population" that delineated the contours of this united front during the March strike included solely the cross-section of laboring "toilers" on the island. At the leadership helm were the students and NCCL strikers of Havana and peasants of Realengo 18 and Realengo 3 in Oriente. Moreover, the Autenticos were lambasted along with their exiled leader, "Grau, who from Miami declared 'that he does not know what to do.'" Again, the Popular Front campaign of unity with Grau and others had not yet come to fruition.[16]

The CPC strike manifesto then went on to herald the "masses" who knew "that the only real solution of the situation … can come only if they overthrow the present dictatorship." In its stead was advocated a "truly revolutionary, anti-imperialist and popular government," which would uphold the rights to

> … nationalization of all wealth in the hands of foreign enterprises; take possession without compensation of all land; working day of eight hours; complete political, social and economic equality for all women; recognition of the right to self-determination of the Negroe [*sic*] nationality of Oriente.

Several months before the May 1935 riots in the epicenter of Harlem in which the CPUSA office was raided and members harassed, the threat of land confiscation in Cuba's "Black Belt" was in rapid acceleration. But this program derived from the March events would be negated in the coming months with obviously grave consequences for the Red-Black alliances then being forged in Cuba.[17]

In August of 1935, a surveillance report on "Communist Leadership in Cuba" was released to the State Department, noting a series of "tactical moves" that were reflected in an article entitled "For a United National Front in Cuba," published in the *Communist International*, official literary organ of the Comintern. Notable was the fact that "the slogan for confiscation of all 'land belonging to Cuban landed proprietors' [had] been amended and now demands the confiscation of land 'owned by foreign companies and by national traitors.'" The *Communist International* of July 20, 1935 went on to articulate the rationale for the Cuban United Front and its adhesion to the Comintern as being associated with "overcoming its left-wing neglect of tasks connected with the struggle for the creation of a united front." This "united front" was characterized chiefly by the fact that the CPC according to Blas Roca had "reconsidered its attitudes toward the national reformist party of Grau San Martin which it considered to be a counterrevolutionary party in process of fascization," and which the Seventh World Congress had declared to be "an entirely unfounded idea." Finally, the conditions leading up to the Cuban adhesion to the Popular Front were compounded by "the shooting of Antonio Guiteras, the leader of 'Young Cuba' by the reactionary government," which itself warranted the rapid popular mobilization of myriad organizations in the political terrain of the island.[18]

The CPC's new stance at the Seventh World Congress was a clear shift from the party's focus during the March general strike which challenged both native and Yankee rulers while upholding the independent fight of the workers and "self determination" of the black majority in Oriente. This decision was seen by Cuban Communists as an opportunity rather than a retreat, a correction of its "isolationist" weaknesses that left it especially vulnerable after the "defeat of the general strike" in March of 1935.[19]

But the Popular Front promulgated national unity in Cuba at the precise moment in 1935 when black laborers in Cuba—foreign and domestic alike— were facing the harshest aspects of the "new measures for greater enslavement and oppression of Cuba"; Blas Roca was very dismissive about the place of Cuba's "Negro population" in the popular campaign. He alluded to the fact that with the onset of the Seventh World Congress, "Such slogans as the self-determination of the Negro nation and the confiscation of the lands of the large estates have been withdrawn as conditions of the united front." These "conditions of the united front" would, on this account, position Communists for "actual leadership of millions toward our objectives." Inevitably these supposed millions precluded a substantial portion of the black laborers on the island.[20]

The 50 Percent Retreat

One must consider how this Cuban intervention in the Popular Front might have been interpreted by black migrant laborers on the island who did not self identify as Cuban. The Jamaican periodical *Plain Talk*, discussed in the previous chapter, had surely documented the plight of migrant Jamaicans in Cuba, and the fact that this paper did not make a point of incorporating the voices of Cuban laborers, much less Communists, suggests that these migrant laborers were considerably alienated from the mainstream Cuban popular movement then under way and vice versa. What implications would a "Cuba for Cubans" movement bear in terms of inter-Caribbean labor solidarity—or even race unity for that matter—if plight of the Cuban was being placed on a higher level of political urgency than the foreign African by the radicals themselves?

Roca acknowledged that "some new questions are cropping up now," particularly the "law of 50 per cent natives on every job, one of the cornerstones of the Grau policy." And it was precisely in Roca's elaboration of this "new question" raised by the 50 percent law that the forces of Communism and black workers clashed most sharply converged most sharply in relationship to the Cuban united front:

> This problem will be raised before the Party for the purpose of breaking the united front. I think that our Party must fight against such proposals and struggle against the inclusion of such a slogan in the united front, fighting at the same time all discriminations against native workers; but as a last resort, we can accept the maintenance of the Grau law "status quo," which, because of its great popularity, even the Mendieta government has not dared to revoke completely ... Our party must fight for the establishment of this government, must be ready to support it and to participate in it, on the basis of the fulfillment of the demand of the united front.[21]

Hence the "last resort" was to "accept the maintenance of the Grau law 'status quo'" because of its "great popularity" across the political spectrum. Nationalism was objectively concession to racism. Such terms of agreement were considered acceptable even though they were premised upon obviously prejudiced and jingoist arguments that functioned to pit "native" against "foreign" laborers in the struggle against racial discrimination.

The CPUSA and the Popular Front in Cuban Context

While the historic role of black and white cross-border solidarity was being undercut in the name of a national unity against Mendieta-Batista reaction, what was considered the necessary mobilization of a broader spectrum of the population was at once more narrow: it was broader in cross-class terms, but more narrow in inter-Caribbean unity from below. The responsibilities placed upon the CPUSA were becoming much more central to the survival of the CPC and the "tasks" of the CPUSA in facilitating this revolutionary process were quite clear. The "last question" on the table, Roca noted, was to outline the "tasks of the Parties of the 'mother' countries with respect to the revolutionary movement in their colonies and semi-colonies." Such were the terms upon which the CPUSA was called to support its political progeny in the semi-colonies, namely in Cuba. Ceding that they had "advanced much," Blas Roca characterized the situation as "far from reaching the point where our Parties of the imperialist countries understand in practice the whole importance of the national liberation movement."[22]

Roca's discussion of this "colonial question," particularly in terms of the specific dynamics of the US-Cuban relationship, reveals the complex interplay between language and political organization in the making of Communist history in this period. He acknowledged that their "great brother Party of the United States has taken the task of the defense of the Cuban revolution as one of its major tasks" and he provided evidence from a "tour by a Cuban comrade throughout the country of mass meeting and assemblies," especially in San Francisco, supporting the Cuban struggles beginning with the viciously crushed general strike in March. Roca's recognition of the CPUSA as a "brother" party certainly signaled toward progressive changes in the language of the Comintern. By 1935, Communists—particularly in Cuba—were now attending these international meetings and making demands themselves on the CPUSA.

The CPUSA had also begun to more directly acknowledge the leadership of Mexican Communists such as Hernan Laborde when he called upon it to reconsider its wholesale dismissal of Roosevelt's "Good Neighbor Policy." In form, the language that was publically being used to generate this political struggle was moving in the direction of more evenly proportioned respect rather than unilateral guidance from North to South. But in essence, the political content of the struggle being waged by Caribbean Communists with their US counterparts was moving in the direction of more class-collaborationist, popular methods for organizing the Comintern and, objectively, a retreat from the anti-racist commitments of yesteryear.[23]

But Roca stated that he was "not yet in a position to declare that this support" was "satisfactory in the aspect of the mobilization of large masses of American toilers in support of the Cuban revolution." In other words, the "popular" movement in defense of Cuba was only powerful if indeed "large masses of American toilers" could show their active engagement and support. Subsequent discussion of the CPUSA reveals that a larger cross-section of the US population than simply the "toilers" would indeed be drawn into this movement. But the day-to-day organizational work of this movement remained to be carried out by the same key organizations and people, primarily in the form of coverage in the *Daily Worker*, which makes one consider whether the qualitative political commitment to advocating for workers' power was worth sacrificing in order to guarantee the quantitative advantage that large numbers of more middle-class, liberal supporters seemed to demonstrate.[24]

CPUSA leaders under the auspices of both the AIL and the ILD were very instrumental in helping to prevent the imminent execution of striking schoolteacher and radical figure Manuel Fonseca in April of 1935. Fully indicative of the political prisoners' campaigns of this period, the Comintern sought to win the first Cuban civil case that was brought up on court martial, denouncing as "terrorist" the Mendieta government which sought to execute Fonseca. News of Fonseca's pending execution hit the pages of the *Daily Worker* in the early days of April, reporting that Fonseca was scheduled to be "shot to death by the firing squad on Saturday morning" for the "crime" of "participation in the general strike." But due to the "Deputations, cablegrams and telegrams" that "flooded" the Cuban government, "On Saturday morning Fonseca did not die!" The work of "only a handful" in New York who "spent the whole day frantically telephoning, rushing about, mobilizing organizations and individuals to protest" alongside "other groups internationally" was considered the reason that they were "able to free Fonseca." To be sure, the memory of such local figures as Antonio Mella compounded by the contemporary cases of Mooney and the Scottsboro Boys was the context that brought the ILD in the US directly into the fold.[25]

According to Lucille Perry in the "Colonial Department" of the ILD in the US, the work of actively trying to build a united front in Cuba with the non-Comintern affiliated socialists began in part with the efforts of the Cuban ILD. Reporting on the activities of the ILD in Cuba since the March general strike and jailing of Fonseca, Perry noted that the CPC had directly reached out to the Cuban Revolutionary Party and Young Cuba though to little avail. Still on "March 30, street demonstrations organized by the Cuban ILD took place in several parts of the island against the threatened execution of Manuel Fonseca, school teacher." In response, from the "center for political refugees" in Miami came word that "Ex-President Grau San Martin head of the Cuban Revolutionary Party (Autenticos) and Antonio Guiteras, leader of Young Cuba, left wing of the Grau group" had "openly denounced" the "military dictatorship, and predicts trouble ahead in the near future." That "trouble" in the "near future" portended the death of Guiteras himself in the coming weeks.[26]

Cuban radicals were arguably operating under a proto-fascist political regime headed by the Mendieta-Batista military apparatus. This was a real historical condition with which all progressive forces had to grapple. The basic conclusion of NCCL leader Cesar Vilar was that the Mendieta government had arisen from the general strike overwhelmingly "victorious" while the people had been crushed. Even in the "blackest days of Machado," recalled Vilar, "the Railway Brotherhood Union of Workers and Employees of the Havana Electric Union of Water, Gas and Electric Workers" had been allowed to exist. But in the aftermath of this March general strike, the "prisons, military quarters, and the notorious prison on the Isla of Pines [were] filled with more than 5,000 arrested workers." Months before the CPUSA made overtures toward the larger US labor movement then led by the AFL, Cesar Vilar wrote an open letter to AFL leaders which was published in the *Daily Worker*, calling upon the AFL to

> ... start a mass campaign, demanding that the Cuban government give freedom to the thousands of political prisoners, the legalization of our unions, the right of free assembly, press and speech, as well as the right to strike ... [and] the abolition of the Court Martial and Emergency Courts.

By seeking to make alliances with the erstwhile vilified AFL, Cuban radicals like Vilar were indeed paving the way for the more popular approach to Communist praxis that would be codified months later.[27]

Vilar had therefore established himself as a leading force in the labor movement between Cuba and the US at a very timely point. In this open letter from Vilar to the AFL, he acknowledged that the AFL had "in its ranks millions of workers" and was a "force capable of helping our masses in their struggle against the military dictatorship and American imperialism." Vilar's days of free speech and unfettered leadership were numbered, but, if only briefly, the CPUSA had helped to build a support network in the form of a united front for the Cuban general strikers that triggered the greater collusion of Cuban and US labor movement forces under the auspices of an emergent Popular Front spanning this entire region.[28]

This movement was met with ever-mounting resistance from the Mendieta government. Manuel Fonseca's release from prison was a temporary victory for the radicals; indeed, his release might have even precipitated the May 1935 shooting death of Antonio Guiteras, leader of "Young Cuba." The assassination of Guiteras became the final decisive factor in encouraging the CPC toward open alliance with Grau San Martin, precisely on the basis of their common-held opposition to the present Cuban political regime. Antonio Guiteras, the 29-year-old leader of the "'Joven Cuba' Party," had been "termed Cuba's 'Public Enemy No.1'" and assassinated, "on Monday evening, May 7th, 1935," according to a "G-2 Report on the Death of Cuban Radical Leader." Plainly, Gimperling's account lays bare the naked defense for Cuba's regime of political and economic repression that American officials had long upheld in their "neighborly" relations with this republic. Gimperling's ultimate conclusion that "the death of Guiteras and the breaking up of his band of gangsters will go far towards purging Cuba of organized terrorism, at least for the present" was a welcome attack from the perspective of US interests in Cuba:

> Antonio Guiteras, twenty nine year old radical, was one of the leaders of the revolution against Machado. It was he who is said to have personally led the attack against the Rural Guard Cuartel in San Luis, Oriente, in May 1933. Numerous reports have been forwarded by this office on this man and little needs be added. He was known to have been not only a narcotic addict, but a smuggler and purveyor of narcotics, and it is known that while he was a pharmacist in Santiago de Cuba several years ago, he was responsible for a number of young men and boys of that town, of the wealthier families, acquiring the drug habit, and he supplied them with illicit drugs at exorbitant prices ....[29]

Allegations against Guiteras went on to include the "kidnapping of Falla Boent (for which a ransom of $300,000 was paid), the robbery of the Municipal Treasury of Havana, [and] several bank robberies and a number of extortions" which were "believed to have been planned by Guiteras and carried out by his large following of gangsters." Clearly, US authorities did not hold Guiteras in high regard.

With figures such as Guiteras being assassinated, it became the opinion of leading CPC members that US radical support for the Cuban popular revolution was not sufficient. Blas Roca informed the CPUSA on May 27, 1935, by way of an open letter in the *Daily Worker*, that "the American comrades have not shown sufficient force in their activities for the Cuban revolution." While ceding that the "*Daily Worker* has given more space and importance to the news of the revolutionary movement in Cuba" in addition to the "Politburo's" use of "influence and leadership in organizations of workers, intellectuals, liberals and anti-imperialists," Roca was not convinced that this was adequate for the degree of repression being faced in Cuba at the time. Roca declared that the "metropolis" was in dereliction of duty given its "insufficient" support for "the national liberation movements in the countries, subject to the bloody boot of imperialism." Moreover, he warned that this hemispheric apparatus that was currently headquartered in New York might lose a "formidable ally" of the "Proletarian Revolution in the United States."[30]

Communist "Liberals" Deported from Cuba

What is retrospectively evident is that the CPUSA, then based in New York, was facing its own conditions of political repression that, while not as severe as those in Cuba, were significant nonetheless. Locals in New York were recovering from a recent police raid of the Harlem-based CPUSA headquarters earlier in May. Still, Earl Browder appears to have anticipated the request from Roca for more solid organizational work in defense of the Cuban movement. Days before Roca's statement had been published, Browder released his own announcement of a united front delegation that was currently making plans to head to Cuba and was soliciting elections from "local trade unions and anti-imperialist organizations." He called upon interested parties to "Prepare, now and immediately a delegation that will go to Cuba whose mission shall be to investigate the conditions of the toiling people, the raging terror, and to report back to the American people." The history of this CPUSA-led delegation sheds some light on the long history of the "*venceremos*" brigades of the 1960s sponsored by radicals in the New Left who sought to express their solidarity with Castro's budding socialist regime.[31]

During 1935, when this delegation or "commission" as it was officially called was in formation, it was the first attempt for CPUSA leaders to test out key aspects of their emerging Popular Front program of action at the very moment when the Seventh World Congress was in session. Composed of a cross-section of US citizens, ranging from professionals to religious figures to CPUSA-affiliated reps from "Spanish Harlem" along with ILD and ALWF members, the demographic shift toward an enlarged base of professionals and intellectuals that was quite literally "on board" for the struggle also reflected similar increases in the representation of professionals and government workers in Cuba's March general strike. Hence, this US delegation's intervention into Cuban radical affairs was at once an outgrowth of, but sharp break from, the delegations during the Third Period led by the CPUSA that sought to bring a largely proletarian base of support to Cuban labor struggles. In the process of this expansion toward a more popular movement, an important anti-racist political focus of the ILD, LSNR and TUUL in the years from 1930 to 1934 was lost. For example, the demand to free the Scottsboro Boys was replaced by a demand for a "free constituent assembly."

The other distinction in this 1935 delegation—in fact inseparable from the wider demographic representation to include artists, intellectuals and non-Communist party members—was that Communists were now pursuing class struggle on much more legalistic grounds and even denying that the delegation was Communist-led, once they were banned from the island and deported back to the US. The open and fierce resistance upon their arrival in Cuba at the hands of an expanded and more centralized military apparatus under the Mendieta-Batista regime in Cuba had become a new condition, indeed a proto-fascist condition, and Communists were forging broader alliances on a political basis that placed revolution and workers' power on the back burner. Delegates from the deported commission who recounted this incident in the pages of the *International Press Correspondence* claimed that the "military dictatorship in Cuba deported our Commission to investigate Social and Labour conditions, composed of 15 persons, representing 20 organizations, papers and magazines," even though these delegates were held "without questioning, without inquiry into our purpose, without any explanation." Charging that the current Mendieta-Batista regime had "withheld recognition from the Grau Government because it passed the eight-hour day," and that the delegation had faced "vague and locally unsubstantiated charges of possession of 'Communistic' documents," *Inprecorr* was now denying that the commission was Communist-led.

In a legalistic approach that was true to form for the Popular Front period, they argued for their right to visit the island on the grounds that the "members of our Commission [were] delegated by the League of American Writers, the Anti-Imperialist League, the American League Against War and Fascism, the International Labour Defence, the National Students' League, the International Workers' Order." Claiming to represent the "honest anti-imperialist sentiments of the masses of the American people," the article reported that the delegation's "very presence in Cuba heartened and strengthened the rapidly growing united front of all anti-imperialist forces in Cuba." That the adjective "honest" was affixed to the "anti-imperialist sentiments" of these delegates demonstrates how Communists were attempting to widen the scope of support for their movement by softening the affective devices used to characterize the aims and intentions of the Comintern. Ultimately, the Commission was barred from the island, local Cuban supporters of the delegation were jailed, and the US representatives were sent home, all under Batista's direct—and Caffrey's tacit—approval. Such acts of aggression on the part of Batista toward the US radicals makes it all the more striking that only four years later, in 1939, US Communist delegates to Cuba would be greeting President Batista literally with open arms.[32]

One thing was for certain: the pro-Roosevelt wing of the bourgeoisie whose perspectives were prominent in the *New York Times* embraced this shift in Comintern approach, characterizing the delegation in a headline as a "U.S. Liberal Group Seized in Havana" with "Fifteen members of a commission of American liberals, including Clifford Odets, playwright" who were reported to have been "arrested here last night when they arrived on the liner Oriente to investigate Cuban labor and social conditions."[33]

The political irony associated with a purported American "Liberal" group arriving on a liner named *Oriente* to "investigate labor and social conditions" seems to have eluded this embedded reporter. Still, the reporter did offer an interesting counter-narrative to that of the Communist presses, one that was based on the perspective of US Ambassador to Cuba, Jefferson Caffery, who "said that he had received no information regarding the status of their mission" nor any "appeal for aid from the Americans" of the delegation. On Caffery's account, "when the Oriente of the New York and Cuba Mail Steamship Company arrived here last night secret service operatives and policemen boarded the liner and first informed the commission ... that its members could not disembark" simply as a preventive measure in case this "liberal" group was not perhaps so friendly, especially considering the fact that their "expected" welcoming committee was believed to have been Communist. Traditionally, US officials had not been very receptive of such enterprises.[34]

From Caffrey's perspective, therefore, it was highly advisable when "200 policemen, soldiers, and marines surrounded the docks to prevent an expected demonstration by local Communist and other radical organizations" even though "the demonstration failed to materialize." Whatever form this "advice" took, the fact that American "secret service operatives" and Cuban "policemen, soldiers, and marines" had amassed in the hundreds and collectively descended on both delegations played no small part in the protest's "failure to materialize." But hardly inexperienced with the problem of political repression at the hands of US authorities, the radicals leading the US delegation mounted a counter-attack though it was articulated in less hostile terms than had been characteristic of Communists in prior years.

The CPUSA had shifted its trope to one of collective "responsibility" in the name of the "American public" for a national project which became increasingly intermingled with its own agenda. Conrad Komorowski, "representing the American League Against Imperialism, in the name of the commission," reported to the *New York Times* that "We came as a delegation of American citizens who feel a responsibility for the actions of the American Government," and moreover as representatives of the "American public" who "came with the frankest good-will." Such language of the "American public" and "citizens" whose "responsibility" it was to foster the "good-will" of the nation was clearly a political jab at the implicitly negative "actions of the American government," but it is also strangely reminiscent of the very language used at that time by the ruling elite to codify its own predominant status in relationship to the republics and nations of the Western Hemisphere, i.e. President Roosevelt's "Good Neighbor Policy." Once Komorowski went on to assert that "[t]hrough us the people of the United States extend their greetings to the Cuban people in the hope that they will obtain their complete freedom," it had become evident that, at least in rhetorical terms, the CPUSA was positioning itself to be presented as a progressive alternative to the State Department for advising on US foreign relations.[35]

This Popular Front coalition of delegates was hardly in favor of seizing state power as the Bolsheviks had done in 1917. In a follow-up by the *New York Times*, Clifford Odets, prominent American actor, playwright and fellow traveler of the CPUSA, demanded the right to a "new inquiry" into the circumstances surrounding the deportation of the delegates back to the US. A minor though not unimportant figure emerged in this political circuit: Reverend Herman F. Reissig, the "pastor of Kings Highway Congregational Church in Brooklyn, who represented the American League Against War and Fascism" in the banned delegation. Popular unity in Reissig's view meant that while "'the forces must stand guard against the inroads of fascism which threaten Cuba as well as the United States,'" it was also compulsory that "'we who are not Communists have got to stop being afraid of being called Communists" since "[w]hat is going on in Cuba today ... is an omen of what will go on in this country tomorrow if we don't take means to stop it.'"[36] How strangely did this obscure Brooklyn pastor's words portend the suffering that the Nazi-turned-anti-fascist German pastor, Martin Niemoller, expressed in his most widely attested poem to the atrocities of Nazi Germany. While Pastor H. F. Reissig was speaking specifically about the relationship between the "50 jailed protesters" under Communist leadership in Cuba and his own frustrated efforts as a member of the ALWF in Brooklyn, he was reflecting the general manner in which fascist aggression was mounting unevenly around the world and, in turn, forcing the hand of those fellow travelers of Communism who were sympathetic but wary of joining the party.[37]

It was not only among religious organizers for the ALWF in Brooklyn where CPUSA-led support in New York for the commission signaled toward an expansion of interest in the Latin Caribbean. Laborers in Harlem apparently pledged to show support for a strike in defense of this delegation's right to entry; in particular, another little-known though potentially important historical figure, Jose Santiago, who was described by the *New York Times* as having represented "several Latin-American clubs" from New York, was among the delegates. Santiago was also at this time the East Harlem sub-district representative of the CPUSA. A flyer which announced an event at the New Star Casino to "protest the arrest of 50 Cuban workers who came to greet the delegation" described Santiago as representing the "Puerto Rican Circle" alongside a representative from Cuba's NCCL with Clifford Odets, author of the play *Waiting for Lefty*. Surely this flyer did not generate a crowd of thousands, and research into meetings that were then held at the New Star Casino at 107th and Park Ave likely would not turn out much evidence that a full house turned out to greet the delegation.[38]

Still the CPUSA had established a network of mini-epicenters of Caribbean-related organization all across New York, from Brooklyn's churches to community organizations in Spanish Harlem. The CPUSA's history in Brooklyn churches dated back to the Haitian gatherings at local AME (African Methodist Episcopal) Zion churches under the ANLC, in support of the "Haitian revolution" of 1929. Spanish Harlem, considered a CPUSA sub-district, had emerged by 1935 as the most recent center of Red activity in support of the popular movements in both Cuba and Puerto Rico which were directed against "Wall Street finance capital."

But this transnational Red-led solidarity remained relatively weak, since Batista's military stronghold over the civilian population was complete by 1936. Surely the fates of the fifty arrested Cuban protesters who supported the US delegation were not significantly altered by this symbolic act of unity held at the New Star Casino in New York. The realities associated with Batista's expanding military apparatus in Cuba were nothing to gamble on. Cuban and US Communists alike began to hedge their bets on increasingly less Red allies, eventually to include Batista himself. By May of 1936, the *Daily Worker* was openly supporting Democratic members of the Cuban House of Representatives such as Antonio Bravo Acosta because he challenged the military's right to prohibit the civil liberties of the Cuban "civilian" population.

Batista's Reactionary Redemption

Rather than cowering before the military regime, the CPC demanded in 1936 a reinvigoration of the September 4th movement begun in 1933 under Grau. An article in the *International Press Correspondence* offered a retrospective analysis of the dangers and opportunities which had to that point emerged since the joint military and civilian movement of 1933:

> The army headquarters under Caffrey's influence have done their utmost to break down the strong bonds of solidarity uniting the people and the army in August-September 1933. They have aimed at converting the Cuban army, which has risen out of the people and is paid by the people, into the strongest pillar of reaction, of the foreign exploiters, of all the enemies of the people. In order to attain this object, they have applied alternate methods of mildness, privilege, and flattery to the masses and the whole army on the one hand, and on the other hand the utmost brutality, driving their persecution to the point of murder (as is the case of Lieutenant-Colonel Hernandez, who had to pay with his life for the attempts to renew the September 4).[39]

An example of Batista's "alternate methods of mildness, privilege, and flattery" on one hand versus "reaction," "foreign exploiters" and "persecution" on the other hand was embodied in the Cuban Olympics celebration of October 1936. According to the *Daily Worker*, "Batista's Hitler-Style Olympics in Cuba" was reportedly funded by American sugar enterprises on the island such that this lavish tournament portrayed a civilized event whose very financial support was generated from the economic super-profits extracted from Cuban laborers.[40]

And yet, with acrobatic twists and turns of Batista's opportunism and the Communists' too for that matter, Batista would soon become the champion of Communists. Indeed, as 1939 came to a close, and Germany invaded Poland, Batista got the last word in the *Daily Worker*. At a meeting of the Cuban Confederation of Workers in 1939, he greeted the labor movement with the utmost reassurance that "The Communist Party in Mexico as well as in Cuba, and in France and the USA where they are recognized as legal forces, instead of elements of disturbance are acting as promoters of democracy." Communists were rejoicing at the fact that after the CPC's legalization, there were nearly 24,000 Communists in Cuba. Moreover, they had determined that the

> ... rulers of Cuba, and especially its outstanding figure, Colonel Batista, understand that the promotion of the well-being of the people and its maintenance, the defence of its democratic institutions, is intimately connected with the struggle against fascism, not in Cuba alone, but in our Hemisphere and throughout the world.

But what had happened to the struggle against racial oppression in this context of Communist collusion with Cuba's rulers like Batista?[41]

The New York-based black Communist James Ford delivered a speech on December 7, 1939 at the Park Palace Casino in Harlem. Standing at his side was Alberto E. Sanchez, General Secretary of the Communist Party of Puerto

Rico (CPPR). "James Ford, an American Negro leader," proclaimed the *Daily Worker*:

> ... knows Cuba intimately. He knows the problems of the hundreds of thousands of sugar workers. He knows Cuba's political leaders and above all he knows the big Communist Party of Cuba, which has won legal recognition by its strength and wise mass leadership.

This ostensible "mass leadership" seems to have ignored the "50 percent" who had been displaced and presumably deported back to Haiti and Jamaica. The exclusion of immigrant black laborers from the work of Communists in Cuba precipitated the eventual lifting of the ban from now President Batista by 1939. The *Daily Worker* reminisced proudly that "Cubans remembered well the time when Ford headed the Communist contingent of a parade of 250,000 people that greeted Batista." Reciprocally, Ford "talked to the everyday Negro workers of Cuba and spoke to such groups as the Atena Club, an influential Negro organization, similar to the National Association for the Advancement of Colored People."[42]

This Atena Club had roots in the Afro-Cuban (especially the well-off Afro-Cuban) community going back several decades. Even Langston Hughes had graced its halls in the 1930s as he travelled throughout the Caribbean in search of Afro-diasporic culture. But why had Ford apparently become acquainted with this organization only after the CPC and CPUSA had dropped their "Black Belt Thesis" approach to fighting racism in the hemisphere? What did these "influential" Negroes now offer to the Comintern that had enriched Ford's experience on the island? Indeed, it was the inclination toward advocating for workers' power and pursuing the more popular approach to mass organizing that to a certain extent made Communists like Ford more amenable to networking with other organizations where Afro-Cubans were prominent such as the Atena Club. And yet the Atena Club was a far cry from Realengo 18 or Realengo 3.

FROM SPANISH HARLEM TO THE COMMUNIST PARTY OF PUERTO RICO: ENTER ALBERT SANCHEZ

Liberal people Cuban condemns oppression crimes Puerto Rico ... let Yankee domination sister island cease ...
International Labor Defense, Cuban telegram to
Secretary of State Cordell Hull, 1937

Unlike the Communist parties of Mexico, the United States, Haiti and Cuba, the CPPR was not officially founded until 1935. In this way, the CPPR was politically born into the framework of Popular Front politics with no official point of reference to prior political approaches to seizing power. But once it had been initiated, the support from its Cuban "sister" party was immediate. Weeks before the general strike that had begun in Cuba in March of 1935, a general strike had rocked the island of Puerto Rico. In the midst of the general strike which began inland among the sugar workers and spread into the stevedore and transportation sectors, the CPC's newspaper, *Bandera Roja*, asserted that "all organizations ought to head to the American Embassy in Cuba." Over and above rallying Cuban workers to denounce "*la dominacion imperialista en el Caribe*," the CPC had found in this Puerto Rican general strike what it considered unchartered territory for the "powerful mobilization of thousands and thousands of new laborers."

Therefore, much like the CPC ten years beforehand, the CPPR had been born into a period of intense class struggle on the island. However, *Bandera Roja* did not appear to grant such rhetorical support for the "thousands of new laborers" engaged in the contemporaneous struggles ripping through St. Kitts and St. Vincent in the Anglophone Caribbean that we discussed in the previous chapter. The inter-Caribbean class solidarity between Cuba and Puerto Rico was essentially an outgrowth of the Communist leadership in these Spanish-speaking islands of the Caribbean. Moreover, Communist activity in Spanish Harlem was also part of the process of party formation on the island and vice versa. And while anti-racism was critical to this movement as it developed in Harlem, this commitment did not seem to reflect as directly toward the various Caribbean islands where black militant workers were more predominant.[43]

Cuban Communists first seized the reins when Albert Sanchez, the CPPR leader and former organizer in New York, was arrested for helping to organize the general strike of 1935 in Puerto Rico. Having been duly seasoned in the art of challenging the US justice system in light of the Scottsboro case, the CPC dispatched a protest message in February 1935 to the US Embassy in Cuba demanding an end to the jailing and charges against Sanchez. US officials noted the relationship between "a large number of protests and threats in connection with the sentencing of Scottsboro and also similar protests from radical organizations and individuals with respect to the persecution of Alberto Sanchez and other strike directors in Puerto Rico." The Cuban party via its street protests and *Bandera Roja* functioned as a geopolitical bridge that linked the oppression of African-American youth in the Jim Crow southern US to the persecution of strike leaders in Puerto Rico. In this way, as Cuban Communists and affiliated radical organizations prepared for the rapid onset of the Cuban general strike of March 1935, they remained at least minimally committed to advancing the struggle against racial oppression in the hemisphere by way of the Scottsboro case and subsequent persecution of anti-colonial nationalists and radicals from Puerto Rico to Spanish Harlem.[44]

Founding of the CPPR in Hemispheric Context

One fascinating dimension of Communist history as it emerged in this Cuban-Puerto Rican context is the difference in how party formation emerged on each island. Both Puerto Rico and Cuba had established sections of the Anti-Imperialist League (AIL) by as early as 1925, as discussed in Chapter 3, and both had Communists organizing in connection with New York.

The "brother" party to the north, as Roca had referred to the CPUSA, was instrumental in supporting the CPPR upon inception of its founding, just as it had been for the parties founded in Mexico, Haiti and Cuba. The *Daily Worker* announced in April of 1935 that the CPPR had been officially founded that year. Chief on the CPPR's agenda was a plan to fight in the "left wing" of the American Federation of Labor in order to strengthen the needle trades union and also to continue their focus on creating a sugar workers industrial union, hence furthering their political inroads from the general strike which had just subsided. Lampooning "The 'New Deal' At Work in Puerto Rico," this article also described the CPPR's plans to expand their work within the Unemployment Councils. Months later, the *Daily Worker* announced that the CPPR had also launched its own periodical, *Lucha Obrera* (Workers' Struggle), which, while a "small paper, eight pages, tabloid size," appeared to carry big weight.[45]

The first issue of *Lucha Obrera* documented the recent successes of this newly formed CPPR, such as its ability to "organize enough mass pressure to force the revoking of the order of the Yankee Major General Governor Winship … from the elections." The "tabloid" form ascribed to the newspaper might have also referred to explicit and shocking—though probably accurate—accounts such as a short exposé about the use of "oil-soaked cats to set the sugarcane fields on fire by the plantation owners to forestall strikes," according to Dr. Jose A. Lanauze Rolon who was described as a "prominent Party leader." This was not a party constituted solely of proletarian forces, though in 1930 the Politburo of the Comintern had strictly stipulated that workers rather than intellectuals or professionals should lead the newly formed Caribbean parties. Neither did the support emanating from Spanish Harlem come from laborers alone; rather, as we will see, Representative Vito Marcantonio, Esq. was quite important for this network.[46]

Above and beyond the deliberate efforts of individual Communists, the larger-context worker- and campus-led struggle was critical. Striking sugar workers and stevedores on the island were a key sector. The students and faculty at the University of Puerto Rico, who were engaged in a series of political campaigns against the racially prejudiced persecution of African Americans, particularly the black young Communist Angelo Herndon, were also important. The *Daily Worker* reported in November of 1935 that the Angelo Herndon Committee based in the United States had received over 2,000 signatures from supporters in France and also that a committee had been established at the University of Puerto Rico. It was not simply the case of the Scottsboro Boys, but also the case of the imprisoned Angelo Herndon, an openly Communist organizer and African American youth whose brother would soon die on the battlefields of Spain while fighting to free it from fascist rule, which inspired the Puerto Rican-based outcry against racism. Relative to Haiti, however, Puerto Rico had emerged fiercely and suddenly as a formidable force in this Red-Black matrix just at the moment when support for the Haitian Communist movement from the US appears to have declined markedly.[47]

While Puerto Rican students were rallying behind the cause of Herndon's release, the chief criticism in the CPPR with their US counterparts was around the problem of insufficient monetary support just as money had been a problem for CPC-CPUSA relations. In October of 1935, only months after the party's formation, Alberto Sanchez wrote to Earl Browder at once thanking him for sending over comrade "Joe K," while criticizing Browder for allowing this individual to be commissioned for work in an island where it was clear that social and economic conditions were dire such that Browder failed to ensure that financial resources from the "central" office were secured for "Joe's" stay. Indeed, "Joe" appears to have been a political asset but a financial liability for the fledgling movement in Puerto Rico. Sanchez's message was clear: send comrades with cash, or send no comrades at all. Monetary support was obviously an expectation of these Puerto Rican comrades from their US allies, even though no such expectations were placed on other parties, namely in Cuba, probably because it was assumed that the party in the US was the most financially secure in the hemisphere.[48]

But even though the CPPR sought monetary support from the CPUSA, party members on the island were primarily focused on Puerto Rico itself and deeply integrated into the nationalist movement for independence, which had long pre-dated the founding of the CPPR. Indeed the "nation" was central to the ideological underpinnings of the Puerto Rican movement. Therefore, Albizu Campos, the long-time Puerto Rican nationalist leader of the independence movement and the island's "public enemy number one" for government officials, played a role for the CPPR that in many ways paralleled the popular alliance between the Communists in Cuba and the progressives aligned with Grau San Martin beginning in 1935. Curiously, however, the Communist "*grupo*" described earlier in this text was created by Communists who had broken with the independence movement and opted instead for a more direct approach to galvanizing for revolution. It is not clear from present research whether those same Communists remained active with the Comintern with the new political approach to Popular Front alliances.

Accordingly, in 1935, Communists in Puerto Rico and the US determined Campos to be an ally in the struggle against President Roosevelt's "New Deal" diplomacy, while the ILD in Oriente, Cuba, also played a role in supporting the Puerto Rican nationalist movement. In short, this burgeoning pro-Campos support was itself a component of the larger Pan-Latino opposition struggle against American empire across the hemisphere—before, of course, the Popular Front dictum became one of peaceful co-existence with bourgeois democracies and their attendant "Good Neighbor" rhetoric. So on what grounds was Campos considered an ally to the Communist cause of anti-fascism as the path towards revolution?

From Opposition to Unity with Albizu Campos

One reason that Campos posed such a challenge to American imperialism was that he had cultivated good neighborly relations on his own terms, terms which were not entirely amenable to US officials and financiers. By May of 1936, the Federal Bureau of Investigation at the issuance of the Office of the Attorney General had contacted US embassies across the region, including the Dominican Republic, Honduras and Panama, to secure a pending indictment against Albizu Campos, "one of the leaders of the Nationalist Party of Puerto Rico" on a charge of selling illegal bonds. After the Attorney General had reportedly

> ... received information to the effect that Pedro Albizu Campos has been successful in distributing a substantial number of the so-called bonds of the Republic of Puerto Rico throughout Mexico, Central and South America and that he maintains one or more Agents at these places for the purpose of effecting additional sales thereof, [his] indictment for conspiracy to overthrow the government [was imminent].[49]

Closer analysis of the circumstances surrounding Campos's subsequent imprisonment, however, gives cause to query such allegations. For even in the case that Campos was engaged in such independent Pan-Latino economic ventures, the much more proximate threat before US intelligence authorities and business interests in the hemisphere was the Communist and nationalist forces that had breathed new life, youth and militancy into the movement for Puerto Rican independence, just as the US military was in the process of expanding its base of operation on the island. All the more pressing was the fact that this radical support for Campos had chosen to drop its bomb in Cuba, where it literally exploded first.

In mid-April of 1936, the US Ambassador to Cuba, Jefferson Caffery, noted that a "[b]omb was exploded at the door of the Consulate at 10 o'clock last night" within minutes after he and a co-worker, "Goodman," had just left the office from a long day's work. While "the police authorities did not advise me of this," he maintained, they were forced to stand guard at the Consulate all night since "the door was blown wide open and completely destroyed." Though Caffery did not affirm that the assailants were ever found, he noted that a "letter was received yesterday morning protesting against the recent conviction of Puerto Rican independence leaders." Perhaps Caffery was referencing the letter dated April 11 addressed to "Al Senor, Jefferson Caffery, Embajador de los EEUU en Cuba" and signed by the "Defensa Obrera Internacional Comite Ejecutivo Provincial de Oriente."[50]

The American authorities had been rendered utterly powerless in determining the origin of this most recent attack on the US embassy precisely because the assumption could not be made that solely Communists or their affiliated DOI (ILD) organization were responsible in this new era of popular alliances. Albizu Campos and the nationalist movement within Puerto Rico had gathered increasing traction and a wide-ranging network of supporters due at least in part to the long history of Cuban political organization in the Oriente Province where this DOI chapter was based. Again this points toward the fact that the conjuncture of Communist organization and black working-class militancy remained a cornerstone of revolutionary praxis in the hemisphere during the interwar period. At the same time, however, there was a negation of the anti-racist component of this network by 1935 insofar as a much more exclusively Latino-centered orientation laid the basis for the movement to defend Campos. Though this movement was led in part by Comintern groups such as the DOI in Oriente, it had emerged precisely at the moment where the "Black Belt" of Oriente thesis had been discarded by the CPC.

The greater concentration of ethno-centric Latino forces seeking a popular alliance for political and economic independence from "Yankee" rule in the north is evident when glancing through the reports that flooded US embassies from across Latin America in outrage against the arrest of Campos and his compatriots. One embassy official stationed in Argentina reported that in regards to an editorial published by the newspaper *La Prensa* of Buenos Aires focused on the independence question in Puerto Rico:

> ... while the newspaper takes no positive stand on the question and states that it would be regrettable if those sponsoring the movement should resort to force, nevertheless it concludes with the statement that "it is necessary to consider the aspirations of the Puerto Rican people in the spirit of equanimity and justice."

Weeks later a translated statement emerged from "La Federacion Universitaria Argentina" addressed to Secretary of State Cordell Hull declaring that "Protests against American armed invasion of Puerto Rico" were underway and moreover that "Spanish America ... is a unit, both in body and spirit, and any invasion of one country is a vital wound to the others." There was an ideological consensus among the organizations and individuals represented by these petitions that "equanimity and justice" in "Spanish America" would dictate the common allegiance to Puerto Rican independence for what were essentially tautological reasons. That is, the ostensibly transcendent goals of "equanimity and justice" were seen by these leaders as derivative of, though not tantamount to, the explicit, class-specific goals of egalitarianism and proletarian internationalism that had been put forward in the years before.

Even the DOI in Cuba had now declared that "Liberal people Cuban condemns oppression crimes Puerto Rico ... let Yankee domination sister island cease." Notably, this familial bond of solidarity was predicated upon ties of language and a common Spanish heritage, ties that Reds in the CPUSA did not entirely identify with, given the largely Anglo-Saxon, Anglophone thrust of the organization—with the exception, of course, of Reds in Spanish Harlem. Therefore, Communists at the time were fast becoming attuned to capitalizing off of this more popular movement as a means of garnering support for the burgeoning Popular Front against fascism around the world.[51]

Editors for *The Communist* placed much more squarely the question of state police terror and Gestapo-like aggression against militant Puerto Rican nationalist youth at the forefront of the "United Front" for Campos: "On October 24, in the university town of Rio Piedras, the first shots in the offense were fired. Four Nationalists were massacred by the police. That bloody action set off the gathering storm" in which the "nationalists publicly swore vengeance and raised the slogan of 'arms, arms, arms!'" The conclusion, determined Harry Robinson, the author of the article, was that "It was in this tense atmosphere that Riggs was assassinated."[52]

Most fascinating about this adventurist call to arms against American empire in Puerto Rico was that it used the same mobilizing trope that had characterized Comintern work linking the US with the Caribbean for years: political lynching. Though Puerto Rican radicals in this particular instance were not decrying the unjust conditions of the Scottsboro Boys at the hands of "judge lynch" in early 1936, Robinson still considered that "the two young Nationalists who did the shooting were immediately lynched by the police in the Central Police Headquarters," and moreover that the "storm of indignation was so great that the police were indicted for murder by the grand jury" with the result that the "General Secretary of the Nationalist Party, Juan Antonio Corretjer, has been imprisoned for one year for 'contempt of court'" along with Campos and others. Whether the article meant to infer that these youths were "lynched" by conventional Jim Crow methods of hanging was unclear, but the fact remained that they were dead at the hands of local police officials. One must wonder whether these Puerto Rican radicals recognized how their own solidarity in defense of the Scottsboro young men and Angelo Herndon the year before formed the ideological backdrop for the comparison to their own most recent "lynching."[53]

Support for Campos then emanating from "Spanish America" also shifted the dynamics of CPUSA activity among Puerto Rican immigrants in Spanish Harlem. This was primarily due to the popular ascendency of Representative Vito Marcantonio in that same region of New York. Marcantonio, a one-time arch-enemy of Harlem-based Communists, had now become heralded in the pages of the *Daily Worker* as the quintessence of Popular Front leadership, the man who represented "the district that sent Mayor La Guardia to Congress several times." During the same time frame, when US Colonel Riggs had been purportedly assassinated in Puerto Rico by local radicals, Marcantonio apparently attempted "to lead an unemployment demonstration out of Madison Square Park and a short time later was held in the East Twenty-second Street police station in 'protective custody.'" In the minutes before his arrest in front of 15,000 demonstrators, he not only "told in his speech of a bill introduced in Congress on Friday, calling for an appropriation to help the unemployed" but he also "denounced the passage in Congress of the War Department Appropriation Bill" since there was "no danger of attack from foreign powers." Patriotically calling upon the crowd to sing the "Star-Spangled Banner" as he was being detained by the police, Rep. Marcantonio was in the process of fast becoming the biggest champion of the cause of Puerto Rican independence among New York-based politicians who were engaged with Popular Front politics of the time. And his links to local Communists based out of Harlem were indispensable in this context.[54]

The All People's Party and the Convergence in Spanish Harlem

Marcantonio had emerged as a formidable leader of the APP in Harlem as a result of the Harlem Riot in March 1935, the same riot that brought Arthur King of the UNIA into closer collusion with local Communists and the subsequent raid on local CPUSA headquarters. This "outbreak served to crystallize sentiment, widespread and deeply felt" and resulted in the "establishment, some months later, of the Joint Conference Against Discriminatory Practices, one of the broadest united fronts in the country," receiving the support of certain elected officials such as Marcantonio. And chief on his agenda was the cause of Puerto Rican independence from his East Harlem base.[55]

The *Daily Worker*'s coverage of Marcantonio increased significantly in the middle of 1936, just as the Tydings Bill on Puerto Rican independence came before Congress; the increase in coverage came about because Marcantonio had been the chief Congressional representative to challenge this bill as the newest "sham" legislation associated with Roosevelt's "Good Neighbor Policy" in the hemisphere. Marcantonio's rhetorical support for Puerto Rican independence undoubtedly helped Communists soften their attacks on Roosevelt's "Good Neighbor Policy" such that they began requesting that the president act in good faith by overturning the Tydings Bill and adopting instead Marcantonio's. "The fight for Puerto Rican independence is an integral part of the American working class struggle," stated Marcantonio to Communist reporters as he prepared to "spend about ten days in the Island [of Puerto Rico] visiting plantations and factories addressing the workers on his bill for Puerto Rican independence and studying labor conditions." In turn, Marcantonio openly acknowledged that his efforts were contingent on the fact that within Puerto Rico, "Communists, Nationalists and other groups have already set up a United Front."[56]

Surely Marcantonio must have been embittered at having been dismissed by Congressional leaders in May of 1936 after declaring that "American imperialism in its thirty-eight year domination of the island, had extracted more than $400,000,000 in profits," namely in the form of "four large American sugar corporations" which owned "half of the good sugar land." But his indictments against US profiteers which were rendered moot on the House floor resounded loudly in the pages of the *Daily Worker.* "'The American people … once a British colony, have no desire to be lords and masters of a smaller nation. Only American tories, banks and sugar corporations … are interested in the island as a colony.'" Communists in Puerto Rico and the United States alike answered to the call of Marcantonio insofar as the *Daily Worker* decried the "ruthless 'dollar diplomacy'" of the "National City Bank and Chase National Bank" said to run the "four huge American plantation companies" that Marcantonio had referenced days before.

The CPUSA dismissed what it considered the Roosevelt "policy of sweet smiles, of abrogating the Platt Amendment in Cuba, of withdrawing the marines from Haiti, of settling the old dispute with Panama, and now of offering independence to Puerto Rico," as a farce and a lie. But rather than entirely negating the possibility for "good neighborly" relations, the CPUSA rallied behind the figure of Marcantonio to meet precisely such ends. Such political maneuvering on the part of the CPUSA during this period was fully indicative of the more popular program for united action against global fascism and Wall Street "reaction" that characterized the policy of the Popular Front.

Openly endorsing the Marcantonio Bill, the CPUSA had now clearly made it a strategy to maneuver politically within the left wing of the established traditional political party system by partnering with "progressive" anti-fascist figures such as Marcantonio. "Ninety days after the bill becomes law the President shall proclaim Puerto Rico free and independent," according to his proposed legislation; moreover, "all American naval and military reservations shall be given up" so that "the people shall be free to set up any government they see fit without any interference from the United States." Indeed this was the quintessence of Popular Front strategy as reflected in the work of the New York-Puerto Rican movement from 1935 to 1939. Or at least this was the social-democratic aspect of this transnational movement in its most explicit form.[57]

Part of the conditions that made Marcantonio's ascendancy possible were generated from the bonds of camaraderie that existed in the community centers, churches and streets of Lower Harlem, or East, or Spanish Harlem, where Communists had a long history of organizing. Indeed, this was the grassroots of the movement. For example, in the last days of August 1936, a "great demonstration called by the Committee for the Defense of Puerto Rican Political Prisoners" based in this Spanish-Harlem community was scheduled to "take place in lower Harlem" and "culminate in a mass meeting at Fifth Avenue and 110th Street," with the joint participation of groups including Nationalist Party Junta, the Puerto Rican Revolutionary party, the Communist Party of Lower Harlem and the Committee for Puerto Rico and supported, of course, by the All People's Party of Harlem. Weeks earlier, a National Congress for the Defense of Political Prisoners had also been formed in Puerto Rico, according to the *Daily Worker*.[58]

Government repression and the economic depression continued to intensify in Puerto Rico, and Communists in New York and Puerto Rico were obligated to respond at the grassroots level. As 1936 came to a close, the readers of the *Daily Worker* heard of "two killed and six seriously wounded" in the streets of Ponce, Puerto Rico, as Puerto Ricans literally gave their lives to enjoy the same constitutional voting privileges accorded to American citizens. But concurrent with this fierce repression in the outposts of American empire was the release of Stalin's report on the Soviet Constitution in December 1936, which announced that the "complete victory of the Socialist system in all spheres of our national economy" had now become an established "fact."[59]

Reports flooding the New York offices of the ILD as of March 1937 indicate that Puerto Rican Nationalists were taking their freedom into their own hands and inspiring their US counterparts toward acts of solidarity. Notable among the agenda items for the ILD in June of 1937 were the plans made for an elected representative to visit US congressmen, senators and government department officials regarding crime syndicalism laws, the Scottsboro trial, and calls for "democratic rights" and self-government in Puerto Rico. From the floor of Congress, such demands were radical, given the state of US political legislation at that time. But the call for "democratic rights" in Puerto Rico paled in comparison to the mass protests that shook the island in March of 1937.[60]

The *Daily Worker* revealed that in New York, the ILD, former Congressman Marcantonio and a politically sympathetic lawyer named Gilberto Concepcion de Gracia, who had also represented Campos in his court case and was also a member of the Nationalist Party of Puerto Rico, had jointly demanded an investigation into reports of "ten people killed in Puerto Rico and fifty eight wounded by police and homes of Nationalist party members raided at the same time as the shootings." Days later, a letter from the National Committee for the Defense of Puerto Rican Political Prisoners, an ILD sub-group, reported a "Palm Sunday massacre in Ponce" in which 15 Nationalists were killed at a protest. With these obscure yet disturbing death tallies, it was evident that Red leaders in New York were embroiled in a wave of violent repression in Puerto Rico that needed international support.

Threats of actual fascism in Puerto Rico loomed larger than this sharpest manifestation of police repression toward the Nationalist protest movement. News in the *Daily Worker* of the recent shootings and arrests came with an adjoining article that drew direct parallels between Governor Winship's social experimentation on Puerto Rican islanders and Hitler's eugenics-based extermination of Jews in Germany: "[Winship] also asked the Legislature to adopt laws leading to the application of 'eugenic sterilization' the same as practiced in Hitler's Nazi Germany against the Jews." In direct response to these reports, the American Committee for the Defense of Puerto Rican Political Prisoners was formed in New York under the leadership of the ILD, a committee whose work kept the ILD busy well into World War II.[61]

The formation of this committee is an example of how militant workers in subaltern epicenters such as Ponce took militant leadership in motivating the work of Communist-led organizations based in New York. In collusion with the CPUSA, this committee for Puerto Rican political prisoners led a mass assembly of two thousand people at Park Palace Casino, which gathered to hear Pat Toohey, a representative of the CPUSA's Central Committee, who demanded the immediate release of all political prisoners and, chiefly, Campos. Toohey had recently met personally with Campos for ten hours in his prison cell in Atlanta, Georgia, and Toohey read out loud a personal address from Campos.[62]

Still, racial and linguistic boundaries were far from overcome in the process of building this international support for Caribbean workers, with respect to the French-speaking people of Haiti. In the very moment when the Latino world was welding its nationalist forces in defense of Campos and Spain, black laborers in Haiti and the British West Indies were arguably under conditions of hegemony on an even grander scale and there was nowhere near such an outpouring of support generated by Reds in New York, who were then rallying behind the cause of Campos and other figures in the Spanish-speaking Caribbean. At the same time, what was ultimately a shortcoming on the part of Communists in New York and the Caribbean to apply even—if not greater—attention to the plight of those in the Black Caribbean should not preclude the Communist commitment to fighting racism in the Latino community based out of Lower East Harlem.

Anti-racism as Anti-eviction in Spanish Harlem: Enter Oscar Rivera

Puerto Rican and other non-state residents facing evictions in Lower Harlem were subject to a racially and ethnically discriminatory Non-Settlement Act. The Communist-led Workers Alliance and local legislators such as Oscar Rivera had decided to challenge the Act aggressively in September of 1938, months before James Ford's announcement of a CPUSA delegation to meet the CPPR in December. Developments in Lower Harlem delineate how race, nation and class interpenetrated in the Popular Front movement, emanating from this subaltern outpost for transnational Red organizations based in Spanish Harlem.

Oscar Garcia Rivera, state assemblyman for the 17th Assembly District in Harlem, alongside that of the Workers Alliance, was indispensable to the direct action campaigns against eviction at that time. On September 3, 1938, the *Daily Worker* reported that Oscar Rivera "went yesterday to the fiat of the Flores family to offer his personal assistance to the destitute family" which was facing imminent deportation as a result of receiving relief in spite of the Non-Settlement Act's stipulation of one year's residency in the city prior to receiving aid. While Puerto Rican mothers such as Mrs. Flores were being deported for trying to feed their children, Rivera went further to add that "It is aimed mainly at Negroes coming from the South and at Latin Americans, including American citizens from Porto Rico." Hence, the struggle against the Non-Settlement Act objectively bound the interests of African American migrants of the US South to those Puerto Rican and other migrants from the other "American South" in the Caribbean.[63]

In the days that followed, the *Daily Worker* ran a rich exposé on the lives of East Harlem's impoverished residents and their resistance, which was said to have been led by the local Communists. Subsequent accounts of the anti-eviction campaigns discussed cases such as the migrant Rodriguez family, composed of an African-American mother and a Cuban father who faced eviction because the mother was a migrant worker who travelled between New York and Florida while leaving her children in Harlem presumably with family members, placing them on relief prematurely according to the stipulations of the Non-Settlement Act. In response to the pending eviction of this migrant black-Latino family, the Workers Alliance began "pressing for the allotment of Federal funds to take care of stranded families, such as the Rodriguez." The plight of the Rodriguez family in many ways personified the very Afro-Latin, Black and Red, New York -Caribbean struggle that Communists had been politically attempting to come to terms with for the duration of the interwar period.[64]

Also at the personal level, Puerto Rican boxer-turned-Communist Fernando Archibald, better known as "Tommy White," provided inspiration to local *Daily*

Worker readers in East Harlem in a moment when Joe Louis and Paul Robeson were breaking racial boundaries in the global cultural and athletic spheres. But Tommy White became a "Red" only because he was privileged enough, or so the story went, to have happened upon

> ... a friend, a Communist. The Communist patiently explained to him that there was no hope for their people till they united. Day by day he told him about the successes of the unions and the unemployed struggle ... and the grand future for labor in a Socialist world. A talk with Armando Roman, now chairman of the Party in Puerto Rican Harlem, completed the job.

Presumably what he meant by "the job" was convincing the boxer to join the CPUSA. Another journalist informed his readers that at the Spanish-speaking branch of the Workers Alliance, "Here come friends of Loyalist Spain with collection cans full of pennies and dimes from the people of Harlem ... I saw 15 such cans on the desk of the branch secretary at one time." The popular cross-section of support ranging from local street fighters to pro-Loyalist fundraisers in this impoverished community had led the *Daily Worker* to proclaim, "The Communist party is deeply rooted among the Puerto Rican people of Lower Harlem." While it is not entirely clear how deep these roots were, there was evidently some degree of Red influence in Lower Harlem.[65]

Jose Santiago's political profile also personified the Communist influence in Lower Harlem. "'The Communist Party in Lower Harlem developed in struggle,'" declared Santiago, who was at the helm of this Communist-Puerto Rican conjuncture. As "Upper Harlem" under James Ford was making preparations for the CPUSA delegation to Puerto Rico, the history of Communist activity in Lower Harlem was being documented through the eyewitness narrative of Santiago, whose own rise to leadership served as an example of this movement which climaxed during the depression years in both Puerto Rico and New York. Santiago's own article in the *Daily Worker* indicated that he had

> ... joined the Communist Party in the midst of these struggles. Son of a shoe maker in central Puerto Rico, he worked on the coffee farms in his childhood, for almost nothing. Mothers picked coffee all day for 30 to 50 cents; children got less for the bare three to four months of the season.

This was the seed of Santiago's political activism which took root in the fertile political soil of Lower Harlem when he arrived, where "life was better and then came the terrible economic crisis of 1929." According to Santiago:

> The Party got its first real start here during the unemployment crisis of 1930 ... Ten to fifteen families were evicted daily. Communists organized a struggle against the evictions ... I remember one struggle at 21 East 110 St. They put the furniture

on the street three times and three times the people put it back. The police drew their guns but the crowd packed the block from avenue to avenue and stopped the eviction.[66]

The streets of Lower Harlem were filled with angry, militant community members suffering from systematic and disproportionate unemployment and homelessness that militarized them to the point that even when "police drew their guns" the "crowd packed the block from avenue to avenue and stopped the eviction." Jose Santiago had joined the ranks of seminal radical leaders like Blas Roca, Alberto Sanchez, James Ford and other people-of-color Reds in this New York-Caribbean network.[67]

In addition to Santiago's decision to become a Communist, one important outcome of the deep suffering incurred during the depression in Lower Harlem was the increase in Puerto Rican representation in the CPUSA. The *Daily Worker* reported that

Today the Lower Harlem section of the Party has more than 870 members in branches, including seven industrial branches. Nearly half the members are Puerto Ricans. There are also other Spanish speaking peoples, many American and West Indian Negroes and New York people of other nationalities

… including Koreans. The global economic crisis which had attracted such migrants as Santiago to New York had become a breeding ground wherein Koreans, West Indians and Puerto Ricans were all living, eating, struggling and organizing together under the banner of Loyalist Spain, the Soviet Union and an independent Puerto Rico—or at least certain clusters of these groups were doing so. Such multiracial, anti-fascist gatherings illuminate the marginal activities of a marginal party with small numbers albeit great historic significance.[68]

By 1938, it was in the labor movement under the National Maritime Union that linkages between the CPUSA and CPPR was more pronounced. Challenging the segregated labor union boundaries with respect to Puerto Rican laborers became an integral factor in CPUSA development during the Popular Front, especially based in New York. From the standpoint of Frederick Myers, one-time vice president of the NMU and Communist, and the Puerto Rican dock workers who ushered in a month-long strike in the early days of 1938, "sentiment among the Puerto Ricans" was paving the way for CIO collusion with, if not control over, the AFL-labor movement in both the United States and Puerto Rico, much to the chagrin of foreign and domestic investors on the island.[69]

The *Daily Worker* reported that "threats of martial law" were "emanating from Governor Blanton Winship" as a result of the "assault on Frederick C. Myers" who was "sent by the CIO National Maritime Union to aid the strikes" which had ensued among the Puerto Rican dock workers. Rather than cowering before authority and waiting for orders as the captain had observed, "the strikers, members of the Union of Puerto Rico Dock Workers" were said to have "stood solid for a month, resisting every provocation of the shipper's agents to split their ranks and smash the strike." These striking workers indeed offered a model of CIO industrial leadership that workers in both the United States and the Caribbean would begin to endorse in their domestic labor disputes.[70]

The *Daily Worker*'s coverage of the AFL and its history in Puerto Rico considerably softened in the weeks following the Puerto Rican strike precisely because the NMU, under the leadership of the Myers and CIO-affiliated organizers, had made significant political inroads among laborers who "stood solid" for weeks on end. What had begun as simply some "native longshoremen [who] walked out demanding a raise from 32 cents an hour to 60 cents," had now resulted in an elision of formerly antagonistic forces in the US labor movement on Puerto Rican soil. Since the AFL and CIO had finally come to sit down at the bargaining table, a 10 percent wage increase for Puerto Rican dock strikers was reportedly agreed upon by "Frederick Myers for the Committee for Industrial Organization, which supported the walkout, and Insular Labor Commissioner Prudencio Rivera Martinez who also is head of the American Federation of Labor in Puerto Rico." Frederick Myers used the *Daily Worker* to explicate the ramifications of this Puerto Rican labor development for the "mainland" laborers when reportedly, "Myers said the cooperation between the CIO and AF of L was 'significant' for American labor and that it pointed the way to mainland workers."[71]

In retrospect, however, what is perhaps more significant is the fact that the CPUSA had cast this vanguard activity now emanating from Puerto Rico as if it were a new development in hemispheric class struggle, yet militant class struggle originating in the Caribbean rather than the US was nothing new. Rather, it was a trend of pendulum-swing politics between the US and Caribbean militancy in which subaltern epicenters were the origins of labor and political uprisings that gave rise to heightened class consciousness in the US: Mexico and Jamaica in 1919, Haiti in 1929, Cuba in 1933, St. Kitts in 1935, Barbados in 1937. Each of these cases had proven time and again to have an impact on radical developments led by Communists in the United States in general, and New York in particular.

In the immediate context of fascist aggression across Europe and into Africa and Asia, the Comintern had considerably narrowed the scope of its class enemies. Communists in the United States had contented themselves with the fact that "one of the most significant labor victories yet won in the Caribbean" was led jointly at the helm by the UMW (Union of Marine Workers), NMU, CIO and ILW (International Longshoreman Workers). All of these labor unions had significant Communist political influence. But also in the transnational "Caribbean Brotherhood" that arose from the Puerto Rican protest was included "Roosevelt progressivism." Rather than Roosevelt's "New Deal" being the chief enemy of Puerto Rican laborers, the CPUSA had determined that the "Puerto

Rican steamship bosses" who were considered nothing more than "colonial office-boys of concerns tied directly with the sixty families which spearheaded the attack on Roosevelt's progressivism" had incited the "Borinquen crew [who] refused to permit the cucumbers to be loaded on the vessel by scabs."[72]

Limits of the Popular Front in Cuban, Puerto Rican and Mexican Context

In the final analysis, however, US rulers were much more amenable to granting socio-economic concessions like higher wages, integrated unions, and acquittals of black youth than to a Communist movement intent on workers advocating for the overthrow of the capitalist system across the hemisphere. US authorities were generally not too perturbed by this Popular Front: "So far as the Communist Party of the United States is concerned it is questionable whether the American Party makes no attempt to conceal its desire to assist similar movements in Puerto Rico and Cuba." According to one official:

> … at the present time, however, it is questionable whether the American Party would care to place such large forces or such a large sum at the disposal of the other parties when it could use them to great advantage in the United States itself.

Ultimately, the year 1939 indeed proved to reinforce the State Department's accurate summation of how it retained the upper hand in containing the movements in Cuba, Puerto Rico and United States:

> With regard to Cuba, it may be stated that the Communist Party will do nothing to disturb the present government. Its policy is to agitate for the strengthening of the present Cuban Government, for the extension of what they term to be "democratic rights" and for the establishment of a People's Front movement there similar to that in Mexico. When this Program is accomplished it may then be expected that the Party will press for passage of laws similar to those in Mexico.[73]

And a fledgling movement spanning this region whose political activities would potentially lead down the path of Mexico's radical movement was not, at this moment in early 1939, seen as the worst political circumstance for the Roosevelt administration.

The Comintern continued to stand behind Roosevelt even as the US military furthered its inroads on the island of Puerto Rico. As late as June of 1939, there was some hesitancy on the part of the US to establish a base there, since military intelligence would need to take extra precaution so as not to disturb its espionage of the fascist Italian, German, Spanish and Japanese forces that were then operating out of Puerto Rico. But by July, it was clear that Puerto Rico had become physically incorporated into the United States military defense system. The *Daily Worker* proclaimed on July 2, days before the United

States would celebrate its own day of anti-colonial emancipation, "Puerto Rico must be held against any invaders who would use it as a stepping stone in an aggressive war anywhere in the Americas." President Roosevelt opportunely enjoyed the explicit consent of Red organizers across the Caribbean Basin as well as in New York precisely at the moment when US military expansion in the Caribbean was on the rise. Even though Puerto Ricans were dying of hunger in 1939, Communists still felt it was better to support the Roosevelt administration since "the employers in combination with certain anti-New Deal elements claim that the Roosevelt laws if they are applied in Puerto Rico would destroy its economy." Even though 100,000 hungry and unemployed protesters flooded the streets in Puerto Rico under the leadership of the Nationalists, socialists and Communists and "banded together in the Protective Union of the Unemployed" under a CIO style of organization, this CIO style of organization had also led the chairman of the NMU to declare that "Be it resolved that we commend our government in its action to strengthen the democratic bonds of the Americas, and we urge the continued cooperation with the democracies and their furtherance of a Good Neighbor Policy."[74]

By 1939, the CPC had become legal, but this was at the cost of building popular alliances that supported the racist exclusion of black migrant laborers from the Cuban work force. Also by 1939, Communist influence in the NMU and CIO was so massive that landmark labor victories had been won for Puerto Rican dock workers, but this was at the cost of the CPUSA granting explicit support to the "Good Neighbor Policy" and implicit support for US military expansion on the island. Even though the Mexican popular movement against fascism was so deeply rooted by 1939 that Spanish Republican veterans were entering in droves for refuge only miles away from the US border, this was at the cost of Mexican Reds showing little if any real support for migrant Haitian laborers in the Dominican Republic who were slaughtered in 1937 under the fascist dictatorship of Rafael Trujillo. Therefore, the remaining pages of this book attempt to assess the significance of the Comintern's response to the massacre of Haitian laborers in 1937 primarily in terms of the activity generated in New York under the leadership of the CPUSA.

as In Cuba
Be Put In
·ation Camps

A Feb. 2,—The Ja-
nbering more than
iow facing another
·m in the matter of
tion, for it is report-
the Cuban Govern-
structing concentra-
in which to house
n labourers who had
g on cuban planta-
now awaiting their
ir native home un-
labour laws of the
·nment.
so·a rumour that is
·here, but without
that the Jamaican
may introduce legis-
port aliens in order
is for the returning

Varring
orld

·t of the bloody
ipain, where the
ne, air crafts, and
torture, pains and
seen and heard—

Continued on page 3—

Continued on page 12

West of !
guerilla :
Fascist
Col

Wr
For
Pl

STRESSI
PUR

The Edit
Sir:—I
letter is, I
you will
written, a
give it p
interest o
any altera
I have i
Talk last
and am v
with you
Movement
Compans
Cont

The N
Work

£72,000,(
PENDE
FOR
OVER
E

Plain Tal
paper, fear
alert in its
other pape
bringing to
readers the

Points To This Scene Of Injustice

The Capitalists' attempt of increasing Newspaper Monopoly to the detriment
of the already oppressed masses.

Jamaica Capitalists Hold Meeting

On Tuesday evening around | ways on the scene of important | money world convened for the
five p.m. the vicinity of Colle- | happenings managed to glean an | purpose of organizing a company
giate Hall was the attraction | ear-ful of just what transpired | to promote a "Daily Newspaper"

---

8 Anti-capitalist critique of the bourgeois press, promoting *Plain Talk* instead as a tribune of the masses. Caption reads "Points to this scene of injustice" (courtesy: NLJ tbc).

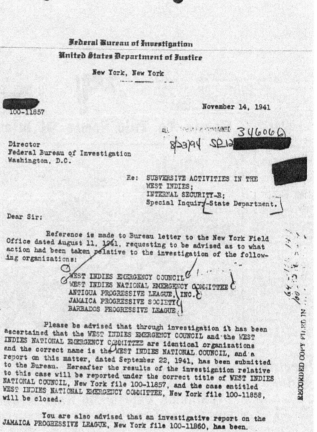

Federal Bureau of Investigation
United States Department of Justice

New York, New York

100-11857

November 14, 1941

ALL ~~~~~~~~ 346060
8/23/94 SP12

Director
Federal Bureau of Investigation
Washington, D.C.

Re: SUBVERSIVE ACTIVITIES IN THE
WEST INDIES;
INTERNAL SECURITY-R;
Special Inquiry-State Department.

Dear Sir:

Reference is made to Bureau letter to the New York Field
Office dated August 11, 1941, requesting to be advised as to what
action had been taken relative to the investigation of the following organizations:

WEST INDIES EMERGENCY COUNCIL
WEST INDIES NATIONAL EMERGENCY COMMITTEE
ANTIGUA PROGRESSIVE LEAGUE, INC.
JAMAICA PROGRESSIVE SOCIETY
BARBADOS PROGRESSIVE LEAGUE.

Please be advised that through investigation it has been
ascertained that the WEST INDIES EMERGENCY COUNCIL and the WEST
INDIES NATIONAL EMERGENCY COMMITTEE are identical organizations
and the correct name is the WEST INDIES NATIONAL COUNCIL, and a
report on this matter, dated September 22, 1941, has been submitted
to the Bureau. Hereafter the results of the investigation relative
to this case will be reported under the correct title of WEST INDIES
NATIONAL COUNCIL, New York file 100-11857, and the case entitled
WEST INDIES NATIONAL EMERGENCY COMMITTEE, New York file 100-11858,
will be closed.

You are also advised that an investigative report on the
JAMAICA PROGRESSIVE LEAGUE, New York file 100-11860, has been.

RECORDED 100-14723-8

NOV 18 1941

RECORDED COPY FILED IN...

9 Federal Bureau of Investigation report on purported "Subversive Activities in the West
Indies," focused on New York-based West Indian radical organizations, 1941 (courtesy
of US National Archives, Washington, DC).

CHAPTER 8

Of "Dogs, Hogs and Haitians"

*Neither communist nor fascist, the Dominican Republic will always be
a pure democracy whose institutional organization is modeled upon the
immortal principles which inspired the patriots of Philadelphia.*
President Rafael Trujillo, 1937

*It took more than prayers to heal me after the slaughter… It took holding
a pretty and gentle wife and three new lives against my chest. I wept so
much when they arrested me. I wept all the time I was in prison. I wept at
the border. I wept for everyone who was touched, beaten, or killed. It took
a love closer to the earth, closer to my own body, to stop my tears. Perhaps
I have lost, but I have also gained an even greater understanding of things
both godly and earthly.*
Edwidge Danticat, words of Father Romain, *Farming of Bones*

*Mid Pleasures and Palaces though we may roam—Be it ever so
humble there's no place like home.*
Plain Talk, 1936

On April 23, 1935, "The Case of Jacques Roumain" was brought before the
American general public with a letter to the editor in the *New York Times*
weeks after the Harlem Riot that resulted in a police raid on the offices of the
CPUSA. This letter, which was authored by one Francine Bradley, disclosed
that "President Stenio Vincent of the Republic of Haiti is gradually moving
toward a dictatorship. A most flagrant and tragic exercise of his powers is the
recent imprisonment of Haiti's leading poet and writer, Jacques Roumain."
Roumain, the great poet, journalist and lecturer, was a founding member of
the Communist Party of Haiti (CPH). His ties to the ILD and other CPUSA-
led organizations based in New York City had already ruffled the feathers of
State Department officials in the recent past. Roumain's network of "friends"
spearheaded by Francine Bradley appears to have been generated from a

demographic centered in the New York artistic and intellectual community and was most probably under the direct guidance of Langston Hughes. A Communist sympathizer and one-time leader of the League of Struggle for Negro Rights, Hughes had stopped in Haiti while in route to Cuba in 1932 and visited personally with Roumain who was then a leading member of the CPH.[1]

Choosing to highlight Roumain's popular appeal as a "leading poet and writer" rather than his Communist affiliations, Bradley insisted that this "brilliant and highly cultured young writer is now lying ill of malaria in a vermin-infested prison in Port-au-Prince, carrying out a sentence of three years for treason." The real crime on Bradley's account was that Roumain, "a member of one of Haiti's wealthiest and most distinguished families, grandson of a former President, educated at the best schools abroad," had been imprisoned for attempting only to "serve his people" by "exercising his supposed right of free speech by opposing the policies of the present government." When Roumain was charged with the "crime" of receiving "materieaux," or what Bradley considered to have been "conveniently interpreted as bombs and ammunition to overthrow the present regime" rather than the radical literature that it was, the result was that "friends in the United States who admire Roumain's outstanding achievements, have formed a committee to work for his release." Hence, contemporaneous with the emergence of political prisoner defense committees in New York for Puerto Rican leaders like Albizu Campos was the formation of political prisoner committees for Jacques Roumain and his peers in Port-au-Prince.[2]

Support from the progressive community in New York for Roumain during his imprisonment was also reflected in the pages of the *Daily Worker*. Roumain himself drew the political connections between the imprisonment of the Scottsboro Boys and his own incarceration. He sent a letter to the *Daily Worker* from what was described as his "Haitian dungeon" weeks after the Scottsboro Boys were each sentenced to serve 75 years in prison, proclaiming "I am glad to stand beside heroic proletariat which defend the Negroes of Scottsboro, Tom Mooney, and so many other victims of class injustice, rather than beside their murderers." Roumain was certainly a formidable figure in the movement for anti-racist proletarian internationalism, so much so that upon his release from prison in the latter half of 1936 the State Department noted that his release from prison had precipitated the intensification of anti-Communist legislation not only in Haiti but even in the Dominican Republic.[3]

The release of Roumain in 1936 took place in the historical context of not only increasing political repression against radical dissidents in Haiti and the Dominican Republic, but also increasing economic hardship for migrant Haitian laborers who had been recently deported from Cuba and forced to work in the Dominican Republic during the world depression. While supporters of Roumain were surely rejoicing at his release, this network of progressives seems to have had an ideological short in its circuit. They were strangely silent when tens of thousands of nameless, faceless, shoeless Haitian migrant peasants and city dwellers without "distinguished" lineage were massacred in 1937—no trial, no jailing nor sentence. More to the point, the Communist network of organizations in New York that had traditionally been aligned with the Haitian masses was essentially absent when Haitians living and working in the Dominican Republic had become political prisoners and economic refugees caught in a matrix of mass deportations and anti-Communist legislation.

This chapter considers some of the contributing factors that account for the minimal effort on the part of New York-based Communists in organizing a counter-attack to the fascist slaughter of Haitian laborers in 1937, during the Comintern era of the Popular Front. Though the National Negro Congress (NNC) helped lead a certain degree of protest in New York during 1937 and into 1938 under the leadership of Max Yergan, ultimately the CPUSA and its organizations fundamentally neglected to respond to the single most important act of fascist aggression in the hemisphere that had been enacted upon black laborers during this period. Such a failure on the part of the NNC in particular and the CPUSA in general suggests that the "Negro question" was at once a strong point and also an Achilles heel of the Comintern during the interwar period relative to the black workers in the Caribbean.

THE POPULAR FRONT'S LIMITATIONS IN HAITIAN CONTEXT

While the anti-fascist Popular Front was designed to place the Comintern in a strategic position to challenge and overpower fascist aggression around the world, the very tenets of class collaboration and leniency toward President Roosevelt as a lesser evil representation of capitalist policy left Yergan, the NNC and the CPUSA more broadly hamstrung in truly mounting a radical campaign of solidarity with Haitian workers. On several counts, barriers of culture, language and race had far from been overcome. First, the Comintern's strategic ranking of granting material defense to Spain over Abyssinia because of the former's socialist-leaning republic and the latter's semi-feudal and monarchical system was objectively necessary from a strategic perspective of consolidating progressive forces and yet inherently problematic: it suggested that the lives of everyday Ethiopians were not as valuable to the interests of advancing global progress as those of everyday Spanish Republicans—many of whom were Communist or pro-Communist on some level. Second, within the hemisphere itself, as illustrated earlier, much more support in the late 1930s was being extended to the progressive movements against oppression in Puerto Rico and

Cuba than in the British West Indies, not discounting those collaborations noted with respect to the NNC and Barbados in Chapter 6.

Changes in the CPUSA's role in mass organization work regarding the "Negro question" during the Popular Front era were also a factor. Even though the NNC purported to be less "sectarian" and "isolated" than the ANLC and the LSNR, the ANLC played a much more transnational, active and popular role in granting support to the Haitian uprising of 1929 than the NNC did in 1937 after Trujillo's massacre. Therefore, the US-centric thrust of the NNC seems to have accounted, in part, for this shift away from the praxis in support of Haitian laborers that the ANLC had exhibited years before. What appears to have been an increasing concentration of black Communist forces in Paris during this same post-1935 period also suggests that a shift away from New York and toward this Francophone metropolis was a factor. French Communists were probably playing a much more direct part in political developments underway in Haiti than the CPUSA by the mid-1930s, and this could partially account for the CPUSA's decrease in support for Haitians after the 1937 massacre. Indeed, Roumain's decision to move to Paris after his release from prison coincided with the move of the ITUCNW's headquarters from Brussels to Paris.

PROTO-FASCIST COMMUNIST BANS IN HAITI AND THE DOMINICAN REPUBLIC

Incipient fascism in both Haiti and the Dominican Republic conjoined to create the conditions for the slaughter of 1937, and anti-Communism was at the core of this political reaction. In the aftermath of the US Marines' withdrawal from both nations on the island, domestic rulers responded by doubling down on their own internal apparatuses for political repression. And the United States was amenable to this process. By late 1936, Haiti was in deep political turmoil. Jacques Roumain's release from prison was directly followed by President Vincent's passage of a Decree Law forbidding Communist activity in any form, according to a November 23, 1936 issue of *Le Moniteur*. US and Haitian authorities were quite cynical toward Communism in Haiti in the wake of Roumain's release from prison:

> The communist bugbear has cropped up periodically in Haiti in recent years and each time has subsided after a brief vogue. It is not improbable that on several occasions, at least, the communist scare was manufactured by the Government as a political distraction; in any event, it is difficult to see what progress communism has made in Haiti, if any, and aside from a few scattered individuals who occasionally publicize in one way or another their communist leaning there is no reason to believe that communism has much following here.[4]

The references to communist activity interchangeably as a "bugbear," "distraction," and a "few scattered individuals" which had apparently "subsided after a brief vogue" indicate that it was hardly considered an imminent threat to the Haitian government at the time of Roumain's release.

Still, Roumain must have had a relatively formidable revolutionary influence since "the President in issuing the aforementioned Decree Law actually had certain persons in mind. Outstanding among these is Jacques Roumain whose recent release from prison ... was reported to the [State] department." The decree banned "Any profession of communist faith ... the dissemination of communist or anarchist doctrines, whether by conferences, speeches, discussion, lectures, private or public meeting" as well as "correspondences," "libraries" and "proprietors of printing houses." At a minimum, this decree demonstrates just how directly the ban on Communist activity was tailored to specific leaders like Roumain and also to organizations like the AIL through which Henri Rosemund had distributed literature from the Crusader News Service several years beforehand. With such seditions directed so clearly at radical individuals and organizations it is quite conceivable to imagine why Roumain had decided to live in Paris shortly after his release.

This decree's denial of the right to free speech to Roumain occasioned his own personal departure first for Brussels then Paris, which, in turn, had larger ramifications for the role of New York in Haiti's political situation for the ensuing period. It appears to have been from Paris that Roumain and other Haitian Communists chose to base their political work for reasons that were at once personal and political. Roumain could have chosen Harlem, where political remnants of the cultural "Renaissance" persisted, and where clearly he had established a base of "friends" who had coalesced to demand his release from prison. But instead he chose Paris where he and his wife could raise their newborn child in a French-speaking metropolis, while recovering from the complications associated with his prison-contracted malaria.

Above and beyond what appear to have been personal decisions on the part of Roumain for moving to Paris, there were also tactical decisions on the part of the Comintern in regards to the headquarters of the ITUCNW that factored into the equation. The ITUCNW headquarters had transitioned from Brussels to Paris as a base of operation between 1935 and 1936 in the very period when Roumain had become active in the Spanish front writers' community based in Europe alongside fellow pro-Communist writers Nicolas Guillen of Cuba and Langston Hughes of the United States. Hence, the balance of Communist forces that weighed in on Haitian political developments shifted toward Europe in the very period when political and labor conditions were worsening for the vast majority of Haitian laborers in both Haiti and the Dominican Republic. The result was a partial though not total eclipse of New

York's prior involvement in Haitian affairs in the era of a hemispheric crisis of holocaustic proportions.[5]

CULTURAL NATIONALISM AND THE SPANISH-ABYSSINIAN MATRIX IN THE HAITIAN CONTEXT

A decrease in the amount of energy that Communists in New York were channeling into the struggles of Haitian laborers accompanied a decrease in the support that former Haitian political allies such as Dantes Bellegarde had previously shown to Comintern groups like the AIL during the turmoil surrounding the Pan-American Congress of 1928. Bellegarde had renounced any Communist influence on the island at the December 1936 Pan-American Conference in Buenos Aires, the same conference where CPUSA members had attended alongside Mexican and other Latin American Communists in order to grant support to Roosevelt's "Good Neighbor" policy.

The racist discrimination against Haiti was far deeper than just Trujillo's negrophobe tendencies; rather, racism across Latin America against Haiti laid the pretext for Trujillo's 1937 massacre. At the Pan-American Conference, US surveillance reports indicated that a "delegate of one of the South American Republics is supposed to have said in an aside" that he "'did not see what contribution of a cultural nature the Republic of Haiti could offer us.'" The outright contempt against Haiti as seen by "us," the other delegates, reflects how the geographical proximity of this "sister republic" could not discount the pervasive anti-Haitian—and by implication anti-African—sentiment that relegated Haiti to the cultural status of a step-sister in the period leading up to Trujillo's mass slaughter.[6]

In this way, Bellegarde's anti-Communism was itself a fatal concession to racial prejudice. For he had finally gained a seat at the Pan-American bargaining table which had been formerly denied to him at the 1928 Pan-American Congress in Havana only to denounce his former supporters on the left and instead assert the same racialized, civilizationist discourse premised upon cultural stereotypes about Haitian people that caused other delegates to resent his very participation at the congress. On Bellegarde's account, Haiti's right to inclusion at this conference was premised upon the idea that "Haiti is indeed the melting pot where different races of Africa and the numerous elements of the French nation have, during many centuries, mixed their blood," thus rendering the "physical properties" and "intellectual culture" of the population "exceedingly interesting to the ethnologist and the geneticist." He went on to critique the "unscientific writings" generated from an "Aryan myth of Nordic superiority" only to construct his own argument for Haitian progress by valorizing the notion of a Haitian "creole" process of miscegenation that served as the basic mark of honor and civilization for the republic.[7]

"Haiti," proclaimed Bellegarde, was "immune to 'racism,' Fascism and Bolshevism" as well as "all doctrines of racial discrimination or of class hatred." Bellegarde's Haitian exceptionalist framework was derived from the very eugenic, anti-African obscurantism he claimed to be challenging. Bellegarde went on to assert that the "Haitian peasant is an individualist and hence strongly opposed to any form of collectivism." He concluded that "if Haiti has known government instability it has always had social stability" which Bellegarde considered "infinitely more important." For the "deep and ineradicable love of the Haitian peasant for his soil," claimed Bellegarde, would forever render Haiti averse in the event that "Communism sought to transform the system of land-ownership" on this island.[8]

The historical irony is that prominent "creoles" such as Jacques Roumain were seeing Red, and Bellegarde's analysis did not sufficiently account for this reality. Even more to the point, Bellegarde's smug dismissal of Communist "collectivism" in relationship to the Haitian peasant inadvertently strengthened Trujillo's anti-Communist ban which, in turn, was the antecedent to the wider attack on Haitian migrant laborers. In the end, Bellegarde's calls for a "collective guarantee" to guard against "any aggression by one of these republics against the other" would fall on deaf ears. President Trujillo had indeed begun to wage a war at first against his own domestic Communists and later against the Haitian diaspora within his country's borders with the tacit consent of the hemispheric leaders gathered at Buenos Aires, including the renowned Haitian patriot Dantes Bellegarde.[9]

But it was not only leaders like Bellegarde who were responsible for putting forward stereotyped, essentialist notions of the Haitian people; even Communists—as evident in the *Daily Worker*—had begun to offer an account of Haitian radicalism that contrasted sharply with the message of class struggle and international, cross-border workers' militancy that groups like the ILD and the AIL had been popularizing at the beginning of the world depression. Apparently Langston Hughes felt he was offering a counter-narrative to that of Bellegarde regarding the revolutionary history and potential of the Haitian people; however, his own sentiments about this "troubled Island" as reflected in the *Daily Worker* were problematic as well. One Sander Voros of the *Daily Worker* made a timely announcement in November of 1936 about Hughes's play entitled *Troubled Island* only days after the release of President Vincent's anti-Communist decree, presumably as a cultural testament to what Voros termed the sustained revolutionary fortitude of "an entire people" in the face of "tyranny."[10] Voros went on to describe the Haitians as a people that were fueled by a "burning desire for freedom but [who were] ignorant of the ways to realize and maintain it." In drawing the mistaken conclusion that the "entire people" of Haiti were "ignorant of the ways to realize and maintain" freedom, Voros's claims seem minimally to have been elitist if not altogether resonant of Darwinian, eugenics-based arguments about natural intelligence which were so preponderant in fascist ideology of the time. Certainly it was problematic for the *Daily Worker* to cast the Haitian masses in such a condescending light only one year before the massacre in 1937.[11]

The *Daily Worker*'s characterization of Haitian people who were "ignorant" of the ways to maintain their freedom contrasted sharply with the fact that Communists were openly praising the pro-Communist fighters for Republican Spain at this same time. The center of gravity in the Popular Front against fascism was shifting toward Spanish soil just as Dominican soil would become drenched in Haitian blood. This Spanish front was preponderant in the international circles of the cultural front, and Hughes, Nicolas Guillen and Jacques Roumain evinced their Caribbean-New York solidarity with the anti-fascist literati attending the Second International Congress for Writers in July of 1937 in Spain. In December of 1937 at the World Writer's Conference in Madrid, a resolution was passed to demand immediate Puerto Rican independence while no such recognition much less resolution seems to have been proposed in response to the Trujillo massacre of Haitian laborers which had transpired in the period since the Second International Congress. If in fact this oversight did transpire, one must ask, how could that have been possible?[12]

Still the problem of differential support in favor of the anti-fascist movement in Spain—and even Puerto Rico—took on greater racial dimensions relative to the struggles underway in Abyssinia and the tragedy that would unfold in Haiti. Epicenters of totalitarian control such as Abyssinia and the Dominican Republic do not appear to have received the support necessary from the Comintern to build a solidly anti-racist movement in the struggle to overturn fascism around the world, and this was reflected in the *Daily Worker* and the *Negro Worker*. In the *Daily Worker*, an update on Italian atrocities in Abyssinia in March of 1937 revealed smuggled photographs of six Ethiopians hanging from the gallows of their Italian occupiers. Days later, William Patterson of the ILD crystallized the Comintern position on the primacy of defending the Spanish Republic as a means of strategically thwarting the Italian incursions into Ethiopia, declaring that "the fate of Ethiopia is being decided upon the battlefields of Spain. This is a fact of tremendous importance." In this black Communist's estimation, and that of the Comintern more broadly, defending Spain was a necessary precondition for breaking the Italian yoke over Ethiopia.[13]

Emanating from within Ethiopia itself was an influential league of nationalist freedom fighters that had joined the ranks of the Spanish front. Several articles in the March 1937 issue of the *Negro Worker* supported Patterson's remarks on the political expediency associated with deferring support for the Abyssinian struggle in the popular movement against fascism. These articles featured the biographies of Ras Imru and his son. The former was proclaimed "the fighter who continued to defend Abyssinia after the fall of Addis Ababa" only to be "captured and taken bound in chains to Italy" and the latter, named Ghyet, was presently "fighting with the Republican forces in defence of Madrid." "What a glorious example he is setting for the youth of the Negro world!" cheered this editorial staff at the *Negro Worker*. But the praise was bittersweet for the article went on to assert—in a manner very reminiscent of the "Troubled Island" analysis of Haiti's "ignorant" freedom fighters—that Ghyet's triumph represented the "tremendous pace at which a backward people can develop in moments of crisis." While it was true that in recent history, Abyssinia had not been a center of workers' militancy as had been the case for black people in many other parts of the world, it was also problematic to dismiss the entire country—full of impoverished peasants—as therefore fated to suffer and take the back seat in Communist support simply because they were still ruled by a monarch rather than a prime minister or colonial governor.[14]

The Comintern's strategic import placed on Spain over Abyssinia was certainly understandable when taking into account the uneven development of radicalism around the world, but it also demonstrates the residual effects of this situation for explaining why Communists in New York were somewhat remiss in their hemispheric duties to the suffering Haitians living in the Dominican Republic. *Negro Worker* editors proclaimed Ghyet's service in Spain to have been "proof of the tremendous value of the united front of all progressive and democratic people supporting Spanish democracy," only to dismiss Ethiopia as a "backward feudal country enmeshed in slavery, superstition and medieval darkness." Given this literally dark rhetorical dismissal of Abyssinia taken by the editorial staff of both the *Negro Worker* and *Daily Worker* in the months leading up to the Trujillo massacre, it is understandable how the ideological pretext of the democratic Spanish front objectively relegated "backward" victims of fascist aggression to the periphery—particularly those enmeshed in the history of "slavery" and "superstition." And Haiti, an important stronghold of African-derived voodoo, certainly bore with it the markers of both slavery and superstition.[15]

Communist support for Spain in 1937, which was articulated in both the *Negro Worker* and the *Daily Worker*, had inevitably placed the Comintern in a race–nation conundrum. Even though it was indeed the case that Emperor Haile Selassie had been "credulous enough to put faith in the word of the ruling class of Great Britain" for relying on British support in thwarting Italian aggression, it was not the case that the entire nation of people living in Abyssinia were responsible for this political decision on the part of their leader. Moreover, even though the struggle underway in Spain was more aligned with the pro-Soviet international movement than that of Abyssinia, a tension between race and nation had arisen for Communists because the lives of everyday black people in

Abyssinia were no less worthy of immediate defense and international solidarity efforts than those of non-black people in Republican Spain. Notwithstanding the tremendous outcries of support in "Hands off Abyssinia" campaigns that the Comintern sparked and supported the world over, it is also true that the Communist movement was on one level ideologically complicit in reinforcing some aspects of the very same racialist and polarizing discourses of "progressive" versus "backward," "scientific" versus "superstitious" peoples that fueled President Trujillo's denunciation of the voodoo-infused cultural traditions of those Haitian migrant laborers living within his nation's borders.

FROM ANTI-COMMUNISM TO NATIONAL-SOCIALISM IN THE DOMINICAN REPUBLIC

In the very period when the Communists were mobilizing a concentration of global Popular Front forces to support the Spanish Republic, the American empire oversaw the process whereby "neighborly" forces in the hemisphere became committed to openly thwarting this Red menace. In response to a State Department query regarding any possible motivations behind the political proscriptions being fostered by President Trujillo in the Dominican Republic, Franklin B. Atwood of the American Legation admitted that it was "not clear" in an October 1936 memorandum:

> According to one well-informed source, President Trujillo is desirous of ridding the Republic of some Spaniards who are suspected of having Communist leanings because of their staunch support of the present Spanish government, and he is employing this means of ensuring their deportation. On the other hand, the new proposal may be related to the basis for current rumors of the intention of President Trujillo to institute a totalitarian State in this Republic, abolishing Congress and other organs of the nominally democratic government established by the Dominican Constitution.[16]

Perhaps the only thing that was "not clear" was Atwood's own ideological vantage point, for his narrative posited a false dichotomy. President Trujillo's aims of "ridding the Republic of some Spaniards who are suspected of having Communist leanings" laid the basis for his plans to "institute a totalitarian State," subsequently eliminating all political opposition by "abolishing Congress and other organs of the nominally democratic government." By the close of 1936, President Trujillo had officially begun to institute a totalitarian dictatorship premised at first upon a nativist policy of anti-Communist sedition only later to re-emerge in the form of a racial bloodbath, all in the name of "God, Fatherland and Liberty!"—and unofficially stamped with the approval of the US State Department.

President Trujillo was a national-socialist. "My Government," he boasted, "for the first time in the Republic, has initiated and carried to completion the qualitative and scientific distribution of all lands apt for cultivation," and "this," he concluded, "is the nature of socialism that I practice." He did not disclose that his pseudo-scientific affinities for the eugenics-based theories of Mussolini and Hitler would provide the ideological rationale for his own strategy of clearing this land for cultivation by carefully yet systematically annihilating the Haitian residents therein. He was therefore opposed to "Communism and other doctrines of the same category" which were "daily inflaming class hatreds" and led to "long and sanguinary armed conflicts." Instead, he was "deeply in sympathy with every proposal to enlarge in the world of conquest of right and the empire of justice." He did not reveal that in the coming months this "world of conquest" and "empire of justice" would drench the rivers of Monte Criste with the blood of Haitian laborers.[17]

Trujillo's assertions that the Dominican Republic had given birth to a new era of egalitarian, classless *civitas,* or citizenry, were strikingly resonant of the manner in which Hitler and Mussolini had built their fascist programs of allegiance to the state for a national project that undermined Communist efforts to foment class antagonism. Trujillo purported to elevate the rights of the average Dominican (unless he or she was a Communist, pro-Spanish, or pro-Haitian sympathizer) to that of the President himself. In essence, the Dominican President's trope of the *civitas* laid the political and cultural groundwork that then enabled him to garner the mass public support for his sole leadership, or "Trujillismo," in order to mitigate any threat of class warfare emanating from progressive Dominicans and Haitian laborers. Such a movement materially placed Haitian migrant laborers into what the contemporary political philosopher Giorgio Agamben refers to as a "permanent state of exception," since as non-citizens they could make no claims whatsoever to the state in the face of Trujillo's dictatorship. The anti-Communist ban that he had successfully imposed in October of 1936 seems to have been the penultimate manifestation of the national-socialist project which had begun to rapidly degenerate in the months leading up to the massacre of October 1937.

The *Daily Worker* did make mention of Trujillo's dictatorship prior to October of 1937, but it did so by reprinting the letter of retired US General Hugh S. Johnson, who submitted a piece to the *Washington Daily News* in which he lambasted the "reincarnated Emperor" of the Dominican Republic who considered to have "attained a dictatorship that should make even Mussolini meek." The *Daily Worker* used Johnson's critique of the Roosevelt administration's "good neighbor aloofness" to make its own case for greater US intervention in opposition to Trujillo's totalitarian regime. Johnson detailed how the "most modern methods of every local and international racketeer" were being carried out in the Dominican Republic:

The press is a controlled echo. Labor unions have been abolished. Strikes are settled with machine guns, and there has been a blood purge of all opposition … In the approved Hitler fashion, a youth was triggered out of existence while strolling with his sweetheart and a man suffering from appendicitis … "Pineapples" have been used to explode the sophistries of opposing statesmen … Under the complacent aegis of our good neighbor aloofness, he diddled American bondholders out of their treaty-guaranteed sureties. There has been diverted by confiscation, assassination and official bulldozing [of] a good deal of private wealth.[18]

Trujillo, on this account, was a tyrant whose wrath of state collectivism and political repression had displaced the entire population from innocent love-struck youths to labor protestors to even "a good deal of private wealth." While interracial childhood sweethearts and striking Dominican laborers were being executed in the streets of Ciudad Trujillo (newly renamed from Santo Domingo), Communists based out of New York were turning out for May Day in 1937 in the tens of thousands, declaring "Up Goes Democracy, Down Goes Fascism!" as well as "Make New York City a Union Town!" Communists in New York were particularly conscious in this era not to burn "popular" bridges in the State Department.[19]

POPULAR ALLIANCES WITH UNPOPULAR RESULTS:
THE NNC AND THE TRUJILLO MASSACRE

No other organization based in New York that was affiliated with the CPUSA would be more caught in the matrix of Red International and Black Caribbean forces that converged in the Dominican Republic in October of 1937 than the National Negro Congress. On October 6, 1937, one of those tragic days wherein the "River Massacre" would run red, black Communist and NNC leader Max Yergan "greeted President Roosevelt's speech calling for international action against the fascist-militarist governments now waging war against China and Spain." Yergan, however, did not mention the "fascist-militarist governments" only several hundred miles to the south "now waging war against" the Haitian population, perhaps, of course, because he had not yet received word of this tragedy. In turn, President Roosevelt expressed his "best wishes" to the NNC in lieu of his direct attendance at their Second National Congress with a personal letter to the NNC which was published on the third day of this convention. In his letter, Roosevelt averred that

… I am glad to extend greetings to the NNC … It seems to me that participation of delegates from the United States and foreign countries in a discussion of such pertinent and major issues as housing, education and employment can not but be significant and productive.[20]

Surely it must have been difficult for black Communists such as Yergan to determine the meaning of terms such as "neighbors" and "good" in a period when global and national political developments were intensifying and complicating almost daily. Under a subject heading entitled "world front," a small, untitled blurb on November 9, 1937—over a month after the massacre had occurred—noted that 3,000 (a low estimate) Haitians had been killed in the "River Massacre." This piece was squeezed into the pages of the *Daily Worker* only weeks after the paper reported on Angelo Herdon's brother, Milton Herdon, who had recently died on the battlefields of Spain and weeks before it discussed how Max Yergan would begin rallying NNC support behind President Roosevelt's "condemning world fascism and pledging full support to the Chinese, Spanish and Ethiopian people." While minimal coverage of the massacre in the Dominican Republic on the part of New York Communists can be understood partially in light of the larger Popular Front mobilizations against fascism that were then preponderant at the time, the other context in which the CPUSA's response must be gauged is the fact that there was an overall lack of disclosure about the incident to the larger public on the part of the Dominican and US authorities.[21]

This lack of disclosure inevitably affected the nature of the response on the part of Communists. In an almost aloof manner, the *Daily Worker* referred to Trujillo having historically "slaughtered 3,000 Dominicans to retain his dictatorial grip" only to have now "dipped his hands in the blood of 3,000 Haitian peasants, men, women and children." Surely these were no "political prisoners" in the strictest, Campos-Roumain-Fonseca sense, but their lives were no less valuable. Insofar as it was apparently "only now that the facts were seeping through," the *Daily Worker* editors roughly charged "a few American bankers and Romana Sugar Mills" and President Stenio Vincent with having been in "complicity of silence over the most barbarous event ever to occur in the Caribbean." A small coterie of bankers and politicians, however, could not have been the sole group responsible for devastation of such mass proportions, but the *Daily Worker* did not address the ways in which many Dominican citizens had been complicit in Trujillo's massacre. Even more to the point, by late 1937—as in the case of Puerto Rico, Cuba and Mexico—the CPUSA and Communists across the hemisphere were averse to challenging very directly the present leadership of their "good neighbors" in the White House and other ruling elites in the region.[22]

Though there was a series of protests against the massacre on the part of the NNC and other organizations connected with the CPUSA, they were nowhere near as forceful as the pro-Haitian campaign of 1929. It is possible that the NNC was distracted with already providing support for the movements in the BWI at the time, since this same time frame was also when the NNC, the ILD and other radical groups were sponsoring dinners on behalf of W. A. Crawford of the *Barbados Advocate*. Notwithstanding the shortcomings of its response, the NNC did still make efforts to rebuke the attack on the Haitians.

The *Daily Worker* indicated that the "Greater New York Council of the National Negro Congress" called for a mass rally in late December of 1937 to protest the killing of (now) 8,000 Haitians in the Dominican Republic, especially "in view of the large number of citizens of Negro origin living both in Haiti and in the Dominican Republic." But Max Yergan, the NNC, and the CPUSA in general were wary of acting too aggressively when approaching the Roosevelt administration about this delicate diplomatic matter of Trujillo's massacre. Max Yergan addressed a letter on behalf of the NNC to his "Excellency" in the State Department attempting to seek redress for the "reported mass killing and deportation of thousands of Haitian civilians in Dominican territory by Dictator Trujillo's military forces."[23]

While Communists like Yergan were hardly expecting the US government to willingly advocate on behalf of the Haitian victims without outside agitation from progressives on the ground, they were also engaged in a process of diplomatic wordplay that carried little if any significance for the very victims in whose name this petition was made. Welles was not convinced that corresponding with progressives—much less Communists like Yergan—was "necessary." He responded to his State Department page, Mr. Dugan, that "I do not know whether any reply to the attached communication is necessary or desirable. If you think it is, please have some appropriate acknowledgement drafted for my signature." Unbeknownst to Communists at the time, Secretary of State Welles had dismissed the plight of the "Haitian civilians in Dominican territory" upon receiving news of the initial figure of 3,000 Haitians dead.[24]

The Secretary of State's indifference to the killings was reflective of an even deeper cynicism and racial prejudice on the part of US intelligence officers in the Dominican Republic. An internal memorandum from Howard Eager, Lieutenant Colonel for the Bureau of Insular Affairs, points toward the ways in which US officials were essentially aware of the long-term and short-term socioeconomic factors that had given rise to the massacre which inevitably implicated American empire in Trujillo's genocidal endeavor. Eager's primary frustration with Trujillo was the fact that "sugar interests directly, and government indirectly, would be seriously crippled by cutting off this source of cheap and reliable labor." It seems Eager's own lens was "insular" to the extent that his only concern was that there was no resale value for dead Haitian laborers who had been cultivating American-owned sugar enterprises like Domino sugar. But Haitian migrant laborers had long been entangled in the transnational web of US business enterprise in Cuba. Guggenheim had not been opposed to the first wave of deportations of Haitian and Jamaican laborers beginning in November of 1933 just as Jamaican "Red Guards" were controlling US sugar mills in Miranda, Cuba.[25]

Most telling about Lt. Col. Eager's own "insular" response to this tragic occurrence was the fact that he had reached a consensus with those on the island who "generally agreed that Trujillo's action in the whole affair was stupid, utterly lacking in reason and likely to have most serious consequences for his government." This "stupidity," Eager explained, lay in the fact that "no adequate substitute for Haitian labor [was] readily available." Moreover, Lt. Col. Eager retrospectively counseled, "If his sole object had been to rid the country of Haitians, he could readily have done so at any time by less objectionable methods," noting the way in which "several thousand Haitians have been repatriated since the massacre, without interference on the part of the Dominican government." On Eager's account, the entire debacle of migration, deportation and repatriation could have been handled with "methods" that were "less objectionable" to the US State Department.[26]

Notwithstanding Eager's blind spots of imperialist ideology, he was correct in asserting that "a systematic massacre of the extent and duration of this one could never have been carried out without [Trujillo's] orders or against his will." Eager correlated the "material increase" in "Haitian banditry" over the course of 1937 with the fact that Cuba had deported thousands of Haitians, forcing them to resort to crime and illegal immigration into the Dominican Republic. Moreover, he also determined that this problem of Haitian-Dominican criminal activity at the border provided much of the rationale for Trujillo's political attack against Haitians in the Dominican Republic:

> President Trujillo of the Dominican Republic is reliably reported to have made on Saturday, October 2, 1937, at Dajabon, a small town on the northern part of the frontier, a violent anti-Haitian speech, capitalizing on the Haitian bandit activities, threatening the perpetrators with death and promising to rid the Dominican Republic of "dogs, hogs and Haitians." Beginning the following day and continuing until about October 10th, in the vicinity of Dajabon and Monte Cristi, a neighboring town near the north coast, there was instituted by Dominican soldiers, local police and immigration inspectors, a quiet, systematic and thorough search for all Haitians in the area.[27]

On this account, Trujillo's "violent anti-Haitian speech, capitalizing on the Haitian bandit activities" became the rallying cry for the subsequent workings of "Dominican soldiers, local police and immigration inspectors" in a "quiet, systematic and thorough" massacre in which "the method almost invariably followed was by clubbing, bayoneting and machete slashing."[28]

But what Lt. Col. Eager characterized as a "stupid" response to Haitian mass migration into the Dominican Republic on the part of President Trujillo, an anonymous Austrian eyewitness named "Mr. X" decried plainly as "the work of a mad man." To Mr. X, the first week in October of 1937 was the scene of a war zone: "X stated that he had spent three years in the Austrian Army during the

World War and that nothing he had seen there was as horrible as the sights he saw at Monte Cristi." Since Dominican civilians were generally prohibited from bearing witness to the killings, Mr. X's personal account which was delivered to the American National Red Cross in a "personal and confidential memo" along with "two corroborative witnesses to this action" from "Mr. Y and Mr. Z, both Europeans," offers an alternative archive for understanding the depth of human depravity that editors at the *Daily Worker* had been unable to convey for lack of knowledge.[29]

Mr. X was an Austrian citizen who had "engaged in various enterprises" that were "connected with German goods and export of hides" while residing in the Dominican Republic for the past nine years. He had borne witness to the massacres in Monte Cristi because his "business had taken him extensively through the Cibao country and the northern frontier, with his principal place of business along the Santo Domingo-Haiti line at Monte Cristi." But whatever long-term social and economic status he had enjoyed had almost seemingly vanished from his perspective once a "Dominican commanding officer of troops in the area sent out a circular letter to all foreigners and to all Dominican citizens" demanding the immediate and unconditional "registration of all Haitians in such persons' employ within three hours." Three hours later, noted Mr. X., the troops had concentrated this literal blacklist of Haitians onto the wharves of the river at bayonet point in a manner akin to the Nazi quarantines of Jewish prisoners in the "chamber of horrors" recounted by Mayor Laguardia in that same year. Trujillo, however, preferred the open air and River Massacre as his site of annihilation.[30]

Mr. X proceeded to describe how "bodies fell into the sea where most, but not all were disposed of by sharks," and those which the sharks had not devoured then "came ashore along the bay of Monte Cristi where they were later seen in large numbers." But Mr. X's historical function as a primary source ends where a whole new archive begins. Some of these apparent cadavers were in reality only staging death as a means of escaping death—a quite surreal experience indeed. Hence we have arrived at the birth of an archive derived from the single most important primary source that can help inform a sound and indeed radical historical perspective of the Trujillo massacre: the Haitian victims who lived to tell the tale.[31]

Statements by Haitian witnesses of and survivors to the week-long killing spree appear to have been received by one Ferdinand L. Mayer from the Division of American Republics in the US Consulate as early as October 7. One survivor, Alteon Joseph, was a field worker who did not know his age. It was very common for undocumented laborers, particularly those who worked in the field, not to know their age. Mr. Joseph recalled that:

> ... having heard the rumor that several Haitians had been killed we got together and decided to leave in a group ... Arriving near Dajabon we met two Dominican

guards who led us near a woods and then they took the men two by two and the women in groups of five or six and saying that the customs gateway was closed … several Dominican guards who attacked me on the neck … They dragged me by one foot and threw me in the ravine where there were already a considerable number of dead Haitians. Men, women and children.[32]

Mr. Joseph's forced repatriation at first began as an escape attempt in response to the "rumor that several Haitians had been killed," and quite quickly he realized that the "several" dead was fast becoming a "considerable number." One 32-year-old dressmaker, a woman named Feneleice Fenay, corroborated Mr. Joseph's account of the occurrences at Dajabon, but her survival mechanisms appear to have been even more intact.

Feneleice Fenay's account demonstrates how women were among the chief victims in the massacre. Ms. Fenay, who said she had "received several blows on my left side and a blow on the head from a machete" and thus decided to silently feign death, also recounted that in the process she had "heard the Dominican guards say it is not necessary that these Haitians cry out like that" at which point "the other one replied this doesn't matter it has all been done well the Haitians won't be able to fight back." The Dominican guards were fundamental to carrying out this massacre and underlying the entire process of annihilation was a desire to ensure that the Haitians "won't be able to fight back." In the all-too-recent past, Haitian laborers had proven themselves to be quite vocal about social, political and economic questions which had impacted the class struggle in the Dominican Republic, and this fact might have haunted the memories of Dominican guards.[33]

But "fight back" many would. Some escaped back into Haiti like modern-day fugitive slaves. Others shed their own blood in the streets of Port-Au-Prince in sacrificial retribution for their brethren that were killed by a leader who subscribed to national-socialist totalitarianism. In the first weeks of December, Haiti would undergo—almost exactly eight years to the day—a similar ripple of student-led strike waves and labor protests as had erupted during the "Haitian Revolution" of 1929. The *Daily Worker* followed up its coverage of the protests to report that over a hundred Haitian student protesters had been killed "in a two-week reign of terror" which had ensued at the auspices of President Vincent (not Trujillo) "after students, workers and government employees began a nation-wide protest strike against the government." Just as the students at Damien College had begun the protests in 1929, in 1937 the protests had "begun by students of the Medical College" chanting "'Down with Stenio Vincent,'" and "'We did not put him in his place, Vincent is an accomplice to the murder of our brothers.'" Most valiant among the freedom fighters who lost their lives in this struggle involved a sister who had lost her brother in the slaughter:

One report which reached New York tells of the brutal killing of a woman demonstrating in Aux Cayes by Vincent's police when she shouted, "Down with Vincent!" She was grabbed, kicked and slugged over the head with a club. She died with the slogan on her lips.

This "troubled island" was hardly plagued with "ignorant" freedom fighters; rather, it was endowed with a militant population of women and men who had continually taken the revolution into their own hands. And now they were being shot down in the streets by their *own* government as if they were nothing more than "dogs, hogs and Haitians."[34]

NNC leaders were not entirely passive in the process of supporting the struggle underway in Haiti and Santo Domingo. In fact, they advocated for an investigative delegation to be sent onto the island just as radicals in New York had successfully made in the cases of Puerto Rico and Cuba throughout the 1930s. Yergan suggested that an "unofficial delegation may be sent from the US to Haiti and to the Dominican Republic" to be "charged with the responsibility of obtaining the complete facts relative to the reported troubles, and of making suggestions for removing the fundamental causes of such troubles." Just as the Cuban delegation in 1935 was composed of professionals, so too was this pro-Haitian support movement in New York derived from "prominent members of the Haitian and Dominican communities in New York City."[35]

But a follow-up article in the *Daily Worker* reporting on one mid-December rally laid bare that the NNC had not grasped the deeply racialized history of intra-island and intra-ethnic antagonism embedded in this essentially fascist crisis on Dominican territory. At this rally, NNC leader A. Phillip Randolph advocated for the unity of Haitian and Dominican people against Trujillo fascism, all the while failing to deal with the reality that some Dominicans were complicit in the slaughter: "The NNC in condemning the massacre of 8,000 Haitians draws a sharp line between the Dominican people and the Dominican government. That government is in the hands of foul fascists. But the people are struggling for freedom.'" Let us recall, however, that for one young Haitian farm worker, it was all of the Dominicans said to have been killing "all of the Haitians," such that the "sharp line" of distinction from his perception was quite different from what Randolph had determined in New York.[36]

Broadly speaking, the myriad eyewitness accounts from the Haitian survivors of the massacre pointed toward the complexity of racial prejudice and this genocidal process, rather than a "sharp line" of distinction within the Dominican population. The hands of the Dominican civilians who witnessed—often in terror but passively nonetheless—as their dictator charged "dogs, hogs and Haitians" with death by machete, or club, or shark were not so clean. The hand of Yergan as he penned words of praise and "spirit" in association with the "Good Neighbor" policy all the while pinning the fates of many suffering Haitians to figures such as Sumner Welles were not entirely clean either. Above all, however, the hands of Trujillo were far from clean.

US officials stationed on the ground in Santo Domingo remarked cynically that Trujillo's dictatorship had gone democratic "at a time when foreign press reports are replete with descriptions of a so-called dictatorship in the Dominican Republic." On the very day that the NNC had requested the assistance of world leaders in "removing the fundamental causes of these troubles," President Trujillo had submitted a request to Congress for lifting the ban on Communism and for "his program for the benefit of the proletariat." Trujillo's program was said to include the following: "giving of lands to poor farmers; laws regulating the conditions of labor and providing for social insurance; the ratification of international labor conventions; and the establishment of agricultural granges for the supplying of tools and scientific instruction to Dominican farmers." "Neither communist nor fascist," Trujillo stated, "the Dominican Republic will always be a pure democracy whose institutional organization" was quite opportunely claimed to have been "modeled upon the immortal principles which inspired the patriots of Philadelphia." The implicit subtext to President Trujillo's national-socialist doctrine was that the "cleansing" of Haitian proletarians in the Dominican Republic had been necessary for the "scientific" advancement of Dominican proletarians.[37]

Moreover, President Trujillo had now considered lifting the ban on Communism based on the principle that the Dominican Republic "does not nor will ever admit the adoption of extremist systems nor of the antagonistic ideologies which today perturb the universal conscience." This "universal conscience," however, was quite hemispheric; indeed, it was American insofar as Trujillo's doctrine of a new nation had been modeled after the "pure democracy" of the American anti-colonialists whose own destiny was made manifest, in part, by the cleansing of the native populations in "American territory." Hence Atwood considered that "all of these steps may, of course be the result of a pure feeling for democracy," but he more deeply found it "remarkable that they come at a time when the Dominican President is seeking to correct the unfavorable press notices he is receiving abroad, characterizing him as an absolute dictator, personally responsible for the acts of his government." But was not Atwood's expressed affinity for a "pure sense of democracy" embedded in an impure, dehumanizing civilizationist discourse that equated the "universal conscience" with Europeans whose gift of modernity had incessantly expressed itself in the form of annihilation, enslavement and domination of darker people in the "New World"?[38]

Even President Roosevelt was complicit with the atrocity during these days of the "Good Neighbor" policy backed by Reds in New York. On December

20, 1937, the President of the United States released a telegram to "His Excellency, General Rafael Leonidas Trujillo," indicating that "I have the honor to acknowledge ... the Government of the Dominican Republic will take part in the procedure invoked by the Government of Haiti" as a means toward reconciling the controversy that erupted between the two nations after the incident. He conveyed his "gratification" that the "Dominican Republic will not give the slightest ground for a disturbance of the peace of America, in the preservation of which all the peoples of the New World have so great and legitimate an interest." Roosevelt went on to label the massacre a regrettable "controversy" whose "rapid, just and pacific solution" could be obtained, he felt, by "utilization of the inter-American peace instruments to which they have now announced their determination to have recourse." What form were these instruments of peace to take, and whose interests would they serve? As we have seen, there had been no "inter-American peace instruments" available to St. Vil as he attempted to cross Massacre River.[39]

Even though Communists in New York had not openly denounced Roosevelt for failure to act in the aftermath of the massacre, they were aware that the "peace instruments" of which he spoke were far from effective. If anything, the *Daily Worker* indicated that US outposts in the Caribbean had abetted Trujillo's regime of terror. For example, an article printed in January of 1938 discussed the interesting case of a Dominican writer named Francisco Firon who, upon releasing a book entitled *Misdeeds of Bandit Trujillo*, fled persecution despite the repeal of the Communism ban; he arrived in Puerto Rico only to be sentenced for libel by a Puerto Rican judge. The article noted that "the issues involved in this case ... go beyond Trujillo's dictatorship and are bound up with the freedom of speech and the press" such that it was "particularly significant when a judge in an American possession becomes the defender of a Dictator in another Latin American nation"—so much for the "instruments of inter-American peace." But Communists based in the United States had also most assuredly lost a degree of political currency in relationship to the plight of the Haitian workers in the Caribbean.[40]

By 1938, the CPUSA was chiefly concerned with the question of fascism in Latin America in relationship to the Brazilian dictatorship under President Vargas of the "Integralistas" Party. An assessment of the state of Brazilian fascism printed in the May 1938 issue of *The Communist* indicates the degree to which the Haitian massacre had been pushed into the background for Communists at the time. In this report on fascism in Brazil, only the last sentence of the multi-page analysis mentioned the Trujillo massacre that had occurred less than one year beforehand. The wholesale killing of these Haitians had been cast as a distant memory. Instead, "Primitive Negro leadership" in Brazil had been identified as a new demographic for hemispheric expansion. The CPUSA had shed "new light" on the struggles of black Brazilians, thus illuminating new terrain wherein the Comintern could try to take up the cause of oppressed black people in the fight against fascism. Through the duration of the interwar period, Communists had indeed remained committed to fighting racism and insisting upon the international, multiracial support of workers around the world for working-class black militancy, even as they made significant strategic errors along the way, errors which can only serve as lessons for what not to repeat in the years to come.[41]

Enclosure No. 7 to
Despatch No. 19
of DEC 17 1937
from the Legation at
Port-au-Prince, Haiti.

C O P Y

INTERROGATOIRE DE AVELINE JOSEPH

D.- Etiez-vous seule en République Dominicaine?

R.- J'étais en famille, père, mère et deux enfants.

D.- Pouvez-vous nous donner les noms, prénoms, âge de ces différentes personnes?

R.- Mon père se nomme Joseph Jean (ignorant son âge), ma mère Genia Aristilde (ignorant son âge) et deux enfants nommés Clerzulie Hes Cayel et Berneus Jean Pierre. Je ne sais pas de quel âge étaient ces derniers, mais ils étaient tous jeunes.

D.- Où sont ces parents dont vous venez de parler?

R.- Ils ont été tous massacrés par des gardes Dominicains.

TEMOINS:

Paul E. Magloire, 1er Lt. GdH.

Josias M. Fontaine (03170) Cpl. GdH.

Sa Marque
Aveline Joseph

(FEMELLE)

****

Ouanaminthe, Haiti, le 6 octobre, 1937.

DECLARATION DU NOMME ST-HUBERT JOSEPH

D.- Déclinez vos nom, prénom, âge, profession et nationalité.

R.- St-Hubert Joseph, âgé de 45 ans, cultivateur, haitienne.

D.- Où habitez-vous?

R.- La Romana, R. D.

D.- Depuis combien de temps demeuriez-vous en République Dominicaine?

R.- Depuis 17 ans.

D.- Pourquoi êtes-vous rentré en Haiti?

R.- Je suis entré en Haiti parce que le mardi 28 septembre 1937, revenant de mon jardin avec mon beau-frère, nous avons été arrêtés et amarrés par quatre (4) gardes dominicains. Pendant qu'ils nous conduisaient, ils nous assaillirent à coups de couteaux. Mon beau-frère fut tué sur le champs et moi

10 Part of the transcript of an interview with a Haitian survivor of the Trujillo massacre, 1937 (courtesy of US National Archives, Washington, DC).

Notes

CHAPTER 1

1 Document 844d.5045/1, 16 May 1919, Box 8895, RG 59, US National Archives; Document 844d.5045/-, 29 June 1919, Box 8895, RG 59, US National Archives.

2 Documents 844d.5045/3–5, 22 December 1919–17 January 1920, Box 8895, RG 59, US National Archives.

3 Document 844b.00/5, 6/30/1920, RG 59, US National Archives.

4 Document 844g.001/1, 1/1/1920, Box 8898, RG 59, US National Archives; Document 844g.001/6, 1/24/1920, Box 8898, RG 59, US National Archives.

5 "Puerto Rican Workers in New York," *Daily Worker*, 8 November 1927, p.4.

6 Document 812.00b/1, 6/16/1920, Reel 90, M274, RG 59, US National Archives.

7 Document 812.00b/5, 9/27/1920, Reel 90, M274, RG 59, US National Archives; Document 812.00b/, 4/13/1921, Reel 90, M274, RG 59, US National Archives; Document 812.00b/39, 9/1/1922, Reel 90, M274, RG 59, US National Archives.

8 Document 812.00b/16, 6/21/1921, Reel 90, M274, RG 59, US National Archives; Document 812.00b/53, 1/23/1923, Reel 90, M274, RG 59, US National Archives.

9 Document 2056-190, 10/6/1919, Reel 6, MID 2056, RG 165, US National Archives.

10 "The Mexican Farmers Joint the Peasant International," *International Press Correspondence*, vol.5, no.14, p.188; Document 821.00b/88, Reel 90, RG 59, US National Archives.

11 Telegram, Document 2056-74, 28 December 1919, Reel 6, MID 2056, RG 165, US National Archives; Telegram, Document 2056-155, 6 March 1919, Reel 6, MID 2056, RG 165, US National Archives; Telegram, Document 2056-133, 3 February 1919, Reel 6, MID 2056, RG 165, US National Archives.

12 Document 2056-190, 10/6/1919, Reel 6, MID 2056, RG 165, US National Archives.

13 Document 812.00b/7, 9/20/1920, Reel 90, M274, RG 59, U.S National Archives.

14 Document 3655-q-5, 10 August 1920, Reel 5, MID 3655-q, RG 165, US National Archives.

15 "Aims of the Crusader," *Crusader* 1 [September 1918]: 5; "Revolutionary Radicalism: Its history, purpose and tactics with an exposition and discussion of the steps being taken and required to curb it, being the report of the Joint legislative committee investigating seditious activities, filed April 24, 1920, in the Senate of the state of New York" (Albany: J.B. Lynn, 1920), vol.2, pp.1483–4; "The Black Man's Burden," *Crusader* 1 [October 1918]: 47–8, 70.

16 In one fascinating portrayal of an African American narrator who had "passed for white" while in Puerto Rico, he was disclosing conditions about the "Jim Crow"

United States to Punta when he "realized that in the words MY PEOPLE I had told of my race. They knew the things of which I had spoke came from a heart that beat with the sufferings experienced before I stepped across the line." But to the narrator's pleasant surprise, Punta himself "had [his] hand in a firm grasp" and looked on "with eyes that bespoke admiration." The almost visceral connection between Punta and this black American narrator who was passing for a white man attempted to capture through literature one dimension of the Afro-Latin question that had been the legacy of racist colonialism: the creation of categories or levels of (non)blackness such that Afro-Latinos like Punta, who as a "mixed blood" represented a less African subject within the social order of humanity.

17 "Punta, Revolutionist," *Crusader* 1 [February 1919], pp.191–3.

18 "Dr. Du Bois Misrepresents Negrodom," 1 [May 1919], p.293; Editorial, "High Rents and Bolshevism," *Crusader* I [May 1919], p.294; "What Does Democratic America in Haiti?", *Crusader* I [June 1919], pp.329–30; Editorial, "The Lusk Committee Makes a Discovery," *Crusader* 1 [June 1919], p.404; For more on the raid of the "Lusk Committee" on New Negros in New York City, see Barbara Foley, *Spectres of 1919: Class and Nation in the Making of the New Negro* (Urbana: University of Illinois Press, 2003), pp.11–13; "The Negro in the West Indies," *Crusader* 1 [May 1919], p.304.

19 Editorial, "Bolshevist!," *Crusader* 2 [October 1919], p.477; "A Volunteer for the African Blood Brotherhood, Cristobal, CZ," *Crusader* 2 [November 1919], p.520.

20 "War With Mexico; What is the Negro Going to Do About It?," *Crusader* 2 [December 1920], pp.952–3, 957, 959.

21 He continued: "I was seething with prejudice and mad with Dominican booze. Now, however, since I have been chastened by the spirit of Socialism, and humbled by Truth, I desire to atone and fight the colored man's battle along with that of other oppressed peoples ... The Dominicans are a brave, musical people ... One of my confederates in crime while digging a trench alongside of me, picked up a large piece of clay and struck a native in the face. I believe it knocked the man's eye out, but nothing was ever done about it, and my friend ate a good supper that night ... In consideration of this fact I sympathize with the Dominicans or Haitians when they protest against the treatment dished out to them by the Democratic administration at Washington." See "A Marine's Confession," *Crusader* 2 [December 1920], p. 961.

22 "Correspondence," *Crusader* 3 [July 1921], p.1231.

23 Rothschild Francis would later work in active collusion with some of the very same black Communists then in the ABB who by the late 1920s were heading Communist mass organizations such as the International Labor Defense, Anti-Imperialist League and American Negro Labor Congress. This alliance would be severed by 1930 due to the political reorientation of the Communist movement worldwide with the "Third Period" strategic decision in the late 1920s to no longer align Communist party organizations and plans of action with those whose commitments lay in strengthening leadership the socio-economic ranks of the national bourgeoisie rather than with working-class independent groups. Where Francis would opt in the 1930s to retain commitment to a more class-based collaboration with local elites in the Virgin Islands for self-government and parliamentary rule, the black Communists who were his former Caribbean militant allies would opt instead for supporting the International Trade Union of Negro Workers and building directly the capacity of the working class for self-emancipation under the leadership of Communist party strategy—at least until 1935.

24 "Foreign Correspondence," *Crusader* 2 [November 1919], p.526.

25 "Overseas Correspondence," *Crusader* 2 [June 1920], p.627.

26 For more on the BSL's Yarmouth Line in Havana see "Report of UNIA Meeting: Honorable Marcus Garvey Speaks, The Yarmouth In Havana" in Robert Hill, *Marcus Garvey and the Universal Negro Improvement Association Papers* 2 (Berkeley: University of California Press, 2003), p.233.

27 "Haiti and the Black Star Line," *Crusader* 3 [October 1920], pp.877, 881.

28 "Overseas Correspondence," *Crusader* 3 [November 1920], p.925.

29 Ibid.

30 Hill, "Reports from the Convention," *Marcus Garvey and the Universal Negro Improvement Association Papers* 2, p.512; The Canal Zone appears to be a case in itself, however, and my project does not elaborate much on the movement in Panama, though it serves as an important example of the convergence of labor and black radicalism by way of the UNIA and ABB.

31 Hill, vol.2, p.517.

32 Editorial, "Black Star Line," *Crusader* 2 [December 1919], p.541.

33 Editorial, "A Paramount Chief for the Negro Race," *Crusader* 2 [March 1920], p.635; "A Letter from Marcus Garvey," *Crusader* 2 [April 1920], p.663.

34 "The African Blood Brotherhood," *Crusader* 2 [April 1920], p.665; "Overseas Correspondence," *Crusader* 2 [March 1920], p.627. At this stage my observations are still very speculative. But more research into the organizing work of the ABB and the UNIA on islands such as the Dominican Republic would shed a tremendous amount of light on the actual development of the New Negro movement in the Caribbean itself post-WWI. At a minimum, the UNIA had not as yet proven to be the only prospect for black international leadership on the island, or even in the Caribbean, and certainly not the hemisphere, much less the globe—at least not in the eyes of this particular member. But the UNIA was the most powerful black political force to be reckoned with in the very region that the ABB was expanding; a look into the August convention of the UNIA in 1920 elucidates this point.

35 "Communists Champion Negro: American 'Reds' Issue Stirring Call to White Labor to Make Common Cause with Colored Workers," *Crusader* 3 [August 1921], p.1212.

36 Editorial, "Stand By Soviet Russia!," *Crusader* 4 [December 1921], p.1314; Editorial, "The American Negro's Duty Toward Haiti and Santo Domingo," *Crusader* 4 [December 1921], pp.1316–17.

37 Hill, "Convention Speech by Rose Pastor Stokes," *Marcus Garvey and the Universal Negro Improvement Association Papers* 3, pp. 675–7.

38 "Greetings from Dominica," *Crusader* 4 [November 1921], pp.1297, 1299.

39 "Biggest Negro Organization Meets Friday: Garvey Tells Plans for 4th Convention," *Daily Worker*, 29 July 1924.

40 Hill, "Convention Report," *Marcus Garvey and the Universal Negro Improvement Association Papers* 5, p.667.

41 Ibid.

42 "Asks Negroes to Unite with International Struggle for Class and Race Emancipation," *Daily Worker*, 31 July 1924.

43 Hill, "Marcus Garvey to President Calvin Coolidge," *Marcus Garvey and the Universal Negro Improvement Association Papers* 5, p.640; ibid., "Marcus Garvey to Ramsay Macdonald," p.641; ibid., "Marcus Garvey to Benito Mussolini," p.643; ibid., "Marcus Garvey to President Borno," p.642.

44 "Negroes Told they are Held in Subjection by US and British Imperialist Rule," *Daily Worker*, no date available, p.1.

45 "Comrade Manuilsky Report on the National-colonial Question," *International Press Correspondence*, vol.4, no. 54, p.20; For more on the relationship between the

movement in South Africa and the "Negro question" in the United States see Ivon Jones, "The Crisis in the South African Labour Movement," ibid., vol. 2, no.16, p.116.; In reference to the American racial context, Jones remarked that "great elements of prejudice among the socialist and Communists of America" was a chief bulwark to the movement therein. Thus the movement among South African comrades themselves was developing at a much faster and more robust pace. In the coming months, in fact, it would be the US-based Black Reds who were to learn much from the South African experience in Red and Black mass organization building.

46 "War on Color Barrier Issue at Negro Meet: Communists Lead Fight with GOP Blocking," *Daily Worker*, 2 July 1924, p.1; For more on the "Negro Sanhendrin" see Joyce Moore Turner, *Richard B. Moore: Caribbean Militant in Harlem* (London: Indiana University Press, 1988), pp.49–50.

47 "Confidential" Memorandum, no date., Opus 1, Fond 515, Delo 400, Reel 26, Document #2. Communist Party of the United States of America Papers [CPUSA Papers], Manuscript Division, Library of Congress; "Programme for the Trade Union Educational League," Reel 26, Delo 405, Document 2–3: CPUSA Papers, Manuscript Division, Library of Congress; Anonymous, Opus 1, Fond 515, Delo 1688, Reel 130, Document 29, CPUSA Papers, Manuscript Division, Library of Congress.

CHAPTER 2

1 "500 Reds Battle Police Here; 5 Hurt," *New York Times*, 15 December 1929, p.1.

2 In reference to the WP before 1929 the organization retains this name, but when referencing this same organization beginning in 1928 it will be referred to as the CPUSA.

3 Anonymous, Opus 1, Fond 515, Delo 1688, Reel 130, Document 29, CPUSA Papers, Manuscript Division, Library of Congress.

4 Ibid.

5 "Letter to All District Organizers from Huiswoud, Director of Negro Dept from Central Com of CPUSA re Haiti," 9 December 1929, Opus 1, Fond 515, Delo 1650, Reel 127, CPUSA Papers, Manuscript Division, Library of Congress.

6 "To Central Executive Committee of Workers Party of America from American Negro Labor Congress Committee of Seven: Whiteman, Minor, Henry, Phillips, Allen, Hall, Doty." 7 August 1925, Opus 1, Fond 515, Delo 504, Reel 34, Documents 7–8: CPUSA Papers, Manuscript Division, Library of Congress.

7 "Unionist Witnesses Tyranny of Marines in Enslaved Haiti," *Daily Worker*, 2 July 1924, p.1; "American Rule in Haiti Held Not Justified: Dr. Leo S. Rose Asserts U.S. Marine Force Should Be Withdrawn Soon," *Christian Science Monitor*, 18 August 1924, p.1.

8 "Mass Meetings to Rally Negro Workers Against Imperialism," *Daily Worker*, 3 July 1925, p.2.

9 "Minutes of the Committee of Negro Work," 24 September 1925, Opus 1, Fond 515, Delo 533, Reel 36, Document 11, CPUSA Papers, Manuscript Division, Library of Congress.

10 "Special Supplement: Imperialism and the American Negro," *Daily Worker*, 14 November 1925, p.5.

11 Fort-Whiteman to General Secretary of Workers Party, Reel 50, Delo 720, Document 10, August 21, 1926, CPUSA Papers, Manuscript Division, Library of Congress.

12 "Negro Organizer Finds Brussels Congress Helps," *Daily Worker*, 5 April 1927, p.2; "Negro Congress Wants US Navy to Leave Haiti," *Daily Worker*, 25 August 1927, p.1.

13 "Negro Congress Wants US Navy to Leave Haiti," *Daily Worker*, 25 August 1927, p.1.

14 Political Committee of the Workers Party of America regarding members of the Anti-Imperialist League Commission, Opus 1, Fond 515, Delo 1533, Reel 116, Document 8a, CPUSA Papers, Manuscript Division, Library of Congress.

15 "Haitian Union Greets Meeting," *Daily Worker*, 18 February 1928, p.7; Cable from All-American Anti-Imperialist League to President Coolidge, Document 810.43-Anti-Imperialism League/57, 16 April 1928, Box 7301, DOS.

16 "Senator King Protests Marine Rule in Haiti," *New York Times*, 14 May 1928, p.29; "Anti-Imperialist Demonstration," *Negro Champion*, 8 August 1928, p.8.

17 "Dressmakers Strike Today," *Daily Worker*, 6 February 1929, p.1; "Negro Workers Cheer Moore, Padmore, at Big Labor Congress Meeting in Brooklyn: 'Only Freedom Lies in Class Organization,'" *Daily Worker*, 28 August 1929, p.2.

18 Minutes of the First Meeting of the Reorganized Negro Committee (National), Opus 1, Fond 515, Delo 1366, Reel 104, Documents 5–7, 14 August 1928, CPUSA Papers, Manuscript Division, Library of Congress.

19 Minutes of the National Sub-committee of the Central Executive Committee on Negro Work, Opus 1, Fond 515, Delo 1366, Reel 104, Document 12, 11 September 1928, CPUSA Papers, Manuscript Division, Flyer for Mass Meeting of the American Negro Labor Congress, Reel 116, Delo 1535, Document 42, 24 August 1928, CPUSA Papers, Manuscript Division, Library of Congress.

20 Flyer, "Work or Meals," Opus 1, Fond 515, Delo 1528, Reel 116, Document 51, no date, CPUSA Papers, Manuscript Division, Library of Congress.

21 "The Revolt Against the Republican Party," *Negro Champion*, November 3, 1928, p.2.

22 "Dressmakers Strike Today," *Daily Worker*, 6 February 1929, p.1.

23 "12,000 Workers Answer Call of Industrial Union: Negro Worker Slugged," *Daily Worker*, 7 February 1929, p.1; "Offer Negro, White Workers Free Scholarships," *Daily Worker*, 16 February 1929, p.2; "Race Prejudice Hit by New Union," *Negro Champion*, 25 May 1928, p. 4.

24 Minutes of Meeting of the Negro Commission, Opus 1, Fond 515, Delo 1685, Reel 130, Documents 1–6, 3 January 1929, CPUSA Papers, Manuscript Division, Library of Congress.

25 "Borno Announces US Change of Face to be Made in Haitian Rule," *Daily Worker*, 29 November 1929, p.3; From National Office of CPUSA in New York City to All Department Heads of CPUSA in the Trade Union, Somen's Department, Negro Department, Agitprop, Agrarian, Communist Youth League, Opus 1, Fond 515, Delo 1691, Reel 130, Document 24, 16 August 1929: CPUS.

26 "Haitian Strike Flares; Marines in Martial Law," *Daily Worker*, 6 December 1929, p.1; "Revolt Against US Imperialism: Battle Marines Who Fire on Peasant, Murder Five," *Daily Worker*, 9 December 1929, pp.1, 3, CPUSA Papers, Manuscript Division, Library of Congress; "Stand by the Haitian Revolution!" *Daily Worker*, 10 December 1929, p.1; "Smash Attack on Haiti, USSR," *Daily Worker*, 14 December 1929, p.5.

27 "Aid Haiti Revolt: Call Mass Meeting for Thursday, December 19," *Daily Worker*, 18 December 1929, p.1; "Defy California Police in Meeting for Haitian Workers; Six Held, Threaten to Deport," *Daily Worker*, 18 December 1929, p.2; "Haitian Demands: Southern White Workers Denounce US Marine Rule in Haiti," *Daily Worker*, 21 December 1929, p.4.

28 "Negro Toilers Join CP at Haiti Meets," *Daily Worker*, 27 December 1929, p.1; "Many Haitians Join ANLC: Marines Withdrawal Demanded," *Liberator*, 11 January 1930, p.4.

29 "World Meet of Negro Toilers at London July 1: International Negro Unionist Committee Calls Meet to Unite Race on Working Class Basis; Revolt of Oppressed Negros in Haiti, Africa and Other Lands Proves Need of Unity," *Daily Worker*, 19 December 1929, p.1.

CHAPTER 3

1 Assistant Secretary of State J.P. Cotton to Cuban Ambassador, Document 337.9324/2, 2 December 1929, Box 3939, RG 59, US National Archives.

2 Document 811c.00B/2 Cross Reference 831.00-Revolutions/11, 1 May 1929, M366, Reel 8, RG 59, US National Archives.

3 Document 811.00B/1020, 18 October 1929, Box 7332, RG 59, US National Archives; Communist Chinese migrant laborers in New York and San Francisco who were circuiting through these US migration capitals at times by way of Havana were often radicalized by the nationalist movements under way in China prior to their emigration. These very same migrants were in turn fundamental to paving the way for the transnational process of inter-party Communist activity between the Caribbean and United States. Moreover, the domestic post-WWI Chinese national liberation movement in the East and subsequent reverberations of Chinese migrant labor radicalism in the West also marked the explicit placing of China at the forefront of the anti-imperialist campaign in the Workers (Communist) Party in the United States. Therefore, Communists in the United States and Caribbean had to calculate increasingly complex demographic variations in the configuration of Bolshevik forces at the local and global levels by 1925 as the Communist movement in China took on ever greater proportions as part of the national liberation struggle against western imperialism.

4 "Comrade Bukharin Report on the Peasant Question in Ninth Section of Enlarged Executive of the CI," *International Press Correspondence*, vol.5, no.35, p.5.

5 "Mexican Communists Greet Daily Worker and Tell of Many Vital Developments," *Daily Worker*, 12 February 1925, p.5.

6 "Unite for the Support of the Chinese People Against Brutal Tyranny of World Imperialists; Where Does American Labor Stand? With the Workers and Farmer of Mexico or with Wall Street?," *Daily Worker*, 4 July 1925, p.1.

7 The distinction in nomenclature between "Pan" and "All" indicates what might well have been substantive divergences between a Pan-Latino thrust of the Mexican-based comrades versus a US-centric notion of All-American leadership based in the United States. Contesting notions of "America" seem to have been embedded in the process of the AAAIL's incipient organizational development, objectively complicating the mission to overturn national chauvinism.

8 "El Peligro; Las Posibilidades; El Proposito," *El Libertador: Organo de la Liga Anti-Imperialista Panamericana*, vol.1, no.1 [March 1925], p.1; "Adios, Socialismo," p.7; "Basta de 'Razas,'" p.9 in Comintern Fond 542, Inv,1, File 2a, European Reading Room, Library of Congress.

9 CP of Mexico and its Third Annual Congress, 7–13 April 1925, Opus 1, Fond 515, Delo 539, Reel 37, Documents 32–38, CPUSA Papers, Manuscript Division, Library of Congress.

10 Ibid.
11 Ibid.
12 Ibid.
13 Ibid.
14 Letter to the Secretary of the Secretary of State from the Central Committee of the Workers Party, Document 812.00b/118, 9 March 1926, Reel 90, M274, RG 59, US National Archives.
15 Manuel Gomez to General Secretary Ruthenberg, 4 May 2005, Opus 1, Fond 515, Delo 717, Reel 50, CPUSA Papers, Manuscript Division, Library of Congress.
16 Ibid.
17 Ibid.
18 Ibid.
19 Manuel Gomez to General Secretary Ruthenberg, Opus 1, Fond 515, Delo 717, Reel 50, Doc.12, 11 May 2006, CPUSA Papers, Manuscript Division, Library of Congress.
20 Ibid.
21 General Secretary Ruthenberg to Manuel Gomez, 16 May 2006, Opus 1, Fond 515, Delo 717, Reel 50, CPUSA Papers, Manuscript Division, Library of Congress.
22 Document 861.00-Congress, Communist International VI/36, Reel 67, RG 59, US National Archives; "'Keep Up the Struggle,' Anti-Imperialist League Urges General Sandino in a Letter," *Daily Worker*, 19 July 1928, p.2.
23 Official Report of the Communist Third International, Reel 101, National Republic Collection, Hoover Institute.
24 More work on the role of migrant laborer Chinese Communists in the Caribbean is necessary to illuminate the long history of Chinese Communist influence around the world even before the ascendency of Communist China post-WWII.
25 "Organize Communist Party of Cuba and Greet Workers Party," *Daily Worker*, 18 August 1925, p.1; ibid., "KKK Shot kills Militant Miner," p.1.
26 Document 837.00B/180, 27 July 1934, RG 59, US National Archives.
27 "Persecution of the Labour Movement in Cuba," *International Press Correspondence*, Vol. 7 no. 57.
28 Circular of the Cuban Section of the All-America Anti-Imperialist League Regarding the Origin and Magnitude of the Crimes Now Being Committed Against the Cuban People, Opus 1, Fond 515, Delo 575, Reel 39, CPUSA Papers, Manuscript Division, Library of Congress.
29 Document 837.00B/6, 8 October 1925, Reel 21, RG 59, US National Archives.
30 "50 Labor Agitators Parade in Wall Street," *New York Times*, 22 December 1925; Interestingly, the AIL in Cuba seems to have sparked the "Red summer" developments of 1925 on Cuban soil, and yet it was the ILD on US soil which first expressed its solidarity for the Cuban cause even before the US branch of the AAAIL. In converse to the Mexican situation where the AIL rather than the ILD initially took up the cause of Sacco and Vanzetti despite the fact that in the United States the ILD was at the helm of this political prisoner's campaign, the US-based ILD appears first to have responded to the defense of jailed Cuban dissidents in the AIL.
31 Document 1437, From Enoch Crowder to Secretary of State, 25 May 1936, M488, Reel 21, RG 59, US National Archives.
32 Document 837.00B/8, Reel 21, RG 59, US National Archives.
33 "Persecution of the Labour Movement in Cuba," *International Press Correspondence*, vol. 7, no. 57.
34 "Anti-Imperialists Denounce Wall St in Cable to Cuba: Latin Americans in Paris Protest Against US Policies; Independence Leaders Speak," *Daily Worker*, 18 January

1928, p.1; "Cuban-American Economic Committee Formed to Intensify Economic Relations Between Cuba and United States and to Increase Reciprocal Advantages," *Evening News*, 12 March 1928; "US Can Help Cuba Develop a Merchant Marine," *Havana Posti* 6 March 1928; "Havana Central Railway Passes to Control of United Railways," *Evening News*, 1 March 1928.

35 Document 812.00B/236, 29 January 1929, M274, Reel 90, RG 59, US National Archives.

36 "Protest the Murder of the Heroic Haitian Workers and Peasants," *Negro Champion*, 14 December 1929.

37 "de etat Rico—Paradise for the Rich But Hell for the Workers," *Daily Worker*, 10 August 1926, p.3.

38 "Washington Warns Moscow Against Support for Porto Rico or Philippines," *Daily Worker*, 25 February 1925, p.2; "American Workers Must Give Heed to the Plea of Porto Rican Labor," 2 December 1925, p.2.

39 Ibid.

40 Letter from N. Sager of General Secretary Ruthenberg, 9 February 1926, Opus 1, Fond 515, Delo 717, Reel 50, Document 1, CPUSA Papers, Manuscript Division, Library of Congress.

41 General Secretary Ruthenberg to Navares Sager, 6 March 1926, Opus 1, Fond 515, Delo 717, Reel 50, CPUSA Papers, Manuscript Division, Library of Congress.

42 Navares Sager to Manuel Gomez, 6 May 1926, CPUSA Papers, Manuscript Division, Library of Congress.

43 Ibid.

44 General Secretary Ruthenberg to Navares Sager, 18 May 1926, Opus 1, Fond 515, Delo 717, Reel 50, Document 15, CPUSA Papers, Manuscript Division, Library of Congress.

45 Ibid.

46 Navares Sager to Manuel Gomez, 22 June 1926, Document 20, CPUSA Papers, Manuscript Division, Library of Congress.

47 Navares Sager to Manuel Gomez, 28 June 1926, Document 21, CPUSA Papers, Manuscript Division, Library of Congress.

48 Navares Sager to General Secretary Ruthenberg, 24 August 1926, Opus 1, Fond 515, Delo 717, Reel 50, CPUSA Papers, Manuscript Division, Library of Congress.

49 General Secretary Ruthenberg to Navares Sager, 5 November 1926, Opus 1, Fond 515, Delo 717, Reel 50, Document 43, CPUSA Papers, Manuscript Division, Library of Congress.

CHAPTER 4

1 Reportage, "A Passport from Realengo 18," *New Masses*, 16 July 1935, pp.155–6.

2 Ibid., p.157.

3 Ibid., p.159.

4 "Cuban Government Held at Bay Before Embattled Peasants," *Daily Worker*, 4 December 1934, p.2.

5 "Cuban Revolutionary Trade Unions Have Achieved Unit, Lead Workers," *Daily Worker*, 12 February 1934, p.6.

6 From Political Secretariat to Communist Parties of the United States, France, Great Britain, and Holland, 29 March 1930, Digitized Comintern files, F.495, Inv 3, File 161, p.48, European Reading Room, Library of Congress.

7 Ibid.

8 Ibid., p.51.

9 "Strengthen Our Party," *The Party Organize* [February 1930]; Organizational Practicant of CPUSA—on Organisation Condition of the CPUSA, 28 April 1930, Opus 1, Fond 515, Delo 1859, Reel 141: CPUSA.

10 International Labor Defense: 1929–1930, 23 January 1930, Earl Browder Papers.

11 ILD Report from the Caribbean Secretariat, 13 March 1930, Opus 1, Fond 515, Delo 2174, Reel 164; Minutes of the National Executive Committee of the ILD, 12 June 1930, Opus 1, Fond 515, Delo 2174, Reel 164, CPUSA Papers, Manuscript Division, Library of Congress.

12 The term "white terror" denoted fascist aggression. However, it was also understood to mean terror inflicted by white people on people of color.

13 Minutes of National Executive Committee of the ILD, 21 August 1930, CPUSA Papers, Manuscript Division, Library of Congress.

14 Letter to "Friends" from Browder, Dun, Baldwin Moreau and Nearing, 8 February 1930, Opus 1, Fond 515, Delo 2202, Reel 165, CPUSA Papers, Manuscript Division, Library of Congress.

15 "Mass Protest Saves Lives of Junco and Other Leaders; DePriest Has ANLC Man Arrested, Porto Ricans Join Fight on Imperialism," *Negro Champion*, 13 January 1930, p.3.

16 "Mexico Before and After the Break with the Soviet Union," *International Press Correspondence*, vol.10, no.12, p.203; "Rupture of Relations Between Mexico and the USSR," *Daily Worker*, 4 February 1930, p.3.

17 "Mexico Before and After the Break with the Soviet Union," p.203.

18 "Problems of the Communist Party of Mexico," *The Communist* [May 1930], vol.9, no.5, p.445; Minutes of the National Executive Committee of the ILD, 12 June 1930, Opus 1, Fond 515, Delo 2174, Reel 164, CPUSA Papers, Manuscript Division, Library of Congress.

19 Document 812.00B/272, 5 February 1932, "The Economic Crisis and the Revival of the Revolutionary Movement in Mexico," *Communist International*, 20 December 1931, M1370, Reel 22, RG 59, US National Archives.

20 From the Politburo to the Communist Parties of the United States, France, Great Britain and Holland, p.50; "The Economic Crisis and the Revival of the Revolutionary Movement in Mexico," *Communist International*, 20 December 1931, M1370, Reel 22, RG 59, US National Archives.

21 Document 811.4066-Scottsboro/189, RG 59, US National Archives; Document 812.00B/276, Reel 22, RG 59, US National Archives.

22 "The Tasks of the CP of Mexico in the Conditions of the End of Capitalist Stability," *The Communist*, vol.12, no.5, p.470; "Race Problem Universal, Says Famous Artist—Painter Tells New York Group that Every Country has its Scottsboro Case, Eastern Stirred by Speech of Diego Rivera in Harlem," *Chicago Defender*, 2 September 1933.

23 "Cuban Worker Killed When Police Fire on Scottsboro Demonstration," *Harlem Liberator*, 8 December 1934.

24 From Anna Damon, International Labor Defense to Secretary of State Hull, 3 December 1934, RG 59, US National Archives.

25 Ibid.

26 Document 800.00B-Junco, Sandalio/1, 3 January 1930, Box 4731, RG 59, US National Archives.

27 Document 837.00B, 13 February 1930, Box 5920, RG 59, US National Archives; "Machado Bans Workers' Meetings," 15 February 1930, p.2.

28 "The Rising Revolt of Cuba: Some Tasks for US Workers," *Daily Worker*, 17 April 1930, p.4.

29 Document 837.00b/30, 29 May 1930, box 5920-2, RG 59, US National Archives.

30 Ibid.

31 Ibid.

32 Document 837.00B/28, 13 February 1930, Box 5920, RG 59, US National Archives.

33 Ibid.

34 "Communist Groups Cheers Cuban Reds," *New York Times*, 17 August 1930.

35 "Letter of the Central Committee of the CPUSA to the Central Committee of the CP of Cuba," *The Communist* [October 1931], p.66.

36 Ibid.

37 Document 837.00B/37, 3 February 1930, Box 55920, RG 59, US National Archives.

38 Ibid.; "The Events in Cuba," *International Press Correspondence*, vol.11, no.44, p.811.

39 Document 800.00B-International Red Day/80, 22 May 1931, Box 4509, RG 59, US National Archives.

40 Ibid.

41 "Cuban Communist Party Hits Legal Lynching of Nine," *Liberator*, 4 July 1931, p.2.

42 "Our Present Tasks in Cuba," *The Communist*, vol.10, no.6, p. 516.

43 Document 837.00/3331, 24 August 1932, Box 5902, RG 59, US National Archives.

44 "Protest Cuban Terror Today: Parade in Harlem to Save Union Leader," *Daily Worker*, 27 August 1932, p.1.

45 "Communist Party Grows Through Leadership of Cuban Workers in Fight," *Daily Worker*, 21 August 1933, p.6.

46 Document 800.00B-Anti-Imperialist League/3791; Box 5904, RG 59, US National Archives.

47 Document 800.00B-Anti-Imperialist League/3758, 8 September 1933, Box 5904, RG 59, US National Archives.

48 "Fifteen Thousand Cubans Mass at Funeral of Young Communist," *Daily Worker*, 7 September 1933, p.3.

49 "American Managers Flee Plantations," *Daily News*, 7 September 1933; "Cuba is Terrorized Anew: Troops Battle Rioting Mobs in Several Cities; Uprising Reported in Ranks of Army," *Chicago Tribune*, 21 September 1933.

50 "'Down with US,' Cheer Moscow: Protestors Honor Slain Student," *Chicago Tribune*, 26 September 1933.

51 Document 837.00B/5045, 30 September 1933, RG 59, US National Archives.

52 Document 2655-q-94, 25 November 1933, M1507, Reel 5, RG 165, US National Archives.

53 Document 837.00/3789, 11 September 1933, Box 5904, RG 59, US National Archives.

54 Document 837.00/3789, 11 September 1933, Box 5904, RG 59, US National Archives; "Negroes Terrorized and Lynched in Cuba," *Harlem Liberator*, 10 March 1934, p.6.

55 Ibid.

56 Ibid.

CHAPTER 5

1 Postcards, Hemina Dumont Huiswoud Photographs Collection, Tamiment Library and Robert F. Wagner Archives.

2 Since the Haitian Red movement was brief yet very intense, it would require a separate investigation and sufficient knowledge of French to conduct enough

research to deeply understand the reasons that the movement in Haiti played out so differently than that in Cuba between 1930 and 1934. For our purposes, we will only discuss several of the major developments in the Haitian Red movement during this period and underscore the key questions about transnational activism between New York and Haiti by way of Comintern organizations.

3 "Many Haitians Join ANLC: Marines Withdrawal Demanded," *Liberator*, 11 January 1930, p.4.

4 "Slavery in Haiti," *Daily Worker*, 15 February 1930, p.4.

5 Document 800.00B-Rosemund, Henry, 7 April 1930, B5920, RG 59, US National Archives; Document 838.00B/4, 7 April 1930, M1246, Reel 6, RG 59, US National Archives; Henry Rosemund seems to have returned to Haiti toward the end of 1929 during the Haitian uprising. More information on Rosemund would be critical to understanding.

6 "Haiti Terror Part of Boss Drive to Crush Sugar Workers' Struggle," *Daily Worker*, 5 January 1933, p.2; Minutes of Meeting at Workers Center, 35 East 12th St of Executive of the Anti-Imperialist League together with Active Workers, 11 January 1932, Opus 1, Fond 515, Delo 3028, Reel 234, CPUSA Papers, Manuscript Division, Library of Congress.

7 Document 838.00B/10-12, Reel 6, M1246, RG 59; "Haiti Wall Street Government Outlaws Scottsboro Defense," *Negro Worker*, vol.4, no.3 [June 1934].

8 "A Trade Union Program of Action for Negro Workers," *The Communist*, vol.9, no.1 [January 1930].

9 "World Aspects of the Negro Question," *The Communist*, vol.9, no.2 [February 1930].

10 Ibid.

11 "Against Bourgeois-Liberal Distortions of Leninism on the Negro Question in the United States," *The Communist*, vol.9, no.8 [August 1930], p.694; "Resolutions of the Communist International on the Negro Question in the United States, October 1930," *The Communist Position on the Negro Question in the United States*, 1932.

12 "The First International Conference of Negro Workers: Its Accomplishments and its future Tasks," James Ford, Hemina Huiswoud Papers.

13 Report on Preparations for London Conference, by James Ford, Reel 5, Earl Browder Papers, Tamiment Library.

14 Ibid.

15 Ibid.

16 Letter to Padmore from ANLC (Briggs), 14 March 1930, Opus 1, Fond 515, Delo 1955, Reel 155, CPUSA Papers, Manuscript Division, Library of Congress.

17 Minutes of Meeting of Negro Department, 25 July 1930, Opus 1, Fond 515, Delo 1966, Reel 155, CPUSA Papers, Manuscript Division, Library of Congress.

18 "US Navy Department Rules Virgin Islands," *Liberator*, 27 September 1930, p.2.

19 Circular from ILD and Patronati Committees of MOPR in the Caribbean and the US to All District Organizers and Sub District Organizers, 16 July 1931, Opus 1 Fond 515, Delo 2222, Reel 194, CPUSA Papers, Manuscript Division, Library of Congress; Organizational Instructions for ILD Caribbean Secretariat—English Section—English Section HQ in NYC, 16 July 1931, Opus 1 Fond 515, Delo 2222, Reel 194. The Patronati were networks of anti-fascist refugee organizations for people suffering in the 1920s from the dictatorship under Italian fascist leader Benito Mussolini. In time, the Patronati were essentially incorporated into the work of the MOPR and chapters of the Patronati were started in the United States under the ILD, US branch of the MOPR.

20 Organizational Instructions for ILD Caribbean Secretariat—English Section—English Section HQ in NYC, 16 July 1931, Opus 1 Fond 515, Delo 2222, Reel 194, CPUSA Papers, Manuscript Division, Library of Congress.

21 The *Caribbean Defender*—Organ of the ILD—Caribbean Secretariat—English Department, June 1931, Opus 1, Fond 515, Delo 2577, Reel 194, CPUSA Papers, Manuscript Division, Library of Congress.

22 The *ILD Builder*, vol.1, no.1. Issued by the National Executive Committee-Organization Department of the International Labor Defense, Opus 1, Fond 515, Delo 2577, Reel 194, CPUSA Papers, Manuscript Division, Library of Congress.

23 Document 800.00B-International Trade Union Committee of Negro Workers/6, 28 December 1931, Box 4150, RG 59, US National Archives.

24 George Padmore, *Negro Workers and the Imperialist War: Intervention of the Soviet Union*, Hamburg, Germany: International Trade Union Committee of Negro Workers, 1931, pp.2–3.

25 George Padmore, *The Life and Struggles of Negro Toilers*, London: RILU Magazine, 1931, pp. 76, 105.

26 Ibid.

27 "Our Aims," *Negro Worker*, vol.1, no.1 [January 1931], p.1.

28 Ibid., "Imperialism in the West Indies," p.16.

29 Ibid., "Workers Correspondence," p.28.

30 Ibid.

31 Ibid.

32 "Special Resolution on Work among Negroes in the United States and the Colonies," *Negro Worker*, vol.1, no.3 [March 1931], pp.14–15.

33 Draft Four Month Plan of Work of the Negro Deportment of the CC as Adopted by Negro Department—October to Feb[ruary] 1932 proceeding from the decision of the 13th Party Plenum, 4 January 1932, Opus 1, Fond 515, Delo 2577, Reel 213: CPUSA.

34 Document 800.00B-International Trade Union Committee of Negro Workers/9, 5 January 1932, RG59.

35 Ibid.

36 Document 800.00B-International Trade Union Committee of Negro Workers/26, 4 May 1932, Box 4150, RG 59, US National Archives.

37 "The Fight For Bread in the West Indies," *Harlem Liberator*, 6 May 1933, p.7; "Negro Toilers Speak at the World Congress of ILD," *Negro Worker*, vol.3, no.2–3 [February–March 1933], pp.1–6.

38 *Negro Worker*, vol.3, no.8–9 [August–September 1933], p.5.

39 "The Labour Movement: Report of Negro Workers' Leader on Soviet Russia," *Negro Worker*, vol.4 no.4–5 [April–May 1933], pp.28–31.

40 Documents 800.00B-International Trade Union Committee of Negro Workers/17-23, Box 4150, RG 59, US National Archives; Document 800.00B-International of Seamen and Harbor Workers Union/69, 30 August 1933, Box 4510, RG 59, US National Archives.

41 Ibid.

42 Document 800.00B-International of Seamen and Harbor Workers Union/70, 15 March 1934, Box 4510, RG 59, US National Archives.

43 "Au Revoir," *Negro Worker*, vol.3, no.8–9, p.18; ibid., "Bravo, British Guiana!," p.4.

44 Document 844g.00/14, 13 September 1934, Box 6221, RG 59, US National Archives.

45 "British Guiana Labour Union Reports," *Negro Worker*, vol.4, no.6 [June 1934], p.18.

46 Document 800.00B-Huiswood, Otto/3, 21 November 1934, RG 59, US National Archives.

CHAPTER 6

1 "Strikers Massacred by British Soldiers on Caribbean Island: Three Die as Guns Are Turned on Peaceful Assemblage," *Daily Worker*, 4 March 1935, p.3.

2 "James W Ford Hails Proposals for a National Negro Congress," *Daily Worker*, 25 May 1935, p.4; "R. Palme Dutt Greets Negro Congress in US: British Communist Leader, in Letter to Ford, Sees Great Influence on World Opinion in View of War being Waged in Africa," *Daily Worker*, 11 January 1936, p.6.

3 Ibid. For more on Dutt's position on the fight against fascism, see R. Palme Dutt, *Fascism and Social Revolution: A Study of the Economics and Politics of the Extreme Stages of Capitalism in Decay* (New York: International Publishers, 1935).

4 Bulletin no.7, The Workers' Bureau of the Negro Workers' Council, National Urban League, 11 December 1935.

5 Bulletin no.2, The Workers' Bureau of the Negro Workers' Council, National Urban League, 26 April 1935; "The Coming National Negro Congress," *Negro Worker*, vol.15, no.2, p.139.

6 "The Fight for the Civil Rights of Negro People in the USA," *Negro Worker*, vol.6, no.6–7 [August–September 1936], pp.3–5.

7 Labor Strikes, Riots and Communist Activity in West Indies, 4 March 1935, United States Department of Justice Investigative Files, Part 2: Communist Party.

8 Ibid.

9 Ibid.

10 Ibid.

11 "Notes and Comments: St. Kitts Shoots Justified," *Negro Worker*, vol.5, no.9 [September 1935], p.23.

12 "The Struggle of the Unemployed in St. Vincent," *Negro Worker*, vol.6, no.9 [November 1936], pp.17–19; Anti-Communist laws in the West Indies, Reel 10, Frame 0533, US Department of Justice Investigative Files, Part 2: Communist Party, Manuscript Division, Library of Congress.

13 Ibid.

14 "The Colonies," *Negro Worker*, vol. 5, no.9 [September 1935], p.14.

15 "The Offensive of Fascism and the New Tactics of Communists (or) Mussolini Says No! Insists on War," *Daily Worker*, 19 August 1935, p.2.

16 *The African Nationalist*, vol.3, no.6 [October 1935], p.105.

17 Ibid.

18 Editorial, "Glory of the British Crown," *Plain Talk*, 18 May 1935, p.4; ibid., "The Problem of Germany to Be Abolished," p.1.

19 Ibid., "Convictions of Scottsboro Boys Reversed," p.2.

20 Ibid., "Herndon Case in High Court," p.5.

21 Angelo Herndon was a young African American Communist and leading member of the Young Communist League who had been imprisoned for his political affiliations and soon became a leading political prisoner within the Communist movement alongside the Scottsboro Boys. For more on Herndon, see his autobiography, *Let Me Live!* (New York: Stratford Press, 1937).

22 Ibid., "Ethiopia Musters Strong Army," *Plain Talk*, 25 May 1935, p.1; ibid., "Ras Tafari Scores Great Moral Victory: Ethiopia Offers Stiff Resistance to Italy," 8 June 1935, p.1.

23 Ibid., "Jamaicans for Ethiopian Frontier," 20 July 1935, p.8.

24 Ibid., "Harlem Recruits 'Legionnaires' to Defend Ethiopia in Threatened War," 3 August 1935, p.8.

25 Ibid., "People of Miranda Cuba Offering Services to Assist Ethiopia in War with Italy; Reply to P.B. Phillips and Others in Ethiopian War," 31 August 1935, p.4.

26 Ibid., "Land and Labour," 25 May 1935, p.4; ibid., "What Can be Done to Improve the Economic Conditions in Jamaica," p.7.

27 Ibid., "Cable Protest Sent the Secretary for the Colonies—Anti Trust Law Advocated," 8 June 1935, p.1.

28 Ibid., "Governor's Protection Necessary," 22 June 1935, p.5.

29 Ibid.

30 Ibid., "Plain Talk Our Racial School Master," 7 March 1936, p.7.

31 "Harlem Shows the Way," *Negro Worker*, vol.6, no.8 [October 1936], pp.20–21.

32 Ibid.

33 Hill, *Marcus Garvey and the Universal Negro Improvement Association Papers*, vol.7, p.lxxxi.

34 "Jamaicans in Cuba May be Put in Concentration Camps," *Plain Talk*, 6 February 1937, p.1; "Bermuda Bosses Ban Birth to Solve Unemployment They Say," *Negro Worker*, vol.7 [March 1937].

35 "1937: A New Year of Struggle for the West Indian Masses," *Negro Worker*, vol.7 [March 1937].

36 "British West Indies," *Chicago Defender*, 19 July 1937.

37 "Link Red Agents with Trinidad's Oil Field Strike: Financed Strike Causing Death of 17 Persons," *Chicago Daily Tribune*, 25 July 1937.

38 Document 844.00b/1, 17 March 1944, RG 59, US National Archives.

39 "Trinidad Oil Strike Spread; Marines Landed," *Daily Worker*, 26 June 1937, p.2.

40 Ibid., "Trinidad Terror Described by Negro," 26 November 1937, p.5.

41 Document 844F.00/12, 3 August 1937, RG 59, US National Archives.

42 Document 844F.00/13, 6 October 1937, RG 59, US National Archives.

43 Ibid.

44 Ibid.

45 Ibid.

46 Ibid.

47 Document 844.00/26, 1 June 1938, RG 59, US National Archives; Document 844.00g/27, 28 June 1938, RG 59, US National Archives; ibid., 8 July 1938. For more on Ferdinand Smith's role as a Communist organizer for the NMU in the Caribbean see Gerald Horne, *Red Seas: Ferdinand Smith and Radical Black Sailors in the United States and Jamaica* (New York: New York University Press, 2005).

48 "Barbados Press Rally Scheduled for Tomorrow," *Daily Worker*, 27 June 1938, p.6.

CHAPTER 7

1 "Red Spanish Forces on the U.S. Border," General, National Republic, Hoover Institute.

2 Albert Gomes, activist, writer and one-time Chief Minister of Trinidad and Tobago, briefly alluded to helping smuggle Spanish Civil War veterans/refugees to Mexico by way of Trinidad in his autobiography, *Through a Maze of Colour* (Port of Spain: Key Caribbean Publications, 1974).

3 "Toward the People's Anti-Imperialist Front in Mexico speech from 7th World Congress," *The Communist*, vol.15 no.1 [January 1936]: 47.

4 "50,000 Mexican Rail Men Strike; Red Flags Raised Over Stations; Government Condemns Walkout and Orders Workers' Return in 24 Hours—Only Mail and

Military Trains to Run on National Railways—Leaders Reported Ready to Yield. Mexican Railway Halted by Strike," *New York Times*, 18 May 1936, p.1.

5 "On the Inter-American Peace Conference," *The Communist*, vol.15 no.9 [September 1936]: 865.

6 "Revolutionary Agrarian Experiment Now Under Way in Mexico: Landowners in Despair, Peons Face Starvation as Government Seizes Land, Introduces Collectivism," *Washington Daily News*, 19 November 1936, Reel 101, General, National Republic.

7 Ibid., "Anglo-American Lands Fall Afoul of Mexican Collectivism," 24 November 1936.

8 Ibid.

9 Ibid.

10 "Text of John L. Lewis Speech At the Auto Workers Convention," *Daily Worker*, 28 August 1937, p.4.

11 A broader discussion of the Trujillo massacre in the subsequent chapter is based upon evidence which indicates that there was little if any substantive response from the Mexican left to this mass racist slaughter of Haitian laborers. But Mexico's decision to act as a national safe haven for Republican refugees of the Spanish Civil War did provide the basis for pro-Republican anti-fascists in the Black Caribbean to locate Mexico as an outpost for "popular" unity in the basin. At the September 1938 convention of the Latin American Confederation of Workers in Mexico, an unnamed labor representative attended on behalf of the Trinidadian labor movement precisely when Trinidad was at the height of its own fierce labor unrest against British colonial authorities.

12 "The National Revolution on the March in Mexico," *International Press Correspondence*, vol.17 no.56, p.1386; "Mexico to Divide Nazi Coffee Farms Among Chiapas Indian Peons," *Daily Worker*, 5 January 1939, p.9.

13 "Cuban Oil Workers Appeal for Support Against Terror," *Daily Worker*, 23 March 1935, p.6.

14 Letter from M. Costella to E. Browder—from Cuban CP to CPUSA, 16 January 1935, Opus 1, Fond 515, Delo 3482, Reel 293, CPUSA Papers, Manuscript Division, Library of Congress; Ibid., From Blas Roca to Browder and CPUSA, 6 February 1935.

15 "Cuban Masses United Against Wall St.-Mendieta-Batista Murder Rule," *Daily Worker*, 12 March 1935, p.6; "Strike Leaders are Executed in Cuba and Demonstrate Today!," *Daily Worker*, 13 March 1935, p.1.

16 "Manifesto of the Communist Party of Cuba Points Road to Liberation of Masses," *Daily Worker*, 14 March 1935.

17 Ibid.

18 Document 837.00B/179, 30 August 1935, RG 59, US National Archives.

19 Ibid; In this way, Cuban participation at the Seventh World Congress of the Communist International in July of 1935 officially occasioned the CPC's dismissal of its own post-strike critique of the "Autenticos" as "counter-revolutionary." As a minority party attempting to seize state power with the forces of "millions," or the "general" population, their rationale was essentially that the "danger" of mass support for Grau-led forces rather than the CPC had proven to become an opportunity for the Reds to widen their own support base within the larger progressive Cuban movement around a trope of national solidarity. The perceived "danger to proletarian struggle" of the Grau San Martin party did not obscure the fact that it remained "still, endowed today with the confidence of the masses of the people," namely the "students," "urban petty bourgeoisie," "toiling Negroes," and the "unemployed." Each of these demographics, when taken in sum total, had come to be seen as the

target constituencies that "Cuba for Cubans" would encompass by way of popular organizations. The CPC had accordingly committed itself to "go with the masses" and "lead them to revolutionary positions on the basis of their own experience," an experience which in their view demonstrated "the important peculiarity of the Cuban revolution as a colonial revolution." This logic had effectively replaced the class-against-class trope so preponderant only months before, now that the successful fight against global fascism and reaction had been declared a popular cause.

20 "Forward to the Cuban Anti-Imperialist People's Front!," *The Communist* [October 1935].

21 Ibid.

22 Ibid.

23 Ibid.

24 Ibid.

25 "How Manuel Fonseca Escaped Death through Mass Protests," *Daily Worker*, 3 April 1935, p.5.

26 "Storm Brews in Cuba as Unbridled Terror Presses on Toilers," *Daily Worker*, 23 April 1935, p.3.

27 "Cuban Labor Appeals to AFL for Aid Against Mendieta Terror Backed by US," 23 April 1935, *Daily Worker*, p.3.

28 Ibid.

29 Document 2657-Q-361-16, 17 May 1935, Reel 2, RG 165, US National Archives.

30 "Responsibilities of the American Communist Party to the Cuban Revolution," *Daily Worker*, 27 May 1935, p.3.

31 "We Must Act Against Brutal Savagery in Cuba," *Daily Worker*, 17 May 1935, p.1. But if Harlem was a bit in flux, then Brooklyn appears to have seized the initiative of defending the "Cuba for Cubans!" movement from Manhattan. While the transnational context of this circuit remained intact, the slight shift into a Brooklyn stronghold, primarily under the auspices of the American League Against War and Fascism (ALWF) and local churches, was reminiscent of the Brooklyn-based initiatives of the ANLC and other Reds groups in the period surrounding the 1929 "Haitian Revolution." And it also appears to have paralleled a shift in "East Harlem" activity associated with the Puerto Rican community of poor, immigrant laborers as well as the contemporaneous and intertwined "Popular Front" movement which was then taking place on a massive scale in Puerto Rico itself.

32 "Deported from Cuba," *International Press Correspondence*, vol.15, no.42, p.1090.

33 "U.S. Liberal Group Seized in Havana," *New York Times*, 3 July 1935.

34 Ibid.

35 Ibid.

36 "Odets, Indignant, Plans New Inquiry," *New York Times*, 7 July 1935; "Workers to Greet Arrival of Cuban Delegation," *Daily Worker*, 6 July 1935, p.1.

37 Ibid. This transnational outcry of clerics against fascist aggression was derived from the personal experiences of these pastors—be they with the imprisoned Reds of Cuba, churches of Brooklyn, or concentration camps of Germany. It offers new possible avenues of exploring anti-fascist religious movements in transnational context.

38 "U.S. Liberal Group Seized in Havana," *New York Times* [1935]; Flyer to greet Delegation of American Workers and Professionals Just Returned from Cuba at New Star Casino at 107th and Park Ave in NYC, 10 July 1935, Opus 1, Fond 515, Delo 3940, Reel 300, CPUSA Papers, Manuscript Division, Library of Congress.

39 "The Cuban Army Must Be on the Side of the People," *International Press Correspondence*, vol.16, no.43, p.1159.

40 "Cuban Sports to Hide Terror: Sugar Barons Run Carnival," *Daily Worker*, 21 October 1936.

41 "The Latin-American Significance of the Cuban Upsurge," *International Press Correspondence*, vol.19, no.18, p.367.

42 Document 811c.00B/7, 13 January 1939, Box 5303, RG 59, US National Archives.

43 "Gran Huelga in Puerto Rico," *Bandera Roja*, 15 January 1935.

44 Document 811c.5045/1, 4 February 1935, Box 4515, RG 59, US National Archives.

45 "The 'New Deal' At Work in Puerto Rico," *Daily Worker*, 3 April 1935, p.4; "Porto Rican Communists Launch Fighting Paper," *Daily Worker*, 16 November 1936, p.2.

46 "Porto Rican Communists Launch Fighting Paper," *Daily Worker*, 16 November 1936, p.2.

47 "University of Puerto Rico Asks for Herndon Petitions; 2,000 Sign Lists in France," *Daily Worker*, 16 November 1935, p.3.

48 From Alberto Sanchez to Earl Browder, 11 October 1935, Opus 1, Fond 515, Delo 3482, Reel 293, CPUSA Papers, Manuscript Division, Library of Congress.

49 Document 811c.51/4, 12 May 1936, Box 4515, RG 59, US National Archives.

50 Document 811c.001/24, 11 April 1936, RG 59, US National Archives.

51 Document 811c.00/31-40, 7-11/4/1936, RG 59, US National Archives.

52 "The Struggle for Porto Rican Independence," *The Communist*, vol.15, no.7 [July 1936], p.629.

53 Ibid.

54 "Marcantonio Seized in Relief Row; Defies Police in March of 15,000," *Daily Worker*, 16 February 1936.

55 "Harlem Shows the Way," *Negro Worker*, vol.6, no.10 [October 1936], pp.20–21.

56 "Puerto Rican Independence Drive Urged," *Daily Worker*, 20 July 1936, p.6.

57 "The Struggle for Puerto Rican Independence," *The Communist*, no date available.

58 "Puerto Ricans plan for March: Campos Was Framed on Charges, Now in Jail," *Daily Worker*, 27 August 1936.

59 "2 Dead, 6 Hurt In Puerto Rico Elections: Islanders, Though US Citizen, Vote Only for Local Officers," *Daily Worker*, 4 November 1936, p.4.

60 "Porto Rico Shootings Protested," *Daily Worker*, 23 March 1937, p.1.

61 "Big Stick Policy of Washington Still at Work in Puerto Rico," *Daily Worker*, 23 March 1937, p.6.

62 "2,000 Jam Meeting for Puerto Ricans," *Daily Worker*, 27 March 1937, p.2.

63 "Relief Ended; Puerto Rican Faces Eviction, Deportation," *Daily Worker*, 3 September 1938, p.3.

64 "Threaten to Deport Family to Florida: Crippled Lad Facing Loss of Operation to Help Him Walk if Relief Bureau's Order Forces Mother Out of Town," *Daily Worker*, 12 September 1938, p.3.

65 "Harlem Puerto Ricans Fight for More Beans to Put Behind the Punch," *Daily Worker*, 29 September 1938, p.4.

66 "Puerto Ricans in Harlem Find CP Fights Their Battle: Communist Party Built Among Struggle Against Evictions, Discrimination," *Daily Worker*, 1 October 1938, p.4.

67 Ibid.

68 Ibid.

69 For more on Frederick Myers see his autobiography, *Home is the Sailor: The Story of an American Seaman* (New York: International Press, 1948).

70 "Aid to the Puerto Rican Dock Strikers," *Daily Worker*, 18 January 1938, p.6.

71 "Dock Strike in Puerto Rico Is Settled: Temporary Wage Scale is 10% Increase Over the Old Rates," *Daily Worker*, 11 February 1938, p.2.

72 "Caribbean Brothers," *Daily Worker*, 11 February 1938, p.7.

73 Document 811c.00B/7, 13 January 1939, Box 5303, RG 59, US National Archives.

74 "Puerto Rico Added to US Military Department," *Daily Worker*, 2 July 1939, p.1; Document 811c.5041/1, 28 February 1939, RG 59, US National Archives; "Puerto Rico Jobless Hold Large Congress," 12 March 1939, p.3; By January of 1939, the War Department had reported a new Dominican Air and Naval Station at Calderas Bay, and President Trujillo would have to prove that his Mussolini-like inclinations would not land this base in the wrong camp. Months later, the *Daily Worker* reported nervously that that since the Panama Canal was a potential passageway for Italian fascists to penetrate the hemisphere, the "Italian fascist press today denounced President Roosevelt and threatened that Italy would regard her frontier as 'the Panama Canal.'" Subsequently, and on the very day that the Japanese seized the Hainan Islands, the now "popular" governments in Mexico and Cuba vowed to defend the Canal Zone along with the United States from fascist penetration.

CHAPTER 8

1 "The Case of Jacques Roumain," *New York Times*, 17 April 1935, p.22; For more on Langston Hughes's first meeting with Roumain, see Hughes's autobiography, *I Wonder As I Wonder* (New York: Rinehart, 1956).

2 Ibid.

3 "Jacques Roumain: Poet in Chains," *Daily Worker*, 28 February 1935, p.7.

4 5 December 1936, RG 59, US National Archives.

5 Nicolas Guillen and Langston Hughes were both prominent literary figures in Cuba and the United States, respectively, and both, along with Jacques Roumain, were deeply implicated in the Communist movements of their time. Moreover, all three of these writers knew one another and essentially formed a literary circuit that was directly and indirectly linked to the organization circuit that the dissertation traces.

6 "Haiti's Role in the Western Hemisphere," Dante Bellegarde at Pan-American Congress, M1246, Reel 6, RG 59, US National Archive.

7 Ibid.

8 Ibid.

9 Ibid.

10 In 1936, Hughes's play *Troubled Island* was produced by the Gilpin Players, the most distinguished black theater company of the early twentieth century. Hughes started to write the libretto for an opera of the same name (and subject), but then gave it up the following year to report from the Spanish Civil War for the *Baltimore Afro-American*. *Troubled Island* wasn't produced as an opera until 1949, when it was performed by the New York City Opera, becoming the first grand opera, performed by a major opera company, to be written by an African American musical composer (William Grant Still) and librettist (Verna Avery, who later married Still).

11 "A Moving Play About Haiti: The Struggle for a Free Haiti Portrayed in Hughes Drama," *Daily Worker*, 28 November 1936, p.7.

12 Document 800.00B Congress of Writers for Defense of Culture, Second International/1, Box 4503, RG 59, US National Archives; "Latin Americans Rally Tonight For Porto Rico," *Daily Worker*, 1 December 1937. Roumain, it is claimed, was lying sick with complications from his malaria at the time and therefore personally

unable to attend the December conference and denounce the atrocities that had been inflicted upon his fellow countrymen.

13 "Mussolini Hanged These Ethiopians," *Daily Worker*, 5 March 1937, p.2; "Ethiopia's Fate at Stake on Spain's Battlefields, Says Negro Leader," *Daily Worker*, 10 March 1937, p.2.

14 "An Ethiopian Fights for Spain," *Negro Worker*, vol.7, no.3 [March 1937]; ibid., "Two Ethiopians: Father Italian Captive, Son Fighting for Spain."

15 Ibid.

16 Document 839.00B/14, 22 October 1936, Reel 5, M1272, RG 59, US National Archives.

17 Ibid.

18 "Trujillo Terror in Santo Domingo Shocking Event to Hardboiled Hugh," *Daily Worker*, 8 February 1937, p.6.

19 "Millions March in Greatest May Day in France, USSR, United States," *Daily Worker*, 3 May 1937, p.1.

20 "People Welcome Roosevelt Peace Call. Browder Says;" *Daily Worker*, 6 October 1937, p.1; "Roosevelt Greets Negro Congress: 800 Delegates Attend Sub-Sessions on Trade Unions," *Daily Worker*, 18 October 1937, p.1.

21 "3,000 in Haiti Slain, Envoy Says: Welles Hears of Massacre in Parley with Haiti Officials Here," *Daily Worker*, 10 November 1937, p.1; "Negro Congress Resolution for Boycott of Japan Against Fascism Released by Yergan, Leader at Session," *Daily Worker*, 18 November 1937, p.5.

22 "3,000 in Haiti Slain, Envoy Says: Welles Hears of Massacre in Parley with Haiti Officials Here," *Daily Worker*, 10 November 1937, p.1.

23 "Haitian Massacre Protest Scheduled Here December 17," *Daily Worker*, 11 December 1937, p.3; Enclosure, Document 738.39/221, 9 December 1937, RG 59, US National Archive.

24 Ibid.

25 Document 2657-q-387, 22 December 1937, M2657-q, Reel 5, RG 165; Document 738.39/217, 19 November 1937, RG 59, US National Archive.

26 Ibid.

27 Ibid.

28 Ibid.

29 Document 738.39/214A, 26 November 1937, RG 59, US National Archive.

30 Ibid.

31 Ibid.

32 Document 738.39/216, 17 December 1937, RG 59, US National Archives.

33 Ibid.

34 "More Than 100 Haitians Killed in Massacre," *Daily Worker*, 7 December 1937, p.2.

35 Enclosure, Document 738.39/221, 9 December 1937, RG 59, US National Archives.

36 "Haiti Massacre is Protested," *Daily Worker*, 18 December 1937, p.2.

37 Document 839.00B/16, 16 December 1937, Reel 5, M1272, RG 59, US National Archives.

38 Ibid.

39 Document 738.39/219, 20 December 1937, RG 59, US National Archives.

40 "Dominicans Protest Porto Rican Jail Sentence," *Daily Worker*, 18 January 1938, p.2.

41 "Fascist Penetration in Latin America," *The Communist*, vol.17, no.5 [May 1938], p.458; "Primitive Negro Solidarity: New Light from Brazil," vol.17 no.11 [November 1938].

Index

Page numbers in *italics* refer to images.